Piagetian Research

Volume Four

PIAGETIAN RESEARCH:
Compilation and Commentary

Volume Four

School Curriculum
Test Development

Sohan Modgil, PhD and Celia Modgil, MPhil

Foreword by Professor Bärbel Inhelder
The University of Geneva

NFER Publishing Company Ltd

Published by the NFER Publishing Company Ltd.,
2 Jennings Buildings, Thames Avenue,
Windsor, Berks. SL4 1QS
Registered Office: The Mere, Upton Park, Slough, Berks. SL1 2DQ
First published 1976
© Sohan and Celia Modgil
ISBN 0 85633 103 1

Typeset by Jubal Multiwrite Ltd.,
66 Loampit Vale, London SE13 7SN.
Printed in Great Britain by
Staples Printers Ltd., Rochester, Kent.
Distributed in the USA by Humanities Press Inc.,
Hillary House—Fernhill House, Atlantic Highlands,
New Jersey 07716 USA.

Contents

FOREWORD

I most sincerely thank Dr Sohan and Celia Modgil for asking me to write a foreword to the series of eight volumes which they are at present compiling. We all know the interest that was shown in, and the success of, the previous book, *Piagetian Research: A Handbook of Recent Studies*. Now, two years later, eight follow-up volumes are being published. We are well aware of what this represents in terms of continuity and devotion to such a long-term task.

The rapid extension of Piaget-inspired research is very impressive; in this series 3700 references are mentioned. It would seem that such an extension is explained by the need for a general theory in fundamental psychology. Another possible explanation is the growing awareness of the gaps in strictly behaviourist theory, on the one hand, and on the other, the continued emergence of new applications for the work carried out in Geneva in the fields of education and psychopathology. Recent studies confirm this trend.

Pleasing though this extension is, however, we are somewhat disturbed by the fact that the replication of our experiments does not always show a sufficient understanding of Piagetian theory on the part of the authors of these new works. We are of course the first to admit that such understanding is not easy to acquire, especially since this form of psychology is closely linked to a certain form of epistemology. Once understood, this form of epistemology appears to be that which best suits genetic psychology, as both are essentially constructivist. Constructivism implies that knowledge is not acquired merely under the impact of empirical experience, as suggested by behaviourist theory, although of course such impact is not entirely excluded from the process. It is also opposed to innate theory, to which, it seems, recourse is frequently had today (maturation being a factor which intervenes, but not exclusively). Constructivism emphasizes the child's or the subject's activity during the course of cognitive development: in other words, everything derives from actions and is eventually translated into coherent and logical thought operations.

In order to promote the necessary understanding, Sohan and Celia Modgil have systematically encouraged the reader to return to the original texts. If authors who have an excellent knowledge of the work of Piaget and his colleagues slightly misunderstand our theoretical position — which is in no way maturationist but rather epigenetic — one can easily imagine the misunderstanding of researchers who are less well informed and further away from Geneva. It is one thing to recognize the necessary sequence of the stages, but another thing altogether to explain them by invoking an innate 'programme'. Piaget's explanation, which is best presented in constructivist terms, deals with the sequence of stages by a process of equilibration or autoregulation. This regulatory activity enables the subject truly to construct knowledge – something which simple maturation does not do.

This point of view is fundamental to the understanding of Piagetian psychology; but more than that, it seems to us to constitute a particularly useful approach to questions of educational application since this form of autoconstruction corresponds more than any other perspective to the ideal called 'the active school', an ideal rarely carried out in practice.

In a constructivist perspective of this kind, it is clearly the sequence of stages which is important and not the chronological ages; the latter vary considerably from one environment to another and also depend on the experimental procedures being used. It is not astonishing that Bryant obtains convservation responses at earlier ages than those noted by us: we ourselves have obtained notable accelerations using operatory learning procedures developed in collaboration with H. Sinclair and M. Bovet (1974). We have recently published the results of a study (Inhelder *et al.*, 1975) which show stable acquisition of conservation notions as of age 5 if the following procedure is used: rather than merely deforming an object such as a ball of clay or modifying a collection of discrete elements, one removes part of or an element of the object(s) and moves it to another spot. In this case conservation appears earlier because the child understands two things he did not grasp during the simple deformations: firstly, that changes in shape are the result of displacements, and secondly, that in the course of these displacements what appears at the end is identical to what was removed at the start (this is what Piaget calls 'commutability'). We highlight this piece of work in order to show the much lesser importance of chronological age which can so easily be accelerated or delayed according to circumstances. The main point is the mode of construction which obeys constant laws and this characteristic is best exemplified by constructivism as we have defined it earlier.

We would also like to add that the recent discoveries of T. Bower and others concerning the innateness of certain behaviours which Piaget had not observed at the sensorimotor level do not contradict constructivism, since these primitive reactions do not directly result in higher-order behaviours but are reconstructed on different levels. These reconstructions are themselves not innate, but evidence of the constructive activities we have already observed elsewhere.

I should like to congratulate Dr Sohan and Celia Modgil on their fine effort in bringing together in these eight volumes the numerous pieces of work, thus rendering them accessible to researchers. We sincerely hope that this will encourage further progress in genetic psychology and all its applications.

Bärbel Inhelder,
University of Geneva

PREFACE

The eight volumes in the present series, *Piagetian Research*, together with the previous publication, *Piagetian Research: A Handbook of Recent Studies*, 1974, are intended to serve a wide range of needs for both teacher and learner at all levels: for university and college lecturers; post-graduate research students; those training to be educational psychologists; teachers and others following a wide range of advanced diploma courses; and education and psychology students at undergraduate level, following Educational and Developmental Psychology options. Research projects have been included which have implications for psychiatrists, paediatricians, rehabilitation and social workers.

In one sense, there are many authors to these volumes. The research evidence included is dependent on the countless efforts of Piaget's followers. In fairness, our gratitude is extended to those followers whose researches contribute immeasurably to the contents of these volumes. In particular, we acknowledge the cooperation of the many researchers personally communicating and forwarding papers for inclusion. Some collaborators have contributed material previously unpublished. These contributions, together with their accompanying correspondence, have resulted in a more comprehensive output.

We owe a very special debt of gratitude to Geneva University, and to universities here and abroad. Likewise, the inspiration of Professors Piaget and Inhelder, together with the general support of Professor Ruth Beard, Dr Gordon Cross, and Professor Marcel Goldschmid, are acknowledged.

It is an honour to have received such distinguished recognition for the volumes from Professor Bärbel Inhelder's gracious Foreword. We offer sincere thanks and gratitude for her interest and involvement and for the pleasant meeting in Geneva.

Enver Carim, an author in his own right as well as a perceptive editor, has provided the expertise necessary for such an ambitious series. Further to these more direct qualities Enver Carim has a profound philosophy with respect to a number of areas of knowledge

including psychology and unusual drive and energy. We are indebted to
him for all his support and acknowledge with gratitude the tremendous
contributions he has made to this series.

Sohan Modgil
Celia Modgil
January 1976

INTRODUCTION

The eight volumes in the present series *Piagetian Research* together with the previous publication *Piagetian Research: A Handbook of Recent Studies*, 1974, are designed to make available a substantial number of Piaget-oriented researches that may be useful for immediate information as well as for long-term reference. The accelerating expansion of Piagetian research has led to an acute need for a source book more comprehensive than the ordinary textbook but more focused than the scattered periodical literature. More specifically, it should give the reader access to source materials that elaborate upon most Piagetian topics. Likewise, such volumes should offer students examples of a variety of approaches utilized by researchers in their efforts to investigate cognitive development. The numerous researches assembled present experimental subjects whose chronological ages range from birth to 98 years. The intended readership is therefore broad, from those interested in the very young, in adolescents, in the elderly.

The present volumes, as well as recording the replications and extensions of Piaget's work, include reflections on, speculations about, and analyses of the various problems of the theory. Hopefully, this should in turn provide inspiration for further elaboration, extension and revision. The research worker is provided with a broad spectrum of original sources from which an appreciation in depth of the theoretical, methodological and practical questions relevant to a Piagetian framework can be obtained. While it is conceded that a secondary source is not the ideal way to comprehend the theory, nevertheless it can provide the reader with a basic direction to the problem at hand.

The material gathered has been heavily drawn from University degree theses, published and unpublished researches up to and as recent as December 1975.* It became apparent that the subject matter was voluminous and that there were many ways to subdivide the Piagetian cognitive researches. In choosing the articles, the criteria were made as

---

* The authors have been alert to studies appearing up to January 1976 (after the completion of the main manuscript) and brief details of further selected researches have been added in order to enrich particular areas of inquiry and discussion. Hopefully, researches within this category will receive full treatment in anticipated follow-up volumes.

objective as possible, while recognizing that a personal slant is bound to influence the selection. Despite an extensive search it is not unlikely that valuable articles have been overlooked. To these researchers apologies are extended. In assembling these researches the principal objective was to include only those which satisfy one of the following criteria: Piaget-oriented (replications or extensions); developmental in nature; or those which have discussed their findings within the Piagetian framework.

The tables of content reflect a broad range of studies, and represent most of the major subdivisions of Piagetian literature. It must be pointed out that while some articles fall naturally into certain specific volumes, others would have fitted simultaneously into more than one volume, this being in part due to the inability to distinguish between the analytic and synthetic. Consequently, it was difficult to select one single scheme that would satisfy all readers and many arbitrary decisions had to be made. There is obviously considerable reliance on the use of cross references.

The compilation covers fifteen areas, assembled in eight volumes — each volume focuses on one/two major aspects of Piaget's work. The main areas covered are: Piaget's Cognitive Theory and his major works, Sensorimotor Intelligence, Conservation, Training Techniques, Logic, Space, Handicapped Children, Cross-Cultural Research, The School Curriculum, Morality, Socialization, Test Development, Animism, Imagery and Memory.

Each volume consists of an integrated review of the range of recent studies followed by abstracts of these researches arranged, in the main, alphabetically. Where details of early research are essential to illustrate the evolution of a particular area of study, these are not represented by a full abstract, but are included in the introductory review. Although many cross references to related abstracts are included, the reviews preceding the abstracts are not intended to be fully critical of the validity and reliability of experimental design. This is partly due to the fact that, unless full details are available (sometimes these have neither been published fully, nor the definition of concepts made meaningful), this would be inimical, and partly because the amount of work involved in a critical evaluation of every study in a work of this breadth would be prohibitive.

In comparison to most publications, an unusual amount of detail of researches is made available, and to accompany this with an equal amount of discussion, although essential, could introduce complexity in the aims of the volumes. Some of the abstracts (indicated by an asterisk) have been written by the authors themselves and reproduced in their entirety. It is realized that some abstracts are of only marginal importance, yet their inclusion is essential to show general developmental patterns. It is the authors' intention that the reader, having investigated the range of available material, would then consult the original research according to his specific interests. Advanced research depends a great deal on what sources and data are available for study, and there is a consequent tendency for some parts of the field to be ploughed over and over again, while others remain virtually untouched.

The list of references included at the end of each volume together form a comprehensive bibliography encompassing over 3,500 references. Volume One additionally includes a comprehensive survey of Piaget's works, arranged chronologically.

Every care has been taken to report the results of the researches as accurately as possible — any misinterpretation of the results is accidental. It must be conceded that all the studies included do not receive equal coverage. While the overall response to the circulated requests was excellent, some shortcomings in the volumes are due partly to some failure of response. While deficiencies of the final product are our own responsibility, they exist in spite of a number of advisers who gave their time generously.

PART ONE

School Curriculum

a. Introduction to the application of Piaget's theory to education

It appears reasonable that a theory which investigates the spontaneous development of human scientific thought might provide a rationale for its systematic pedagogical development; however Piaget has not until recently explicitly addressed himself to education.

Piaget (1971) in *Science of Education and the Psychology of the Child*, makes it clear that he supports what he calls the 'new methods of education' and the 'traditional school' is strongly disfavoured. Further, that the new methods have their origin in the psychological developments of the 20th century and that it was the 'great movement of modern genetic psychology' that was the beginning of the new methods (*ibid.*, p. 145). Himself being the leading exponent of this movement, Piaget traces the development of the new methods through three stages. He acknowledges the contribution to modern education of Rousseau, Pestalozzi and Froebel, but asserts their failure to establish a psychological framework necessary for the working out of educational techniques that are truly adapted to the laws of mental acquisition. Such psychologist-educators as Dewey, Claparède and Decroly contributed to the second stage of the emergence of the new methods of education. The strength of the contribution of this 20th-century psychology lay in the fact that it was 'from the outset, and in all its aspects, an affirmation and an analysis of activity', and that 'everywhere we find the idea that the life of the mind is a dynamic reality; intelligence a real and constructive activity', (*ibid.*, p. 146). However the final source of the new methods, 'whatever the connection in the case of each of our principal innovators between child psychology and their key ideas in the field of education', was in the 'great movement of modern genetic psychology', (*ibid.*, p. 145).

The distinction between the 'traditional' and the 'new methods' is made explicit by Piaget. The former 'imposes his work on the student:

it makes him work' and while a good teacher may teach in such manner as to make provision for genuine activity, nevertheless Piaget is convinced that 'in the logic of the system, the students' intellectual and moral activity remains heteronomous (subject to external law) because it is inseparable from a continual restraint exercised by the teacher', (*ibid.*, p. 151). While asserting that active education does not mean that children should do anything they want, 'The new school, on the contrary, appeals to real activity, to spontaneous work based upon personal need and interest', (*ibid.*, p. 152).

The implications of Piaget's theory for education as extracted by Ginsburg and Opper (1969) have been restated and expounded by Dale (1975, pp. 135–138) as follows: '*Principle one:* New ideas and knowledge should be presented at a level consistent with the child's present state of development of thinking and language. This could be regarded as an educational truism: most teachers would regard such a principle as basic to good teaching practice ... as Piaget has shown ... most adults, including teachers, do not know the limitations of a child's thinking and language, nor do they know how to find out these limitations ... *Principle two:* A major source of learning is the activity of the child ... Duckworth in ... *Piaget Rediscovered*, presents Piaget's view that "good pedagogy must involve presenting the child with situations in which he himself experiments in the broadest sense of that term"... *Principle three:* Classroom practice should be tailored to the needs of individual children and should present moderately novel situations ... *Principle four:* Children learn by social inter-action ... they should share experiences, discuss their discoveries and argue out their differences of opinion ... *Principle five:* Children should have considerable control over their own learning ... Duckworth presents Piaget's view of education as follows: "The principle goal of education is to create men who are capable of doing new things, not simply of repeating what other generations have done – men who are creative, inventive, and discoverers ... to form minds which can be critical, can verify, and not accept everything they are offered ... to resist individually, to criticize, to distinguish between what is proven and what is not ... pupils who are active, who learn early to find out by themselves ... who learn early to tell what is verifiable and what is simply the first idea to come to them." '

Dale concludes, 'Piaget has not developed new educational ideas: very similar ideas were put forward by John Dewey (. . . .) many years ago and by many others since. His contribution is the provision of a cohesive theory supported by extensive observation and experi-mentation. It is a theory which provides a sound basis for development of a "progressive" approach in schools', (*ibid.*, p. 138)

i. Piagetian-based curriculum/programmes for young children

Case (1972) analyzed a kindergarten programme aimed at the development of conceptual skills within the framework of the neo-Piagetian model patterned after Pascual-Leone (1970). It was predicted, on the basis of the analysis, that experimental kindergarten Ss would perform 'at the same level as regular grade-IV children on a verbal classification task, and at the same level as regular grade-II children on a gestural classification task. The success of the predictions was interpreted as evidence that the neo-Piagetian model can provide a conceptual link between Piaget's developmental theory and Gagné's learning theory', p. 339. (Details appear later).

Owens (1973) viewed his study as 'basic research in the application of Piagetian cognitive development theory to curriculum used in the primary school classroom. Small-group activities were provided to improve the abilities of the children to use mental processes which Piaget has concluded are prerequisite to the development of a concept of number'. The sample comprised 47 kindergarten and grade one children from an economically disadvantaged urban community. Sixteen lessons in which the matching relations, 'as many as', 'more than' and 'fewer than', and the length relations 'as long as', 'longer than', and 'shorter than', were given to the Ss. One-half of the Ss received pre-tests. 'Then the full treatment group had four lessons on conservation of the matching relations and five lessons on the transitive property of the matching relations. The partial treatment (control) group continued with regular class work. Twelve structured interview post-tests were given to all Ss . . . '. Owens concluded that the treatment was not effective in enhancing the ability of the Ss to conserve matching relations. The treatment facilitated the ability of the Ss to perform transitivity tasks very much like the treatment activities. However, such an improvement did not transfer to the more difficult Transitivity Problem or to the logically parallel Transitivity of Length Relations. Pre-testing had no effect on the abilities of the Ss to employ the relational properties. There was a positive but weak relationship among the variables with the exception that Length Relations and Transitivity of Length Relations were not related to each of the others. (Details follow).

The intent of Newby's (1973) study was to discern implications for elementary curriculum inherent in Piaget's theory of the development of concrete logical thinking. Five generalizations regarding concrete operational thinking were employed as a basis for discussing the Piagetian implications for an elementary school curriculum. Implications focused on operational thinking, learner participation, and social involvement. Attention was paid to alterations in the goal; learning experiences provided in mathematics, science, reading and the language arts, and social studies; the means of evaluation required to make a conventional school curriculum consonant with Piaget's theory and research. Newby concluded that Piaget's research has provided a detailed description of the manner in which a child structures his intelligence to allow logical reasoning and that the theory should guide educators in planning elementary school curricula. (Details are given later).

Kamii (1974) who developed a detailed 'Piagetian-based' programme for young children, has described teaching procedures without specifically conceptualizing the teaching strategies employed (Parker, 1972 and Frost, 1973). Kamii stresses that the teacher 'set up a situation sometimes proposing an activity, and see how children react', Frost (1973, p. 157). She uses such other terms as 'exploratory method', 'skilful', and figuring out what the child is thinking, to elaborate his way rather than disrupt it. She stresses avoidance of sudden imposition of a line of reasoning different from the child's. Basically, Kamii represents the teacher roles as primarily environmental structuring and unobtrusive interaction to help children test out their ideas, by 'differentiation and integration of previously constructed schemes'. Encouragement, rather than teaching, is Kamii's characterization of the teaching roles. 'Stress is on the use of activities which emphasize physical knowledge, with negative feedback from objects, but not from people, to stimulate child curiosity and confidence. Kamii's richly sophisticated descriptions are suggestive but not specific', Robison, Jagoda, and Blotner (1974). In continuation, Kamii (1974a) elaborated on Piaget's principles of interactionism and constructivism with a discussion of his theory of intelligence, the biological origin of intelligence, and the development of structures. She described the varied influences that affect the child's own development of intellectual structures, relating these to the nature of his educational experiences.

The goals of the Cognitive Developmental Early Childhood Education Programme (Willis, 1975) fall into three general categories: social-emotional development, cognitive development, and psychomotor development. Willis includes the proviso however that Piaget views all learning as a unified process and that the classroom teacher incorporates all phases of development as a whole in the activities. The emphasis is on giving children opportunities to attain objectives rather than the imposition of fixed requirements. (Details follow). In a paper entitled 'Formative evaluation in a cognitive developmental programme for young children', Willis, Cohen and Clement (1975) describe the attempt to establish an evaluation system for the Cognitive Developmental Early Childhood Programme consistent with the Piagetian assessment approach. (Details follow).

More recently, Selman (1975) reports research which suggested that stage progression in social reasoning 'occurs through mechanisms similar to those proposed by Piaget in logical-mathematical thought. The development of social reasoning involves experiences of conflict in the child's attempt to apply his current level of thought to social problems, and exposure to moderately higher levels of thought. The aim of our research, following Piaget's framework, is descriptive — to describe a sequence of levels of social thought from the egocentric to the sociocentric. The educational application in the domain of social development is based upon evidence of a natural progression of social thought from an initial level at which the child confuses the perspectives of self and other (level 0), to subsequent levels of development at which he realizes that other's subjective thoughts and feelings are distinct from self's (level 1); that other can consider the self's objective attitudes and feelings (level 2); that self and other can view self's and other's point of view mutually and simultaneously (level 3); and that there is a general social viewpoint that transcends individual perspectives (level 4). For the last three years we have been developing a curriculum model for primary school children based on this research. The assumption of the curriculum is that children's functioning in areas such as social problem-solving, interpersonal awareness, communication and persuasion skills, and moral thought and behaviour can be improved by helping children apply their level of social reasoning to these areas and by helping to stimulate movement through the levels. With these considerations in mind we constructed a set of dilemmas designed to stimulate the child's ability to perceive and understand perspectives other than his own. The dilemmas are presented to children through filmstrips and recordings . . . The teacher then asks the children to discuss in small groups what should be done to resolve the dilemma, to give reasons for each choice and to debate about whether some reasons are more adequate than others. Role-playing and class debates are also used. Teachers are encouraged to use these discussions as models for dealing with real-life dilemmas that arise in class', p. 132.

Jimenez (1976) envisages the system of synectics as being a 'highly practical and positive way of making Piaget's theories an effective part of education'. He considers that the ideas of the inventor of synectics, William Gordon, may be applied in making Piaget's theory operational, rather than leaving to chance the development of intelligence. Jimenez focuses on Piaget's theory as 'the most solid theory we have of the development of learning skills from childhood to adulthood', but which seems 'paradoxically to be also the least usable . . . Taking in too simplistic a sense Piaget's insistence on the impossibility of skipping developmental stages or of rushing growth, some teachers understand him to mean that stimulation and challenge are like an excess of Vitamin C, to no avail at all. And so, Piaget, whose essential achievement has been to recognize that immature intelligence nevertheless is intelligence, that the child in his own fashion truly thinks, can be and is being subverted to justify the understimulation and the underexercise of the young mind.' Jimenez therefore, examines the ideas of Piaget and Gordon on the mechanisms at work in both the developing mind of the child and the developed mind of the adult. He concludes by indicating with actual classroom examples, the kind of practical contribution to teaching and learning that can be expected from the sustained use of Piaget's and Gordon's systems. (Details follow).

ii. Enrichment intervention programme

Kohlberg (1968a) examines the Piagetian contributions to pre-school programmes with specific reference to academic linguistic training. Kohlberg attempted to demonstrate how Piagetian theory leads to the conclusion that it is futile to teach cognitive skills. 'The conception of the pre-school period as a critical period for the environmental stimulation of general intelligence is examined, considering general intelligence in both psychometric and Piagetian terms.' Kohlberg further recalls the contributions of Piaget and associates in the 'development of pre-school children's play, their conversations with one another, their conceptions of life, of death, or reality, of sexual identity, of good and evil. The implications of these and other themes for the broader definition of pre-school objectives are taken up elsewhere', (Kohlberg and Lesser, in preparation).

However, Bereiter (1970, pp. 25—31) responded critically to Kohlberg's conclusion against specific instruction. Bereiter accuses Kohlberg of treating instruction as if it were an alternative to experience when the issue concerns only a half-hour per day of structured interaction between teacher and child within the day of free activity. Kamii (1970. pp. 33—9) argues that Bereiter did not succeed in making a convincing case in support of specific instruction, but at the same time Kamii considered that the educational implications that Kohlberg drew from Piaget's theory were too general. She maintains that 'the two schools of thought converge with regard to the teaching of social knowledge, but not with regard to logico-mathematical knowledge . . . The relative merits of the two approaches can be determined only through long-term longitudinal comparisons'. However, Kohlberg (1970 pp. 40—8) reiterates the points of his 1968a article, which he directs to the criticisms of Bereiter and Kamii. (For the full dialogue among Kohlberg, Bereiter and Kamii, refer to 'Interchange', *A Journal of Educational Studies*, 1, 1, 1970).

An investigation of the efficacy of Piaget curricular elements integrated into a traditional Head Start programme was carried out by Diamond (1973). Specifically, the author was intent to determine whether Piagetian elements when added would enhance classification and seriation skills and conservation of discontinuous and continuous quantities in more Head Start children than a programme without such elements. The samples consisted of 23 in the experimental group and 19 in the control group. In order to help Ss progress from pre-operational to concrete operational thought, 'curricular elements were added to the daily class routine. The daily five minute sessions were with a group of three children and the teacher "aide" playing with materials physically and verbally . . . Nine separate activities, using a variety of toys . . . spread over the school year, specifically addressed the seriation, classification and conservation concepts . . . Building a general climate of inquiry was attempted: open-ended questions on the part of the adult encouraged various physical and verbal responses from the children. Direct intellectual confrontation within a social framework so that discovery was inevitable was the exact process in the treatment'. Seriation skills developed more in Head Start Ss who were taught in the traditional curriculum with Piaget curricular elements integrated than in the traditional curriculum without such elements. Classification skills developed more in Head Start Ss who were taught in the traditional curriculum with Piaget curricular elements integrated than in the Head Start Ss who were taught in the traditional curriculum without such elements. The third and fourth hypotheses stated that conservation of discontinuous and continuous quantity will develop in more Head Start students who are taught in the traditional curriculum with Piaget curricular elements integrated than in Head Start students who are taught in the traditional curriculum without such elements. The former was confirmed, while the latter was rejected. 'The four essential factors for intellectual growth according to Jean Piaget are maturation, physical and social interaction and equilibration. This study's method incorporated these elements . . . It does appear that in the hands of a teacher . . . such curricular elements integrated into the traditional classroom facilitates intellectual growth', (Diamond, *op. cit.*), p. 168—A. (Details are given later).

To examine the patterns of inducements in cognitive development in 48 children aged three to five years and to compare the effects of two contrasting pre-school programmes on the development of logical operations abilities, Bingham-Newman (1975) administered an experimental and a comparison programme. The former incorporated a theoretical framework and a teacher education component built on Piagetian theory. The latter used a conventional nursery school programme. A 'representative' battery of Piagetian tasks and two standardized non-Piagetian measures: the Raven's Coloured Progressive Matrices and the Peabody Picture Vocabulary Test were administered in a pre-test-post-test design. Typical age patterns for the Piagetian task performances for the three- and five-year-old Ss were noted. The percentages showed an overall increase in Ss' responses in the higher response categories in the post-test for both the Piagetian and non-Piagetian tasks. Cross-sectional analyses demonstrated no marked differences between the performances of the experimental and control groups. Longitudinal analyses revealed that significant gains were made on several of the seriation subtasks and the length comparison measurement subtasks. T-test comparisons of the non-Piagetian tests pre- to post-test indicated significant gains for all Ss on the Peabody Picture Vocabulary Test and only for the 'wave two' control groups on the Raven Progressive Matrices. (Details follow).

The Early School Admissions Programme is a pre-kindergarten programme for the four-year-olds. Reid (1975) asserts, 'This programme was concerned with the development of cognitive and verbal abilities. With this in mind, credence was given to many avenues opened for experimentation and a Piagetian based curriculum. It became paramount to place emphasis on thought processes and assimilated language in order to enhance logical thinking among these four-year-olds . . . The measure, based on the nine programme objectives, maintained the concepts of Jean Piaget, as he traced the stages of development of children as they entered the pre-operational period at about the age two and through age seven. A measure such as Programme Evaluation Measure, locally constructed and administered at monthly intervals was apparently far better suited for the disadvantaged and/or inner-city child than the commercial standardized tests. More than that, the Piagetian concepts of child development seemed a more logical measure of pupil growth. It meant that a child's growth could be measured in terms of his own individual rate rather than by national or even local norms for that matter. Moreover, by providing teachers in the programme with data concerning each child, the teacher could plan and adjust the programme to meet the needs of the individual. Also information could be provided for the future kindergarten teacher that would enable her to plan to build on strengths and to boost weaknesses of the individual child . . . The use of a Piagetian scale measure has enabled us to be more objective in observing and respecting the learning process as such applies not only to the group of pupils, but to the individual pupil as well.' (Details follow).

De Meuron (1974) described a collaborative effort made between a psychiatric clinic and a school district administration, to provide an atmosphere of change for children and their families from an inner-city slum area. Detailed observation and study of the affective and cognitive (Piagetian) characteristics of the children were undertaken. Meetings with teachers concerned and the medical, social and psychological services were also involved. She discussed the social and intellective functionings of the children which operate, in effect, to alienate them from all that school might offer them. De Meuron presented specific illustrations of changes in classroom practices aimed at modifying the obstacles to learning experienced by the 57 children (CA = seven to 11) exhibiting such psychiatric categories as: borderline retardation, hyperactivity, brain damage, minimal brain dysfunction, behaviour problems, emotionally disturbed, and schizoid. Ethnically they included: Puerto Rican, Black Americans, Chinese, Jewish, Polish and Italian.

More recently, in a study entitled, 'Faciliating psychological growth in post-adolescents: a cognitive-developmental curriculum intervention and analysis', Brock (1975) using the broad theoretical underpinnings of Dewey, Piaget, and Kohlberg, a six week curriculum intervention was designed to deliberately promote 'structural' cognitive development using a group of 41 genuine college physical-therapy-assistant students. This intervention followed the 'deliberate psychological education' model of pairing direct action and structured reflection. 'However, it was distinct from other interventions of this type in that the students were actively involved in a highly structured and supervised physical therapy clinical situation, as opposed to the rather ambiguous or open action situations employed in other deliberate psychological education studies', p. 4140—B. Programmatic results showed the experimental group intervention well' liked and seen as moderately useful in a personal and professional sense for the students. Measures of cognitive developmental growth showed no significant change from pre- to post-tests, or between experimental and control groups however. Students tended to remain at 'conventional' levels of development as measured by the Kohlberg and Loevinger tests. (Details follow).

iii. 'Piaget for Teachers' and teacher training programmes

Piaget (1971) emphasizes 'But from the point of view of the teachers and their social situation, those old educational conceptions, having made the teachers into mere transmitters of elementary or only slightly more than elementary general knowledge, without allowing them any opportunity 'for initiative and even less for research and discovery, have thereby imprisoned them in their present lowly status', (p. 124).

Furth (1970) in *Piaget for Teachers*, addresses himself to teachers in a series of letters and states that Piaget's findings point to the need to 'strengthen his (the child's) thinking so that the child will develop to the point where he can use the verbal medium intelligently'. Furth believes that teachers concentrate too much on imparting specialized skills such as reading and that thinking comes before language and adults have little idea of the quality of thinking that goes on in the child. The reason being partly the exaggeration of the role of language in the development of logical development. He is convinced that the ability to think and to learn can be cultivated, and describes a number of thinking games built on symbol-picture logic which are devised to challenge the child's operative intelligence and reinforce his spontaneous thinking development. Furth's interpretation of Piaget's theory of intelligence as a basis on which to construct the educational treatment of the child may prove difficult for teachers. Selman (1975) in a review of Furth and Wach's (1974) book *Thinking Goes to School*, states, 'Furth and Wachs challenge the reader to sharpen his conception of "thinking": first by emphasizing that thinking involves action as well as reflection; second by specifying that thought is involved in sensorimotor activities; third by showing that the physical activities need not be thought of as mere gymnastics drill; and fourth by showing that thought is more than verbalization. Furth and Wachs use Piagetian theory to lend validity to activities other than reading and maths in the elementary grades. The collaboration of developmental psychologists and clinician leads to some good results. There is nothing wrong with vintage wine in a new bottle; that is, worthwhile sensorimotor exercises cast loosely within a Piagetian framework. But the authors face a dilemma. On the one hand, they do not want a "teacher proof" cookbook; on the other, they want to be concrete, to get away from the standard, "Here are some general ideas for you teachers, go out and transform your school . . ." Both extremes are offensive to them and to the Piagetian conception of development, which involves active construction on the part of the teacher as well as the child. But the middle ground the authors seek is elusive — they might have had better success if they could have shown how to link qualitative or Piagetian levels of reasoning to levels of performance in each of the games or activities they present', pp. 133—4. (An outline of *Thinking Goes to School* appears later).

Piaget in the Classroom, is edited by Schwebel and Raph (1973). Examples of actual classroom practice are included so that teachers can assimilate a great deal of information and gradually build meaning. Sinclair, Duckworth, and de Meuron were especially effective. Sinclair has reported several learning experiments involving conservation and demonstrated their relationship to teaching arithmetic. She suggested numerous ways in which Piagetian insights could be employed to arrange the child's encounters with number in an ordered and facilitated way. Duckworth has shown how the teacher could work with children so as to provide more material for the learner to try to put things together in his head. De Meuron demonstrated how the classroom environment and a seasonal learning unit could include Piagetian concepts. (Details follow). (See also Boyle, 1975, details of which are, more appropriately, given in Volume One in the present series *Piagetian Research*).

Sime (1973) discussed the significance of Piaget's work and stated that a study of his findings made many intending teachers aware that they did not themselves have some of the fundamental concepts, such as conservation, on which the understanding of number depends. Such awareness made a more competent guide to children's learning ' . . . a student needs experience in diagnostic testing (à la Piaget) and of attempting, under tutorial guidance, to relate his teaching to the results of the testing. To this one must add a *caveat*. In the schools teachers will not have clinical conditions in which to do Piagetian testing. Unless, in the colleges, students are given experience in adapting the testing to non-clinical conditions most will cease to do such diagnostic work once they qualify', p. 273.

Tursi (1973) attempted 'to analyze selected "organismic" presuppositions inherent within Piaget's theory of the ontogenesis of human scientific thought in order to discern the epistemological consequences of these presuppositions. If some of these epistemological consequences can be made more explicit, application of the theory can be better evaluated by teacher educators who can be in a better position to decide if these consequences represent beliefs which they share and wish to implement', p. 673–A. The mode of analysis constituted four features: (a) exposition or presentation of Piaget's own ideas in his own terminology, (b) analysis with a view to examination and interpretation, (c) epistemological and ontological aspects of the presuppositions, and (d) implications for early childhood education. Presuppositions were analyzed at the 'world view' level; the 'paradigm' level; and the theoretical level of genetic epistemology. Tursi concludes, 'Eclecticism appears to be incompatible with a Piagetian holist viewpoint. Since Piaget's "world view" appears to be incompatible with the dominant world view extant in academic psychology and psychological foundations of education, it is not surprising that it is misunderstood. The dominant view with its concomitant view of man would rationally justify different teaching strategies and practices than would the Piagetian view . . . these differences . . . would appear to require considerable modification of current dominant educational practices', p. 674–A. (Details follow).

Robison, Jagoda, and Blotner (1974) stated, 'with the New York State mandate that teacher training programmes within the state be competency based by 1975, it seemed appropriate to assess the extent of improvement, both in teacher performance and in children's learning, over traditional methods of training teachers. The area of children's classification behaviour was chosen as a target, and student teachers were trained to teach classification, with teacher training either competency-based or traditional in format. Additionally, we were attempting to independently evaluate whether classification could be more effectively taught by teachers using a Piagetian, or teachers using a Skinnerian philosophy of learning ... there were four treatment conditions: Piaget Modular ... Piaget Traditional ... Skinner Modular ... and Skinner Traditional ... The modules featured such activities as, independent reading, self-testing, self-selection of material to be covered, viewing of videotapes, listening to audio-cassettes ... , optional conferences with college supervisors, discussion with colleagues ... The traditional format trained students in teaching classification, primarily via classroom lecture, discussion, and quizzes, during seminar ... The Skinnerian approach emphasized such teacher behaviours as use of behavioural objectives, small steps, children proceeding at their own rate, reinforcement ... , preassessment and diagnosis of errors to determine the child's starting point ... The Piagetian approach featured such teacher strategies as cognitive dissonance acceptance and encouragement of children's play, absence of evaluative, judgmental or reinforcing statements, encouraging manipulation on the part of the learner, and post assessment'. In continuation the relationship of teaching competence to teacher performance and children's learning of classification skills was studied by Jagoda and Robison (1975). Two studies were conducted. The first study was a two x two factorial design which compared competency based vs. traditional approaches, and Skinnerian vs. Piagetian philosophies. Four treatment conditions were utilized: Piaget Modular, Piaget Traditional, Skinner Modular, and Skinner Traditional which were evaluated for effectiveness with regard to: (a) student teacher performance; (b) advancement of children's classification skills. Seventeen student teachers participated and their videotaped performance was evaluated. 'Only with regard to use of behavioural objectives and appropriate implementation were the differences marginally significant in favour of the modular groups. Children in 17 early childhood classes were pre- and post-tested on the Sigel Classification test. Although there was a paradoxical decline in Sigel score from pre- to post-test overall, this decline was significantly less for children taught by the traditionally trained student teachers', Jagoda and Robison (*op. cit.*). A replication study with several improvements was also conducted. The authors concluded that ' ... we are as yet unable to determine any advantage for children, in training teachers according to the CBTE format'. ('CBTE refers to a behaviourist conception of teaching skills and evaluation of those skills in public, objective and criterion-referenced ways'.) (Details are given later).

Charlesworth (1975) presented at the philosophical, theoretical, research and practice levels a model for guiding the teaching of young children in the cognitive areas of language and conceptualization. A description of the primary theories which underlie early childhood programmes: Piagetian, Behaviourist and Traditionalist is given. The author has suggested that the theories can be combined in a complementary way followed by examples of research studies in conceptualization, language, and psycho-social realms which bring theory and practice closer to each other. The nature of the learner is placed in a Piagetian framework. The concepts which should be developing in early childhood were outlined as the source of curriculum objectives. The study concludes with a demonstration as to how the principles may be used in practice no matter what materials, guides, or teaching kits the teacher has available. (Details are given later).

Implications of Piaget's theory for in-service education were examined by Tamburrini (1975). She maintains, 'There is first a question of values. Although Piaget's evidence supports a position of the human individual as an active learner constructing reality, that does not mean that you have necessarily to base what you do in education on that. You can choose to do that, or you can choose to forget all about it and concentrate on children acquiring skills, on conditioning, or on behavioural objectives. What you first have to do is to make a decision about your values in education. There is no doubt a great deal of evidence to suggest that we can condition children. There is also evidence to suggest that we can produce more autonomous human beings . . . In the in-service education of teachers we therefore need to help them to scrutinize their values and to be aware of what the range is. There is a second question of values. Teachers need to scrutinize values and make decisions about whether they are going to go for cooperative individuals or competitive individuals . . . A third principle is that when a teacher has provided a classroom with a diversity of materials, each of which has within them a potential for diversification, children can and will operate at different conceptual levels, but they will also operate in relation to different concerns and preoccupations. So what is needed is that a teacher is then able to relate to children diagnostically to find out what they are paying attention to', Tamburrini (*ibid.*, pp. 8–9).

The author then cites a 'good' example of the ongoing diagnosis by a teacher in a context which was highly diversified. 'The teacher's notes give a glimpse of her educational dialogue with those children. She provides just the right accommodative gap and continually learns from the children's words and actions. What this teacher is doing is extending the children's thinking appropriately in the context of their activities.

She knows about symmetry and balance but she also has an understanding of developmental principles which leads her to engage successfully with the children', Tamburrini (*ibid.*, p. 9).

iv. Closed and open systems of education

Wickens (1974) contrasts the primary features of closed and open systems of education, the former generally associated with the S—R model and stress on traditional, hierarchically organized learning of content; the latter on the individual learner and the interactional processes among children, teachers, and the broader educational environment. Wickens utilized three basic features derived from the Piagetian work to provide a theoretical framework for open-system programmes. These include the role of active involvement in learning on the part of the child, the maintenance of a social system in the classroom as an integral part of learning, and lastly, the progressive development of representation.

More recently, Mai (1975) described a comprehensive theoretical framework for Open Education built upon the epistemological, psychological, and philosophical premises of Dewey and Piaget. The theoretical discourse assumes that Open Education requires for itself a more rigorous understanding of the psychological notions and their philosophical implications than currently seem to inform Open pedagogy. 'It also assumes that Open Education, like the Progressive Movement in education before it, faces as its major task that of getting beyond the phase of self-advocacy through polemical, rhetoric and sentimental theorizing, so as to evolve a consistent and workable body of pedagogical prescriptions for elementary teachers'. (Details are given later).

v. Critical studies

A critical study of the applications of Piaget's theory to education was undertaken by Barros (1972) who raises several questions 'what relevancy might genetic epistemology have to education? Are there any gaps in the theory which may hinder or infer educational implications? What is the role of education and . . . instruction in Piaget's theory?' Barros maintains that Piaget's attempt to establish a scientific basis for epistemology is grounded on a structuralist view which understands knowledge as a process of construction and proposes a methodology that considers logistic formalization as its fundamental resource. However, the models which Piaget employs to describe and account for the stages of development in cognitive functioning have been criticized for the lack of precision and its formulation. Moreover, that educationists have overlooked formal (axiomatic) aspects of the theory and by so doing have created severe problems in attempted applications. (Details are given later).

Gaudia (1974) contended that the contribution of Piaget to educational theory and practice is minimal. Almost none of his writings deal directly with education and pedagogy themselves. According to Piaget, development is the process essential to learning and each element of learning occurs as a function of total development. The teacher's dilemma is whether to be wary of Piaget's conclusions or to agree with the current acceptance of his viewpoint. Piaget refuses to be pinned down on the question whether or not the cognitive development of a child can be modified through formal intervention, labeling this problem an 'American question.' Educators are confused about Piaget's position as to the relative influence of heredity and environment on development. Piaget's comment on this problem has frequently been, 'I refuse to be concerned'.

However, Hawkins (1973) emphasized what Piaget himself has often asserted, 'that (this) developmental framework is not directly relevant or adequate to the practical and theoretical perspective of a teacher. In particular, there is a certain danger in the unimaginative use of Piagetian interviews to check off children's conceptual "attainments" and thus provide a sort of profile of individual developmental level. It would be very poor credit indeed to the thought of a great investigator if such very limited diagnosis became a sort of administrative substitute for the widely abused IQ, which, in turn, was poor credit to the early great investigations of Binet', pp. 133–4.

Boyle (1975) promotes the view 'that psychology's contribution to the teacher lies primarily in offering conceptual schemes . . . in terms of which the interactions between teachers and learners can be analysed; and in providing a source of ideas on children's cognitive development. With respect to the latter, the views of Piaget as applied to education are discussed, and it is argued that their use to the teacher is negligible'. (The study is described more fully in Volume One, in the present series *Piagetian Research*).

b. Mathematics

Fischbein (1973) maintained that Piaget's 'work shows very clearly that intelligence develops through a series of stages . . . The essential idea for our discussion is that each fundamental system of knowledge must be anticipated and prepared for in earlier stages by means specific to these stages. According to this law, the learning of mathematical structures during the period of the final equilibrium of formal operations must already be prepared for during the period of concrete operations by means appropriate to this period. This will permit the structures to become efficient instruments in mathematical thought', p. 227. He further commented that Piaget has demonstrated 'the close relationship between the important mathematical structures and the organization of human intelligence. According to him, mathematical structures are closely related to the main operational. structures of intelligence gradually built up during the subject's ontogenesis, and group structure is at the core of this relationship. At the concrete operational level, intelligence has already acquired, although only partially, characteristics that are analogous to those of a group', p. 228. Hawkins (1973) stated that the epistemological and historical origins, or the systematics of 'those basic mathematical structures we know and seek to regenerate in our teaching . . . is very much alive today, thanks in large measure to the work of Professor Piaget . . . Piaget has brought about a long-overdue revitalization of the philosophical framework of Immanuel Kant, who developed the first coherent account of knowledge as the product of a self-regulating synthetic activity. With respect to the proto-deducing style of mathematical thinking, . . . Piaget has made an important theoretical argument which is thoroughly Kantian in spirit, though grounded also in his own empirical studies of intellectual development. This argument concerns the origin and nature of our sense of logical entailment or necessity. Like Kant (and Hume), Piaget argues that contingent generalizations derived from factual observation can never, of themselves, give rise to this idea of necessity. This sense of necessity is first operative, Piaget argues, in the habitual use of those schemata by which infants and children develop, with increasing competence, their ability to control and transform their material surroundings by systematic means. In still later intellectual development the distinction between the necessary and the contingent gains recognition by a kind of reflective abstraction; our knowledge can be traced partly to perception and partly to a growing awareness of our own active transformation of that experience into a stable and organised system of intellectual resources', pp. 132—3.

Kessen and Kuhlman (1962) addressed the first of their conferences entirely to the work of Piaget concerning cognitive processes in children and Flavell (1963) has summarized both Piaget's psychological and epistemological views. In 1964 Piaget elaborated his views at the Cornell and California conferences which addressed their inquiry to the implications of current cognitive development researches for the mathematics and science curriculum (Ripple and Rockcastle, 1964). Various issues were discussed: for example, the appropriate sequence of the presentation of specific concepts in curricula; relative usefulness of direct instruction, as opposed to self-discovery in the formation of concepts; and the role of language in such formation.

Kilpatrick (1964) describes the curriculum programme of the School Mathematics Study Group. He discussed the issue of spontaneous development in children's thinking versus acceleration of this development through formal instruction and experience. However, it is essential to point out that the features of this curriculum scheme are not entirely compatible with the findings of Piaget's studies. Kilpatrick speculates that the child's ability to understand may be changed by new curricula, and that the issue of stages, therefore, remains an open one. Bruner (1966) has provided a psychological rationale for the major ideas of this new mathematics curricula and the work of Dienes (1959) is especially relevant in this respect. Similar research efforts have been undertaken by Fischer (1964). He maintains that Piagetian work has indicated 'the need for following a plan designed in accordance with the child's developing thought structures. Providing the requisite concrete experiences which undergird abstract and symbolic learning presents a challenge to the teacher, and calls for changes in much of the traditional curriculum'. (See Piaget, 1973, discussed later).

A significant contribution to mathematics curriculum development has been made by the Nuffield Mathematics Project aimed at ages five through to ' 13 years. An Australian programme acknowledging and espousing Piagetian theory is the Victorian Primary Mathematics Courses (1966). Piaget's influence, likewise, is acknowledged in references on how to teach mathematics in such books as Biggs and MacLean's *Freedom to Learn*, (1969).

Collis (1971), attempted to distinguish mathematical material most suited to the abilities of concrete operational and formal operational level pupils, respectively. He concluded that educationalists should be familiar with the characteristics of the mental strategies manifest at the various Piagetian stages and that curriculum content should be adjusted accordingly. Collis (1971) reported that concrete operational Ss were performing at the lower levels on problems in mathematics which involved working within a set of axioms. When a problem of the type 'a and b are two numbers such that $a \times b = a$ and $a \times b = b$' was administered and Ss asked to make a series of deductions, 10 to 11 years concrete operational SS found a partial solution and proceeded on this basis regardless of the fact that this leads to conflicting results. Subjects of brighter ability (CA 10 to 11 years) when given problems of this type demonstrate what Festinger (1957) has termed 'psychological discomfort', (Collis, 1972). Neimark and Lewis (1967, 1968) investigating on the acquisition of logical problem-solving strategies substantiate findings reported by Collis (*op. cit.*). Neimark and Lewis's Ss were of normal and bright abilities aged nine and 16 years. The Ss were administered a series of eight problems and their information-gathering behaviour was evaluated by means of a strategy score. They concluded, ' . . . the increase in logical-information-gathering strategy with increasing mental age was best described in terms of an increase in the number of Ss who develop and use a logical strategy', (*ibid.*, p. 107). The studies of Collis (1971, 1972) implied that one could not expect a full comprehension of any inconsistency involved in a simple mathematical system before age 16 years. In extending his 1971, 1972 studies, Collis (1973) in a study of children's ability to work with elementary mathematical systems asserted that, 'Previous studies using mathematical material and the Piagetian model seem to imply that Ss are not able to work within a closed abstract system before they have attained the capacity for formal-operational reasoning. The studies described here support this implication. They show also that Ss below the formal level of thinking tend to ignore a given defined system and reason by analogy with a familiar system. Although items with less abstract elements operated upon appear to be attained first there are grounds for believing that the basic problem lies in the difficulty S has in controlling the variables which define the operations allowable within the system. The studies are seen being of interest to psychologists working with the Piagetian model as well as to teachers and curriculum planners', p. 121. (Details are given later). In extending his earlier works, Collis (1974) studied the development of a preference for logical consistency in school mathematics, by sampling the behaviour of 127 Ss between the ages of nine and 16 years on tasks involving the necessary consistency of a mathematical table. One set of tables was self-consistent and the other gave inconsistent results. The eight-year-old Ss gave preferences and justifications which demonstrated that they were either unaware of the inconsistency or considered it irrelevant. On the other hand, 16-year-old Ss preferred the consistent set of tables and gave 'consistency' explicitly as their reason for preference. 'Groups of Ss in between these ages responded in terms that showed a preference for the consistent table but were not in general able to give explicit reasons for their choice', Collis (*ibid.*, p. 978). (Details follow). (Details of Collis, 1971 study are given in Modgil, 1974, p. 269).

720 mathematics O-level items from pre-tests written for two different syllabuses were assessed for 'concrete' or 'formal' demands by two judges, using Piagetian criteria by Malpas and Brown (1974) 'The mean difficulty indices for items placed in concrete and formal categories were compared in order to test the hypothesis that items classified as making higher demands would be found more difficult'. While there was some variability, there was significant agreement between the judges in the placing of the items, 'and a significant correlation between classification category and the difficulty index of the items. An unexpected difference between the two syllabuses in the distribution of items over concrete and formal categories was also discovered'.

An application of Piagetian research to the growth of chance and probability concepts with 23 low achievers in secondary school mathematics was made by McClenahan (1975). Five tasks as outlined by Piaget and Inhelder in *La Genese de L'Idee de Hasard chez L'Enfant*, were individually administered. A training study was then designed and implemented. The majority of the Ss advanced responses indicative of stage II for the majority of the experiments. There was a strong indication that the low achiever in mathematics may not have attained the formal operational stage, at least as far as the topic of probability was concerned. The author concluded with some implications for curriculum development. 'When selecting subject matter for the low achiever, the level of development should be considered. Piaget's developmental psychology appears to give some understanding of what can, and what is not likely to, be taught profitably to low achievers in mathematics at the secondary level', p. 686–A. (Details follow).

Cathcart (1971), in an investigation into the relationship between conservation and mathematical achievement with primary school children, emphasizes that for success in mathematics the child should be able to analyse a problem from different points of view. The implication for teaching is that there should be a more general problem-solving approach, rather than the teaching of particular rules for particular types of problems. (Details of the study appear in Modgil, 1974, pp. 267–8).

The sequence of development of some early mathematics behaviours was studied by Wang, Resnick, and Boozer (1971). The battery of tests, administered to kindergarten children, assessed the ability to perform a specific task involving counting, use of numerals, or comparison of set size. The data gathered were subjected to scalogram analyses to test hypotheses concerning sequences of acquisition of these behaviours. The results demonstrated: '(a) a reliable sequence of skills in using numerals; (b) the dependence of learning numerals upon prior acquisition of counting skills for sets of the size represented; (c) acquisition of numeral reading for small sets before learning to count larger sets; and (d) the independence of counting and one-to-one correspondence operations in young children', p. 1767. The authors discussed the implications of the findings for designing an introductory mathematics curriculum. (Details appear later).

Concrete operational thought and developmental aspects of solutions to a task based on a mathematical three group were investigated by Sheppard (1974). The learning of a mathematical three group, rotations of an equilateral triangle, and nine Piagetian tests of concrete operations were administered to 25 lower-middle class children aged six, eight, and 10 years. 'Except for an initial phase in which the fundamentals of the task were learned, the six-year-olds were significantly inferior to the older children in their success in learning to combine two rotations, learning to replace combinations by a third element, and being able to retain their skill with a closed mapping when tested on the learning material and on transfer material. Operativity correlated with performance on all the tasks of the mathematical group except for the initial preparatory phase. The data were seen as supporting the conclusion that if concrete operations can be described by groupings, operational subjects can establish closure in a mathematical group', p. 116.

In a study entitled, 'Do mathematical group invariants characterize the perceptual schema of younger and older children?', Gyr, Willey, Gordon, and Kubo (1974) explored whether perceptual processes of children can be viewed within a Structuralist frame of reference and, whether the concept of the group of transformations, and related notions can be used to formulate perceptual phenomena and to predict experimental results. 'The paper discusses (1) the benefit for perception theory to be derived from having its processes described in terms of group theory, (2) past work in perception which has used group theory, and (3) some studies by the authors which explore whether the invariance structure which underlies groups of transformations is reflected in the perceptual functioning of children', p. 176. (Details follow).

The development of concepts of infinity and limit in mathematics was studied by Langford (1974). 'Under the most favourable conditions a majority of nine-year-olds can conceive of the arithmetical operations of addition, subtraction and multiplication being indefinitely iterated when applied to numbers. In the case of division this is put off until age 13. The way in which children answer questions about indefinitely iterated division indicates it is not until age 13 a majority of children have a concept of limit. Even at age 15 the overwhelming majority of adolescents continue to think of limits from the standpoint of potential rather than of completed infinity. This points to the conclusion that while concepts relating to potential infinity develop between the ages of nine and 15, concepts of completed infinity do not develop until after this period. It also indicates that the claim of Piaget and Inhelder (1956), based only on the results from tasks involving division, that the concept of indefinite iteration does not develop until the period of formal operations, needs to be reassessed'. (Details are given later).

The effects of a Piagetian geometry model on young children were investigated by Barton (1975). The sample comprised of 24 'beginning' school children, 12 five-year-olds, and 12 eight-year-olds. The group was identified according to high mathematical ability or low mathematical ability as determined by standardized tests. A test instrument, a pre-test and post-test composed of three topological, three projective and three Euclidean ideas was abstracted from Piaget and Inhelder (1956), and developed by Barton. A topological, projective and Euclidean progression as advanced by the Geneva school was substantiated. Recommendations were advanced for incorporating selected geometric ideas into the elementary school curriculum, and for providing additional developmental research in mathematics education. (Details follow).

In a Paper entitled: 'Spontaneous *vs.* scientific concepts in mathematics', Fleckman (1975) states that Piaget has provided two important ideas that can help one learn and teach more effectively: a comprehensive examination of children's cognitions show a maturation of children's thought processes; and task analysis enable one to follow how internalizations of cognitions take place. 'Teachers feel that the discoveries made spontaneously during lessons mean that the student has attained meaning and understanding of a concept. What the student is exhibiting is the very first accommodation of which Piaget speaks and has not attained in depth assimilation. Cognitions that are on the level of awareness do not occur spontaneously. Rather, the group of concepts entails step by step, sequential learning to allow for progress and interaction of accommodation and assimilation. Emphasis in the classrooms in the teaching of mathematics has been mainly the accommodation of the student to presentations of concepts or computations in mathematics. Cookbook approaches even when replaced with inductive, discovery techniques are insufficient for internalization of meaning. There has to be a maturational process such as described by Piaget whereby concepts on the accommodation level proceed to the assimilation level; where spontaneous learning becomes scientific (psychological learning). Vygotsky has used the spontaneous and scientific terminology to distinguish the types of learnings involved in mastery of concepts . . . this is a vitalization of Piaget's ideas of task analysis so that sequential presentation may be accorded the content, and also maturation of cognitions are provided', Fleckman (*op. cit.*). (Details are given later).

More recently, Martin (1975) concluded that, Piaget does not always use mathematical language as precisely as a mathematician might desire; because what mathematical concepts Piaget's tasks are measuring is often not clear, inferences for mathematics education from his research should be made with caution; and Piaget's evidence that topological representation precedes Euclidean and projective representation, while often tantalizing, is not unequivocal and occasionally may be based on assumptions which are mathematically incorrect. An example of such an erroneous assumption is that figures can be classified into topological and Euclidean shapes', p. 6368—A. (The study is described more appropriately in Volume Two under the present series, *Piagetian Research*).

(i) 'Children's Mathematical Concepts: Six Piagetian Studies in Mathematics Education.'
M.F. Rosskopf (Ed.), 1975

The results of Genkins (1975) study indicated that as early as the kindergarten level, children have sufficient ability to learn some of the behavioural features of geometric figures. As a result of paper-folding children were able to classify 'point-symmetric non-bilaterally-symmetric figures and asymmetric figures as non-bilaterally-symmetric. Although they apparently did not improve their ability to identify bilaterally symmetric figures, paper-folding appears to be a worthwhile experience to provide for kindergarten children although the "mirror method" was not appropriate'. Through the mirror task second graders learned to discriminate all types of figures except vertically oriented bilaterally symmetric figures. They learned about regularities of figures as well as their irregularities and to identify figures as non-bilaterally-symmetric and bilaterally-symmetric. 'This was in contrast to the case of the kindergarten children, who learned to classify non-exemplars as non-bilaterally-symmetric but did not learn to classify exemplars as bilaterally symmetric', p. 41. Paper-folding supplemented the second-graders work with the mirror. The conjecture therefore that the concept of bilateral symmetry was an appropriate one both mathematically and psychologically with which to introduce young children to transformation geometry was supported.

In a study entitled 'Topological Understanding of Young Children' Bass (1975) concluded that the concept of enclosure seemed to mature earlier than the concept of order, which precedes the concept of equivalence. She drew implications for teaching geometry in early childhood with respect to development ('a gradual, step-by-step process of structural accrual and change') and further to the affective aspects of 'readiness': the child's interest, appreciations, attitudes and values. A further focus was placed upon 'the wealth of children's literature' involving mathematical ideas to help provide 'the spark needed to intensify children's interest in topics related to mathematics and increase the possibilities for varied and meaningful experiences', pp. 68—9. A selected list of such children's books is provided. She likewise refers to the importance of the diagnosis of the child's informational and operational level and cites Hunt's (1969) statement that 'the best cues for an appropriate match of circumstances and child are the evidences of spontaneous interest and surprise'.

In studying the child's conception of area measure, Wagman (1975) drew implications for school programmes. She comments that normally, the first significant presentation of area is made when pupils are about ten- or 11-years-old. 'Conventional texts assume that the pupils already have discovered independently the (unit) area, congruence, and additivity axioms and can conserve area. (Almost all of the material in such textbooks is concerned with the unit postulate; the other axioms are discussed only briefly). This underlying assumption is not consistent with the empirical findings of this investigation. About a third of the ten- and 11-year-olds in the sample either failed to apply at least one of the neglected axioms (area, congruence, and additivity) even in perceptually easy cases, or did not conserve area,' p. 109. The prevalence of the confusion of area and perimeter indicated the importance of clear differentiation of these two functions. 'Children in the third grade who conserve (who are in the majority) should be ready for some instruction concerning the area axioms. Those who do not conserve might benefit from conservation training techniques,' p. 109. The author further emphasizes the importance of concrete materials, especially in the earlier grades which only add to the interest and enthusiasm but acknowledge that concepts are learned first concretely and then abstractly.

The concept of limit is basic to the study of a branch of mathematics called analysis. Mathematics educators have begun to introduce topics in analysis much earlier in the school curriculum.

Taback (1975) focuses on the studies of Davis (1964): The Secondary School Mathematics Curriculum Improvement Study (1968); the Cambridge Conference on School Mathematics (1963); and Smith (1959). Taback considers that as mathematics educators concern themselves with the child's readiness for such instruction, they must, necessarily, consider his awareness of the concept of limit. Taback concludes that by stressing the importance of Piaget-type research in mathematics education, 'it is becoming increasingly popular to investigate the child's insights into mathematical concepts through individual interviews, that is, by presenting him with tasks, probing his answers, and categorizing his thought processes. Future researchers, however, will need to know if and when it is advantageous to structure their questions within situations that are overtly non-mathematical', p. 144 (details of Taback's study are given more appropriately in Volume Two in the present series *Piagetian Research*).

The concept of function was investigated by Thomas (1975) and concerned the learning by seventh and eighth grade subjects of high ability, of the concept specifically taught and applied in a modern programme of instruction. 'The study did not deal with the concept of function in the broad sense of functionality, nor with "functional thinking". Rather, it dealt with the learning of a formal contemporary concept of function as exemplified by the text materials of the Secondary School Mathematics Curriculum Improvement Study (SSMCIS, 1966)', p. 146. 'Certain aspects of the concept of function were not specifically dealt with in the final analysis of stages. Among these is the concept of a one-to-one function. The difficulties that some subjects had in distinguishing the concept of a unique assignment from a one-to-one assignment indicates that, in teaching, care must be taken to discriminate the allowable types of assignments for a function. Furthermore, the interview protocols suggest that subjects need more practice in discriminating instances and non-instances in varied settings and representations', *ibid.*, p. 169.

In a study of low achievers' understanding of logical inference forms, Carroll (1975) concluded that, 'In the process of gleaning some information about students' reasoning abilities, many questions have been raised. This in itself seems fruitful, since the factors influencing the subjects' attempts to reason logically are undoubtedly many, and knowledge concerning any of these factors could shed light on the reasoning process. This process, important to all engaged in education, is especially pertinent to the task of the mathematics educator, who must be involved in helping students to develop skill in drawing conclusions, in forming and recognizing proofs, and in avoiding fallacious reasoning', (*ibid.*, p. 207).

ii. Comments on mathematical education
J. Piaget, 1973

Piaget asserted, ' . . . it would be a great mistake, particularly in mathematical education, to neglect the role of actions and always to remain on the level of language. Particularly with young pupils, activity with objects is indispensable to the comprehension of arithmetical as well as geometrical relations . . . There exist, in fact, two types of "experience", one very different from the other which are related to the subject's actions . . . there is what is known as "physical experience" . . . which consists in acting on objects in order to discover the properties of the objects themselves . . . But there also exists . . . what could be called "logico-mathematical experience"; this type of experience gathers its information, not from the physical properties of particular objects, but from the actual actions . . . carried out by the child on objects — these two types of experience are not equivalent,' pp. 80–1. Piaget continued to give reasons for the role of actions and logico-mathematical experience in the later development of deductive thought. ' . . . first is that mental or intellectual operations, which intervene in the subsequent deductive reasoning processes, themselves stem from actions; they are interiorized actions and once this interiorization, with the coordinations it supposes, is sufficient, then logico-mathematical experience is the form of material actions is no longer necessary and interiorized deduction is sufficient. The second reason is that coordinations of actions and logico-mathematical experience, whilst interiorizing themselves, give rise to the creation of a particular variety of abstraction which corresponds precisely to logical and mathematical abstraction: contrary to ordinary or Aristotelian abstraction which derives its source from the physical properties of objects and for this reason is called "empirical", logico-mathematical abstraction would be referred to as "reflective abstraction",' p. 81.

Piaget demonstrated that characteristics of both the concrete- and formal-operational children are important for the psychologist and the teacher and that 'having established the continuity between the spontaneous actions of the child and his reflective thought, it can be seen . . . that the essential notions which characterize modern mathematics are much closer to the structures of "natural" thought than are the concepts used in traditional mathematics', pp. 82–83. 'It can, of course, happen that certain people will try to teach young children "modern" mathematics with archaic teaching methods, based exclusively on verbal transmission from teacher to child with a premature use of formalization. With such methods there are bound to be a certain number of failures and these help to explain the scepticism of certain great mathematicians such as J. Leray. However, it is not the "modern" character of the mathematics programmes that is at fault but the methodology and psychology used in such cases. In fact, it is often particularly difficult for the teacher of mathematics, who, because of his profession, has a very abstract type of thought, to place himself in the concrete perspective which is necessarily that of his young pupils. However, from the developmental point of view and in relation to the progressive assimilation of the structures . . . , there would seem to be no contradiction . . . between the initial concrete phases of structures and the final stage when they become formal and abstract. The teacher can only be aware that there is no contradiction between these two levels of thought if he is fully acquainted with (and this is the difficulty for the teacher) the details and functioning of these successive spontaneous thought structures . . . In order to make this necessary conjunction between the logico-mathematical structures of the teacher and those of the pupil at different levels of his development, certain . . . general psycho-pedagogical principles should . . . be mentioned. The first is that real comprehension of a notion or a theory implies the re-invention of this theory by the subject . . . A second consideration should constantly be present in the teacher's mind: i.e., at all levels, . . . the pupil will be far more capable of "doing" and "understanding in actions" than of expressing himself verbally . . . the representations or models used should correspond to the natural logic of the levels of the pupils in question, and formalization should be kept for a later moment as a type of systematization of the notions already acquired . . . We do not believe with Pasch that formalization goes in the opposite direction to that taken by "natural" thought but so that there may be no conflict between the former and the latter, formalization should be allowed to constitute itself in its own time and not because it is forced to by premature constraints', Piaget (*ibid.*, pp. 84—7).

c. Science

Piaget's theory for science teaching suggests that the attainment of scientific concepts is a gradual one for the child, that all concepts are not necessarily attained at the same time within an individual, and that inter-individual differences play their part in their acquisition. Science teaching in primary schools should be such 'as to promote the continued development of the overall cognitive structures . . . this means the provision of a variety of tasks, materials and problems appropriate to the anticipated current cognitive structure of each child so that through self regulatory behaviour the child will make the cognitive match appropriate to his developmental state and will therefore maximize his interest and motivation . . . It would be quite reasonable to expect under these circumstances that different children would be doing different things, or the same things at different rates which is, in effect, simply restating for a particular subject area one of the important principles of the integrated day which seems so clearly implied in Piaget's work . . . in common with the method of inquiry, the structured environment approach implies the opportunity for interpersonal interaction, discussion and disputation . . . Science in the infants and primary school should be essentially activity and discovery, but true activity in the sense that while objects and ideas will be manipulated and hence experienced, providing real opportunities for significant and meaningful sensory experience, children should be encouraged to explore texture, appearance, sound, odour, and to sense movement with the emphasis on formal abstraction of attributes and relationships of objects and events', McNally (1973, pp. 136–7).

Duckworth (1974) described how her Piaget-oriented study has relevance for classroom work. She pointed out that skills of being able to watch and listen to children yielded valuable insights into how children see a problem, what intellectual difficulties they face, and how they come to make significant steps forward in their thinking — 'the having of wonderful ideas'. She concluded with a description of a primary science project conducted in Africa together with the approaches she developed for evaluating the effectiveness schools can have on the continuing development of novel ideas in children.

Watson (1974) after a brief account of the Piagetian stages of intellectual development, draws attention to the Geneva school efforts which have been largely devoted to examining how the basic concepts of mathematics and science — and of everyday life — such as those of volume, weight, area, density, or velocity develop, for the most part in the stage of concrete operations. He maintains that it is only recently that detailed studies of the development of science concepts at the secondary level have been undertaken and cites the work of Inhelder and Piaget (1958), Mealings (1963), Peel (1970), Shayer (1972) and Ingle and Shayer (1971). (Details follow).

Haysom and Sutton (1974) maintain that much of the pupils learning in science involves them in thinking in the abstract, when they manipulate ideas and possibilities in their minds. 'Teachers often introduce such abstractions as mass and volume early in their courses, and follow these by the even more intangible relationships between them, such as density. Pressure, which involves the concepts of force and area, and quantity of heat, which involves both temperature change and mass, are also derived quantities of this sort. Reasoning about them may well be presented using algebraic or graphical symbols. Arguments comparing one possibility with another become commoner as the course progresses, and so do higher order abstractions such as proportion (a comparison of ratios, which themselves are abstractions). Most of these mental processes fall within the category which Piaget called "formal" operations', p. 27. The editors cite the Piagetian experiments of the pendulum problem, the problem of floating and sinking and problems of spatial perception. (Details follow).

Jenkins and Whitfield (1974) have edited readings in science education and after an outline of Piaget's stage of cognitive development maintain, 'It is now possible to see how Piaget's work could be used to assess a projected course. First, the stages of the course ought to follow the same order of increasing logical complexity as are present in the pupils own development. Secondly, the age range over which the course is taught should match the age range over which these stages develop (even as one recognizes that the course may be a partial means for the pupils' development)', p. 43. The editors then discuss relating cognitive development to science courses and cite the findings of Mealings (1963), Shayer (1970, 1972). (Details appear later).

The Nuffield Junior Science materials employ a predominantly Piagetian approach and have made a significant contribution to science teaching approaches. A further significant series of resource materials and guidebooks for teachers have been provided by the Schools Council. Dale (1975) refers to the Victorian Education Department's Primary Science Materials together with the Australian Science Education Project, also designed according to Piagetian development levels and have adopted a learning approach consistent with Piagetian theory (p. 116).

Dale continues: 'Once a teacher is in a position to judge the level of mental development of a child he can depart from his shotgun approach (fire a lot of information to the "average" level of the class and some of it is sure to stick!) and select the information and procedure most appropriate for that particular child. The art of tailoring teaching to suit individual children is still in its infancy but Piaget's work does provide some guidelines. Since most of the teaching of science at primary and secondary levels is to children at concrete and formal stages, the following information is restricted to these two stages. The information could be used by a classroom teacher in preparing learning situations in science. It provides some guide on "what" and "when" to teach', Dale (*ibid.*, p. 131). A summary of the features of thinking at concrete and formal stages is provided: Dependence on concrete information; ability to completely solve a problem; ability to isolate variables and test them systematically; ability to control unwanted variables; ability to develop rules and procedures and models; ability to deal with probability and correlation; ability to specify position; understanding of area and volume; understanding of density; understanding of time and time intervals; ability to handle proportion; and ability to explain a happening in terms of what has caused it. (Full details appear in Dale, *op. cit.*, pp. 131—4).

Among the early attempts to illustrate the significance of Piaget's work for curriculum development is that of Banks (1958). He examined formal reasoning in students using experimental situations drawn from Piaget's *The Child's Conception of Physical Causality* (1930). The author concluded that secondary modern school pupils should be inspired to analyze and reason concerning scientific phenomena as opposed to formal presentation of scientific principles. (Fuller details appear in Banks, 1958, and Lunzer, 1960).

A study by Ross (1959) involved children drawn from two junior schools and one secondary modern school. He employed a demonstration method to explore the principles of sound involving relations between sound and movement of the vibrating body; frequency and length; length and pitch; conduction of sound; and interrelated topics. Through experimental demonstrations, children were asked to predict the results following procedural variations. The majority could not comprehend sound, detecting only its relationship with movement. (Fuller details appear in Ross, 1959, and Lunzer, 1960).

Karplus (1964) developed the 'Science Curriculum Improvement Scheme' (SCIS) (1970). The aim of the scheme is described as 'that of enhancing the development of thinking to the formal operational level' – an aim which lends itself to the use of Piagetian concepts. Karplus argues that in his experience with teachers and children, there are some who enter adulthood without reaching the formal level (*cf.* Hughes, 1965, Tomlinson-Keasey, 1972). If and when this is achieved, the areas of acquisition are restricted. The author specifically mentions Piaget's experiments on the concept of conservation of volume, as an instance.

The study of Linn and Thier (1975) was undertaken to explore the effect SCIS has on the development of logical thinking in children. 'In order to investigate this effect, comparisons were made between fifth graders who had studied at least the Energy Sources unit from SCIS and fifth and eighth graders who had not studied SCIS.' The authors found that 'fifth graders who studied Energy Sources appeared to be better logical thinkers than comparable fifth grade students who did not. Also, students of Energy Sources had scores that were close to those of eighth graders in comparable areas. Gains on an important measure of logical thinking resulting from a commercially available science program are very encouraging. These gains are even more noteworthy since the teachers of the classes in this sample represent a cross section of all teachers using the SCIS program. Although most teachers of SCIS have some contact with science coordinators who have been introduced to the program by SCIS staff members, these teachers do not ordinarily have extensive special training.' It appeared that logical thinking was affected as a result of the learning to explicitly name variables and the use of materials to do experiments while interacting with peers.

Field and Cropley (1969) attempted to clarify the relationship between science achievement and four cognitive style variables – mental operations, originality and flexibility and category width – among 178 subjects, aged 16 to 18 years, all following Science Courses. The questionnaire developed by Tisher (1971, described in 'Test Development', Part II of this volume) was employed to measure the stage of mental operations. A highly significant relationship existed between operations classifications and level of science achievement for each sex. High science achievement was therefore associated with the ability to apply formal operations in processing science information. The boys' performance was superior to that of the girls on all variables. The superiority of the boys with regard to the development of formal operations was considered by the authors to be of interest, particularly as little has been attempted to date in this area with pupils beyond 15 years. No sex differences were reported by Inhelder and Piaget (1958) and Tisher (1971). Field and Cropley comment that the apparently slower development of formal operations by the girls is perhaps, 'a contributing factor to their general inferiority to boys in handling science information at this stage of schooling and in later stages also'. The study implies that 'teachers should become better informed of their pupils' abilities or modes of cognitive functioning and endeavour to programme the class work both to capitalize on and extend these'. Furthermore, that 'a multidimensional view of intellectual functioning might provide more useful information about interpupil differences in science achievement than any univariate approaches'.

An active attempt towards the fulfilment of the Cornell Conference issues (*op. cit.*) was made by Almy and associates (1971). The authors' aim was to investigate the effects of instruction in the basic concepts of mathematics and science on logical thinking abilities of second grade children. They argue that the group of children who had no prescribed lessons in either kindergarten or first grade operated equally well in the Piagetian tasks as did the groups who had prescribed lessons beginning in kindergarten. But the latter groups performed better than did the groups whose prescribed lessons began only in the first grade. However, Almy and associates conclude: 'The ambiguity of the findings precludes the drawing of final conclusions, either as to the major questions of the study, or as to the more subsidiary questions having to do with the relative efficacy of different ways of presenting science concepts to children and also with the relative effectiveness of different kinds of teaching strategies'. Nevertheless, the study provides evidence as to the nature of the children's thinking at this age and illuminates the complex interactions that are involved when early instruction is undertaken. The authors conclude their investigation with a full discussion on curricula content and its timing together with instruction and the assessment of the individual. Almy, Chittenden and Miller (1966, p. 121, and described more fully in Modgil, 1974, pp. 263—4) maintain: 'Of most importance, there are indications of the different ways that children in the same grade view phenomena and problems that the adult regards as similar or even identical. The significance of such diversity for the early childhood curriculum and for the instruction of the child remains to be explored'. (Criticism of the methodology of this study has, however, been advanced by Gaudia, 1972 — see abstract Almy, Chittenden and Miller; *cf.* Figurelli and Keller, 1972; Little, 1972).

Recent studies which have attempted to illumine the significance of Piaget's work for curriculum innovation, design and development include Colton's (1972) study, with its dual aim: to determine the relationship between the ability to perform a concrete operational task at the pre-operational level and the acquisition of classification skills based on a systematic task analysis of that specific operational task; and to examine the relative effectiveness of a science curriculum based on systematic task analysis on the development of classification skills related to a learner's ability to accomplish a specific task. The concrete operational task of predicting floating objects, patterned after Piaget, was administered. A series of instructional sequences were derived out of the floating objects test. 'The short-term instructional sequences were taught to children in the first and third grade, half of whom had had long-term instruction based on Science — A Process Approach, an elementary school science programme designed to teach the processes of science by means of lessons based on task analysis and behavioural objectives'. Colton concluded that given long-term instruction, or short-term instruction in classification skills, children can be helped to acquire concrete operational thought which they do not demonstrate when denied such instruction. 'The design of curriculum must be based on both what is feasible, "what can be" and what is desired, "what ought to be". While the findings of this study provide assistance with the former, answering the latter requires that the curriculum designer give consideration of what values of the total school and societal setting ought to be reflected in the curriculum that is implemented by the educational complex. In this study task analysis has been found to be a functional tool in designing curriculum. It is the responsibility of the educator and curriculum designer to decide when to apply this tool of task analysis in order that it will be most beneficial to the learner', (Colton, *op. cit.*), p. 5658–A. (Details are given later).

In a study entitled, 'Curriculum design for junior life sciences based upon the theories of Piaget and Skinner', Pearce (1972) had a twofold purpose. 'First, to develop experimental curriculum materials utilizing concrete and formal operations levels with secondary reinforcement to facilitate concept attainment in seventh grade life science. Second, to investigate these experimental curriculum materials to determine if they facilitated the learning of more science knowledge than the current classroom learning situation and also facilitated the movement of students into the formal operations level of intellectual performance. The experimental curriculum materials were based upon the theory of intellectual development as couched by Piaget and the theory of secondary reinforcement postulated by Skinner'. Four classes were selected as the experimental group. Ss in these classes used the experimental life science curriculum materials while the control group Ss did not use the materials. The sample which comprised 72 Ss were at the concrete operations stage of intellectual development by the pre-test results. Four Piagetian tests and the Metropolitan Science Test, Advanced Level were administered in a pre-post-test situation. No significant difference between the experimental and the control groups for science achievement was computed. There was a significant difference between pre- and post-test results for each group. Ss in the experimental group showed significant change in intellectual performance in the formal operations stage from pre-test to post-test, while the control group did not demonstrate a significant difference in this area between pre- and post-test results. 'The comparison of the frequency of responses recorded in concrete operations and formal operations between pre-test and post-test results indicated significant change for both groups tested. This significant change, indicated for the control group, did not represent entry into formal operations but represented gain from stage to stage within concrete operations (disequilibrium, Stage II—A to equilibrium, Stage II—B) and formal operations (disequilibrium, stage III—A to equilibrium, Stage III—B) as noted by Inhelder and Piaget (1958). A comparison of . . . study indicated that the change for the experimental group was significantly greater than the change in intellectual performance for the control group for all four Piagetian tasks. The results . . . indicate that students learned as much life science content in a curriculum designed for experiences in concrete and formal operations with secondary reinforcement as students in a "traditional" curriculum. The findings support the hypothesis that science experiences in concrete and formal operations facilitate the change of intellectual performance into the formal operations level . . . that an active method of instruction which provides experiences for students to operate at their ability levels can be superior to the "traditional" method in providing experiences that facilitate the transition from concrete to formal operations level of intellectual performance', (Pearce, 1972, p. 5537—A). (Details are given later).

In a study entitled, 'A test of a theory of development in Uganda: implications for intellectual growth of school children in less technologically developed nations', Kimball (1972) was intent 'to describe variables and to propose hypotheses relating educational experiences to development outcomes; to analyze the results of testing these hypotheses and to evaluate their relevance to the prediction of future trends; to produce viable suggestions describing some methods through which primary schools can be improved to increase an individual's chance for raising his level in development-specific structures through creative growth, given the set of alternatives and resources at his command'. The variables considered were: educational experience, type of school, age, location of school, 'outreach', and SES. Dependent variables included: cognitive and affective development, school achievement and economic return. The sample of 1228 children and adults (all male) were interviewed in the four ecological settings. Twenty school children each from grades one, four, and six from new science curriculum and old science curriculum schools were selected. Twenty non-school boys with age and socioeconomic backgrounds similar to those of the pupils were the comparison group. Adults from these role categories completed the sample in each setting: farmers, labourers, craftsmen, shopkeepers, officials and teachers. The hypotheses and the results of their testing related to children and adults are discussed separately. 'The results show that the new science curriculum in its first year of operation does contribute significantly to psychological development. It is speculated that science education is strongly associated with development-related learning outcomes (adult results), a new science education may contribute even more to these outcomes as these children become adults . . . From observations in the classroom and an analysis of teaching strategies the new science curriculum classrooms exhibit a tendency toward more flexible approaches to teaching. This flexible approach includes use of materials for each individual to interact with, evaluation of results of experiments, teacher as colleague instead of authority, effective growth as well as cognitive, process over content, freedom of exploration, creativity as well as logical processes, teaching for an unknown future . . . This research brings out the need for researchers and curriculum developers to he in Piaget's "formal operations" stage of development so that future accomplishment may add even further significance to our understanding of change and growth', (Kimball, *op. cit.*). (Details follow).

To compare the effects of various units of an activity-based curriculum, Elementary Science Study — ESS (1966, 1969, 1971) and a textbook approach, Laidlaw Science Series (Smith, Blecha, and Sternig, 1966) upon 54 third grades and 56 fourth grades student classification skills (Piagetian tasks, patterned after Allen, 1967), science achievement, and scientific attitudes were studied by Vanek and Montean (1975). One third grade and one fourth grade group were randomly assigned to the instruction in the ESS Units and the remaining groups were instructed using the textbook series. Results demonstrated that the teaching method or materials make a difference in achievement or classification ability. 'The effectiveness of a programme cannot be judged on its theoretical framework alone . . . Science, with its emphasis on critical questioning, experimentation and control of variables can lead to significant learning, regardless of a child's ability or achievement as measured by standardized tests. The affective domain has been ignored too long in education at the elementary levels. It appears that the teaching method makes a difference in scientific attitudes. Children using an activity-based curriculum (ESS) seem to be more willing to explore their world and happier learning about that world. Differences in scientific attitudes also appear for grade and sex differences. A more critical look must be taken at these variables, especially with the trend toward multi-graded classrooms and the abolishment of socialization along sexist lines', Vanek and Montean (*op. cit.*)'. (Details follow later).

To develop a concept classification scheme based on the Piagetian model, Bautista (1975) administered two tasks to students enrolled in 'CHEMS and Project Physics.' Piagetian tasks of conservation of volume, separation of variables, and equilibrium in the balance and achievement tests which were a part of 'CHEMS and Project Physics' materials were given. Each of the concepts involved in the achievement test items was subjected to the operational criteria for evaluation. Formal students performed significantly better on 57 out of 61 formal questions than concrete students and no significant difference was computed in the proportions of formal and concrete students responding correctly to 38 out of 39 concrete test items. The classification system designed by the author was supported. (Details follow).

In an article entitled, 'How to assess science courses', Shayer (1970) argues that when planning new science courses, one must necessarily think of the science first. However, that in structuring a five-year school course, it is important to bear in mind that the mental capacity of the pupils increases year by year. 'If taking account of this is not to be merely intuitive, a technique to assess the concepts suggested for different stages of the course is needed. Piaget's work might form a basis for such assessment . . . ', p. 182. Shayer cites examples from the Nuffield O-level Chemistry in an attempt to demonstrate how this might be done. (Details follow). This technique of assessment of science courses based on Piaget's conceptual stages was extended by Ingle and Shayer (1971). In the light of estimated conceptual levels for each of the topics in the Nuffield O-level Chemistry course the authors suggested modifications to the sample scheme which might be necessary to provide courses for pupils of different intelligence. (Details appear later). In continuation, Shayer (1972) in a paper entitled, 'Conceptual demands in the Nuffield O-level physics course', suggested some conclusions about the style and structure of the O-level physics course. The author attempted to answer two questions 'what is the minimum conceptual level that the pupil must have attained without which his interest cannot be sustained? And what conceptual level is needed to enable the pupil to extract from the experiment what is suggested in the teacher's guide?', p. 26. (Details follow). Although the individual topics of the Nuffield Foundation courses in the sciences have been assessed in Piagetian terms (Shayer; Ingle and Shayer; and Shayer, *op. cit.*), Shayer and Wharry (1974) attempted to develop a method of testing a class which would demonstrate the level of thinking of the individual pupil in the context of the science teaching that the pupil was receiving. 'It was hoped that this method would both serve as a source of information about pupils and about the suitability for them of the work we have given or plan to give them', p. 447 (Details follow).

Linn, Chen and Thier (1975) undertook to investigate whether learners allowed to choose their own apparatus-centered activities would work at these activities at their own logical level. The authors developed a science enrichment center to test this hypothesis. Activities designed for the center focused on scientific reasoning. Trials of the center with fifth and sixth graders revealed that children worked at an appropriate logical level and made gains in scientific reasoning ability. Characteristics of activities which tended to foster scientific reasoning were discussed. Observations concerning appropriate formats for presenting personalized experiences and possible organization of a personalized enrichment program are reported. The various types of leadership which are congruent with personalization and enrichment were discussed together with the role of the paraprofessional leader in a choice environment is explored. (Details follow).

Knott (1974) drew a random sample of 10 pupils from four classes in two different schools and administered Piaget and Inhelder's (1958) tasks of the Projection of Shadows and the Equilibrium in the Balance. Knott stated, 'In the secondary schools the rate of change has been slower than in primary schools where a great deal of experimentation has been going on to provide more child centred and child oriented work. Teaching methods have been changed somewhat by the Nuffield Projects and the School Councils Projects. New programmes of science teaching have been introduced but the innovations have been less marked than in schools for younger children. From the findings of the developments of these two science concepts in two secondary schools it seems to suggest that considerable changes in teaching methods are desirable. Curriculum development is not simply a matter of devising new syllabuses but is linked to the study of methods most appropriate to the needs of the pupils at local level'.

On the assumption that conservation of chemical identity; composition and mass were essential to basic understanding of chemistry, Hall (1973) was intent to discover the extent to which these conservation principles were present in a sample of 23 boys and girls aged from 11 years one month to 12 years 10 months and within the IQ range from 108 to 140. Ss had experienced a course of teaching similar to the first three sections of the Nuffield O-level chemistry scheme, which involved the study of chemical reaction through a consideration of the effects of heat on substances and of combustion and which seemed to assume that relevant concepts and schemata could be developed without difficulty. The results make this doubtful and suggest a need to re-examine the ideas underlying courses of this kind. (Details follow).

The study of the cognitive development of science students in introductory level courses was undertaken by Griffiths (1974). The Ss were selected from chemistry and physics courses at a state university and an inner-city community college. The test administered was the Piagetian test of the inclined plane, to demonstrate the development of the INRC group or the combination of colourless liquids, to test the combinatorial system. All responses were tape recorded. Griffiths concluded that the majority of the students at the level of introductory science courses had a major handicap in terms of the development of their cognitive structures. Moreover, that 'the strategy of developmental work at the college level may best be directed in terms of the students' cognitive development and not in the imposition of vocabulary and skills upon a less developed structure', p. 3989A. (Details are given later).

In, 'Conceptual demands in the Nuffield O-level biology course', Shayer (1974) argues, 'It is more difficult to assess the thinking involved in a biology course than in one in physics or chemistry. Much traditional O-level biology teaching has been of a descriptive kind, and it is possible to achieve a creditable pass without any mathematics or hypothetico-deductive thought at all. This is not to suggest that the activity of organizing information is not a process of thinking: on the contrary, I think its development is of equal importance, for the intelligent adolescent, to the "possibilistic" thinking described by Piaget as Formal Operational. And it shows up neither in the method of teaching intelligence of the psychometric school nor in the very different methodology of Geneva. But because of the presence of so much Formal thought in the Nuffield course makes an analysis possible, I do not want it to be concluded either that I am taking sides in favour of the course for that reason, or because of its apparent difficulty, recommending the traditional approach instead', p. 1. (Details follow).

That logical operations, critical thinking, and creative thinking are all components of science content comprehension were investigated by Polanski (1975) in 220 fourth and sixth grade subjects through the administration of the Piaget Comprehension Test using Piaget's operations of classification, seriation, logical multiplication, and comprehension; Raven Test of Logical Operations; Iowa Comprehension Test; Roberge Critical Thinking Test; and the Torrance Creative Thinking Test. Science content comprehension had both a logical operations and a critical thinking component, but little support was found for a creative thinking component. The use of Piaget's logical operations in the construction of a model of science content comprehension was strongly supported and recommended. (Details are given later).

d. Social studies

Taba *et al.* (1971) in *A Teacher's Handbook to Elementary Social Studies*, contributed to rethinking with respect to what should be taught and how it should be taught in social studies. Taba *et al.* cite the work of Piaget and Szeminska when outlining educational objectives, curriculum content, learning activities, teaching strategies and evaluation in relation to the role these give to thinking generally.

McNally (1974) in a discussion of Piaget's views on moral development for social studies and teaching in general states, 'It is difficult to see . . . how primary school children especially in the early primary grades . . . could develop anything but a superficial understanding of such concepts as "law and order", and "economic and social interdependence of the community", to take but two aspects of topics recommended by a current Australian social studies curriculum for third grade. In fact this curriculum suggests that "Children should be helped to realize that they have a part to play in the class and school organization similar to the part played by adults in the community outside". When it is realized that some children in that particular state enter third grade at the age of seven plus, and that children at this age are only beginning to appreciate the rules governing the game of marbles, in which all of the physical elements are present, expectations of the amount of real understanding of the role of adults in the community outside must be small indeed. In fact, one of the criticisms that can be levelled at much of the teaching of social studies in primary schools is that despite the frequent suggestions by various curricula concerning the relevance of experience and activity in building genuine understanding appropriate to the developmental level of the child, abstract political, social and moral concepts are frequently presented in verbal fashion with the remedy for incomplete understanding or lack of understanding simply being to present more words. When Piaget's views on cognitive development are related to his findings on moral and social development the utility of such an approach becomes obvious. Again,

Piaget's views of moral and intellectual development suggest that effective group work in the primary school must of necessity develop slowly in response to the progressive integration of intellectual, moral and social development. The development of the ability to appreciate rules and to cooperate in conjoint activities seems to await the development of the ability to adopt the perspective of another, i.e., to relinquish the egocentric view of the world, just as the full development of concrete operations awaits the coordination of perspectives and an objectification of the child's view of the world', pp. 133—4. (An outline of McNally, 1974: *Piaget, Education and Teaching* appears later).

Kowitz (1975) in a review of Rest (1974) 'Developmental psychology as a guide to value education: a review of "Kohlbergian" programmes', stated, 'Kohlberg has contended that moral education should not be aimed at teaching some specific set of morals but should be concerned with developing the organizational structures by which one analyzes, interprets, and makes decisions about social problems. Cognitive developmental value education thus differs from the socialization or indoctrination approaches. The focus is upon acquisition of structured competencies that transfer to later life and have a cumulative effect in enhancing and enriching life. The cognitive developmental approach does not make ethical relativity and value neutrality the corner stones of value education as the value-clarification approach does. Programmes designed to implement value education have depended heavily upon group discussion of personal dilemmas. Much of the advice given by specialists in value education is difficult, if not impossible, to carry out in the classroom. In practice, teachers are often reduced to teaching basic principles of general, developmental psychology. Most suggestions concerning value education are based upon assumptions concerning the sequence of human development, especially in the capacity to acquire patterns of behaviour. Unfortunately, precise statements of developmental sequences are not available. However, the potential of value education strongly recommends it as a field for continuing research and development', (*ibid.*, p. 196).

Allman (1973) was intent to examine the possibility of diagnosing community college students' cognitive functioning abilities, in social science content areas, by means of a Piagetian type clinical diagnosis. 'Observation of the results of the factor analysis confirmed the expectations regarding the Piagetian aligned factor structure of the diagnosis and offered a construct validity and reliability estimate of approximately .86 ... Twelve factors or constructs aligned with Piaget's theory were isolated. The constructs represented both a concrete operational and an abstract operational level of cognitive functioning for most of the cognitive tasks diagnosed. Seven of the factors discriminated significantly ($p < .001$) between the strata and in all cases, discriminated in favour of stratum three, the stratum with highest past level of academic performance. The Ss in the stratum with the lowest level of academic performance, stratum one, and frequently stratum two Ss were functioning at a concrete operational level during the diagnosis . . . findings of this research necessitate immediate and continuous research of Piagetian remediation approaches based on the diagnosis and remediation of the learner's cognitive functioning abilities', (Allman, *ibid.*, p. 5343—A). (Details follow).

'The Place of Maps in the Junior School', an investigation undertaken by Prior (1959) draws its experimental tasks from the later experiments reported in *The Child's Conception of Space* (Piaget and Inhelder, 1956). Prior was intent to obtain guidance for appropriate curriculum content. Prior concludes that 'while experiences using actual models and simple maps provide the necessary material on which to base true concepts, they should enter only incidentally in the junior school programme'. However, it must be stressed that Prior's presentation of results lacks the clinical Piagetian depth. (Fuller details appear in Prior, 1959, and Lunzer, 1960).

The relationship between children's classification-class inclusion abilities and geographic knowledge as measured by Piaget's spatial stages was examined by Rand (1974). The sample comprised 120 elementary school children stratified by age, sex, residence and socioeconomic status. The tests administered were the Geographic Stages Test and Piagetian tests of general classification and class-inclusion. The data was subjected to chi-square, analysis of variance and correlational analyses. Results demonstrated that children's 'observed responses are significantly different from theoretically expected responses for total sample and for all subsamples on all subtests and the total test with the exception of total score for girls. Further, results indicate that while children progress through age-stage relationships similar to those originally proposed by Piaget, there is wide variance in children's performance . . . that children do differ significantly according to age, giving support to Piaget's original contention of age-stage progression. In addition, while few significant differences were found between groups of children, evidence clearly suggested that trends were apparent. Boys out-performed girls, urban children out-performed rural children, and higher SES children out-performed lower SES children . . . that the largest single predictor of total geographic performance was age, which contributed approximately 50 per cent of the variance . . . analysis indicates significant relationships do exist between children's performance on general classification-class inclusion measures and that of geographic concepts of classification and inclusion. Low correlations ($r = .20-.36$) exist between single classification abilities and geographic performance, while moderate correlations (r = .35–.54) exist between multiple classification abilities and children's performance on geographic concepts. Moderate to high correlations (r = .50–.65) exist between general class inclusion abilities and geographic spatial abilities, suggesting that geographic classification-class inclusion abilities may be a special instance of those more general abilities', Rand (*ibid.*, p. 4886A). (Details follow).

Case and Collinson (1962) reported that with respect to verbal material, the emergence of formal thought in adolescents was not uniform across subject matter, in that examinees found history passages more difficult than geography or literature. The authors interpret the result due to the difficulties children have in handling time as a variable, especially when ideas appear in sequences other than that in which the events occurred.

Lodwick studied inferences drawn from reading historical passages and the responses advanced by children. He contends that the reasoning inherent in Piagetian tasks may be appropriately transferred to other areas of the curriculum. He identified three stages corresponding to the three Piagetian levels. After giving a short paragraph setting out the story of King Alfred and the cakes he asked the question 'Could Alfred cook?'. Peel (1972) stated 'some explanations were given which demonstrate an increasing maturity of understanding of the anecdote'. It is intended here to cite only two such explanations: 'Answer A: "Yes" (Why?) "Because he's the King". (Can every King cook?) "No". (Why could Alfred cook?) "Because he can fight". This answer reveals fragmented thought. One aspect of the situation is focused upon and refers to concrete material; hence his combined statements often contain inconsistencies. It also reveals that maturity of thought is a factor in understanding. Answer E: "No I don't think so, because in the olden days the King didn't have to know how to cook at all. It's like today he has servants to wait upon him. If he could cook, he would know approximately when cakes were done. He was thinking about the Danes but some instinct would have told him, if he could cook, when the cakes were done. We can't really tell." This explanation shows that the thinker is able to judge the statements formally and logically and is not put off by their content. Thought is said to be reversible, resulting in consistent argument. Hypotheses are examined systematically', p. 166.

Hallam (1969a) cited his 1967, 1969 work in which Piaget's work on logical thinking and moral judgements had been used as 'a basis for investigating children's thinking and judgements in history'. Scalogram analysis indicated that the level of formal operations was reached after a chronological age of 16.2 years and a mental age of at least 16.8 years. Hallam considered that syllabuses should be organized to take account of the limitations in pupils' reasoning and forwarded suggestions for the prevention of 'paralysis in thinking in history'. With respect to younger pupils the history taught should not be over-abstract in form, nor should it contain too many variables. Hallam elaborated that if children are dealing with material that is largely concrete in nature they will not necessarily lose the intellectual values associated with the study of history. 'Statements will still need to be queried and confirmed. Simple cause-effect relationships can be appreciated in studying such topics as the development of lake villages or the punishments meted out to sixteenth century criminals... The cultivation of an inquiring spirit is easier to stimulate in younger pupils through the study of concrete topics such as writing, houses, entertainments, clothing, transport and so on than in trying to force them to understand abstract political, constitutional and religious changes'. Pupils in the 'third year' should be ready to tackle the more abstract type of history presented in a simple form but there should usually be only four variables. Those pupils reaching the formal stage at 14-plus years should be able to use inductive and deductive thought and will often be sitting for external examinations. Too much examination work has entailed the repetition of learnt facts and opinions although questions are being set which demand inferential thought. 'A compulsory section on historical documents might give examination candidates the opportunity to exercise their historical judgement and thus avoid excessive dependence on memory work'. Progress towards the formal operational stage may be accelerated by a conscious effort to present at least four viewpoints in any historical topic, thereby leading to a 'cognitive conflict'. There is however the proviso that there must be the right amount of discrepancy between the work, and the pupils' thinking skills. Group discussion among pupils with the necessary cognitive skills and preliminary information, and written work involving reflective thought are advocated as part of the general approach to improving thinking in history. (Full details appear in Hallam, 1969a.)

Goldman (1964) reported that there are Piagetian levels of religious thinking through which children pass. The pre-religious, comparable with the Piagetian intuitive stage is marked by unconnected guesses. Sub-religious is the second stage and parallels Piaget's concrete operational stage. The stage was marked by answers evoking cause and effect. Goldman's last stage — the religious stage — is characterized by abstract thinking and corresponds to Piaget's formal operational level. In continuation, Goldman (1966) examined the final stage in relation to the biblical story material he had previously employed. He concluded that since religious thinking is essentially an interpretation of experience, children must have had primary mental stimulation, undergone some form of perceptual activity and developed some capacity for abstract thought before the profound truths of religion can be appreciated. Further, that this was not the same as acknowledging the truth of them in terms of commitment.

Individual and group responses of 14- and 15-year-olds to short stories, novels, poems, and thematic apperception tests: case studies based on Piagetian genetic epistemology and Freudian psychoanalytic ego psychology were examined by Petrosky (1975). The study identified and described five variables that influence response to works of literature: stage-specific operations, identity theme, past experience, expectations, and reading ability. The cognitive and affective parameters of any response in any form were determined by the respondent's stage-specific operations and by the respondent's personality. Moreover, stage-specific operations and identity theme were intra-individual variables constructed within and with past experiences. The response to literature took a form that was learnt, and 'response to literature evolves into a genuine dialectical experience when the respondents are given the opportunity to articulate and share personal impressions and interpretations in group situations', Petrosky (*ibid.*, p. 852—A). (Details follow.)

e. Conservation as a predictor of reading comprehension

Piaget's formulations have implications for the teaching of reading. Schwebel and Raph (1974) focus on the matrix of conceptions based on the active engagement of the child in the first year of life which comprise the precursors to reading: 'Reading is an activity that requires the mental capacity to represent objects with conventional signs that are distinct from the objects for which they stand. The means through which the child develops this mental capacity evolve gradually from an active interaction with the concrete world . . . Although the idea of reading's being related to experience has been around for a long time there is still a tendency to assume that the six-year-old entering first grade should have sufficient experiential background to grasp the meaning of words in charts, workbooks and readers. Piaget's careful observation of how knowledge develops in children has given us a better understanding of the nature of the sequential experiences a child has had prior to age six which enable him to approach the goal of school learning. Piaget's system also provides us with clues to use in discovering a child's level of thinking and, accordingly, the adequacy of his preparation for reading', p. 17. Goodacre (1971) has applied some of the Piagetian ideas to the teaching of reading. With respect to Piaget's stages in relation to reading, Goodacre described the sensorimotor stage as being characteristically concerned with books as objects to be handled with reliance on someone in the environment to demonstrate the turning of pages, and to identify the objects represented in two-dimensional form, with possibly some connection being made with the written symbols representing familiar objects. At the transductive stage children are unable to see more than one or two factors in a situation and cannot reverse their thought or test if it is true conversely. It is therefore difficult for 'children to break up the slowly acquired sound pattern of words in order to relate phonemes to graphemes or even to hear and distinguish morphemes'. However, 'visually words are more and more accurately observed and eventually seen as total configurations and possibly overall shape does become an important clue'. Goodacre suggested that the child discovers the principle of phonetic analysis during the intuitive stage. He may realize that certain letters have more than one sound although it may be some time before he realizes the reverse of this, that similar 'sounds' (phonemes) can be produced by different letter combinations. At the concrete phase with the developed abilities to conserve, to carry out the act of reversibility, to classify, and to seriate, the child 'gradually learns to ignore irrelevant variations; e.g. differences in shape of letters related to script or type; sounds related to accent. He learns from experience that letters can produce different sounds, but the usual or correct pronunciation is determined by inclusion in a word. He learns to deal with more than one factor simultaneously. For instance, variation in the vowel sound (long or short) may lead to the reader trying internally several pronunciations very rapidly until by trial and error the right "fit" is reached which is in line with the signals from the contextual clues'. 'Passing out of the concrete stage, children operate at a formal level, using their skill in a flexible and mature manner; e.g. they adjust their reading rate to the level of difficulty of the reading matter, and they mentally organize what is read so that they obtain an overall meaning'.

Furth (1970) in applying Piaget's ideas to education drew the distinction between 'reading' schools and 'thinking' schools. He suggested the teaching of reading is so time-consuming in the concrete-operational period that it actually impairs cognitive development. Furth asserted that the more meaningful and varied the encounters the child has had with the real world the better will be the 'thinking foundation' on which learning to read is necessarily based. Raven and Salzer (1971) suggested that any reading programme that recognizes the validity of Piaget's theory will be heavily activity-oriented.

The relationships between a child's performance of selected tasks of conservation and selected factors in reading readiness were studied by Brekke (1972). Eighty-one first grade children were administered the Gates-MacGinitie Reading tests; Reading Skills, SRA Primary Mental Abilities Grades K—L; and conservation task patterned after Piaget. The results demonstrated that a child's performance of selected tasks of conservation were significantly related to selected factors in reading readiness. Mental age and sex were significantly related to conservation and reading readiness. CA was positively but not significantly related to conservation and reading readiness. Teacher prediction was significantly related to reading readiness. (Details follow).

In continuation, the patterning of conservation and reading readiness was studied by Brekke, Williams, and Harlow (1973). Conservation operativity was positively and moderately correlated with reading readiness and only slightly less correlated with reading readiness than intelligence as measured by the Primary Mental Abilities Test. Likewise, a moderate correlation was computed between conservation and intelligence. 'Most primary school teachers have only a general awareness of intelligence testing, but it would also seem that Piagetian principles have not been widely disseminated at the practitioner level. While the intelligence test ratings may be helpful in assessing readiness, a new focus of attention might also be placed on conservation. Conservation should be taken into account as an additional measure of readiness for beginning reading instruction. Attendant with this recommendation is the need to acquaint primary level teachers and reading specialists with Piagetian principles and ways of evaluating the child's operational level', p. 138. (Details appear later). It is interesting to note that in Almy, Chittenden and Miller's (1966) longitudinal study, the same conservation tasks were administered at six-months intervals for a two-year period. Among their findings was that, while reading readiness was moderately related to reading growth (r = .46, in middle class schools; r = .54 in a lower class school), conservation nevertheless was somewhat related to reading (r = .37 in a middle class school; r = .39 in lower-class schools). Brekke, Williams and Harlow (*op. cit.*) reported conservation to be positively and moderately correlated (r = .52) with reading readiness and only slightly less correlated with reading readiness than intelligence.

To determine if there were a relationship between reading achievement and the ability to conserve, Stanfill (1975) tested 160 second grade students on Piagetian conservation tasks of number and continuous quantities. The Stanford Reading Test and the Otis-Lennon Mental Ability Test were also administered to group Ss as achievers or low achievers. Other variables explored included: years of formal school, sex, CA, and SES. Conservation proved an appropriate measure to employ in diagnosing a student's readiness to read when used concurrently with other data. That the formal teaching of reading should not precede the child's ability to conserve. Students of lower SES who were unable to conserve tended to be unsuccessful with formal reading experiences. (Details follow).

Relations among perceptual-motor skills, ability to conserve, and reading readiness were studied by Ayers, Rohr, and Ayers (1974) among 94 kindergarten and first grade children. Tests administered were the Purdue Perceptual–motor Survey, the Metropolitan Reading Readiness Test, and six Piagetian tasks of logical thinking. The Purdue scale and Piagetian scores demonstrated no correlation. However, both sets of scores were moderately correlated with school readiness as measured by the Metropolitan test. (Details are given later).

It was hypothesized that, in a reading readiness programme,

intervention with specific, hierarchically taught, Piagetian-based Symbol Training (Weisz, 1974, Think * A * Ling Programme) will prepare children better for visual discrimination of word forms than intervention with relevant but random symbol training (Weisz, 1975). An experimental and a control group of first grade children were administered: Test of discrimination of word forms (adapted from Croft); Test of discrimination of Piagetian-based symbols (Weisz, 1974); and Test of discrimination of word-like forms (adapted from Slingerland). Weisz concluded that training with a Piagetian-based Symbol (Directionality) Series may prepare children to differentiate figures in all symbol systems. 'The instructions for such a programme are so elementary that they can be given in "any language" and to very young children', Weisz (*op. cit.*). (Details are given later).

The relationship between conservation abilities on selected Piagetian tasks and reading abilities was studied by Hurta (1973). Reading disabled and non-reading disabled children were studied to determine whether differences in conservation abilities could be identified. Two groups of 25 children within the age range from seven to eight years five months comprised the sample. 'The children classified as reading disabled were enrolled in a special education class for the language-learning disabled and read at a level six months below their anticipated reading level. The non-reading disabled children read at a level which ranged from less than six months below to above their anticipated reading level'. Each S was administered the Concept Assessment Kit Conservation (Goldschmid and Bentler, 1968b) and the Durrell Analysis of Reading Difficulty test. The study concluded that 'The only statistically significant differences which exist between children classified as reading disabled and non-reading disabled were found in the conservation of length on Task A and in the stage of development on all tasks administered. Regardless of the reading classification of the child there appeared to be a significant relationship between the child's level of functioning on specific conservation tasks and specific reading sub-tests of the Durrell Analysis of Reading Difficulty', (*ibid.*, p. 4942—A). (Details appear later).

Conservation and reading comprehension of second grade bilingual American Indian children was investigated by Brekke and Williams (1974). The sample of 38 children were administered two tasks of number conservation and three tasks of substance conservation. Additionally, they were given the Draw-A-Man Test and the Classroom Reading Inventory. The mean grade placement level was 2.39, 31 of the children were operational on all the tasks. Correlations ranging from .27 to .42 were computed between the three measures of reading level (independent, instructional, and frustration) and operativity on the conservation tasks. Draw-A-Man Test scores were then partialled out from these correlations; 'the correlations were essentially unchanged, mainly because of a low correlation of the Draw-A-Man Test with the scores on the Classroom Reading Inventory', p. 65. (Details appear later). In continuation, conservation as a predictor of reading comprehension was studied by Brekke and Williams (1975). The authors stated that, 'conservation and intelligence have been found both singly and in combination to be positively related to two measures of reading given seven months after the administration of the conservation measures. However, neither conservation nor intelligence made any significant independent contribution to the prediction of the reading measures when a reading readiness test, administered at the same time as the conservation tasks, was considered in the prediction of reading achievement. When intelligence and reading readiness were separately partialled out of the relationship between conservation and the two measures of reading achievement, the partial correlations dropped to a near-zero value', p. 40. (Details are given later).

The relationships of reading comprehension, conservation ability, auditory discrimination, and visual-motor development of the third grade pupils were studied by Kent (1973). One hundred and seventy-nine Ss were categorized into one of two groups: the high reading comprehension group and the low reading comprehension group according to performance on the comprehension subtest of the Gates-MacGinitie Reading Tests. The Slosson Intelligence Test was administered to the low reading comprehension group, in order to eliminate intelligence as a factor in poor reading comprehension. Ss were also given six Piagetian conservation tasks, the Wepman Auditory Discrimination Test, and the Bender Gestalt Test for Young Children. These measured conservation ability, auditory discrimination, and visual-motor development respectively. Results demonstrated that Ss in the high reading comprehension group performed at the higher levels of visual-motor development when compared to Ss in the low reading comprehension group. High reading comprehension female Ss surpassed low reading comprehension female Ss in visual-motor development and conservation ability. Relationships between reading comprehension and visual-motor development were observed with all Ss as were the relationships between reading comprehension and auditory discrimination. Likewise, relationships were also computed between reading comprehension and conservation ability. (Details follow later). However an investigation of the feasibility of using a measure of conservation as a predictor of reading comprehension was undertaken by Brauchler (1975). The sample of 106 children were tested on a Piagetian conservation task, the PIAT reading comprehension test and the Stanford-Binet Test of Intelligence. Overall, the results did not establish the utility of the conservation measure used as a predictor of reading achievement. (Details are given later).

An investigation to test Piagetian theory by validation of a reading comprehension test was carried out by Morgan and Esposito (1976).* A random sample of 80 children were administered the Kretschmer reading comprehension test, reading–thinking exercises, and six Piagetian tasks. Multitrait-multimethod correlation analysis of 31 research questions stated in null hypotheses sought to satisfy four requirements for convergent and discriminant validity. As an additional test of construct validity, a factor analysis was computed on the 32 items.

Analysis of the data yielded (a) few significant correlations, and (b) no clearly interpretable factor pattern. It was concluded that the experimental test lacked both convergent and discriminant validity and, in a larger sense, construct validity. The results supported Piagetian theory concerning the cognitive functioning of the concrete operational child. Pedagogical implications were discussed. (Details follow).

* Gratitude is extended to Dr R.F. Morgan of Old Dominion University and to Dr J.P. Esposito of Virginia University for sending the results of their work to be included.

f. 'The Nature of Adolescent Judgment,' E.A. Peel, 1971 (Abstracted)

The justification for including a summary of this book is that Peel attributes his work at a fundamental level to the investigations of Inhelder and Piaget (1958) into the growth of logical thinking in adolescence. He emphasizes, however, that whereas Inhelder and Piaget used practical science situations, he has constructed verbal situations for assessing the maturity of judgment. 'The substantive part of the book is concerned with the elaboration of a theory about the psychological nature and development of judgment and with attempts to materialize this theory by devising measures to investigate the conditions under which adolescents make judgment'.

Peel asserts: 'Above all else the adolescent and young adult apprehend the inconsistencies between the actual and the possible. They are impelled to the opinion and action which characterizes their lives by a drive to reconcile this actuality of their existence with the possibilities they themselves envisage. Usually they strive to modify the actual. This going forward and outward to conceive of possibilities beyond the limits of their environment is the central feature of their intellectual life.' He acknowledges that this view of adolescent thinking emerges from a speculation by Piaget and Inhelder (1958) and has been implied in the writings of many educationists, but has received no empirical investigation. Further, that there have been 'few systemic investigations into the growth of thinking during adolescence, despite the fact that learning during the secondary . . . years is most important and formative for real understanding in the upper school and higher education'. He emphasizes, however, that understanding is not sufficient; the ability to make effective judgments for appropriate action is also needed. He defines judging in relation to thinking as 'a form of thinking and is therefore invoked whenever we are in a situation for which we have no ready-made answer learned off pat'.

The test material designed to assess the developmental changes in adolescent thinking consisted of passages relating to topical, social or intellectual problems followed by a question demanding more for its answer than the information given in the passage. A second question 'Why do you think so?' provided the insight into the maturity of the judgment. The resulting answers were grouped into three main categories: 'Restricted', which were 'tautological, premise-delaying and irrelevant'; 'Circumstantial', which were 'bound solely by the content of the passage, often taking account at first of only one element'; and 'Imaginative-Comprehension', answers which involved the 'invocation of independent ideas and the consideration of the problem in their terms'. These three categories were subdivided into finer divisions where necessary, in the various investigations carried out by Peel and his students. He considers that the distinction between 'content-dominated' answers and imaginative answers involving explanation, is crucial.

Peel (1966), in an investigation with pupils nine-plus to 15-plus in New Jersey, confirmed that answers involving thinking beyond the evidence given in the passage are not prevalent before 13½ to 14½ years. 'Circumstantial' answers were associated with the ages of 12 to 13½ and there was little evidence of restricted answers. A number of Birmingham University students have supported Peel in his investigations. Rhys (1964) investigated adolescent thinking in terms of geographical material. On the premise that 'the understanding of geographical material at the secondary stage compels the adolescent to place a person other than himself in an environment other than his own and further more, he must take into account the complex interplay of a miscellany of factors within that foreign environment', Rhys obtained four main categories of answers ranging from the tautological to the imaginative. The highest level of mature judgment occurred at CA 15 years and MA 16 years.

Davies (1964) found that average mid-adolescents have difficulty in dealing with problems involving the selecting and eliminating of hypotheses, even when the hypotheses and the supporting evidence is provided. Similarly Mealings (1961; 1963) revealed the difficulties in choice and rejection of hypotheses in practical science problems. Peel comments: 'Teachers at all levels tend to streamline the learning process by presenting the most acceptable hypothesis and neglecting to eliminate the remainder . . . teachers should not forget that it is part of their task to promote thinking and that the complete act of selecting a best judgment entails rejecting the others. To this end they might more often draw attention to alternate explanations in order that the pupils may themselves reject them'.

The results of a study by Thomas (1967), indicated that 'we may expect immature causal judgments from pupils as old as 15 years of age in relatively non-technical situations where a multiplicity of factors operate over a long period of time'. Peel draws attention to the necessity of understanding in many fields of knowledge of the 'wide class of changes which appear to be dominated by a process of transforming random elements into ordered structure and the reverse process of going from order to disintegration'. In considering this 'Order-Disorder' change Peel comments that test situations are needed where ordered material can be presented and where the equivalent of a spontaneous change can be carried out, with the request for predictions of the outcome. He envisages these tests being concerned with a wide field including human affairs.

With respect to the promotion of mature judgment, Peel cites the work of Suchman (1961, 1964), who investigated the classroom conditions necessary to develop the inquiring mind. He initiated 'learning to think' sessions in which pupils were encouraged to inquire and discover concepts autonomously. Biran (1968) constructed a successful learning programme which demonstrated to pupils how to design experiments, to test hypotheses and to draw conclusions. Gray (1970) found that adolescents subjected to programmed texts for training judgment obtained higher scores on thinking problems. Anderson (1967) administered instruction in thinking to pupils and the results showed a considerable influence on the maturity of judgment. Stones (1965) gave programmed instruction in relevant historical concepts and increased the maturity of historical judgments in a group of secondary pupils. Peel (1967) discusses the possibility of using the actual responses obtained in the investigations of persons' judgments as a means of teaching individuals how to judge. Peel (1972) has edited a monograph entitled, *The Quality of Thinking in Secondary School Subjects* incorporating consideration with respect to the understanding of school material: the formation of historical concepts, geographical learning, the growth of mathematical thinking, adolescents' thinking in science, and religious judgment. The monograph concludes with an analysis of thinking abilities as objectives in curriculum development. (Details follow).

Of recent interest is Peel's (1975) paper addressed to the 'Predilection for Generalizing and Abstracting'. Peel reports 'the development of a sentence preference test designed to contrast tendencies to abstract, generalize and particularize in thinking'. It was observed that certain terms carry both general and abstract meanings and Peel reports that 'using such words in sentences bringing out these differing meanings provides an indication of readiness to use abstractions and generalizations. Validity and reliability data is reported among secondary school pupils and is further considered to confirm earlier works (1971a, 1971b, 1975a) which showed that tendencies both to generalize and abstract increase during adolescence. Peel discusses his findings in application to language usage and comprehension and to higher level thinking processes required during secondary school and in higher education. Peel (1975a) focused on the understanding of pupils' comprehension of textual material involving a unit consisting of the text, question asked and the response made. He considered for an adequate analysis, semantic, psycholinguistic and logical sources need to be consulted. The main difficulty lies in the inclusion of the responders previous experience when he comprehends or judges from a text.

g. 'A Structural Foundation for tomorrow's Education', J. Piaget (Abstracted)

Piaget (1972), in a recent article written for a series of studies prepared for the International Commission on the Development of Education, at UNESCO, draws attention to the proportionally small number of students choosing a scientific, as opposed to a liberal arts, career. Piaget considers that, in order to bring education into line with the needs of society, it is necessary to undertake a complete revision of the methods and aims of education. Piaget proposes that this reorganization would involve the question of the role of pre-school education; the true significance of active methods ('which everyone talks about but which few educators effectively apply'); the application of child and adolescent psychology and 'that of the necessarily interdisciplinary nature at every level of the subjects taught as opposed to the compartmentalization still so widely prevalent both in the universities and secondary schools.'

Piaget comments that in his investigation of the development of physical causality, he found no evidence of the existence of special aptitudes. 'Consequently our hypothesis is that the so-called aptitudes of "good" students in mathematics or physics, etc., consist above all in their being able to adapt to the type of instruction offered them, whereas students who are "bad" in these fields, but successful in others, are actually able to master the problems they appear not to understand — on condition that they approach them by another route. What they do not understand are the "lessons" and not the subject. Thus it may be — and we have verified it in many cases — that a student's incapacity in a particular subject is owing to a too-rapid passage from the qualitative structure of the problems (by simple logical reasoning but without the immediate introduction of numerical relations and metric laws) to the quantitative or mathematical formulation (in the sense of previously worked-out equations) normally employed by the physicist. Nevertheless, we willingly admit certain aptitudes (once sufficient maturity is attained) which distinguish strictly deductive from empirical and factual minds, but even in mathematics many failures in school are owing to this excessively rapid passage from the qualitative (logical) to the quantitative (numerical)'.

Piaget emphasizes that the use of active methods giving broad scope to the spontaneous research of the child or adolescent requires that the teacher be far from dispensable; the teacher will be involved in creating situations and constructing initial devices in order to present problems to the child. Further, to 'provide counter-examples which compel reflection and reconsideration of over-hasty solutions'.

With respect to the teaching of mathematics Piaget states 'if mathematics teachers would only take the trouble to learn about the "natural" psychogenetic development of the logico-mathematical operations, they would see that there exists a much greater similarity than one would expect between the principal operations spontaneously employed by the child and the notions they attempt to instil into him abstractly'. (For further details see Piaget, 1972, p. 19.). In connection with science, Piaget's views again centre round the importance of active methods. If an experiment is not carried out by the individual himself with complete freedom of initiative it will no longer fall within the category of an experiment but will be mere drill with no educational value.

At the pre-school level Piaget considers that it appears possible to provide a 'kind of propaedeutic to scientific instruction' consisting of exercising the powers of observation. Piaget elaborates that certain actions can be successfully executed at age four to five, but good descriptions cannot be given before nine to 11 years: therefore practice in observation would be very useful. He cites Karplus, who 'considers these observation exercises to be so useful, even at the pre-school age, that he has devised situations with two observers in order to instil at a very early age an understanding of the relativity of observation'.

Piaget further draws attention to the increasing interdisciplinary nature of research in every field and the lack of preparation for this on the part of the researchers. Teaching should stress structuralism which with its interdisciplinary vision is gaining more and more acceptance and support' (Piaget elaborates on structuralism on p. 23). 'What is needed at both the university and secondary level are teachers who indeed know their subject but who approach it from a constantly interdisciplinary point of view, i.e. knowing how to give general significance to the structures they use and to reintegrate them into over-all systems embracing the other disciplines'. Further, there is a need to look closely at the future relations between the human and natural sciences and for students to be encouraged to pass freely from one section to another and be given a choice of many combinations. With respect to teacher training Piaget recommends that the teaching profession should be upgraded at all levels: that there should be full university training for all teachers at every level ('for the younger the students are the more difficult the teacher's task if it is taken seriously') and that such training is necessary for full psychological knowledge.

Piaget finally recommends 'a close union of training and research, the students being associated with the latter right from the start. Team research which is not supervised by a single professor but by representatives of neighbouring fields working closely together . . . (in spite of the difficulties attendant on such collaboration). These are not insurmountable as our experiments in Geneva have shown'.

Abstracts

A validation study of a Piagetian type diagnosis of community college students' cognitive functioning abilities
P.D. Allman, 1973

The author was intent 'to examine the possibility of diagnosing community college students' cognitive functioning abilities, in social science content areas, by means of a Piagetian type clinical diagnosis. In addition, analyses were made to determine the relationships between isolated constructs of cognitive functioning and certain demographic variables. The initial expectation was that factor analysis would yield constructs aligned with constructs of cognitive functioning delineated by Piaget. It was also expected that the diagnosis would significantly distinguish between the three strata of subjects as the strata were formed on the basis of the subjects' past levels of academic performance. On the other hand, it was not expected that the diagnosis would be discriminatory in reference to other demographic variables studied. Observation of the results of the factor analysis confirmed the expectations regarding the Piagetian aligned factor structure of the diagnosis and offered a construct validity and reliability estimate of approximately .86. Observation of the results of the relational studies served to support the stated expectations except that measures related to three of the constructs were discriminatory along the dimension of sex. Twelve factors or constructs aligned with Piaget's theory were isolated. The constructs represented both a concrete operational and an abstract operational level of cognitive functioning for most of the cognitive tasks diagnosed. Seven of the factors discriminated significantly . . . between the strata and, in all cases, discriminated in favour of stratum three, the stratum with highest past level of academic performance. The subjects in the stratum with the lowest level of academic performance, stratum one, and frequently stratum two subjects were functioning at a concrete operational level during the diagnosis.

The important findings of this research necessitate immediate and continuous research of Piagetian remediation approaches based on the diagnosis and remediation of the learner's cognitive functioning abilities', p. 5463A.

Perceptual — motor skills, ability to conserve, and school readiness
J.B. Ayers, M.E. Rohr and M.N. Ayers, 1974

AIM / To determine the relationship between perceptual—motor tasks, conservation skills, and readiness for school.

SUBJECTS / N = 94. Fifty-six children were enrolled in the first grade and 38 children were enrolled in kindergarten. The children were 'above average in intelligence.'

METHOD / The various tests administered were (a) The Purdue Perceptual-motor Survey, which measures five areas of perceptual-motor activities, including balance and posture, body image and differentiation, perceptual-motor match, ocular control, and form perception, (b) The Metropolitan Readiness Test (Hildreth, Griffiths and McGauvran, 1969), (c) Form A of the Peabody Picture Vocabulary Test (Dunn, 1965) in order to assess intelligence, and (d) Piagetian Conservation tasks of number, liquid amount, solid amount, weight, length and area. These were administered following procedures utilized by Stafford and Renner (1971).

RESULTS / The eta correlation technique (Walker and Lev, 1953) was used to determine the relationship of Piaget tasks to Purdue subtests, Metropolitan subtests and IQ. Significant correlations were observed between the Piagetian tasks and IQ and the listening and Numbers subtest of the Metropolitan test. Likewise, a significant value was noted between the Piaget tasks and the Balance and Posture subtest of the Purdue. 'This seemed to indicate that ability to conserve is related to the elementary motor responses (balance beam and jumping) but not to tasks requiring integration of perceptual-motor functioning . . . both perceptual-motor skills and logical thinking can develop separately. Therefore, complete development of motor functioning, as suggested by Kephart (1964), may not be necessary for children to develop all conservation skills. Children who have not developed fully in certain perceptual-motor areas should not be excluded from experiences designed to develop conservation skills but should be exposed to special programmes or given special emphasis', p. 494.

Applications of Piaget's theory to Education: a critical study
N. R. A. Barros, 1972

Barros maintains that Piaget's 'main concern has been centered on the elucidation of epistemological problems and his theory attempts to solve these problems at a scientific level. However, the genetic epistemology that he proposes has attracted the attention of educational researchers, i.e. curriculum specialists and academicians interested in the problems raised by the impact of the recent scientific trends on curriculum development, more than that of philosophers or psychologists . . . In the critical examination of the main trends followed by the implementation of Piaget's genetic epistemology to education, interesting inferences can be drawn for the conduct of Piagetian research in education for the establishment of some starting points for what might become an educational theory based upon cognitive research . . . aroused by Piaget's work . . . .' However, Barros maintains that Piaget himself has offered relatively few references to possible educational applications and that the theory does not offer clear answers to 'good pedagogy'. Barros maintains that before an attempt is made to apply Piaget's epistemological ideas to education it is important to consider what relevancy genetic epistemology may have for education, whether there are any gaps in the theory which might hinder in the inference of educational implications; and the role of education and instruction in Piaget's theory. Piaget's theory is examined as a whole to solve such issues. Piaget's attempt to establish a scientific basis for epistemology is grounded on a 'structuralist' view and 'logistic formalization'. Barros cites Witz's analysis and research which might clarify 'the meaning of Piaget's axiomatic model, it opens . . . perspective for Piagetian research in education.' Other evidence cited is that of Almy and associates (1971).

The effects of a Piagetian geometry model on beginning school children
P.C. Barton, 1975

AIMS / The author was intent 'to provide an in-depth investigation of a young child's understanding of selected geometric ideas through a descriptive, subjective evaluation. Specifically, the objective was to determine . . . if understanding of selected geometric ideas parallel Piaget's topological, projective, and Euclidean thesis; to investigate which geometric ideas the group learned easiest as a result of intervening and teaching certain concepts; and to examine the relationship of geometry understanding of the factors of age, ability, and approaches', p. 4972—A.

SUBJECTS / N = 48 from kindergarten, five-year-olds, and eight-year-olds. Ss were identified according to high mathematical ability or low mathematical ability as determined by standardized tests.

METHOD / A test instrument, a pre-test and post-test composed of three topological, three projective, and three Euclidean ideas was abstracted from Piaget and Inhelder (1956), and developed by the author.

RESULTS / A topological, projective and Euclidean progression as advanced by the Geneva school was substantiated. Recommendations were advanced for incorporating selected geometric ideas into the elementary school curriculum, and for providing additional developmental research in mathematics education.

The relationship between intellectual levels and achievement in the comprehension of concepts classified according to a scheme derived from the Piagetian model
L.B. Bautista, 1975

AIM / To develop a concept classification scheme based on the Piagetian model.

SUBJECTS / Students enrolled in 'CHEMS and Project Physics'.

METHOD / Operational criteria delineated for identifying concrete concepts were: seriation, transitivity, class inclusion, one-to-one correspondence, and conservation. For formal concepts the operational criteria of propositional thinking, combinatorial operations, proportional reasoning, separation of variables, reciprocal implications, and exclusion were established. The two types of tasks administered were: (a) Piagetian tasks of conservation of volume, separation of variables, and equilibrium in the balance, and (b) achievement tests which were a part of 'CHEMS and Project Physics' materials. Each of the concepts involved in the achievement test items was subjected to the operational criteria for evaluation.

RESULTS / Formal students performed significantly better on 57 out of 61 formal questions than concrete students and that no significant difference was computed in the proportions of formal and concrete students responding correctly to 38 out of 39 concrete test items. The classification system designed by the author was supported.

Development of logical operations abilities in early childhood: a longitudinal comparison of the effects of two preschool settings
A.M. Bingham-Newman, 1975

AIM / To examine the patterns of change in cognitive development in young children and to compare the effects of two contrasting pre-school programmes on the development of logical operations abilities.

SUBJECTS / N = 48 aged three to five years.

METHOD / The experimental programme incorporated a theoretical framework and a teacher education component built on Piagetian theory while the comparison programme used a conventional nursery school programme. Each programme was evaluated with two successive 'overlapping waves of pre-school children', each group remaining in the programme for two years. The Ss were evaluated using a representative battery of Piagetian tasks and two standardized non-Piagetian measures: the Raven's Coloured Progressive Matrices and the Peabody Picture Vocabulary Test in a pre-test-post-test design. Seriation, transitivity, double seriation, measurement, and conservation abilities were examined.

RESULTS / Typical age patterns for the Piagetian task performances for the three- and five-year-old subjects were noted. The percentages showed an overall increase in subjects' responses in the higher response categories on the post-test for the Piagetian tasks. Likewise, higher scores were also noted on the post-test for the non-Piagetian measures. Cross-sectional analyses demonstrated no marked differences between the performances of the experimental and control groups. Longitudinal analyses revealed that significant gains were made on several of the seriation subtasks and the length comparison measurement subtasks. T-test comparisons of the non-Piagetian tests pre- to post-test indicated significant gains for all subjects on the Peabody Picture Vocabulary Test and only for the 'Wave two' control groups on the Raven Coloured Progressive Matrices.

An investigation of the feasibility of using a measure of conservation as a predictor of reading comprehension
C.E. Brauchler, 1975

AIM / It was hypothesized that children showing concrete operational intelligence would perform adequately on a test of reading comprehension.

SUBJECTS / N = 106 children.

METHOD / A Piagetian test of conservation, the PIAT reading comprehension test, and the Stanford-Binet Test of Intelligence were administered.

RESULTS / No significant difference among the means of the conservers or non-conservers was computed. The sample studied differed significantly from the norm group presented in the achievement test manual. Correlations for both conservation and mental age scores with the reading comprehension measures were not above the critical value for significance at the alpha level of .05. However, conservation correlated higher than MA with the reading comprehension scores. Generally, the results did not establish the utility of the conservation measure used as a predictor of reading achievement.

An investigation of what relationships exist between a child's performance of selected tasks of conservation and selected factors in reading achievement
W. Brekke, 1972

AIM / The author was intent to determine what relationships exist between a child's performance of some conservation tasks and selected factors in reading achievement.

SUBJECTS / N = 81 first grade children.

METHOD / Children were administered the Piagetian tasks of number and substance. Gates-MacGinitie Reading Tests: Readiness Skills, SRA Primary Mental Abilities Grades K—L were also given.

RESULTS / The study demonstrated that the child's performance on selected tasks of conservation was significantly related to selected factors in reading readiness. Mental age was significantly related to conservation operativity and reading readiness. Sex differences were significantly related to conservation and reading readiness and chronological age was positively but not significantly related to conservation and reading readiness. Teacher prediction was significantly related to reading readiness.

Conservation and reading achievement of second grade bilingual American Indian children
B. Brekke and J.D. Williams, 1974

Brekke and Williams point out the research efforts which have investigated the relationships of Piaget's stages to reading instruction. They cite the work of Raven and Salzer (1971) who demonstrated that reversibility and decentration are important for beginning reading. Almy (1964) indicated that the child's comprehension of reciprocal relationships may be related to his stability of perception, necessary for visual discrimination in beginning reading instruction. Elkind *et al.* (1965) found a correlation between reading achievement and recognition of words and further that decentration is involved in the recognition of words.

AIM / The authors were intent to determine what relationships existed between conservation and the progress in beginning reading among bilingual Indian children.

SUBJECTS / N = 38. The children, 17 females and 21 males ranged in age from six years five months to nine years four months. The children's first language was Zuni and their second was English and their standard scores ranged from 78—118 for the Draw-A-Man Test.

METHOD / Children were administered the following tests:
  (a) Conservation of Inequality of Number.
  (b) Conservation of Equality of Number.
  (c) Conservation of Equality of Substance.
  (d) Conservation of Inequality of Substance.
  (e) Conservation of Equality of Substance.

Each test was individually administered and all responses were recorded verbatim. Full details of the experimental procedure including scoring techniques are described elsewhere (Brekke and Williams, 1974, p. 67).

Intelligence and reading level were obtained through the administration of the Goodenough Draw-A-Man Test (Harris, 1963) and the Classroom Reading Inventory (Silvaroli, 1972).

RESULTS / Conservation scores were significantly related to the three measures of reading level. This relationship remained true when the Draw-A-Man Test was partialled out. Low correlations of the Draw-A-Man Test with the reading levels were low and the authors question the usefulness of the Draw-A-Man Test as a measure of intelligence for the bilingual child.

Conservation as a predictor of reading achievement
B.W. Brekke and J.D. Williams, 1975

AIM / To determine to what extent conservation may be used as a predictor of reading achievement.

SUBJECTS / N = 72 and ranged in age from 70 to 91 months. The mean MA for Ss was 80.44 months.

METHOD / The tests administered included: Gates-MacGinitie Reading Tests: Readiness Skills; SRA Primary Mental Abilities Test, Grades K—L; and five tasks to assess the attainment of conservation, including two tasks with conservation of substance.

RESULTS / Despite a significant relationship between both conservation and intelligence regarding success on a reading test administered seven months later, neither was a significant predictor when a reading test had been included in the initial test battery. 'On the other hand, there is a strong relationship between conservation and intelligence with reading readiness, which accounts for a lack of the independent contribution of either conservation or intelligence with the two measures of reading achievement. Both singly and in combination conservation and intelligence were significant predictors of reading achievement. When the partial correlations between conservation and reading achievement were analyzed, all values dropped to near zero. Apparently the relationship between conservation and reading achievement is not independent of reading readiness and intelligence', p. 98.

Conservation and reading readiness
B.W. Brekke, J.D. Williams and S.D. Harlow, 1973

The authors draw attention to Piaget's views on reading readiness by quoting Hall (1970, p. 30), 'So the concept of readiness is not bad but I am not sure that it can be applied to reading. Reading aptitude may not be related to mental age. There could easily be a difference of aptitude between children independent of mental age. But I cannot state that as a fact because I have not studied it closely.'

AIM / An investigation of the relationship between conservation and reading readiness.

SUBJECTS / N = 81. Of these, 46 were male and 35 were female, with a mean age 77.3 months and mean mental age 80.3 months.

METHOD / Each subject was administered the following tests:
   (a) Gates – MacGinitie Reading Tests: Reading Skills
   (b) Primary Mental Abilities Test: Grades K–L
   (c) Conservation of Inequality of Number
   (d) Conservation of Equality of Number
   (e) Conservation of Equality of Substance
   (f) Conservation of Inequality of Substance
   (g) Conservation of Equality of Substance

Each child was tested individually and all responses were audio-taped and transcribed on record sheets for scoring.

RESULTS / Conservation was positively related to the reading skills of the Gates-MacGinitie Test, and only slightly less correlated with reading readiness than intelligence as measured by the Primary Mental Abilities Test.

A moderate correlation was noted between conservation and intelligence. The authors finally conclude, 'Conservation should be taken into account as an additional measure of readiness for beginning reading instruction. Attendant with this recommendation is the need to acquaint primary level teachers and reading specialists with Piagetian principles and ways of evaluating the child's operational level', p. 138.

Facilitating psychological growth in post-adolescents: a cognitive-developmental curriculum intervention and analysis
S.A. Brock, 1975

AIM / To explore educational and theoretical questions in the area of promoting post-adolescent cognitive psychological development.

SUBJECTS / N = 41 junior college physical therapy assistant students.

METHOD / Ss were divided into an experimental (N = 22) and a control group (N = 19) on the basis of class scheduling. 'This "non-equivalent control group design" provided a comparison between the standard curriculum of "talking about" the clinical situation and aspects of communication, and the experimental curriculum of activity engaging in role-played and group applications of (1) relationship building, (2) communication processes, and (3) moral reasoning. These elements of the "action-reflection" curriculum are aimed at (a) increasing the development of "active-listening" skills; (b) differentiating multiple causes of behaviour, (c) increasing perceptions of personal choices of action; (d) recognizing multiple role behaviours, and (e) identifying levels of moral and ethical reasoning. All of the foregoing elements relate directly to promoting structural psychological development such that individuals come to move through the hierarchical stages of cognitive development, thus viewing themselves and others in more complex, and adequate ways. A series of proximate measures aimed at formative evaluation were used to assess the programmatic and cognitive-developmental growth aspects of the intervention. They included daily session evaluations, and overall feedback questionnaire and "active-listening" skill test, student boys, other impressionistic data, the Kohlberg Moral Judgment test and the Loevinger Sentence Completion test on ego-development . . . the broad theoretical underpinnings of Dewey, Piaget, and Kohlberg (were used)', p. 4140–B.

RESULTS / Programmatic results demonstrated that the experimental group intervention was well liked and seen as moderately useful in a personal and professional sense for the students. Measures of cognitive developmental growth indicated no significant change from pre- to post-tests, or between experimental and control groups. However Ss tended to remain at "conventional" levels of development as assessed by the Kohlberg and the Loevinger tests. Brock finally concluded, 'Implications of the data . . . point to suggestions for maximizing interventional gain within a deliberd's psychological education curriculum. First "action" situations with some ambiguity would seem to facilitate the questioning and risk-taking responses needed for cognitive growth. Second, specifying building-in norms of accepting individual differences would allow more productive cognitive disequilibrium to merge from student interaction. Third, pre-testing individuals would allow known heterogeneity to be maximized. Finally, analyzing an intervention's inherent level of cognitive development could provide a linkage of student and intervention stage, facilitating an optimal growth producing cognitive mismatch', p. 4140—B.

Learning and development: a neo-Piagetian interpretation
R. Case, 1972

AIMS / Three hypotheses were formulated as follows:

(1) 'For the verbal encoding task, the specially instructed children will do as well as normally instructed grade-IV children (nine to ten years), and better than normally instructed grade-II children (seven to eight years)'.

(2) 'For the encoding gestural task, the specially instructed children will perform at least as well as normally instructed grade-II children (seven to eight years), and better than normally instructed kindergarten children'.

(3) 'Like the normally instructed children from grades II and IV (and unlike the normally instructed kindergarten children), the specially instructed children will do as well on the encoding verbal task as on the decoding verbal task'.

SUBJECTS / Ten schools who used the Conceptual Skills Programme (Pascual-Leone, 1970) were considered. Out of these schools, the one which served a middle-class population participated in the study. Subjects were selected from kindergarten, grade II, and grade IV.

METHOD / The overall design consisted of the administration of four tests developed by Pascual-Leone and Smith (1969). These subjects had already completed the Conceptual Skills Programme. The objective was to compare their performance with that of the regularly instructed kindergarten, grade-II, and grade-IV subjects already tested by Pascual-Leone and Smith. The two decoding tasks were administered first. Half the children received the decoding verbal (DV) tasks first; half received the decoding gestural (DG) tasks first. (Details of the various tasks are given in Pascual-Leone and Smith (*op. cit.*) and Case, 1972, pp. 352—3).

RESULTS / 'The specially instructed kindergarten children performed at about the same level as the normally instructed grade-IV children on the encoding verbal task, and intermediate between the normally instructed grade-II and grade-IV children on the encoding gestural task. The specially instructed kindergarten children also showed little difference in their performance between the encoding and decoding verbal tasks. All these trends were significant', p. 353. Case concludes, 'Pascual-Leone's model embraces both a learning and a developmental perspective within one theoretical framework . . . its main developmental construct (M space) is formulated in such a fashion that precise developmental predictions can be made about the effects of particular learning experiences . . . , the model gives added predictive power to Piaget's developmental theory in the area of learning, and may also prove able to give added predictive power to Gagné's learning theory in the area of development', p. 357.

Cognitive development: guiding principles for early childhood programmes
R.N. Charlesworth, 1975

The author presented at the philosophical, theoretical, research and practice levels a model for guiding the teaching of young children in the cognitive areas of language and conceptualization. The opening discussion centres on the reasons for having a theoretical rationale, definition of cognition, concept and language and describes her basic assumptions regarding heredity and environment, maturation and learning and the concept of teaching. The primary theories which underlie early childhood programmes: Piagetian, Behaviourist, and Traditionalist were compared and it was suggested that the theories may be combined in a complementary way. Examples of research studies in conceptualization, language, and psycho-social realms which 'bridge the gap' from theory to practice were cited. The nature of the learner was placed in a Piagetian framework. The concepts which should be developing in early childhood were outlined as the souce of curriculum objectives. The nature of teaching was described as a systematic diagnostic process which proceeded in a sequential manner. The author concluded with a demonstration as to how the principles may be used in practice no matter what materials, guides, or teaching kits the teacher has available. 'There are two appendices. Appendix A is for the reader who wishes to pursue in more detail the current trends in early childhood education and Appendix B lists many of the current available guides and kits.'

A study of children's ability to work with elementary mathematical systems
K.F. Collis, 1973

AIMS / Three hypotheses were formulated by the author as follows: (a) 'Responses to items in all tests for Ss below 16 years would show a tendency to ignore the given system and reason by analogy with a familiar system'. (b) Subjects below 16 years of age would tend to be non-operational on the various tests. (c) Operativity on items one and two in test one would be preceded by operativity in the parallel items in tests two and three.

SUBJECTS / N = 330, with an age-range from seven to 17 years and 11 months.

METHOD / Three tests were administered adapted from Collis (1971, Test 9). 'Each test set up the same mathematical system by defining an operation, "*", and indicating that the elements to be operated on were zero and the positive integers (0, 1, 2, . . .). Ss were required to make deductions about the truth or falsity of five statements. The definition of the operation in each was: "*" is an operation such that a * b = a + 2 x b, and the five statements, set out in table one, were in parallel in that, from test to test, they involved the same operations in the same order — the only changes were in the level of abstractness of the elements and the method of making responses. In test one Ss were told to indicate when the statement would be true. As this form of response was not suitable for tests two and three, Ss were asked in these tests to mark the statement true or false', page 122.
Sample items in test one included: a * b = b * a; a * x = a; test two comprised such items as 5 * (4 * 6) = (5 * 4) * 6; 3 * (4 + 6) = (3 * 4) * 6; test three items included: 982 * (475 * 638) = (982 * 475) * 638; 572 + (865 * 749) = (865 * 749) + 572.

RESULTS / All three hypotheses stated above were substantiated. Utilizing mathematical material and the Piagetian model seem to imply that Ss must attain the capacity for formal-operational reasoning if Ss are to work within a closed abstract system. 'They show also that Ss below the formal level of thinking tend to ignore a given defined system and reason by analogy with a familiar system. Although items with less abstract elements operated upon appear to be attained first there are grounds for believing that the basic problem lies in the difficulty S has in controlling the variables which define the operations allowable within the system', p. 121. The findings are discussed with other related studies, Collis (1971); Inhelder and Piaget (1958); Peel (1966, 1967); Scandura (1968, 1970).

The development of a preference for logical consistency in school mathematics
K.F. Collis, 1974

AIM / The author was intent to study the development of a preference for logical consistency in school mathematics.

SUBJECTS / N = 127 at four different age levels: nine, 11, 14, and 16 years.

METHOD / 'Two sets of two-element tables were constructed ... Tables A_1, A_2 and A_3 were such that (a) the result obtained by operating on any pair of elements was always the same; (b) when combined into one three-element table, they gave consistent results for all combinations; and (c) when used for mapping either two or three elements into one, they gave nonconflicting results. It will be recognized that table A reflected a typical group structure in which the axioms of a group held. Tables B_1, B_2 and B_3, ... were such that (a) the result of operating on any pair of elements was not always the same, for example, 1 * 1 = 1 and 1 * 1 = 0; 2 * 0 = 2 and 2 * 1 = 2; (b) when combined into one three-element table, inconsistent results were obtained for some combinations; and (c) when used for mapping either two or three elements into one, they gave conflicting results. Table B did not conform to the structure of a mathematical group', p. 979. One set of tables was self-consistent, and the other gave inconsistent results in some of the cells. After training in which Ss used both sets of tables, they were asked to show which set they preferred to work with and to give their reasons. (Fuller details of the two- and three-element tables and the experimental procedures are described in Collis, 1974, pp. 979–980).

RESULTS / Eight-year-old Ss gave preferences and reasons which demonstrated that they were either unaware of the inconsistency or thought it not relevant. On the other hand, the 16-year-old Ss preferred the consistent set of tables and advanced 'consistency' explicitly as their reason for preference; 'groups of Ss in between these ages responded in terms that showed a preference for the consistent table but were not in general, able to give explicit reasons for their choice', p. 978. Collis finally draws attention to the educational significance of his results. 'It is still far too common to see curricula and teaching methods used on cognitive processes with which the primary and early secondary school child is not equipped. If the procedures used in this experiment are taken to mirror certain systems which the child is expected to master in primary and early secondary school — e.g., grammar in English, remote and proximate causes in history, fractions and mensuration in mathematics — then some obvious limitations both in curriculum and method appear. This study suggests that the child is only beginning to have a feel for the need for consistency in a system at about the age of 11 years and that he is well into the junior secondary school years before this "feeling" becomes rationalized to the point where he is able to verbalize his ideas; yet a number of curriculum topics and teaching procedures used during these years seem to imply that the child is capable not only of recognizing inconsistency but of being able to give explicit reasons for some element not conforming to the system', p. 983.

The role of classification skills in children's acquisition of concrete operational thought
T. Colton, 1972

AIMS / The author was intent to investigate the relationship between the ability to perform a concrete operational task at the pre-operational level and the acquisition of classification skills based on a systematic task analysis of that specific operational task. Further, to explore 'the relative effectiveness of a science curriculum based on systematic task analysis of the development of classification skills related to a learner's ability to accomplish a specific task'.

SUBJECTS / Children in the first and third grade.

METHOD / The Piagetian task of predicting floating objects as described by Almy *et al.* (1966, pp 54—55) was administered. 'Based on a systematic analysis of this task a series of ordered skills and processes were developed. This analysis of skills and processes was used to develop behaviour objectives for a series of instructional sequences. These short-term instructional sequences were taught to children in the first and third grade, half of whom had had long-term instruction based on "Science-A Process Approach", an elementary school science programme designed to teach the processes of science by means of lessons based on task analysis and behavioural objectives'.

RESULTS / All subjects who had experience in the short-term instructional programme enhanced their performance of the concrete operational tasks when compared with their control counterparts. Only third grade subjects who had long-term instruction exhibited operativity on the prediction of floating objects task. No such evidence emerged with respect to the first grade subjects. The study demonstrated that children can be helped to acquire concrete operational thought which they do not show when denied long-term instruction or short-term instruction.

Colton finally concludes, 'The design of curriculum must be based on both what is feasible, "what can be" and what is desired, "what ought to be". While the findings . . . provide assistance with the former, answering the latter requires that the curriculum designer give consideration of what values of the total school and societal setting ought to be reflected in the curriculum that it implemented by the educational complex . . . task analysis has been found to be a functional tool in designing curriculum. It is the responsibility of the educator and curriculum designer to design when to apply this tool of task analysis in order that it will be most beneficial to the learner'.

An investigation of the efficacy of Piaget curriculum elements integrated into a traditional Head Start programme
H. Diamond, 1973

AIM / The author was intent to study if Piaget elements added to a traditional Head Start programme would enhance classification and seriation skills and conservation of discontinuous and continuous quantities.

SUBJECTS / N = 42. There were 23 subjects in the experimental group and 19 in the control group.

METHOD / The sample was pre-tested in October, 1971 and post-tested in June, 1972 on Piagetian tasks of classification, seriation, discontinuous and continuous quantities. 'The method was designed to aid the children in their intellectual progress from pre-operational to concrete operational thought as defined by Piaget. The curricular elements were added to the daily class routine. The daily five minute sessions were with a group of three children and the teacher "aide" playing with materials physically and verbally. The materials were toys, inexpensive and used in the classroom only for these prescribed activities. Nine separate activities, using a variety of toys (cars, beads, checkers, chess sets) spread over the school year, specifically addressed the seriation, classification and conservation concepts. The instructions given to the teacher and "aide" by the author explained the specific objective of each task and the broad range of behaviour that might bring about the achievement of the concept addressed. Building a general climate of inquiry was attempted: open-ended questions on the part of the adult encouraged various physical and verbal responses from the children. Direct intellectual confrontation within a social framework so that discovery was inevitable was the exact process in the treatment'.

RESULTS / Seriation skills were more developed in more Head Start students taught in the traditional curriculum with Piaget curricular elements integrated than in the traditional curriculum without such elements. Classification skills and conservation of discontinuous quantity were more developed in more Head Start students taught in the traditional curriculum with Piaget curricular elements integrated than in the Head Start students taught in the traditional curriculum without such elements. However, conservation of continuous quantity did not show any such evidence. Diamond finally concludes, 'The four essential factors for intellectual growth according to Jean Piaget are maturation, physical and social interaction and equilibration. This study's method incorporated these elements — the children were at a pre-operational level on the brink of concrete operational thought, and the curriculum spread over eight months provided cognitive conflict within a physical and social daily framework. It does appear that in the hands of a teacher :.. such curricular elements integrated into the traditional class-room facilitates intellectual growth', p. 167A.

*Spontaneous vs. scientific concepts in mathematics**
B. Fleckman, 1975

Piaget has given us two very important ideas that can help us learn and teach more effectively. These are:

(a) A thorough examination of children's cognitions shows a maturation of children's thought processes.
(b) Task analysis enables us to follow how internalizations of cognitions take place.

Mathematics, whether new or the old, is still being taught with little or no consideration for these Piagetian concepts. Rather miscon-

* Published by the kind permission of the author. Gratitude is extended to Professor Bess Fleckman of Miami-Dade Community College, Florida.

ceptions of how learning takes place can account for the incorrect internalizations of mathematics by yet another generation of students. One of the misconceptions concerns the use of the discovery method in mathematics. Teachers feel that the discoveries made spontaneously during lessons mean that the student has attained meaning and understanding of a concept. What the student is exhibiting is the very first accommodation of which Piaget speaks and has not attained in depth assimilation. Cognitions that are on the level of awareness do not occur spontaneously. Rather, the grasp of concepts entails step by step, sequential learning to allow for progress and interaction of accommodation and assimilation.

Emphasis in the classrooms in the teaching of mathematics has been mainly the accommodation of the student to presentations of concepts or computations in mathematics. Cookbook approaches even when replaced with inductive, discovery techniques are insufficient for internalization of meaning. There has to be a maturational process such as described by Piaget whereby concepts on the accommodation level proceed to the assimilation level; where spontaneous learning becomes scientific (psychological learning).

Vygotsky has used the spontaneous and scientific terminology to distinguish the type of learnings involved in mastery of concepts. To me, this is a vitalization of Piaget's ideas of task analysis so that sequential presentation may be accorded the content, and also maturation of cognitions are provided.

The basic materials for building a thought structure in mathematics are concepts. Teachers are inclined to forget how very vague are the concepts of children due to past oversights in the area of solid development towards generalization and discrimination. Often the quantitave operations on the part of the youngster were considered the behavioural manifestation of learning of concepts but, in reality, this may be only representative of a possibility for learning. It is not a guarantee!

The child uses concepts constantly but the use made is that which is labelled 'spontaneous use'. This use does not examine nor define. This use is not on the conscious level for the child becomes *conscious* of his spontaneous concepts relatively late; the ability to define them in words, to operate with them at will appears long after he has acquired the concepts. (Vygotsky, 1962, p. 92).

It is the work of the teacher to develop the related, organized structure with the child, where teacher and child use his verbal responses as a means for working consciously toward concept attainment. This situation is a learning situation that is far different from an instance where the child uses the concept in a spontaneous fashion where the concept is ill-defined and where the user is not conscious of his own act of thought. The scientific concept develops not from direct teaching of the concept but rather from an evolutionary process of going from percept to concept.

Instruction is the key to this development. The teacher plays a decisive role in this evolutionary process by guiding the child to become conscious of his own mental processes. It is this inner process of thought which becomes a conscious thing to the youngster which distinguishes spontaneous from developed or scientific concept formation. The spontaneous concept focuses on the object itself and never on the act of thought itself.

For example, a child doing the division below may work it out, yet not be aware that the 23 in the example is really 2300, the 2300 being the product of 100 x 23.

$$114\ 2/23$$
$$23\overline{)2624}$$
$$\underline{23}$$

Only when the child has had the experiences of learning the number system, the meaning of place value, and is able to discriminate that the zeros in 2300 do not affect the subsequent subtraction, only then, will his abstraction of writing the 2300 as 23 be on the conscious level of control. Then, discrimination and definition are possible by the child. It is only then that we can say the scientific concept is attained.

This conscious level of control allows for the concept to be placed into a relationship of the total structure of the mathematics and makes of this new concept a sub-structure.

Using the example above, the youngster now has the sub-structure of meaning for the 23 as 2300 and can now go on to using the divisor and the first two numbers of the dividend for the obtaining of a trial divisor which is meaningful, rather than rote.

Errors in attaining concepts do occur. It is possible that there is a confusion in the images, memories and percepts of the child. These faulty images, memories and percepts may come about from lack of experience or lack of validation of the child's observations. Again, the teacher plays the central role to help the child avoid errors and overcome them when they occur. She must be sure that the material of the task be organized so that it is appropriate to the capabilities of the learner and that the material is related to previous learnings. She uses the structure of mathematics to categorize, to fit in, to relate, the new learnings to previously attained concepts. She may use a combination of methods, a combination of inductive or deductive method to guide the learner. The inductive method proves helpful in sustaining interest and activity, and for the understanding of the function of the concept. The deductive method can be valuable for clearing up the internal structure of the concept. This approach allows that through teacher assistance, the child can do more that he could have done by himself, though, again ... only within the limits set by his development. The instruction can lead the child to new developmental levels. Thus, in the example above, the inductive method could be used during development as:

$$
\begin{array}{r}
4 \\
10 \\
100 \\
\hline
23)\ 2624 \\
\end{array}
$$

```
        4
       10
      100
23) 2624
    2300      100 x 23 = 2300
    ----
     324
     230       10 x 23 =  230
    ----
      94
      92        4 x 23 =   92
    ----
       2   remainder which can be
             divided as: 2/23
```

The deductive method used by the teacher would effect the 'short-cuts' after generalizations were on the scientific concept level. Thus the teacher leads her students as she guides. Vygotsky has said that the only good kind of instruction is that which marches ahead of the development and leads it. (*ibid.*, p. 104). Many times this means that the scientific concept, having had the help of teacher development sometimes runs ahead of the spontaneous concepts, since these latter lack the awareness that the teacher brings to the learning situation. This may be difficult to comprehend. It is possible that the youngster may have the understanding of the division above, on the scientific concept basis but still need further relating and development to spontaneous situations, experiental situations. When the awareness is brought to bear on the spontaneous situation then it, too, becomes enriched, related, and categorized into the already existant knowledge field of the child. This can be illustrated by examining the remainder in the above example in a concrete situation involving yards of material where the answer would be expressed 114 2/23 and in a situation involving books where the answer would be expressed 114 and two books remaining.

The teacher seeks the lowest threshold of the child's development and then guides the student to reach the upper thresholds. There is constant interaction of spontaneous and scientific concepts, each contributing towards building understandings which allow the youngster to operate on higher intellectual levels.

When the teacher has the knowledge of the difference between spontaneous concept and scientific concept, she will not be apt to accept a child's operations without inquiry. The youngster may be using the term 'one-half' and even perhaps doing computation involving 1/2 yet not be able to define the process and verbalize his own act of thought. The concept then is still not at the conscious level for the child. Here, there would be need for the teacher to use concrete situations to make the mathematics meaningful. If the time is taken to approach the arithmetic in this developmental fashion, later on the youngster at college level would not be writing one-half of 12 as: $12 \div \frac{1}{2}$*

The differentiation of spontaneous and scientific concept development is vital for understanding.

Thinking goes to school: Piaget's theory in practice
H.G. Furth and H. Wachs, 1974

The authors summarize the book as ' . . . a description of how to structure a first or second grade classroom to bring about an atmosphere for thinking'. The authors describe the 'Thinking School' project set up in a school in West Virginia (Kindergarten and First Grade one) — the objectives ranging through 'creative independent thinking, positive self-image, social cooperation and moral responsibility, knowledge of people and environment, (to) basic academic skills'. Furth and Wachs denounce an academic approach for five-year-olds (i.e., rote learning, and didactic teaching), and set the scene for a progression of kinaesthetic and sensorimotor exercises that will orientate the child towards manipulative skills, discrimination exercises, visual thinking games, eye—hand and ear—hand games, and finally lead to games in logical thinking that give classroom life to the classical ideas of Piaget, Bruner, and Vygotsky. The final chapter assesses the project and its implications.

Dolan (1975) while reviewing the book asserts, 'Teachers of infants in British schools will probably find little that is unfamiliar in the curriculum practice suggested by the authors in the early part of the book. Few, however, would consider Piaget's theory as the root of this practice, even though his ideas lend powerful support. Teachers may be more interested in the compendium of games outlined in the body of the test. The classification of some of the games is a matter of debate, as is some of the labelling. Nevertheless, many are novel and ingenious, may give new ideas to teachers, and will certainly appeal to children', p. 97. Loughran (1975) thinks that the book was worth writing for two

---

* Recently, the author gave this question to nine college students and two of the nine wrote it as given above.

important reasons: 'first a real attempt has been made to make systematic, rational educational provision for the "pre-conceptual" age group; secondly, an extensive programme of "lessons" and activities requiring sensory discrimination and/or conceptual thinking is provided for the teacher's use . . . ("the implication for the teacher of Piaget's theory of intuitive thinking" that so bemuse the many student-teachers who can give Piaget, almost verbatim, on the irreversible out-pourings of pints of lemonade, has been worked out in practice). Nor is there any danger if the system is carefully used, of waiting for "readiness" to appear for not only are the discrimination exercises tapered into formal reading, writing and number skills, but the claim seems justified that low-level and high-level thinking are both possible in many of the exercises, as in Piaget's "transition stages" . . . a "thinking hour" or daily "thinking time" might be a better thing than "free activities", because it would be child-centred in much more than an emotional sense', p. 81.

The study of the cognitive development of science students in introductory level courses
D.H. Griffiths, 1974

AIM / To ascertain the level of cognitive development of college students following science courses.

SUBJECTS / The subjects were selected from chemistry and physics courses from a state university and a college.

METHOD / Each subject was tested twice — first by the E and later by another member of the research team. All responses were tape recorded. The subjects were administered one Piagetian task; the inclined plane, to demonstrate the development of the INRC group or the combination of colourless liquids, to test the combinatorial system (Inhelder and Piaget, 1958). The tape recorded responses were validated by two independent techniques. 'Randomly selected tapes were given to persons familiar with Piagetian scoring methods but not with the hypothesis of this paper and secondly, tapes were transcribed and given to science faculty members to score from the framework of the student's intuitive grasp of the science concepts involved in the problem'.

RESULTS / Griffiths concludes, '1) The composite results of the total sample failed to meet the Piagetian criteria that 75 per cent should have scored at the stage IIIB. Only 39 per cent of the subjects scored at this level; 2) A non-parametric analysis of the two subsamples indicated no significant differences in the subjects' performances; 3) Both subsamples scored significantly higher on the chemical combination task compared to the plane task, but significantly below the Piagetian criteria; 4) No significant differences were found in the performance of distinctly different racial subsamples. An analysis of the tapes in terms of the parameters of scoring at the stage IIIB formal level and the usage of a technical vocabulary showed that subjects possessing a technical vocabulary, but not the formal stage of operations, were severely limited in their performance with the experimental equipment because of their tendency to resolve conflicts with the superposition of words that did not apply . . . concluded . . . that the majority of the students at the level of introductory science courses have a major handicap in terms of the development of their cognitive structures . . . that the strategy of developmental work at the college level may best be directed in terms of the students' cognitive development and not in the imposition of vocabulary and skills upon a less developed structure', p. 3989A.

Do mathematical group invariants characterize the perceptual schema of younger and older children?
J.W. Gyr, R. Willey, D. Gordon, and R.H. Kubo, 1974

The authors argue that, 'In spite of the availability of theories which conceptualize perceptual systems within a framework of group theory and in spite of the arguments about the power of such concepts by Structuralists (Piaget, 1970), much experimental work remains to be done. Some such work suggests that perception does not manifest group properties. Piaget (1969) argues that perceptual processes do not possess mathematical group structures since they prevent the child for some time from attaining cognitive group structures on "conservation" tasks. Or, again, he suggests that the absence of perceptual group structures accounts for some of the perceptual illusions (Piaget, 1969)', p. 178.

AIMS / The authors were intent to investigate whether perceptual processes of children can be viewed within a 'structuralist' frame of reference. Further, if the concept of the 'group' of transformations can be employed to formulate perceptual phenomena and to forecast experimental outcome.

SUBJECTS / N = 96 within the age-range one to seven years. The Ss were assigned to two groups: young subjects, age one to two years, and older subjects, age three to seven years.

METHOD / The apparatus used and the stimuli presented were patterned after Gyr *et al.* (1973). The procedure comprised showing the movie to each child and 'consisted of four main pairs of events: (1) an 18 sec. presentation of I followed by a 26 sec. transformation, r, of that object; (2) an 18 sec. presentation of I followed by 26 sec. of p'; (3) 18 sec. of t, followed by 26 sec. of r, and (4) 18 sec. of t followed by 26 sec. of p'. In order to reduce effects of each pair on the next, each pair of stimuli, including the first, was preceded by a blank screen of 10 sec . . . S's mothers were told that all the subject had to do was to watch the movie. His or her attention was to be directed to the circular screen upon first being seated in front of it, but from then on, viewing or not viewing the screen was to be left up to the subject. The beginning of each member of each pair was accompanied by ringing of a bell to facilitate the subject's viewing of at least the very beginning of each new event', p. 183.

(Fuller details of the apparatus, stimuli and experimental procedure are described in Gyr *et al.*, 1974, pp. 182–3).

RESULTS / The correlation between the complexity of the stimuli and attention paid was substantiated for all children. Subjects in the age-range three to seven demonstrated 'priming of the rotation stimulus by the translation stimulus . . . some kind of schema for motions was developed in these Ss and persisted across phenomenally different stimuli . . . There seem to be two major reasons why younger subjects might manifest a perceptual invariant structure in the case of complexity (prediction I), but not when differential priming effects of t on r and t on p' are examined: perhaps younger subjects' internal hierarchical structures are too weakly formed, or the demand on memory posed by the priming experiment is too high to allow for priming to take a hold . . . our predictions, based on the assumption that perceptual schema of subjects have certain invariance structures predicted by group theory, were supported. However, such support is at best partial', p. 185.

*Conservation concepts in elementary chemistry**
J.R. Hall, 1973

AIM / On the assumption that conservation of chemical identity,

---

* Written and prepared by the author for inclusion in this volume. Gratitude is extended to Dr J.R. Hall of the University of Newcastle-upon-Tyne.

composition and mass were essential to basic understanding of chemistry, this pilot study was intended to discover the extent to which these conservation principles were present in a small sample of first year secondary school pupils.

SUBJECTS / N = 23 boys and girls, age 11.1 to 12.10, IQ 108 to 140 from grammar school, who had completed an introductory course in chemistry in nine months preceding tests.

METHOD / Subjects were individually presented with experiments involving simple chemical transformations and asked to say whether new substances were formed and to give reasons for their judgements.

RESULTS / Responses indicating non-conservation were given as follows: mass six Ss, identity 12 Ss, composition 17 Ss. *

DISCUSSION / Subjects had experienced a course of teaching similar to the first three sections of the Nuffield O-level chemistry scheme, which involved the study of chemical reaction through a consideration of the effects of heat on substances and of combustion and which seemed to assume that relevant concepts and schemata could be developed without difficulty. The results make this doubtful and suggest a need to re-examine the ideas underlying courses of this kind.

Theory into practice: activities in school for student teachers
J. Haysom and C. Sutton (Eds.), 1974

Under the Science Teacher Education Project Series, *Theory into practice: activities in school for student teachers*, the editors Haysom and Sutton state that pupils' learning in science involves them in thinking in the abstract, when pupils manipulate ideas and possibilities in their minds. They maintain that most of the mental processes (e.g. introduction to such abstractions as mass; volume; density; pressure involving the concepts of force and area; and quantity of heat involving both temperature change and mass) fall within the category of Piagetian formal operations. Reviews by Peel (1967), Ausubel and Robinson (1969), and Shayer (1972) show that few pupils use formal reasoning before CA 13. 'It is important for a teacher to know how his pupils stand in this respect, for only then can he make appropriate decisions,

---

* Further data from 36 subjects is given in — J.R. Hall. Research into the Teaching and Learning of Science in the Classroom, Part III: a Comparative Study. University of Newcastle School of Education, 1974 (unpublished).

such as postponing the topic, or handling it in a manner which is more tangible and less abstract', p. 27. The editors go on to cite three of Piaget's experiments: the pendulum problem (ability to investigate a problem involving several variables); the problem of floating and sinking (ability to eliminate contradictions in explanations of observation); problems of spatial perception (ability to use an intangible frame of reference) as assignments designed to help teachers 'to get some insight into your pupils' abilities in this respect . . .', p. 27. Haysom and Sutton provide worksheets and diagrammatical representations of the above experiments, together with questions for discussion which teachers working in the secondary schools can use in the assessment of their pupils' formal reasoning.

The relationship between conservation abilities on selected Piagetian tasks and reading ability
M.J. Hurta, 1973

AIM / To determine the relationship between the child's ability to conserve and reading ability. Reading disabled and non-reading disabled children were examined to establish if differences in conservation abilities could be pinned down.

SUBJECTS / N = 25 within the age range from seven years and eight years five months. 'The children classified as reading disabled were enrolled in a special education class for the language-learning disabled and read at a level six months below their anticipated reading level. The non-reading disabled children read at a level which ranged from less than six months below to above their anticipated reading level'.

METHOD / The Concept Assessment Kit-Conservation (Goldschmid and Bentler, 1968b) was administered to assess the child's performance in two dimensional space, number, substance, continuous quantity, weight, discontinuous quantity, length and area. Durrell Analysis of Reading Ability was also administered. Each subject was classified according to his level of function and to his stage of development on all tasks.

RESULTS / A chi-square value was computed for each hypothesis formulated. The conclusions were: 'The only statistically significant differences which exist between children classified as reading disabled and non-reading disabled were found in the conservation of length on Task A and in the stage of development on all tasks administered. Regardless of the reading classification of the child there appeared to be a significant relationship between the child's level of functioning on specific conservation tasks and specific reading subtests of the Durrell Analysis of Reading Difficulty'.

*Conceptual demands in Nuffield O-level chemistry**
R.B. Ingle and M. Shayer, 1971

Shayer (1970) devised a technique of assessment of science courses based on Piaget's conceptual stages. Ingle and Shayer were intent to determine, 'What is the minimum conceptual level that the pupil must have attained without which his interest cannot be sustained? And what conceptual level is needed to enable the pupil to comprehend the course in a well-integrated way? – for this he must grasp the chemistry of the sub-topic in relation to the course as a whole'. These issues were important for each sub-topic of the Nuffield sample scheme.

The copper task provided an instance of the assessment: 'In the introduction, topic A2–5, the pupil conducts a series of experiments and proceeds by elimination until the two sources of the black deposit on copper are isolated. Unless he can appreciate the first stages of formal reasoning this process of elimination will seem arbitrary and pointless, and he will not be interested. Thus this topic is estimated as requiring stage 3A. When he comes to topic 3.2 he needs to be thinking in terms of some simple model (stage 3A) of elements as constituents of compounds to make any sense of the experiment by generating oxygen by heating lead oxide, i.e. to grasp the concept of gas density, his formal reasoning needs to be fully developed (3B)', p 182. Ingle and Shayer discuss the difficulties and propose remedies when investigating the conceptual demands in Nuffield O-level chemistry with the Piagetian stages of conceptual development as the anchor.

*The relationship of teaching competence to teacher performance and children's learning of classification skills ** ****
E. Jagoda and H. Robison, 1975

AIM / The national trend toward competency based teacher education (CBTE) in the United States is spreading rapidly despite the

*   Gratitude is extended to Dr M. Shayer of the University of London, Chelsea College for sending his work to be abstracted.

**   Written and prepared by the authors for inclusion in this volume. Gratitude is extended to Professors Eleanor Jagoda and Helen Robison of Bernard M. Baruch College, City University of New York.

***   This research was supported by a Faculty Research Grant, CUNY Research Foundation Grant No. 10081.

lack of an empirical base. CBTE refers to a behaviourist conception of teaching skills and evaluation of those skills in public, objective and criterion-referenced ways. For two semesters, Fall 1973 and Spring 1974 we were engaged in an attempt to establish some empirical basis for CBTE, which has been mandated by New York State to begin in 1975. Our efforts have included two field studies which, although they overlap, will be described separately.

SUBJECTS / The first study was a two x two factorial design which compared competency based vs. traditional approaches, and Skinnerian vs. Piagetian philosophies for the training of student teachers, to teach classification in early childhood grades, chiefly to children aged four to seven years. This gave rise to four treatment conditions, PM, PT, SM, and ST, which were evaluated for effectiveness with regard to: 1) student teacher performance; 2) advancement of children's classification skills. (PM = Piaget Modular; PT = Piaget Traditional; SM = Skinner Modular; ST = Skinner Traditional). The 'Modular' term refers to a packaged unit of instruction, usually with behavioural objectives, learning activities and assessment procedures, with considerable student independence in pace of learning and in choice of learning activities. Modules are very popular in CBTE programs.

METHODS / Seventeen student teachers participated in the study. Their videotaped performance was evaluated by the two principal researchers with regard to: 1) use of behavioural objectives; 2) use of materials; and 3) appropriate implementation.

RESULTS / Only with regard to use of behavioral objectives and appropriate implementation were the differences marginally significant in favor of the modular groups. Children in 17 early childhood classes were pre- and post-tested on the Sigel Classification test. Although there was a paradoxical decline in Sigel score from the pre- to post-test overall, this decline was significantly less for children taught by the traditionally trained student teachers. The overall decline was thought to be attributable to boredom on the part of the children, and to the haste with which the student teachers completed the post-tests. The superior performance of student teachers in the modular conditions, however, was not reflected in the classification skills of the children they worked with. Finally, student teachers were tested on the Minnesota Teacher Attitude Inventory. Although our students scored at very conservative levels, performance on the videotaped teaching sample was highly correlated with scores on the MTAI, more liberal students being evaluated more favorably.

Replication study

In our second study, the design of the first was replicated, with several improvements in implementation. Eight of the 13 student teachers were second-semester students, who had participated in the previously described study. They were assigned to treatment conditions such that they experienced different training from their previous semester training: M were shifted to T conditions; P were shifted to S conditions; and vice versa. The remaining five student teachers were assigned so as to roughly equalize the groups.

METHODS / With the exceptions that the placement of the student teachers shifted to a different school district, and children's testing was carried out by the two principal researchers, using the Raven Progressive Matrices Test (PMT), all other factors of the study remained unchanged.

RESULTS / Regarding differential effects of training condition on children's classification learning, no significant differences were noted. Regarding student teacher performance on the videotape samples, no differences could be associated with different training techniques, M vs. T, P vs. S, with the exception that the Skinner Modular student teachers were superior in their use of materials.

As in the previous study, student teachers who scored high on the MTAI were evaluated more favourably on the videotapes, but no relationship was found with children's learning or with satisfaction by the student teachers with their training. Among those student teachers who were in the study for two semesters, those who were rated high on videotape evaluation in the first semester retained high ratings the second semester, although the training condition changed. This raises the question of whether qualities of the student teacher carry more weight than training techniques.

A further analysis was carried out, making explicit the difficulties encountered in carrying out this type of research in the field. In summary, we are as yet unable to determine any advantage for children, in training teachers according to the CBTE format.

Readings in science education: a source book
E. Jenkins and R. Whitfield (Eds.), 1974

The editors, after an outline of Piaget's stages of cognitive development, maintain, 'It is now possible to see how Piaget's work could be used to assess a projected course. First, the stages of the course ought to follow the same order of increasing logical complexity as are present in the pupil's own development. Secondly, the age-range over which the course is taught should match the age-range over which these stages develop (even as one recognizes that the course may be a partial means for the pupil's development)', p. 43. The editors then discuss relating cognitive development to science courses and cite the findings of Mealings (1963) and Shayer (1970, 1972). Shayer by means of examples demonstrates that the Nuffield Chemistry O-Level Sample Scheme comprises much conceptual material which is taught too early for the majority of pupils for whom the course was designed. The 'copper problem' (topics A2 and A3) is taught in schools usually at the age of 11 to 13 and ' . . . requires the use of formal operations twice. If done heuristically . . . it involves making alternative hypotheses. And the formulation of a theory of chemical combination in which the weight of elements is preserved, as a compound is formed, while all their other properties disappear, is itself symbolic and not concrete. So we have a piece of work in the course which demands formal operations at a time when the pupils can only operate concretely . . . Inevitably, pupils must take a lot "on faith" for the first couple of years until they can think symbolically', *(ibid.,* p. 184). After arguing with topic 11 on g-atoms and topic 13 on the Periodic Table, Shayer maintains, 'I think that the gradient of increasing logical complexity steepens too abruptly at this point', *(ibid.,* p. 184). After presenting detailed analyses of Piaget's concrete and formal operations stages, Jenkins and Whitfield (1974) assert, 'If one teaches science in a highly selective school, and rarely below the third year at that, one will rarely meet any pupils below the 3A stage of formal operations: if one teaches science to average classes in a comprehensive school, and rarely above the fourth year, one is unlikely to have met any pupils whose thinking goes beyond the concrete operations stage. If you try to make someone participate in a process which is taking place at a more complex level than that to which they have access, communication breaks down. Your words may be simple, but the relationships they point to are not', p. 45. The editors then cite the findings of Shayer (1972). The latter author, after a detailed analysis of the Nuffield O-Level Physics course, goes on to comment on the conceptual demands in the light of Piaget's stages of cognitive development. 'It is clear both from the spirit and the detail of the Nuffield Physics course . . . that the fact of conceptual development in children was both known and allowed for in a more conscious way than in the planning of the chemistry or biology courses. Not only is there a smoothly progressing standard of complexity visible from the first year to about half way through the fourth, but the principle is consistently observed throughout that any abstract or symbolizing work is introduced via the experimental situation to which it refers, and by which the situation is interpreted or correlated with other experience. This . . . style . . . can be seen as one that allows the maximum of integration, for the pupil, of experience gained concretely with the formal or abstract language developed to handle deeper relationships, whereas much traditional physics teaching could more properly be classified under the pathology of thinking — the handling of formal relationships as symbolic games hardly related to experience at all', *(ibid.,* pp. 31—32). The article is concluded by citing an extract taken from Mealing's (1963) research which Shayer refers to — an example of relevant educational research in which it is possible for science teachers to collaborate.

*Piaget and synectics**
J. Jimenez, 1976

The most solid theory we have of the development of learning skills from childhood to adulthood seems paradoxically to be also the least usable. It is the 'genetic epistemology' of Jean Piaget. Even when the theory is taken as a guide to practice, as it increasingly seems to be among teachers, it tends to have an unexpected regressive effect. Taking in too simplistic a sense Piaget's insistence on the impossibility of skipping developmental stages or of rushing growth, some teachers understand him to mean that stimulation and challenge are like an excess of Vitamin C, to no avail at all. And so, Piaget, whose essential achievement has been to recognize that immature intelligence nevertheless is *intelligence,* that the child in his own fashion truly *thinks,* can be and is being subverted to justify the understimulation and the underexercise of the young mind. If he successfully has worked against artificial speed in education, he has less successfully worked against artificial delays. I say 'he', but I mean of course those who use and abuse him.

By one of the more remarkable coincidences in the world of education, a highly practical approach to teaching and learning has been developed which coincides almost perfectly with Piaget's developmental theory and which may well be among the best ways to deal with both of the difficulties we have mentioned, namely, making the theory operational, and using the operationalized theory to stimulate rather than to retard or to leave to chance the development of intelligence. This highly practical and positive way of making Piaget's theories an effective part of education is called Synectics. So far as I am aware its inventor, William J.J. Gordon, was not trying consciously to put

* Published with the kind permission of the author. Gratitude is expressed to Dr Jacques Jimenez of Middlebury College, Vermont.

Piaget's theory into practice when he was developing his own approach. Still, Gordon's work may be the best way to make Piaget a practical and positive force in the classroom. For the two men have addressed themselves in complementary ways to the same central questions about the learning process: What is it? And how do we cooperate with it?

We will first examine the ideas of Piaget and Gordon on the mechanisms at work in both the developing mind of the child and the developed mind of the adult.

We will then briefly test the validity and usefulness of these ideas in a discussion of what seem to be the two dominant modes of thought in our culture. The first might broadly be called Platonic, in that it argues from some pre-existing form or mental structure to empirical reality. It tends to recognize as real whatever is a direct example or a transform of the pre-existing idea. Whatever does not conform to the idea is either criticized as false, or is simply ignored. Martin Luther, for example, thought largely in this fashion. The second mode of thought might broadly be called Aristotelian in that it argues from empirical reality toward form or structure. Meanings are more variable here, being always in the process of becoming. They are held to for as long as they are useful, or pleasing, or promising of further insight; after that they are put aside as being neither true nor false in themselves, only no longer fertile. Leonardo da Vinci, for example, thought largely in this style. The two modes of thought have been in our culture from at least the age of Pericles. For purposes of our inquiry we will use as examples of them Luther and Leonardo, who lived at the dawning of the modern mind – who *were*, if anybody was, that dawning.

Finally, we will indicate, by actual classroom examples, the kind of practical contribution to teaching and learning we can expect from the sustained use of Piaget's and Gordon's systems. For such thinking is not limited to geniuses, it belongs in varying degrees to all.

Piaget and Gordon:
Genetic epistemology and synectics

Underlying all of Piaget's grids and complicated syntax is a very simple model of what experience is. The model is starkly biological. Piaget sees experience as the interaction of an organism and its environment. But 'interaction' is less simple than it sounds. It can go two ways:

organism——————	modifies——————	environment
environment————	modifies——————	organism

In the first, the organism alters its surroundings to suit itself; in the second the organism is altered (or alters itself) to suit its surroundings.

In the first, external reality is changed so that the organism may remain the same. In the second, the organism is changed so that external reality may remain the same. Piaget calls the first kind of interaction 'assimilation' because in this process reality is assimilated to the organism's point of view or way of operating. The second he calls 'accommodation' because the organism accommodates its point of view or way of operating to some new reality.

The whole extraordinary collection of Piaget's research is little else than an investigation of how these two modes of interaction develop from infancy to adulthood. According to Piaget, at the earliest (sensorimotor) phase they occur only in nerves and muscles; then in the phase of 'egocentric representative activity' they occur in images and in symbols built up from the materials or schemas of the first phase, and so on until one achieves conceptual and logical thought.

Gordon's terms do not imply the biological framework of Piaget's, nor the same concern for exhaustive theoretical discourse. Instead, they reflect Gordon's experience as an inventor and professional consultant, a man who is paid to get results. He says, the mind has two basic jobs to perform. One is to 'Make the Strange Familiar', that is, to incorporate new facts, events, experiences, etc., into the frameworks already established by previously appropriated facts, events, experiences, etc. We learn the new by connecting it to, or realizing it through, the old. The other process of intelligence is the opposite. It is to 'Make the Familiar Strange', that is, to free something already known from the stereotypes we have put onto it, or what is the same thing, to alter one's angle of vision to meet new realities. This is the essential thing needed for creative insight.

Piaget's and Gordon's schemes are fundamentally identical

But there are deeper convergences between the two systems. Piaget has determined that the process of pure assimilation for a child is what we call 'play'. That is, in play a child is not gathering in anything really new about the world around him, he is merely testing and celebrating the already achieved systems of behaviour he had available within him. Nothing fundamentally new is learned in play; 'it is only a happy display of known actions,' (Piaget, 1962, p. 93). At most, an increasingly large range of external people, things, and events are assimilated into the pre-existing patterns of thought and behaviour. In play, the child uses the world as an extension of himself, and celebrates himself as the paradigm of the world. 'Symbolic play is merely egocentric thought in its pure state,' (*ibid.*, p. 166).

Accommodation or 'imitation' in the child is the opposite process. Here, the child adapts himself to what he sees, and tries to understand it by imitating it, getting the feel of it from inside. Piaget gives a charming example of this process in a child of one year and four months:

> L. tried to get a watch chain out of a match-box when the box was not more than an eighth of an inch open. She gazed at the box with great attention, then opened and closed her mouth several times in succession, at first only slightly and then wider and wider. It was clear that the child, in her effort to picture to herself the means of enlarging the opening, was using as 'signifier' her own mouth, with the movements of which she was familiar tactually and kinesthetically as well as by analogy with the visual image of the mouths of others *(ibid., p. 65).*

Children's play is a form of 'Making the Strange Familiar,' or of simply keeping everything as familiar as possible. Children's imitation is a form of 'Making the Familiar Strange,' of exploring the unknown.

There is one more thing to say about Piaget's analysis before we are ready to see the extraordinary relevance here of the psychological mechanisms defined by Synectics. Piaget is not satisfied to state *that* such and such processes occur. He wants also to explain *how* they occur. Throughout the course of development in both play and imitation Piaget sees the same simple process at work:

> The mistakes the child makes in his interpretations reveal the inner mechanism of his imitative technique and provide clear confirmation of the findings we gave earlier. The most typical example is that of the eyes. In response to my movement of opening and closing my eyes, J. at o; 11 (14) opened and closed her mouth (obs. 25), L. at o; 11 (5) opened and closed her hands, then her mouth (obs. 29), and T. at o; 9 (30) did likewise with his hands and mouth (obs. 31). In our view, mistakes such as these are extremely illuminating. It certainly cannot be a question of considering the visual perception of the movements of someone else's eyes as a signal which sets in motion the child's schemas of the hand or mouth, for no bond of contiguity in space or time has caused him to make a connection between them. The child's mistake is due to confusion, it is true, but it is intelligent confusion: the model is assimilated to an analogous schema susceptible of translating the visual into the kinesthetic, *(ibid., p. 44).*

What Piaget has done in this passage is to give a description of metaphor at work. In assimilation/play the work of metaphor is to reduce the world to the child — to 'Make the Strange Familiar.' In accommodation/imitation the work of metaphor is to expand the child to the world — to 'Make the Familiar Strange.' It is precisely Gordon's discovery that metaphor is the simple device by which the human mind, both child and adult, accomplishes its twin prodigies. The difference between child and adult is not that the child thinks by metaphor and the adult without it, but that the child does not know he is thinking metaphorically while the adult does know, and the child cannot completely control or balance the metaphor while the adult can. Piaget's circular system of assimilation and accommodation is therefore explicitly: a description of the workings of metaphor.

The difference between the two men on this point in only one of degree of explicitness. Gordon distinguishes three kinds of metaphor which, depending on how they are used, can either assimilate reality to the personality (MSF) or accommodate the personality to reality (MFS). The most basic form of metaphor he calls Direct Analogy:

> DIRECT ANALOGY is a simple comparison of two objects or concepts: 'A *crab* walks sideways like a sneaky burglar' ... the subject of the analogy is the first part of the comparison — 'a crab.' The analogue of the analogy is the thing to which the subject is compared — 'a burglar,' (Gordon, 1971, p. 18).

According to Gordon the function of Direct Analogy as the basic kind of metaphor is to enable the mind to think in comparisons and contrasts, that is, to think both synthetically and analytically in the same act. Direct Analogy compresses many functions into a single complex act, and it does that in such a way as to enable the mind to control all parts of the process. Piaget has detected this kind of activity in one kind of children's game which he defines as 'simple identification of one object with another.' (Piaget, 1962, p. 123). He gives an example of it:

> At 3; 4 (0), talking to a safety-pin: *'She's going into her house: she's a grandmother.'* But already at this stage the symbols, apart from a few residual exceptions, tended more and more to be used in varied combinations. For instance, at 3; 11 (24): *'I've seen a dead frog. —* Where? — *Here you can see its eyes and its mouth. Look, there's a big hole in its back.* — No, I can't see anything. *I was only joking: it's a basket,'* (*ibid.*, p. 124).

Shakespeare, in comparing the morning to a forehead and the evening to a buttock did exactly the same thing as that child: 'I am one more familiar with the buttock of the night than with the forehead of the morning.'

A second kind of metaphor Gordon calls Personal Analogy:

PERSONAL ANALOGY is a description of how it feels to identify with a person, a concept, a plant or animal, or a non-living thing, (Gordon, *op. cit.*, p. 21).

The new element in this kind of analogy is that 'I' am one of the terms of comparison. My feelings, movements, etc., are the analogue to which something else is being compared, or vice versa. The more profound my identification with the other, the more genuine the Personal Analogy is. According to Gordon, the purposes of making oneself one of the terms of the comparison are twofold: either (1) to generate terms for defining *oneself* through the exploration of the activities of some external but analogous being; or (2) to generate terms for defining some *external being* through an exploration of one's own analogous activities and feelings.

Piaget has discerned Personal Analogy in the games of children in which there is 'identification of the child's body with that of other people or with things,' (Piaget *op. cit.*, p. 124). He gives an example of it:

> Again at 4; 3, L., standing at my side, quite still, imitated the sound of bells. I asked her to stop, but she went on. I then put my hand over her mouth. She pushed me away angrily, but still keeping very straight and said: *'Don't. I'm a church'* (the belfry), (*ibid.*, p. 125).

King Lear, seeing in the storm the condition of his own mind and in his mind a version of the storm, did the same thing.

Gordon has also distinguished a third kind of metaphor, which he calls Compressed Conflict. Classically this was known as paradox or oxymoron. It is a highly conceptual and explicit statement of the paradox latent in the other forms of analogy, and operates in the way Piaget says concepts do, as an abstract summary of more concrete images or behaviours. Gordon defines it as:

> a poetic, two-word description on a high level of generality where the two words don't seem to fit and sometimes actually contradict each other, (Gordon, *op. cit.*, p. 26).

It is, then, a summary of the opposing principles which, in the manner of Hegel, make a thing work. For example, a spinning top can be viewed either as a straight line (the axis) or as a circle (the revolution around the axis). Plato, somewhere in *The Republic*, insists that these two perceptions about a top are separately true but mutually exclusive, hence that they should be stated in two separate propositions. But Gordon would join them in one proposition as mutually true. One would not be thought of without the other. A top, then, could well be defined as a 'straight curve' or a 'static spin.' This is precisely the sort of thing Piaget calls the dynamic equilibrium of opposing mental processes. Assimilation and accommodation taken together are a compressed conflict. Piaget considers that compressed conflict to be the main characteristic of adapted intelligence; Gordon considers it to be the main characteristic of *all* systems, whether physical or mental.

And so, putting Piaget and Synectics together, we may well have a three-word definition of intelligence: the complementary processes of assimilation and accommodation, both accomplished by means of metaphor. Piaget has spent his time defining with ever greater precision what is meant by the first two terms; Gordon and his colleagues at Synectics Education Systems, have spent theirs defining with ever greater pragmatism what is meant by the third.

It would seem that in Gordon's explicit, teachable treatment of metaphor we may have the key to bringing the richness of Piaget's developmental theory into the classroom.

Two styles of thought

If Piaget is right, mature human intelligence consists of a dynamic equilibrium between assimilation and accommodation. It has, in other words, two basic styles. They may work now and again for each other, against each other, or simply apart from each other. Now one may be stressed, now the other, now their combination. But all their combinations and transformations still are reducible to the two basic styles which assume each other and finally balance each other. If this is so, we should be able to see them at work in the various people who have shaped our culture. And indeed that is the case. There are two basic types of thinkers: those whose primary style is assimilation, and those whose primary style is accommodation. It turns out that both kinds of thinkers work by metaphors.

Martin Luther can stand for the first and Leonardo da Vinci for the second.

1. *The assimilators: Luther and company*

In pure assimilation, no new experience, fact, feeling, problem, or behaviour is allowed unless it fits rather neatly into an older and even primordial experience, fact, feeling, problem or behaviour. People whose style it is to think mainly in terms of such master patterns — Jung called the most commanding of these patterns archetypes — spend a great deal of their energy finding more and more subtle repetitions or transformations of those patterns in the world. Luther was one such thinker.

Erik Erikson says of him:

At its height, Luther's rebellion centered in the question of man's differential debt of obedience to God, to the Pope, and to Caesar — or rather, to the multitude of Caesars then emerging. At the beginning of his career another and, as it were, preparatory dichotomy preoccupied him: that between the obedience owed to his natural father, whose views were always brutally clear, and the obedience owed to the Father in heaven, from whom young Luther had received a dramatic but equivocal call. The earlier dichotomy actually followed Luther far into the manhood of his theological struggles, (1972, p. 49).

An awful moment for Luther came during his first Mass, when he balked at the first words of the Canon: 'You, therefore, most merciful Father . . . ' Addressing the heavenly Father before him as 'merciful' in the presence of his earthly father behind him, Martin, now himself invested with the mystical fatherhood of priestly ordination, found himself at the center of the great, indeed the central problem of his life. As time went on Luther made headway toward solving the problem, but not before he had enlarged and deepened it to include the Holy Father the Pope and the secular father the Prince. He even had to wrestle with it increasingly in himself. For he himself became one version of the problem when, as a figure of enormous authority, he took his harsh paternal stand against the peasants and also when, as a physical father, he faced his firstborn son — whom, amazingly enough, he named Hans, after his own father. All the huge questions of Luther's theology for which he is so justly famous — sin, guilt, faith, grace, conscience, salvation — were questions developed ultimately out of the hurt confusion of a boy who was trying to make sense of the man — and by expansion the cosmos — that had begotten him.

Clearly for Luther a larger and larger universe of concerns was assimilated into the primordial pattern which itself never fundamentally changed. Luther proceeded outward from the primordial pattern by a series of metaphorical extensions of the original problem, reliving and reconsidering in different circumstances the same model. Piaget explains the process:

> In a word, all those with whom the child lives give rise to a kind of 'affective schema,' summary or blending of the various feelings aroused by them, and it is these schemas which determine the main secondary symbols, as they often determine later on certain attractions or antipathies for which it is difficult to find an explanation except in unconscious assimilation with earlier modes of behaviour, (Piaget, *op. cit.*, p. 176).

The mechanism of this kind of thought is clearly metaphor. In the terms used by Synectics, we can see all three kinds of metaphor at work in it. First there is the ever broadening Direct Analogy between Luther's original and private family experiences and his subsequent political and religious involvement. There is, in this widening Direct Analogy, also an expanding Personal Analogy, that is, an expanding empathy, as Luther identifies *himself* over and over again with the problem element in each situation, now on the son's side of his basic metaphor, and now on the father's side. He constantly projects *himself* into the pattern and thereby achieves an emotional, participatory understanding before he has achieved a logical, conceptual one. And finally, at every stage there is the third kind of metaphor identified by Synectics, Compressed Conflict. Paradox is everywhere: fathers as givers and stranglers of life, sons as joyfully dependent or dreadfully brutalized, fathers as benign and capricious providers, sons as the sustained and the betrayed. By ever-widening Direct and Personal Analogies Luther assimilates more and more of reality into this central Compressed Conflict, which it is his vocation somehow to resolve.

The dominance of a single metaphor, to which an increasingly wide range of experience is assimilated, is a frequent thing among highly creative men. The pattern is there in Carl Jung, Dag Hammerskjöld; it is there, too, even in the watchworks physics of Isaac Newton and of the 18th and early 19th Centuries generally. Indeed, it is there in any instance of what Thomas Kuhn calls 'normal science,' whose foundation is to assume the universal validity of the established paradigm, and whose task is to find ever widening application of it.

On the negative side, this style of thinking tends to be reductive of reality rather than respectful of its variety. Its depth is equalled only by its narrowness, and its intensity of personal involvement easily leads to fixation and obsession. As a consequence, for example, Luther's became a reform rearward; it was oblivious of the emerging science of his day which was pointing the future, and lost itself in an attempted return to 'original,' pre-ecclesiastical Christianity. The metaphor blocked out for him a great deal that was happening in his world. In its extreme form, this kind of thinking finds itself incapable of breaking out of its own metaphors. All Direct Analogies from the outer world to the inner personal one are made, not for the sake of finding something new *in the world,* but for the sake of confirming — even of celebrating — something old *in the self.* In its extreme form, it comes terribly close to what Freud meant by neurosis.

The examples given above of this kind of thinking are all, despite their rather grandiose dimensions, essentially examples of what Piaget calls assimilation, and of what Gordon calls Making the Strange Familiar, or simply learning. They have more in common with perfectly ordinary modes of learning than might appear to be the case at first sight. They are, in fact, only extreme instances of what happens in any learning experience, the essence of which is the assimiliation of new experiences by analogies to more established patterns of knowing and feeling.

II. *The accommodators: Leonardo and company*

In accommodation, old experiences, facts, feelings, problems, and behaviours are interesting to the extent that they prepare for new ones. The thrust is towards the startling, with the commonplace supplying some initial framework in which to begin to conceive it. People whose style is to think mainly through such unsettling associations spend much of their energy in what Einstein called 'combinatory play,' (Hadamark, 1949, p. 142). Leonardo da Vinci was such a thinker.

Even in his less magnificent moments — when, for instance, he was merely constructing or quoting riddles — Leonardo's taste for taking the familiar as something to be made strange is evident.

Men will take pleasure in seeing their own works worn out and destroyed. (Of Shoemakers)

Oxen shall by their horns protect the fire from death. (Lanterns)

Those which have done best will be most beaten, and their children will be carried off and stripped or despoiled, and their bones broken and crushed. (Of nut trees which are beaten)

Innumerable lives will be extinguished, and innumerable vacant spaces created upon the earth. (Of the mowing down of grass)

Flying creatures will support men with their feathers. (Of feathers in beds)

A great part of the sea will fly towards the sky, and for a long time it will not return, (Clouds), (McCurdy, 1923, pp. 270–85).

In each case the riddle is created — the Familiar Made Strange, the mind accommodated to new views of reality — by the introduction of a startling metaphor. The disquieting masochism in the first riddle, the attribution of intentionality to oxen in the second, the terms borrowed from slavery in the third, etc., are all instances of Leonardo's intrinscially metaphorical style by which he tried to tease his world into yielding something other than the conventional wisdom.

Leonardo used precisely the same process in his more substantial enterprises. He argued constantly as though the known were a metaphor to help us to leap to the unknown. Not surprisingly, he made some splendid mistakes by trusting too much to the prophetic power of his metaphors: 'Dissect the bat, study it carefully, and on this model construct the (flying) machine,' (*ibid.*, p. 152). It didn't work, but Leonardo insisted that, despite a most significant discrepancy that he was himself aware of, the analogy *would* work, so confident was he of the validity of the approach.

> You will perhaps say that the sinews and muscles of a bird are incomparably more powerful than those of a man . . . But the reply to this is that such great strength gives it a reserve of power beyond what it ordinarily uses . . . Man is also possessed of a greater amount of strength in his legs than is required by his weight, (*ibid.*, p. 154).

The same mistaken trust in a metaphor happened when he thought he saw in the ebb and flow of the ocean the image of the blood's circulation. Leonardo's mistakes — like the children's mistake cited by Piaget above — reveal with particular clarity the mechanism at work in his thought: look to Direct Analogy for insight, i.e., for accommodation to new realities.

Trying to understand what happens to the body in old age, Leonardo dissected an old man's corpse and discovered the 'thickening of the skin of the veins,' (*ibid.*, p. 79). He concluded, rightly, that this thickening of the veins diminished the amount of nourishment available to the skin, which therefore toughened and wrinkled. He went on to say, 'and this network of veins acts in man as in oranges, in which the peel becomes thicker and the pulp diminishes the more they become old,' (*ibid.*). It is important here to note that the orange skin is not a metaphor used to explain what is happening to the old man, but quite the opposite. The old man's veins, circulatory ststem, and skin, which Leonardo understood already, helped him to understand the fate of the oranges. It is a splendid example of thought proceeding by accommodation.

Leonardo, like any balanced thinker, was as adept at assimilation as at accommodation. Probably no man of his day understood as well as he the flight of birds. That is because no one had so completely assimilated the poorly understood mechanics of air and wings to the well understood play of water and oars: 'All the movements of the wind resemble those of the water,' he said, and he realized that a bird turns around in mid-flight 'by taking a stroke with the wing in the direction of the tail, like a man rowing in a boat with two oars, who takes many strokes on that side from which he wishes to escape, and keeps the other oar fixed,' (*ibid.*, p. 141).

As we have already seen, Leonardo tried to accommodate this brilliantly simple assimilation to the invention of artificial, mechanical flights. Its failure in this instance does not diminish the power of his essentially correct accommodating method. For example, in one astonishing — and correct — statement, Leonardo jumped from his painter's intimate knowledge of the behaviour of black and white paints to something of worldwide, even of astronomical, importance: 'The atmosphere is blue because of the darkness which is above it, for black and white together make blue,' (*ibid.*, p. 227). No one actually *saw* what Leonardo said would be there until the first man went from the white through the blue and into the black in the 1960s.

Leonardo was nowhere more explicit than in the following passage about how we can find in the commonplace the sufficient source of all the new ideas we need, if only we know how to use it metaphorically:

I will not refrain from setting among these precepts a new device for consideration which, although it may appear trivial and almost ludicrous, is nevertheless of great utility in arousing the mind to various inventions. And this is that if you look at any walls spotted with various stains or with a mixture of different kinds of stones, if you are about to invent some scene you will be able to see in it a resemblance to various different landscapes adorned with mountains, rivers, rocks, trees, plains, wide valleys, and various groups of hills. You will also be able to see divers combats and figures in quick movement, and strange expressions of faces, and outlandish costumes, and an infinite number of things which you can then reduce into separate and well conceived forms. With such walls and blends of different stones it comes about as it does with the sound of bells, in whose clanging you may discover every name and word that you can imagine, (*ibid.*, p. 172).

It is easy to see everywhere in Leonardo's work the presence of Direct Analogy — as, for example, when he draws in the margin of his notebooks a heart with the artery and vein systems spreading up and down from it; right next to it he draws a seed with root and branch system growing out of it. But Paul Valéry in his groundbreaking essay on Leonardo decades ago saw more than Direct Analogy at work. He saw also Leonardo's extraordinary ability to project himself into the forms he was thinking about — to project himself, as it were, into the spots on the wall. Commenting on what we here are calling Leonardo's instinct for Personal Analogy, Valéry wrote:

Nothing seems more deliberately absurd when described than the temerity of a person who declared he *is* a certain object and feels its impressions — especially if the object is inanimate. Yet there is nothing more powerful in the imaginative life. The chosen object becomes as it were the center of that life, a center of ever multiplying associations, depending on whether the object is more or less complicated. Essentially this faculty must be a means of exciting the imaginative vitality, of setting potential energy to work, (Valéry 1971, p. 26).

Here Personal Analogy is used for the sake of accommodation, that is, one's own feelings are used as a basis upon which to go out to something in the world until now not understood. The list of those who have worked with both Direct and Personal Analogy in the manner of Leonardo is long and illustrious, including such men as Kepler, Matisse, Einstein, Robert Frost, and Alexander Graham Bell. These men not only worked this way, they knew that they worked this way. Their style was accommodation, their technique the metaphors of controlled fantasy.

On the negative side, this style of thinking can easily lack a stable center, a principle of coherence. Indeed, Leonardo himself, though unquestionably a genius, was a very scattered genius. His treatise on painting is no treatise at all; it is a disorganized series of inspired but almost random jottings. His famous notebooks are filled with glorious doodles that in no fashion amount to a coherent image of the world. This most famous painter of them all has been destroyed several times by nature and by war, but above all by a fatal flaw within the painting itself; the experimental paints Leonardo used simply disintegrated. Accommodation unbalanced by assimilation is its own form of mental disarray.

In any case, accommodation, like assimilation, works by metaphor. The application is different, but the mechanism the same. Leonardo and the others actively and deliberately played with Direct Analogy to see what new combinations they could come up with, and equally actively threw themselves by Personal Analogy into the new metaphors they envisioned, in a search after the dynamic element within those metaphors — the Compressed Conflict implied within them — that give the metaphors their energy and interest. If Piaget has told us what accommodation is about and has sometimes explicitly and always implicitly identified analogy as its main tool, Synectics has explictly told us what that analogy is about, and how to use it, and — no small thing — how to teach it.

We turn now to the subject of teaching it and of teaching by it. The Luthers and Leonardos did their main thinking by metaphors, and so do the rest of us everyday — less grandly, but no less consistently.

Piaget, Synectics, and the schools

Essentially the use of Synectics as a way of implementing Piaget in the classroom comes down to the use of metaphor – here identified as Direct Analogy, Personal Analogy and Compressed Conflict – in the service either of assimiliation (MSF) or of accommodation (MFS). For present purposes, what this means can better be expressed through anecdote than through abstract statements. I will offer six brief anecdotes as examples of teaching and learning which, by the deliberate exploitation of metaphorical thinking, put Piaget's model of intelligence to practical and positive work in educational settings.

(1) The members of a second grade class were given a bean, a kernel of corn, and a pea to plant in a dish of dirt on their desks. They were to water and watch, that is all. The teacher did not feel the children could do much more than that 'because, you see, of their developmental stage.' I spoke with one of the children and, to see how far toward insight she would go if guided by the help of metaphors, I asked her: 'Are the seeds alive?' 'I don't know,' she said. Moving her toward a Direct Analogy, I asked, 'Are you alive? And how do you know?' She answered that she moved, breathed, drank water, ate, felt the heat and saw the light of the sun, and so forth. 'Do the seeds do that?' She thought each one through, and concluded with triumph and a real delight for the seeds, 'They're alive!' So far this is an example of assimilation, or making the strange familiar, by means of a Direct Analogy. I decided to push for more. I told her that now we knew the seeds were like her in that they were alive; but in what ways might she be like them? I asked, 'Are *you* a seed somehow?' She stared at them – without doubt, though she said nothing out loud, she was putting herself in their place by Personal Analogy – and finally she said, 'I'm growing but I don't know what I'm going to grow up to be.' She grappled with an idea too big for her, became confused, and finally gave it up; but the seeds, for a moment, gave her a new viewpoint on herself. This is an example of accommodation, of making the familiar strange, in this case by means of a Personal Analogy. Utterly respectful of her developmental stage, the metaphorical approach to teaching and learning can activate whatever is there to activate, and also reveals better than preconceptions to where the real limits of real children are.

(2) Two five-year-old boys were playing with small toy trucks around the rim of a toilet bowl. The trucks had a mock accident and plunged into the water. Carried away with the dramatic possibilities, one boy flushed the toilet. When they both saw the trucks disappear the boys began screaming and howling. The adults tried to come to the rescue by telling the boys they could buy new trucks, but the boys continued to cry because they were not crying for the loss to themselves. One adult aware of the ubiquity of metaphor in children's

thinking, sensing that the boys were crying for the trucks themselves, asked 'do you think they're alive?' The boys said yes, the trucks were alive and it was a terrible thing they were feeling now, drowning in the dark. She explained very carefully that, although the trucks in some ways *seemed* alive, in fact they were not; and she asked the boys to give examples of the ways the trucks were not like, say, themselves. The boys did so, and were immediately consoled about the fate of the trucks. As the adult well knew, the boys were experiencing the perils of incomplete and immature metaphorical thought, what might be called runaway Personal Analogy. Having identified themselves with the trucks they could not dis-identify themselves; the analogy was all comparison and no contrast. It was all assimilation, without any reality control. It was what Piaget would call purely egocentric, nonadaptive assimilation in a state of disequilibrium. The adult familiar with the workings of Personal Analogy was able to help the boys break out of it — or give it the quality of 'reversibility,' as Piaget would say. These boys learned as much by rejecting an analogy as the little girl earlier on did by accepting one. In both cases real learning took place because an adult was there to help the children with their metaphor.

(3) A group of junior high school students were to study the era of Slavery and Emancipation. The teacher wanted to use analogy to help the students to insight, but rejected any specious and misleading analogy that might be based on their own experience with and reaction to authority figures. Such an analogy would assume that slavery was already directly familiar to them, where in fact it was very strange indeed. But that is not to say that *nothing* in their experience could serve to bring it home. Accordingly he asked for a Direct Analogy: 'What inanimate thing do you own that is your slave?' After many suggestions the class voted on one as the answer they liked best: yo-yos. He then asked them to put themselves in its place as he played with imaginary yo-yo. He asked what they felt about going up and down, up and down: what they felt toward the string, toward the hand, and so forth. The answers ranged from comfortable compliance on through to bitter rage, as the children got more and more in to the Personal Analogy. What began to come out were two sets of contradictory attitudes — a Compressed Conflict, in fact. The teacher went on. He said, 'I do a fancy trick with you, the string breaks, and you go flying into the bushes. What do you feel now?' Again, the answers to this Personal Analogy question ranged from delight at being rid of stupid tasks and confining strings to sudden feelings of impotence and worries for the future — again, a Compressed Conflict in the making. A student finally said, 'That's not yo-yos — that's slavery and emancipation.' The teacher then helped the class review what they had said and to put it into a formal, logical statement. They then went on to study the

history itself, to see whether it bore out their own Personal Analogies and Compressed Conflicts – in other words, they tested their hypotheses against the facts, ready to change them if and as necessary. First an assimilation, and then a willingness to accommodation, but it is highly doubtful they would have come so close to it if they had not been helped to think in metaphors.

(4) Another junior high school class was given an almost impossible problem: to describe the relative motions of the earth, the moon from four different perspectives, (a) as viewed from the earth, (b) as viewed from the moon, (c) as viewed from the surface of the sun, and (d) as viewed from a point *above* the sun looking down on the solar system. For a mature adult this is a formidable conceptual task. But the teacher was not out to confuse his students or convict them of ignorance. He told them they had all the information they needed in their own heads already. All they would have to do is to think back to a few of the rides they had all taken at the last country fair. He provided them with a Direct Analogy by which to help them make the strange familiar. We have no time here to explain just how the octopus, the spinning barrel, and the race track helped to solve the problem; suffice it to say they did. The important thing is that the students did their own thinking, and on a problem that could easily have been judged too sophisticated for their developmental stage and it would have been so indeed if they were not helped to think by metaphor.

(5) Tenth grade biology students came into a class to learn that 'tomorrow you will dissect an animal that is the shape of fear.' The teacher asked for situations of helpless fear that his students had experienced – and there were surprisingly many of them. He then asked what their bodies did, what shape they took, in those situations. The general pattern was to make oneself small, even spherical, to protect the soft parts by presenting the hard parts, and so on. He asked them for any animals they knew that had been shaped by fear. Pushing the Direct Analogy harder he asked for fear-formed human inventions, and then asked which of these animals went with which of the inventions. All of this amounted to a veritable inventory of the shape – or rather, the shapes – fear takes. The next day the students were given a clam, dissecting equipment, lab manuals, and a one-sentence task: 'Identify 10 fear-formed structures.' Instead of doing a code-book laboratory exercise they were trying to demonstrate the validity of their own ideas – again, an exercise that would have been beyond them were it not for the metaphor. The teacher threw in a final assignment after the labs were done, partly for the fun of it and partly to test for concept attainment: 'What building in your town is a clam?'

(6) And finally, a 12th grade class, this one in English, on the subject of Cyrano de Bergerac. The problem was not only to understand

analytically but to accept emotionally the implausible relationship of Cyrano and Christian in the wooing of Roxanne — Cyrano poetical but ugly, Christian beautiful but nonverbal. The teacher began by pointing out that Cyrano and Christian had a partnership and — grabbing a pair of scissors — said, '*This* is a partnership. How?' Among the ideas stimulated by the analogy were that one blade had what the other lacked, that neither could work apart from the other, that from one point of view each blade was the cutting edge and from another point of view each one was the necessary resistance to the cutting edge — a system, in other words, of opposing forces — in other words, each blade implied a Compressed Conflict. The two blades of the scissors taken together were therefore a double set of paradoxes. The problem in the play is the same thing, a double set of complementary paradoxes in the two characters. It works out so that one man experiences vicariously through the other what he himself lacks.

Once the idea of a complex and paradoxical relationship was cleared up, the concept of vicarious experience needed further reflection. The teacher took up the scissors again and a piece of paper and, asking 'What does this feel like?' cut the paper. Several students winced, proving how vivid Personal Analogy — or empathy, or vicarious experience — can be, as it had also been for the little boys and the flushed trucks. But the older student could go on to see also that vicarious experience, though it indeed is *felt* from another point of view is not felt. It is both real and fictitious, participatory and distanced, intense and safe — again, a Compressed Conflict. Without the aid of Direct Analogy and Personal Analogy, finally refined into Compressed Conflict, such abstractions as 'partnership' and 'vicarious experience' would have remained for these students what most academic abstractions remain for most students — words. The metaphor grounded the abstractions in imagination and experience without for an instant sacrificing conceptual clarity and generality. It is safe to say that we have in this example what we do not find in the others, namely, the use of metaphor in the mature — or nearly mature — mind. It is as pertinent here as for little girls reflecting on peas and beans.

What Luther and Leonardo did is not so different in kind from what these students, kindergarten through 12 did, however different in loftiness of purpose and skill of application. If the examples from geniuses of old and non-geniuses of the present do anything, they tend to confirm the assimilation/accommodation model of intelligence put forward by Piaget and the place of metaphor in those processes as identified by Synectics. Teachers, parents, and counsellors who know Piaget are better off than those who do not, but those who know the Synectics approach to metaphor as well are better off than those who know only Piaget. For they can not only analyze the mind at work, they can help it to work: they can not only respect its limits, they can help it to reach its limits; they can not only say that the growth of intelligence is natural, they can also apply the art and the artifice that will help nature grow.

The relationships of reading comprehension, conservation ability, auditory discrimination, and visual-motor development of third grade pupils. A.H. Kent, 1973

AIM / To investigate the differences and relationships of reading comprehension, conservation ability, auditory discrimination, and visual-motor development in children.

SUBJECTS / N = 96 third grade children in elementary schools. Twenty-four boys and 24 girls were in the high reading comprehension group; 24 girls and 24 boys were in the low reading comprehension group, as assessed on the comprehension subtest of the Gates-MacGinitie Reading Tests. In the low reading comprehension group, the Slosson Intelligence Test was used to eliminate intelligence as a factor in poor reading comprehension.

METHOD / Each child was seen individually on six Piagetian conservation tasks, the Wepman Auditory Discrimination Test, and the Bender Gestalt Test for Young Children.

RESULTS / Kent concludes, 'Subjects in the high reading comprehension group surpassed subjects in the low reading comprehension group in visual-motor development. High reading comprehension female subjects surpassed low reading comprehension female subjects in visual-motor development and conservation ability. Relationships between reading comprehension and visual-motor development were found with all subjects; with male subjects; with female subjects; and with reading comprehension and auditory discrimination with all subjects; with the high reading comprehension group; with high reading comprehension male subjects. Relationships were found between reading comprehension and conservation ability with all subjects, and with female subjects in both the high and low reading comprehension groups', p. 2924A.

*A test of a theory of development in Uganda: implications for intellectual growth of school children in less technologically developed Nations**
R. Kimball, 1972

Creative growth is the man-induced, systematic, creative form of change that produces improvements in existing structures or originates totally new ones. Creative growth is a methodology for producing outcomes that are productive, predictable and controllable.

This study asks the following question: If progress is to be maintained and problems solved by carrying out a program of creative growth, how is this program to be implemented? Any improvement in developmentally-relevant levels of progress within socio-cultural, economic-technical, political, psychological or constitutional institutions, is due not only to the resources at hand but in the opportunities for change that are available.

Resources include the human and the natural. Human resources are made of several dimensions including the psychological: affective and cognitive.

Schools are one of the most prominent institutions in any community for implementing development and progress. If a program that reinforces those features that produce creative growth could be implemented, improvements may be possible in the young that would greatly influence activities in their later life.

The Uganda Government has been developing new curricula, especially in science, which they hope will significantly contribute to creative growth. The influence of a new science curriculum on the intellectual and emotional growth of children forms the main content of the research of this study.

In what ways would a change in the curriculum in the primary schools lead to a change in development levels? Many authors (J. Piaget, P.C. Vernon, T. Husen, T.W. Schultz, D. Smith, A. Inkeles among others) have implied that rational thinking and planning, a creative approach to problem solving and an emotional control that allows for empathy, are necessary (but not necessarily sufficient) psychological conditions to maximizing the utilization of resources with flexible alternatives for creative growth.

The objectives of this study are as follows:

A. To describe variables and to propose hypotheses relating

* Published by the kind permission of the author. Gratitude is extended to Professor Richard Kimball of Educational Science Consultants and California State University.

educational experience to development outcomes.

B. To analyze the results of testing these hypotheses and to evaluate their relevance to the prediction of future trends.

C. To produce viable suggestions describing some methods through which primary schools can be improved to increase an individual's chance for raising his level in development-specific structures through creative growth, given the set of alternatives and resources at his command.

The variables being considered here as most influential in producing changes in development-relevant learning are as follows: educational experience (years of school, attendance-nonattendance), type of school (new science curriculum, old science curriculum), age, location of school (Buganda rural and urban, Bugisu rural and urban), outreach (trips to urban areas, exposure to media), socioeconomic status (SES).

The following dependent variables are measured: cognitive development (rationality, creativity), affective development (self-image, want fulfillment), school achievement and economic return.

Test questions which were used to measure the above variables were devised by the author in previous research in East Africa and Mexico and by other researchers in cross-cultural studies. These questions were modified in a pre-test of 144 students, pupils, adults and non-school children near Kampala, the capital of Uganda. Three research assistants, two from Buganda and one from Bugisu, were chosen from over 35 university applicants. They collected classroom, ethnographic and census information as well as the interview data used in testing the hypotheses.

The sample tested was all male. 1228 children and adults were interviewed in the four ecological settings. Twenty school children each from grades one, four, and six from new science curriculum and old science curriculum schools were selected. Twenty non-school boys with ages and socioeconomic backgrounds similar to those of the pupils were the comparison group. Adults from these role categories completed the sample in each setting: farmers, laborers, craftsmen, shopkeepers, officials, teachers.

These relationships among independent variables are proposed:

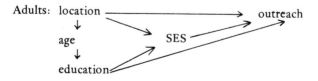

Outreach generally is dependent on a person's SES. The richer can afford radios, television and newspapers. They tend to live in the urban areas and have more education. Outreach is also a direct function of location. An individual who lives in an urban area is more likely to be influenced by 'modernizing' forces than one living in a rural area. Generally, the younger the adult the higher his education level.

Non-school children:

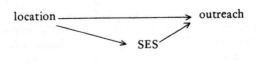

age

Location, SES and outreach are related similarly for non-school children as adults. Age is independent of location.

Pupils;

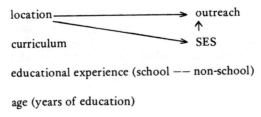

educational experience (school — — non-school)

age (years of education)

Note: Variables without arrows are fully independent. Variables at the beginning of a causal link can also be considered independent.

The following are the hypotheses and the results of their testing. *Related to children:*

1. Pupils in all schools teaching the new science curriculum will score significantly higher on measures of affective and cognitive development and school achievement.

Hypotheses one is confirmed. Results are significant at the .001 level.

2. Pupils in urban schools will score significantly higher than pupils in rural schools on measures of affective and cognitive development and school achievement.

Hypothesis two is confirmed. Results are significant at the .001 level.

3. Pupils from higher SES homes will score significantly higher on

measures of affective and cognitive development and school achievement.

When controlled for location, hypothesis three is not confirmed.

4. School children will score significantly higher than non-school children of the same age and background on measures of cognitive and affective development.

Hypothesis four is confirmed. The results are significant at the .001 level.

5. Children taking more trips to an urban area, using the radio, television and newspaper more will score significantly higher on measures of cognitive and affective development and school achievement than children not so oriented.

Hypothesis five is confirmed. The significance level falls from .001 to .01 when location and SES are controlled for.

6. The older the child (the higher the grade level) the significantly higher will be his score on measures of cognitive and affective development and school achievement.

Hypothesis six is confirmed. The results are significant at the .001 level.

7. The six variables (curriculum location, SES, outreach, education and age) will explain a significant portion of the variance in scores measuring cognitive and affective development and school achievement in children.

Regression analysis yields these results.

Per cent variation explained by each independent variable (school children)

		Independent Variable						
		curriculum	location	SES	outreach	education	age	TOTAL
	rationality	7.9	2.3	.1	.1	20.00	8.1	38.5
	creativity	1.3	7.0	1.1	.7	21.50	8.7	39.3
Dependent	self image	6.0	3.6	.2	.1	7.7	4.5	22.1
Variable	want fulfillment	2.0	.7	1.3	.3	16.4	1.5	22.2
	school achievement	.6	.3	.1	.1	20.0	5.8	26.9

Percent variation explained by each independent variable (non-school children)

		location	SES	outreach	age	TOTAL
	rationality	11.1	1.1	1.4	37.4	51.0
Dependent	creativity	8.7	.2	1.3	27.8	38.1
Variable	self image	16.6	1.0	3.5	11.0	32.1
	want fulfillment	7.1	2.6	4.0	2.7	16.4

Hypothesis seven is logically confirmed in that a significant proportion of the dependent variables (especially the cognitive variables) is explained by the independent variables.

Hypotheses related to adults:

1. Adults in urban areas will score significantly higher than adults in rural areas on measures of cognitive and affective development and economic return.

Hypothesis one is confirmed. Results are significant at the .001 level.

2. Adults coming from higher SES homes will score significantly higher on measures of cognitive and affective development and economic return.

Hypothesis two is confirmed. The significance value reduces from .001 to .01 when location is controlled for.

3. Adults living in or taking more trips to urban areas, using radio, television and newspapers more will score significantly higher on measures of cognitive and affective development and economic return than those not so oriented.

Hypothesis three is confirmed. The significance value reduces from .001 to .01 when location and SES are controlled for.

4. The more years of school completed by adults the significantly higher will be their scores on measures of cognitive and affective development and economic return.

Hypothesis four is confirmed at the .001 level of significance.

5. The older the adult the significantly higher the score on measures of cognitive and affective development and economic return.

Hypothesis five is not confirmed. The relationship is positive until age 35 and then becomes negative. Each effect cancels the other for the total sample.

6. The five variables (location, SES, outreach, education and age) will explain a significant portion of the variance in scores measuring cognitive and affective development and economic return in adults.

Per cent variance explained by each independent variable (adults)

		Independent Variables					
		loca-tion	SES	out-reach	edu-cation	age	TOTAL
Dependent Variable	rationality	0.9	1.0	.1	30.2	4.7	36.9
	creativity	3.0	1.6	.1	21.0	2.4	28.1
	self image	6.9	0.1	.1	10.0	0.1	17.2
	want fulfillment	1.3	0.1	.3	60.0	2.2	63.9
	economic return	0.1	0.5	5.0	38.0	1.2	44.8

Hypothesis six is logically confirmed. A significant portion of each dependent variable has been explained.

The results show that the new science curriculum in its first year of operation does contribute significantly to psychological development. It is speculated that since education is strongly associated with development-related learning outcomes (adult results), a new science education may contribute even more to these outcomes as these children become adults.

Further findings include a reduced inclination of the educated to want to live in the cities and to have large families. As education level increases there is the tendency to accumulate and manipulate those materials and human resources that are prerequisite to increasing development levels and subsequent progress.

Hopefully the new science curriculum will lead to changes in other curricula so that a more rational and creative approach can be used to solve the problems that are within man's control.

From observations in the classroom and an analysis of teaching strategies the new science curriculum classrooms exhibit a tendency toward more flexible approaches to teaching. This flexible approach includes use of materials for each individual to interact with, evaluation of results of experiments, teacher as colleague instead of authority, affective growth as well as cognitive, process over content, freedom of exploration, creativity as well as logical processes, teaching for an unknown future.

Further studies should shed light on whether or not these observations form significant influences in the education process. Is it the style of teaching or the scientific process or both? Can this approach be used in other subject areas? Will the results then be multiplied?

This research brings out the need for researchers and curriculum developers to be in Piaget's 'formal operations' stage of development so that future accomplishment may add even further significance to our understanding of change and growth.

*Development of concepts of infinity and limit in mathematics**
P.E. Langford, 1974

Experiment One

INTRODUCTION / Previous studies of the development of concepts of infinity in children have failed to distinguish potential infinity from completed infinity, although this has traditionally been an important distinction in mathematical philosophy (Boyer, 1939). Potential infinity is involved in such notions as that mathematical operations can

---

* Published by the kind permission of the author and the editor. Gratitude is extended to Dr Peter Langford of Birkbeck College, University of London and the Editor, Archive de Psychologie, Geneva. Ref: 1974, 42, 311–322.

be indefinitely iterated or that there can be no largest or smallest number. Completed infinity is involved in the concept of an infinite set or an infinite decimal. The concept of a limit can be considered from either point of view. If it is said that a function can be brought indefinitely near a limit point, this is a statement about potential infinity. If, on the other hand, we speak of the limit of an infinite sequence being reached, that is a statement about completed infinity. It seems likely that concepts of potential infinity develop before those of completed infinity as many adults have difficulty with completed infinity, but not with potential infinity.

Three studies of the development of concepts of mathematical infinity and limit have been reported. One of these, Smith (1959), suffers from the drawback that results are reported in terms of scores on a 'limits test' which involves many questions relating neither to infinity nor limits, most notably questions asking for the text term of a sequence. This makes interpretation of his data impossible.

The earliest study was that of Piaget and Inhelder (1956). Their task involved showing children a figure — either a square, triangle or line — and requesting them to draw repeated bisections of the figure. When the figure became too small for further bisection the child was asked about the possibility of continuing the process in his mind. Questions were asked about three aspects of this process. First, to see if the child appreciated the operation of bisection could be continued indefinitely. Then to see whether he thought the end product of the process would have a shape, or whether it would be a point. Finally, to see whether the child thought the original figure could be reconstituted from its 'constituent' points. It was found at 11 or 12 years of age children believed in the possibility of indefinite bisection of the figure, that the end result would be a point and that the original figure could be reconstituted from its 'constituent' points. If valid, these results would indicate that children develop concepts of potential infinity, in this case indefinite bisection, at the same time as they develop concepts of completed infinity, in this case the notion that the end product of the bisection would be a point. However, the children's notion that the original figure could be reconstituted from points provides immediate occasion to doubt this conclusion. This erroneous idea would indicate that the child had failed to appreciate that the nature of a point is to have no extension. This doubt about Piaget and Inhelder's conclusions will be returned to later.

Taback (1969) again used tasks involving indefinite iteration of operations applied to geometrical figures. His investigation was more broadly based in that it involved operations other than bisection, including operations that increased the size of the figure as well as those that diminished it. He concluded it was only at age 12 a majority of children were able to conceive of indefinite iteration or the limit point of a sequence. He points out that there was, however, a very marked discrepancy between results on his various tasks testing for the concept of a limit point. He suggests that in tasks involving representation of the limit point in the figure shown to the child, such as in a task involving bisection of a line, children do much worse than in tasks where the limit point is not represented, as where a series of figures are drawn one inside another. However, another aspect of Taback's results suggests an alternative explanation.

Taback notes that in two of his tasks many children of 10 and 12 years would assert that the limit point would be reached in a finite number of steps. One of these was the bisection of a line task. Taback rightly rejects this as evidence of a genuine limit concept of any sort. In fact, subjects who gave responses judged correct by Taback on these tasks would deny that the figure ever reached the limit point and would say the figure could get as near the limit point 'as you like'. This is interesting for two reasons. First, it suggests that on these tasks the children were responding in terms of potential infinity rather than completed infinity. Second, it suggests an alternative explanation for the apparent success of 11- and 12-year-olds on some of the tasks calling for an understanding of limits in the studies of Piaget and Inhelder (1956) and Taback (1969). For inspection of the criteria for success used in these tasks shows that 11- and 12-year-olds only succeed when the criterion for success is identification of the limit point and no check is made upon whether or not the child believes it is reached in a finite number of steps. It may be, therefore, that 12-year-olds have difficulty with even the concepts of indefinite approach to a limit and are far from having any notion of completed infinity. On those tasks where Taback tested for belief in an infinite process he found only a minority of 12-year-olds succeeded. This view is not without problems, as a small study conducted by Taback in relation to the apparent conflict between his own and Piaget and Inhelder's results suggests otherwise. This study of Taback's provided the starting point of Experiment 2 and will be discussed more fully in that connection.

Experiment 1 tested the hypothesis that 12-year-olds have little concept of completed infinity, but are developing a concept of potential infinity. This was done by testing their concept of indefinite iteration in relation to the four arithmetical operations applied to both space and number. Particular attention was paid to the form in which questions were asked and care taken to ensure that questions asked in relation to limit points being reached were also accompanied by questions to find out whether the child thought they would be reached in a finite or in an infinite number of steps.

METHOD AND PROCEDURE / The study was conducted by means of questionnaires. All questions were asked without reference to figures or diagrams. This seemed appropriate in view of Taback's (1969) finding that while children of eight years are hindered by lack of a figure in an indefinite iteration task, children of 10 and 12 are not. Interest here was in children from nine to 15 years of age.

An analysis of variance design was used in which subjects were assigned to seven matched groups on the basis of mental age as measured by Cattell's 'Test of "g": Culture Fair' test, scale 2, form B. The groups had mean mental ages corresponding to the ages nine to 15 inclusive. There were two between group factors, mental age and an instructional variable, and three within group factors, the type of question asked, the type of operation it was asked about and the domain, either spatial or numerical, to which the question related. The questions were assembled into two questionnaires, one for each instruction type. These were given as group tests.

The nature of these questionnaires can be most easily appreciated by reference to a nuclear question from which all others were derived:

'You take the number one and add one. That makes two. You add one again, that makes three. If you go on adding one again and again will you ever have to stop?'

The question given here is from the questionnaire with 'difficult' instructions. That is to say, the questionnaire was preceded by no particular instructions, other than one not to hurry. In the 'easy' instruction questionnaire the following passage was read out by the tester before the children began.

'These are questions about what you can imagine. You can do a lot of things in your mind. If one of your schoolmates is better than you at a game, you can still beat him in your mind, even though you can't really. When you answer these questions try to use your imagination.'

These instructions were modelled on those used by Piaget and Inhelder (1956) to assist children in adopting an abstract attitude towards the task. When these instructions were presented, all questions were phrased in the grammatical passive, to further reduce concrete connotations in the questions.

Within each questionnaire, questions varied as follows. To produce variation over operation types the question would be adapted to deal with subtraction, multiplication and division. In multiplication and division questions the operator was two rather than one. To produce the variation relating to type of question asked, the end of the question would be replaced by 'what is the biggest/smallest number/length you can reach?' Each description of an infinite process would be followed by the two types of ending in random order labelled (a) and (b). Questions asked about space would be phrased in terms of operations performed upon the position of a point B, initially one inch to the right of a point A.

SUBJECTS / N = 140 subjects were assembled into groups matched for mental age, as previously described. Chronological ages of subjects ranged from nine to 15 years. Subjects were selected from primary and comprehensive secondary schools in the Greater London and Hertfordshire areas of England. In the case of comprehensive schools where streaming took place selection was from the middle streams.

RESULTS AND DISCUSSION / Two kinds of analysis were performed on the results. The first was an analysis of variance on the total score for groups of ten subjects on each question type. In connection with this, age trends were examined. A second analysis was performed to isolate the tendency noted by Taback (1969) for children in early adolescence to believe the limit of an infinite sequence is reached in a finite number of steps.

(a) Analysis of variance and age trends

At each mental age level, ten subjects performed on each of the two questionnaires. The total score for these groups of ten subjects on each question was subjected to the appropriate analysis of variance. The following criteria were used in judging whether an answer was correct or not.

A correct answer on a question asking for the biggest or smallest term in a sequence was made to depend on the subject giving a correct answer to the corresponding question as to whether the sequence would ever stop. The removal of this restriction did not affect any of the significance levels in the analysis of variance. The most frequent correct answer to questions asking for the biggest or smallest term in a sequence was 'there isn't one' or some equivalent. 'Infinity' or 'one divided by infinity' were also scored as correct.

All five factors had a significant effect on the score for each group of ten subjects, $p < .01$ in each case, except the between group instruction variable. This produced an F ratio, $p = .10$. The only significant interaction was between operation type and domain of application. This was apparently caused by the breakdown of the general tendency for spatial operations to be easier than numerical operations in the case of subtraction, where the two domains were about equally difficult. It seems reasonable to suggest that in this case the tendency for numerical operations to be easier was counteracted by the particular difficulty of negative numbers.

Subjects were assisted by instructions to use imagination and the phrasing of questions in the grammatical passive, although as we have already seen this effect did not attain significance. Questions asking whether a sequence would ever stop were found easier than questions asking what the smallest or largest term would be. In terms of the theoretical interpretation being suggested here, this would be because of the adolescent thinking in terms of potential infinity the latter question has misleading implications.

Numerical questions were found easier than spatial ones, probably because they have less concrete connotations. This has the implication that the use of number lines in the explanation of indefinite iteration may be more of a hinderance than a help to children in early adolescence.

Division was markedly more difficult than the other operations. Average scores for groups of ten subjects on addition, subtraction, multiplication and division were 4.8, 4.2, 4.3 and 2.6 respectively.

In considering the effect of age upon score, it seemed best to detail scores under both the easiest and under the most difficult conditions of instructions and phrasing. The easiest condition for the subject was when he was instructed to use his imagination, the question was phrased in the passive and he was asked if the sequence would ever stop. The most difficult condition was when no instructions were given, questions were phrased in the active and the subject was asked the biggest or smallest term of the sequence. Table 1 shows scores for these conditions.

The figures in Table 1 show that, in the case of numerical operations, even at mental age nine years a majority of children were able to conceive of addition, subtraction and multiplication being indefinitely continued when they were asked about them in such a way as to discourage concrete interpretations of the questions. Under difficult conditions, where such concrete interpretations were possible, this did not occur until mental age 14 or 15. In the case of division, under easy conditions it was not until mental age 13 and under difficult conditions not until mental age 15 the children could conceive of indefinite iteration. All these accomplishments were about two years of mental age retarded in the case of spatial operations.

Partial correlations were run between individual subjects' scores, on whichever questionnaire they were given, their mental age and their chronological age. The partial correlation between chronological age and score, with mental age constant, was .42 (p<.01), whereas the partial correlation between mental age and score with chronological age constant was only .16 (p<.05). This suggests that chronological age is more important than mental age, measured by the intelligence test used here, in determining childrens' grasp of concepts of infinity and that the ages mentioned above might be more meaningfully seen as chronological rather than mental ages.

Table I: Scores per group of ten subjects as a function of age, question type, operation type and domain of application.

Easy Question Type (See text for Explanation).

Mental age		A	S	M	D
9	Sp.:	5	4	5	6
	No.:	6	6	7	3
13	Sp.:	8	10	8	3
	No.:	8	5	7	6
10	Sp.:	4	6	6	2
	No.:	7	5	6	3
14	Sp.:	4	6	3	3
	No.:	9	5	7	6
11	Sp.:	5	5	5	7
	No.:	10	10	10	8
15	Sp.:	7	6	7	6
	No.:	10	8	10	9
12	Sp.:	5	8	3	3
	No.:	8	4	4	3

Difficult Question Type

Mental age		A	S	M	D
9	Sp.:	1	1	1	0
	No.:	0	1	0	0
13	Sp.:	0	0	1	0
	No.:	1	0	1	0
10	Sp.:	0	0	0	0
	No.:	0	0	0	0
14	Sp.:	2	2	1	0
	No.:	6	2	6	2
11	Sp.:	1	1	1	0
	No.:	2	1	2	1
15	Sp.:	9	9	8	2
	No.:	9	8	7	5
12	Sp.:	2	2	2	0
	No.:	1	1	1	0

A = Addition, S = Subtraction, M = Multiplication, D = Division. Sp. = Space, No. = Number.
Note: Under the easy condition the group of mental age 11 years scored abnormally highly on all items including those shown above.

(b) The tendency to believe limits are reached in a finite number of steps

---

Table II: Cases in which the limit was said to be reached in a finite number of steps compared with correct answers.

		Operation Type			
		A	S	M	D
	9	7(2)	7(1)	9(0)	4(10)
	10	8(3)	7(1)	9(3)	1(12)
	11	10(0)	9(0)	11(0)	7(2)
Mental	12	9(4)	10(0)	8(2)	1(12)
Age	13	14(1)	10(1)	14(2)	5(12)
	14	18(2)	11(3)	13(4)	6(8)
	15	29(1)	28(3)	29(3)	14(1)

A = Addition, S = Subtraction, M = Multiplication, D = Division.
Unbracketed figures show a number of correct answers to questions asking for the limit of a process (either infinity or zero) summed over instruction type (whether instructions to use imagination and passive phrasing were given or not) and domain of application (spatial or numerical). Thus each figure corresponds to 40 questions. Bracketed figures show the corresponding figures for number of answers in which the limit was said to be reached in a finite number of steps. This could be ascertained as every question asking for the limit of a process had a corresponding question asking whether the sequence would ever stop.
Note: Figures for mental age 11 are atypical as they include a group who did abnormally well (see note to Table 1).

Table II shows that in the case of division there is an inverse relation between correct answers and the tendency to believe the limit of the process will be reached in a finite number of steps. This relation is not seen in the case of the other operations and in their case the tendency to believe the limit will be reached in a finite number of steps is less marked, particularly in relation to the number of correct answers. This suggests that the tendency to believe that zero can be reached in a finite number of steps in the division problems is actually responsible for the difficulty of these questions. Why do children believe zero is reached in a finite number of steps?

This seems to arise from a tendency to consider the magnitudes removed in the process of division, accompanied by an inability to realize that the increasing number of magnitudes removed is compensated for by their decreasing size. In interview this inability to compensate sometimes takes the extreme form of an argument that the initial magnitude is composed of a number of parts and when these have all been removed there will be nothing left. An alternative argument the adolescent may turn to focuses on what remains after each step in the division process, rather than on what remains.

According to this line of reasoning, at each step in the division process there is something left, therefore the process can be continued indefinitely and the magnitude will never be exhausted. It seems to be through a resolution of these two lines of argument, by means of the realization that the increase in the number of magnitudes removed is compensated for by their decreasing size, that the adolescent arrives at a concept of indefinite iteration as applied to division.

An interesting implication of this analysis is that the division problem seems to involve both a concept of sequence, in this case the sequence 2^{-n}, and also series, in this case the sum from 1 to n of 2^{-n}. Most limiting processes involved in secondary school mathematics can be seen as involving both sequence and series, irrespective of the form in which the problem is explicitly presented. This suggests that the difficulty children have with such limiting processes may arise from the inability to compensate in relation to series, whether or not the problem is explicitly expressed in terms of series.

Experiment Two

INTRODUCTION / Before drawing any general conclusions about the adolescent's concept of infinity there is one question to be resolved. This relates to a small study performed by Taback (1969) in order to attempt to resolve the conflict between his own and Piaget and Inhelder's (1956) results on the bisection of a line task. Piaget and Inhelder found, using just a question about the end product of the process, that 12-year-olds could perform the task. Taback found that if he counted only responses in which the child said that the process could be continued indefinitely, only a small number of 12-year-olds succeeded. Taback (1969) suggested that the conflict of results might have arisen from his own use of a task encouraging a concrete attitude, in which the problem was presented in the form of a story about a rabbit hopping along the line. Removing this concrete aspect of the task and presenting it as it was presented in Experiment One in terms of a line and a point, Taback found that of the five 12-year-olds he tested four said that the process of bisection could continue indefinitely and would result in a 'point, speck, dot or atom'.

The only significant aspect in which Taback's task appeared to differ from Experiment One was that he asked for the end product of the process of bisection, while in Experiment 1 the corresponding question was as to how near the limit point the remainder would approach. Experiment II was an attempt to replicate Taback's (1969) findings using his form of this aspect of the questioning.

METHOD AND PROCEDURE / Experiment II was a partial replication of Experiment One, with some modifications. The division questions from Experiment One for number and space were given in questionnaire form with the same instructions as used in Experiment One to encourage imagination. The section of each question asking 'What is the smallest number/length you could reach?' was replaced by Taback's (1969) question 'What would be the end product of this process?' Two forms of the questionnaire were prepared, in one of which this question was always asked before the question 'Will it ever have to stop?' In the other, the order was reversed. Thirty 12-year-olds and 30 15-year-olds were given the questionnaires, half at each age being given one question order and half the other.

SUBJECTS / These were similar to those used in Experiment One, except that they were selected on the basis of chronological age alone.

RESULTS AND DISCUSSION

Table III: Classification of answers of children of 12 and 15 years to two kinds of question about indefinite iteration of division

		12 years		15 years	
		Sp.	No.	Sp.	No.
	O	5	1	3	0
	N	0	0	9	13
Infinite	S	4	4	1	5
Process	L	1	1	3	0
	M	2	2	6	7
		12	8	22	25
	O	11	14	5	1
	N	1	0	2	2
Finite	S	3	6	0	1
Process	L	0	0	0	0
	M	3	2	1	1
		18	22	8	5

Finite Process indicates the process was said to stop, Infinite Process that it was said not to stop. Sp. = Space, No. = Number. O = Zero will be reached, N = You can get as near zero as you like, S = Some particular fraction will be reached, e.g. 1/8, L = The magnitudes will become increasingly negative, M = Miscellaneous answers, mostly 'don't know'.

The order in which questions were asked had no influence on results, and this variable is not shown in Table III. Table III indicates that, as found in Experiment One, the majority of 12-year-olds believe the operation of halving cannot be continued indefinitely. Most of those who say this believe the end product of the process will be zero. A number of 12-year-olds who believe the operation can be indefinitely continued do say zero will be reached, but Taback's (1969) sample of only five children greatly exaggerated the incidence of this type of response.

Results from the 15-year-olds also confirm the findings of Experiment One. Here we find a majority of children believe the operation of halving can be indefinitely iterated. The majority of these say there will be an indefinite approach to zero, rather than that zero will be reached.

The most striking finding from Experiment Two was that a small number of children at both 12 and 15 years said the end product of the process of halving would be an increasingly negative number or negative distance. This confirms the view discussed earlier that many children focus upon the magnitudes removed during the process of bisection and think the result of adding up all these magnitudes will get larger and larger. This causes many children to think that the process will be halted when the initial magnitude is exhausted, but some evidently believe the result will be the production of negative magnitudes. Notice that all responses involving the production of negative magnitudes also assert the process can be continued indefinitely.

CONCLUSIONS / Under the most favourable conditions a majority of nine-year-olds can conceive of the arithmetical operations of addition, subtraction and multiplication being indefinitely iterated when applied to numbers. In the case of division this is put off until age 13. The way in which children answer questions about indefinitely iterated division indicates it is not until age 13 that a majority of children have a concept of limit. Even at age 15 the overwhelming majority of adolescents continue to think of limits from the standpoint of potential rather than of completed infinity. This points to the conclusion that while concepts relating to potential infinity develop between the ages of nine and 15, concepts of completed infinity do not develop until after this period. It also indicates that the claim of Piaget and Inhelder (1956), based only on the results from tasks involving division, that the concept of indefinite iteration does not develop until the period of formal operations, needs to be reassessed.

*Personalization in science: Can we teach children to interpret experiments? * *
M.C. Linn, B. Chen, H.D. Thier, 1975

Introduction
Many psychologists and educators, notably Bruner (1966) and Piaget (1970) have stressed that children are most likely to develop intellectually when they are encouraged to work with equipment

---

* Published by the kind permission of the authors. Gratitude is extended to Drs Marcia C. Linn, Benjamin Chen and Herbert D. Thier of the University of California, Berkeley.

(objects and organisms) at their own level. It has been pointed out by people studying aptitude treatment interactions that even children of the same age and general ability level may not profit from the same experiences (Cronbach and Snow, in press).

Rather than attempting to diagnose the experiences appropriate for each child, we are currently exploring the feasibility of allowing children to choose their own experiences within a general framework of possible choices. The assumption is that children, in this atmosphere, will choose activities which will help them learn. If most 10-year-olds are given dolls and trucks or geiger counters and centrifuges they will probably not choose experiences which will foster logical development. The materials must, in some way, relate to the children's available knowledge and stimulate them to uncover new relationships.

We are developing a program which allows children to use their full potential to uncover relationships, to find out for themselves, to come up with ideas for testing their own hypotheses, and to try to unravel complex phenomena. We feel that the equipment and general framework in this sort of program determines the type of progress children will make. We are concentrating on equipment and activities which will foster children's understanding of variables, designing investigations, and interpreting data from experiments. We are attempting to create materials which will facilitate such an intellectual awakening without much dependence on the program leader. Naturally, we do not envision a leaderless situation but rather a situation where the leader might be a paraprofessional, parent volunteer, or other person not necessarily trained in teaching.

We made a number of assumptions and several decisions when we embarked on this project. We assumed that our responsibility to help prepare children for the 21st century would be partially fulfilled by helping children learn to interpret experiments, design simple investigations, and recognize variables that affect the outcome of observed events. We also assumed that some proportion of the variance in the performance of students who have participated in an educational program can be attributed to the design of the program. We decided to aim our program towards nine- to 13-year-olds both because Inhelder and Piaget's (1957) research indicated that this group would be likely to profit from instruction in interpreting experiments and controlling variables and because no such program was currently available. Additionally we decided that an introduction to science concepts might be necessary before children could be expected to carry out experiments on their own. This decision was based on classroom observations of children using science apparatus for the first time. A similar hypothesis has been partially confirmed by Duckworth (1974). Our idea was that an introduction would help the child organize his available knowledge for coping with experimentation and provide a few useful concepts such as variable, evidence, and interaction.

In the investigations we have carried out thus far we have been interested in:

1) How do children respond to the invitation to do their own experiments?

2) What method of presenting activities to children leads to independent investigation?

3) What sort of activities are most successful?

4) What apparatus design is easiest to use?

5) Do children adapt an individualized science situation to their own intellectual level?

6) What level of understanding of experimentation and variables do nine- to 13-year-old children display?

7) What sort of progress do students invited to do their own experiments make?

8) What sort of student background in science is likely to lead to learning from doing independent investigations?

9) What sort of student interaction while working on science activities is likely to foster learning?

10) What are the possible roles for the leader of the program?

11) What responsibilities can be handled by the students?

Pilot Study

A pilot study was carried out to determine how children react to being allowed to choose their own apparatus and perform experiments (Linn, Chen, and Thier, in press). This trial involved whole classes of children in their regular classrooms.

Development of activities

Activities in an individualized program must reflect the interests of the children. Therefore, we asked a group of 11-year-olds to list the science activities they would most like to do. From these lists, which were quite general, like 'work with chemicals,' 'make things fly,' and 'investigate oil spills,' we developed apparatus for about 30 different activities including testing the acidity of various substances, flying rubber band powered airplanes, and saving goldfish from oil spills.

Classroom trial

In keeping with our assumption about a need for an introduction to science concepts, in this study children first participated in 18 one-hour structured sessions where they were introduced to materials-centered scientific exploration. Concepts such as evidence, variable, histogram, and interaction were explored. The students were then asked to choose their own apparatus from the 30 projects, carry out experiments, write a report, and change to new apparatus for an additional 18 one-hour sessions. Using earlier versions of evaluation measures described below for the Enrichment Center trial we found that children learned to identify variables during the introductory sessions and made significant progress in ability to design and control experiments as a result of the total 36 hour program. The results are reproduced in Table 1. A more complete discussion is found in Linn, Chen, and Thier (in press).

A number of problems arose when the students worked on their own experiments in this program:

1) All the students tended to request the same apparatus
2) Children frequently changed from one activity to another
3) Most investigations were quite superficial, few students followed up on preliminary findings.

We wondered if the problems which arose might be alleviated by providing some structure for each set of apparatus. Additionally, problems of space and organization of large amounts of apparatus in a regular classroom convinced us that a program such as this required some physical space of its own. It should be noted that others such as Lindvall and Light (1974) have observed similar space problems with individualized programs. Lindvall and Light (1974) chose to simplify and consolidate apparatus so they would occupy a smaller area. We, instead, developed and evaluated the Science Enrichment Center described below to evaluate methods of structuring activities and to accommodate the apparatus. One major factor leading to our decision is that many schools have space for such a center now that the lower birth rate has reduced the number of students.

Enrichment center trial

Children in American elementary schools today frequently leave their classes for music, art, drama, and many other activities. Generally these activities are physically separated from the regular classroom because special equipment, special kinds of space, or unusual noise demands are involved. Similarly, individualized science requires equipment storage space, working space, and a conversational noise level. Additionally, it is economically desirable to insure maximum usage of available equipment by having it centrally located. Although we used an empty classroom, we could just as easily have used a portion of a multipurpose room and can imagine situations where a corner of the library or a section of a large classroom might be used. If children come to a special place for the program then every child need not be involved; thus children can choose whether or not they wish to participate.

Table 1: Results of Pre-test, Post Introduction Test, and Post-test for Controls (N = 51) and Experimentals (N = 52)[1]

Evaluation Measure	Pre-test				Post Introduction Test				Post-test			
	Control		Experimental		Control		Experimental		Control		Experimental	
	m̄	SD	m̄	SD	m̄	SD	m̄	SD	m̄	SD	m̄	SD
Science Process Test (SPT)												
Variables	3.2	2.1	3.9	4.1	2.8	2.9	7.9*	5.9	3.9	3.6	6.4*	4.2
Experimentation	5.2	2.9	4.7	2.6	4.7	2.4	5.4	2.5	5.7	2.3	7.4*	3.2

* $p \leq .01$
[1] Also reported in Linn, Chen, Thier (in press).

Activity format

During the pilot study we observed that the structured introduction seemed to help students begin their investigations. Students were better able to identify variables after the introduction; they also, during the individualized sessions, appeared to carry out more complex investigations with apparatus they had first encountered during the introduction than with unfamiliar apparatus.

In the Enrichment Center trial we were attempting to develop a program that students might attend for variable time intervals and that would be led by a paraprofessional. We, therefore, attempted to include the advantages of the introduction in the instructions for each activity. It should be noted that this introduction provided a subset of the experiences included in the Science Curriculum Improvement Study (SCIS) elementary school program. Thus the SCIS materials might provide the same sort of introduction. We are currently investigating this possibility along with other possible approaches for providing this information in the introduction.

In providing printed directions for each set of apparatus we also hypothesized that if a student were directed to solve one problem with a particular set of apparatus he would be more likely to come up with ideas for his own investigation. Basically, children were challenged to 'Make a four layered rainbow of liquid,' 'Find out which solution is absorbed the fastest,' or 'Determine which glue is strongest.' They were told that once they had solved the initial challenge they could use the equipment to try to solve new challenges suggested by their investigations, their leaders, or eventually by the printed directions for the activity. Examples of activities used in the center are given in Figure 1. In general, directions involved as little reading as possible. Usually one or two questions to help the student focus on the variables in the situation relating to the solution were included; students were not required to answer these. Students could request additional equipment as they needed it and were encouraged to think of new challenges and ask for the necessary equipment. Over 40 activities were developed in this format.

Center operation

Folding chairs and large tables were placed in the classroom. Much of the floor area was left open for experimentation. The various activities for the students were posted on the walls. All equipment was shelved in one area of the room.

Fifteen students at one time came to the center from various classrooms once a week for an hour. One member of the staff served as the center director and was present for nearly every session. One or two other members of the project staff were present. One leader supervised

Figure 1: Example of Activities

ABSORPTION

CHALLENGE: Which liquid is absorbed fastest: water, alcohol or oil?

Materials

paper clips	newsprint
water	alcohol
2 stands	oil
4 containers	blotter paper

Solution

Here is a way to set up this experiment:

blotter paper

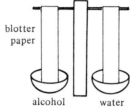
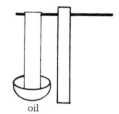

alcohol   water   oil

What kind of paper will you use for water and oil? ——————————

Explain why? ————————————————————————

NEW CHALLENGE: Set up an experiment to find out if newsprint absorbs faster than blotter paper.

INCLINED PLANE

CHALLENGE: Get a block of wood to slide down an inclined plane that is 10 centimeters high at one end.

Materials

1 rubber coated sliding board	salt
15 spacing blocks	sand
1 formica coated block	flour

Solution

1. Set up the inclined plane with 5 spacing blocks. (Each block is 2 centimeters.)

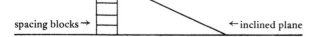

spacing blocks →   ← inclined plane

cont'd

2. Try sliding the block down the board, sprinkle flour on the board.

3. One variable is the height of the inclined plane. Another is the surface that the board slides on. Try using sand, salt, and flour on the plane. Try other variables that you think of.

NEW CHALLENGE: Do an experiment to show whether a heavy or light block slides down an incline more easily.

SNAIL WALK

CHALLENGE: Try to get a snail to walk across a plastic circle placed on a table. Start the snail three feet away from the circle. See if the snail will cross the circle three out of five trials. Complete the experiment in one hour.

Materials

   2 lights
   2 reflectors

Solution

1. Set up a light source and reflector and turn it on. Place two or three snails in front of it.

Which way do the snails move? (Describe or draw a picture.)
What variables are affecting the snails in this experiment?

2. Hold a turned on light source *behind* a snail and keep moving it towards the snail as the snail moves.

What happens?

What variables do you think the snail is responding to in this experiment?

Using the light source in this way, see if you can solve the problem of getting the snail to walk across the circle.

Describe your solution.

Try to find another way to solve the problem.

the students and interviewed them when they completed their experiments. Another kept track of which students were working on which activity, dispensed equipment, and solved equipment problems. A third leader circulated around the room and offered encouragement. It should be noted that this program was not designed to simulate a realistic school situation. During the course of the study we did, however, devise procedures for students to check out and return equipment without leader help thus making it conceivable that a single leader could supervise the group. At this point the project was in a developmental stage and project staff were present to observe and evaluate the activities, the design of equipment, and the organization of the center. Staff were also exploring procedures for use in a regular school setting.

At the first center meeting, one leader gave a brief introduction to the mechanics of the center operation. He instructed the students to read the challenges, choose one to work on, and get equipment and instructions from the other leader. Since there were over 30 activities to choose from, we requested that only one set of equipment for each activity be in use at one time. This kept the total amount of necessary apparatus within reason. Children were requested to finish one activity before starting another, to make a report in words or pictures on the appropriate form (Figure 2), and to be interviewed by the leader (interview questions are shown in Figure 3) before proceeding to the next activity.

Figure 2: Report form

Name _____ Date _____

Title of Experiment:
Description of Experiment: (What you are going to do.)
Variables:
What you changed. How you changed it:
Results:

Figure 3: Interview form

Interview

What project did you choose?
About how long (how many hours) did you spend on this project?
What did you like the least about this project? Why?
When did you need help from the leader? Why?
What other challenges for these materials did you try?
What did you find out about that wasn't asked for in the instructions?
Now, tell me in your own words what you did while you were working on this project, and how you felt about it. (The answer will be TAPED. In taping, first give your name, the date, and the activity used before answering the questions.)
What do you want to work on now?

Some of the experiments, once they were set up, required only observation for several weeks. In this case students were allowed to start on a second activity while waiting for results from the first. Additionally, some activities involved short (10 to 15 minutes) delays while something happened. A large number of mathematical puzzles, logic games, and topology problems were always available for students to use at these times. A more ideal solution would be to have students come to the center for a flexible time period.

Treatment conditions

From pilot work it appeared to us that students who worked in groups on the same project had different experiences than those who worked alone. Our hypothesis was that children who worked alone would be more likely to fit the experiment to their own intellectual level and would thus be more likely to learn about experimentation. We imagined, however, that children who had a choice of working alone or in a group would have one more way to tailor the total situation to their own taste and would find the situation more pleasant than those who were required to work alone. We also hypothesized that by working in groups children would be encouraged to discuss problems together and possibly learn from these discussions.

Thus, in the Enrichment Center trial we set up two types of experimental conditions. In the *Independent* condition each child was asked to work on his own project by himself. In the *Peer* condition children were told that they could work with one or two friends or work alone.

Trial school

An urban school in a generally lower middle class, racially mixed area agreed to participate in a trial of the Enrichment Center. The teaching staff was interested in educational approaches which cater to the needs of a diverse student population. Various types of individualized or self-paced programs were used by the teachers. These children had not participated in any laboratory science program in the past; the enrichment center was their first introduction to activity-centered science.

All fifth and sixth grade children participated in the study. There were 132 fifth and sixth graders in five different classes. (Some fifth graders came from a fourth-fifth combination class.) Children were assigned to classes on the basis of ability and personality characteristics.

SELECTION OF GROUPS / Teachers agreed to have groups of five to 10 students absent from their class two one-hour periods each week. They suggested that these periods be 11 to 12, one to two, and two to three on Monday and Wednesday. Pupils from each class were randomly assigned to the control group or one of the two experimental conditions. Our plan was to have 15 students representing two different classes at each enrichment center session. By convincing two teachers to have children at the center during three of the sessions we succeeded in always having two classes represented. It proved impossible to arrange a schedule whereby an equal number of children from each class were assigned to each experimental group but a close approximation was made as shown in Table 2. Six students left the school during the course of the study. An equal number of fifth and sixth graders and boys and girls were assigned to each condition.

Table 2 : Number of students completing all evaluation measures

Class	Control Group	Independent Experimental Group	Peer Experimental Group
A	4	5	4
B	8	13	7
C	10	10	10
D	10	6	11
E	9	10	10
Total	41	44	42

The two experimental conditions were run on different days of the week to minimize staff confusion. Groups for each day were formed from the same classes, thus students from classes A and C came at 11:00 on Monday and at 11:00 on Wednesday. We are aware that differences between experimental conditions could be attributable to the day of the week they occurred, but we chose not to control this variable.

CONTROL SUBJECTS / Subjects were told that the center was not large enough to accommodate all the fifth and sixth grade students at once. Therefore some students, selected by chance, would come for the first 10 weeks, and the others would come for the following 10 weeks. Control subjects were disappointed when the center began. Before we gave the post-test we assigned controls to enrichment center sessions, told each student when he would be coming, and posted schedules in each classroom. Thus we felt that, if anything, controls tried harder than experimentals to do well on the post-test.

Controls were aware of what happened in the center. Some even came in to tell the leaders which project they wanted to start with when it was their turn to come to the center. This situation precluded formation of a control group that, say, used the equipment without the directions. It is clear, in fact, that no pure control group could be formed for this study. We might have used students in another 'comparable' school as controls but then we encounter the question of random assignment. Rather than avoiding this sort of research altogether, we have tried to 'overcontrol' or err in favor of the controls when a choice arose.

Measures of variables and experimentation A pre-test and post-test of Variables and Experimentation, designed to measure children's ability to name variables and interpret experiments were devised by the project staff. The pre-test was administered to each class before the center began and the post-test was administered after the experimentals had come to the center ten times.

These variables and experimentation tests were presented on film; students wrote their answers to each question. They were similar to measures used in the first experiment (Linn *et al.*, in press). The procedure was to bring in the apparatus for the test such as a ramp and rolling sphere, identify each element, demonstrate the apparatus, show a short film segment which gave a more detailed demonstration, read the first question, show a film illustration of the question, allow all students to answer the question, and read, watch, and answer the remaining questions. Some typical questions are shown in Figure 4. Questions covered recognition of variables, controlling variables, recognizing uncontrolled variables, and interpreting experiments. Four questions were administered in one 30 minute session for the pre-test. Eight questions were administered in two 30 minute sessions spaced a week apart for the post-test. The pre-test was composed of parallel forms of a subset of the post-test items.

Scoring for responses to these questions was established by the authors. For the first question shown in Figure 4, responses were scored as follows: Zero points--circles unequal positions, answers 'I don't know', 'Because high is better' or describes what was done. One point--circles unequal positions, discusses the role of one variable 'high goes farther' or attempts to set up a compensation 'I think red is heavier so make it low.' Two points--circles equal positions, gives general reason like 'so you can find out.' Three points--chooses equal positions and says position must be the same to find out about the spheres.

For the second question shown in Figure 4, the two parts were scored separately. The first part (Why do you think she said that?) was

---

Figure 4: Examples of science process test items

1. Suppose you want to find out whether the *red sphere or the tan sphere* might make the target move farther. To find out you could release each sphere and let it hit the target as shown below.

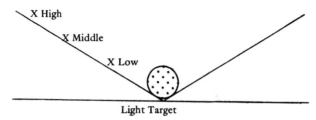

Light Target

At which position would you start the red sphere? (Circle your choice)

High   Middle   Low

At which position would you start the tan sphere? (Circle your choice)

High   Middle   Low

Please explain how you choose your answer _____

---

2. Suppose Bill wants to prove that *the high position is better than the low position* to make the target go far. He does these experiments:

Trial 1

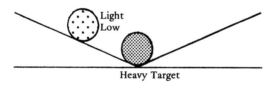

Heavy Target

Trial 2

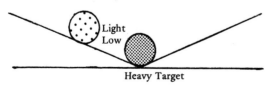

Heavy Target

Barbara says he can't find out by doing these experiments. Why do you think she said that? _____
How could you improve the experiments? _____

scored as follows: Zero points—'I don't know' or 'I think you could'. One point—'Both experiments are the same.' Two points—'The positions used in both experiments are the same'. The second part (How could you improve the experiment?) was scored as follows: Zero points—'I don't know'. One point—'Change position of one sphere.' Two members of the staff independently scored all responses. Agreement was reached on 80 per cent of the papers. Disagreements were resolved by a third rater.

Summary of procedure for trial

To evaluate the effectiveness of the enrichment center all the fifth and sixth grade pupils in one school were given a *Variables and Experimentation* pre-test. Subjects were randomly assigned to three groups: Control, Peer condition, Independent condition. Subjects in the Peer condition came to the center in groups of 15 for one hour on Monday; these subjects worked on the projects of their choice with one or two friends or alone. Subjects in the Independent condition came to the center in groups of 15 for one hour on Wednesday; these subjects worked on the project of their choice by themselves. After 10 weeks, the *Variables and Experimentation* post-test was administered. The controls then came to the center for 10 sessions.

RESULTS AND DISCUSSION/

Student response to the Center

Students showed a great deal of interest in the center. Many students came in during their lunch time and after school to talk to the leaders and check on experiments. On several occasions students chose the center over school assemblies. Although they were never reminded, few students forgot to come to the center. All but two students wanted to continue to come to the center after the experimental sessions were over — one of these two had trouble getting to the center on his broken leg.

In general, students concentrated on their experiments and tried to solve the challenges. Most students attempted at least 10 different activities during the course of the center. They were less interested in recording results than in working with the apparatus. They tended to make reports so they could go on to new apparatus. The problems which occurred in the pilot study (all subjects doing same experiment, frequent changes from one experiment to another, superficial investigations) were lessened by the new format.

Only a few students invented their own challenges while attending the center. Most seemed to find the available activities challenging and usually knew what they wanted to do when they finished their current project. They tended to identify activities by the objects that were used for their solution (e.g., eggs, snails, buzzer, grape juice, food colors). Examples of challenges invented by students included: Inflate a sealed bag, make a rubber cement ball, and grow a blue crystal.

When the center was in session most students were actively involved in doing their activity. Leaders were called on to assist when the apparatus or the directions were confusing. Problems were recorded by the leaders so that they could be solved when the activity was revised.

Leaders noted that students enjoyed repeating experiments they had observed being done by their peers and were often unable to predict the results. For instance, they were surprised when they sprouted seeds in moist paper, or discovered which ball bounced highest. Leaders also noted that students tended to investigate transitive relationship using trial and error when the variables were unfamiliar. Thus when students found that solution A was denser than solution B and B was denser than C, they still did not know if A was denser than C.

Students at the center engaged in a lot of informal discussion whether they were in the Peer or the Independent group. Every member of the Peer group worked with another child on at least one activity and the majority worked in groups for all challenges.

There were fewer activities going on at any time in the Peer group than in the Independent group, although, in contrast to the pilot study, at least five activities were being done simultaneously. Thus, students who were waiting for something to dissolve, change, etc., in the Peer condition might have had only four other activities to observe while those in the Independent condition might have had 12 others to observe.

Students working in groups in the Peer condition were encouraged to make their own reports. In general, however, one member was perceived by the others as the spokesman. It was rare for members of the group to disagree even when a response was clearly wrong. It appeared that each group informally chose a leader and the activity was conducted at the intellectual level of that person. Other members of the group might be challenged, confused, or bored with the activity at the peer leader's level.

The activities designed for the enrichment center were devised so that one student could carry them out. Rather than assigning such an activity to a group of students, it would be more meaningful to design activities specifically for the group. We have not yet attempted to develop an approach which would allow multiple users to work together, each at their own level.

Interviews and reports

Responses from reports and interviews were combined to determine whether students were describing variables and explaining how variables affect results. A teacher unconnected with the project was asked to read the directions for each activity and each report and interview. This rater determined whether the report and interview included a description of a variable discovered by the student and/or a description of the effect of variable on the outcome of an experiment. In over 70 per cent of the cases descriptions of variables were observed by the rater; in over 50 per cent of the cases descriptions of the effects of variables were observed by the rater.

Looking at the results by activity we observed an interesting phenomenon. For many activities, students tended to both name variables and describe the effect of the variable on the outcome of the experiment. Activities which led to over 75 per cent of the students naming variables *and* over 60 per cent of the students explaining the effect of the variables were Bouncing Balls, It's a Gas (effect of temperature on freon), Magnetic Interaction, Rusty Nail (effect of salt and water on rusting), Pendulum, and Eggostrength (weight needed to break an egg). Activities which led to over 75 per cent of the students naming variables but less than 40 per cent of the students describing the effects of the variables were Crystals (growing alum crystals), Stopper Popper (shooting corks from various angles), Liquid Separation (using salt to keep 2 colors of water separated), and Mixed Up Powders (using filters and evaporation to separate salt, sand, and cornstarch). We felt that the major difference between these two groups of activities was that the first group involved mainly variables that children at this age understand intuitively such as height, weight, and temperature while the second group involved less familiar variables such as density, angular trajectories, and filters.

Of the 40 projects, the one chosen most often was 'Eggostrength' which involved mainly breaking eggs. Making bubbles, alarms, crystals, and rainbows and popping a stopper were the next most frequently chosen projects. (Chosen 30 or more times.) Activities which were chosen the least often (10 times or less) include Coloured Wheels, Liquid Separation, Rusty Nail, Absorption, and Duckweed. The more popular activities, therefore, did not necessarily involve familiar variables but tended to involve a product (bubble, crystal, alarm) or an interesting result. It did appear that children concentrated on the result of experiments and thought of the center as a place to make things happen. Naturally, many factors influenced student choices and student interest including availability of apparatus, choices of friends, opinions of others at the center, quality of apparatus, and clarity of the instructions.

In responding to the questions about how they liked the activities, students would recommend activities to a friend about 80 per cent of the time. Only five activities were recommended by less than 70 per cent of the users. Students reported that activities were interesting about 55 per cent of the time. The most interesting activities were Bubbles, Crystals, Eggostrength, Liquid Separation, Mouse Alarm, and Mixed Up Powders. The least interesting were Bouncing Ball, Coils (making an electric magnet) Magnetic Interaction, Pendulum, Snail Walk (guiding snails), and Sticky Stuff (finding out which glue is stronger). All the activities which were *both* popular and reported to be interesting involved a product (broken egg, bubble, crystal, alarm) but did not necessarily involve familiar variables.

In each activity the median time spent by the students varied between 1/2 hour and 2—1/2 hours. It appeared that students preferred to finish a project in one visit to the center (one hour) although many students spent three or more hours on selected projects. Students tended to change projects when they completed the challenge, had great difficulty with the apparatus, or lost interest. Since it was necessary to put apparatus away at the end of the hour's visit to the center there was reason to finish in that time period. Clearly a more flexible time schedule would be preferable for this sort of program.

One general observation was that all the most popular activities except crystals were used on the average for one hour while the less popular activities except absorption were used, on the average, for two hours. While using activities for a long time precludes its use by others, in fact, crystals were used for 2½ hours on the average and still had 35 users. Thus, it seems that activities which last longer than one class period are less popular than those which can be done within one class period.

Student comments about printed directions and apparatus were passed on to activity authors and incorporated into revisions. When comments were unclear, students were interviewed by the activity author. Many improvements in activities resulted from student comments. It should be noted that project popularity was not a major criterion for keeping or dropping an activity. In fact, the most popular activity, eggostrength, was dropped because it resulted in little intellectual stimulation.

Evaluation of student progress

Results for pre-tests and post-tests are given in Table 3. Although students were randomly assigned to groups, the Independent group had somewhat higher pre-test scores than the other groups. Correlations between pre-test and post-tests were .42 for Controls, .59 for Peers, .65 for Independents. Since the correlations were similar we used analysis of Covariance to adjust the post-test means for pre-test differences. Analysis of Covariance, as shown in Table 4 yielded an F with probability of .07. While close to the .05 level, this is not significant. It should be noted that Analysis of Covariance for Peers and Controls yielded a significant F while Analysis of Covariance for Independents and Controls yielded an insignificant F.

Table 3: Means and standard deviations of pre-test and post-test scores

Group	Pre-test[1]		Post-test	
	Mean	*SD*	*Mean*	*SD*
Control	10.4	5.8	11.2	7.1
Independent	11.9	6.5	13.5	8.1
Peer	9.5	6.2	13.7	8.4

[1] Since the pre-test was half as long as the post-test, pre-test scores were doubled to simplify inspection of the data.

It is interesting to note that the standard deviations for experimental subjects are higher than those for controls on the post-test. This is consistent with the pilot study. Inspection of scatterplots of pre-test vs. post-test scores indicated that this was probably due to a floor effect on the test. Scores were bunched at the bottom of the distribution which had more of an effect on controls (who had lower overall scores) than on experimentals.

Looking at the results for individual questions we see that only about 10 per cent of the subjects successfully answered question 1 in Figure 4 while about 50 per cent successfully answered question 3 in

Table 4: Analysis of covariance for control, peer, and independent subjects

Source of Variation	*Sum of Squares*	*DF*	*Mean Square*	*F Value*	*Signifi-cance of F*
Covariate	2333.9	1	2333.9		
Between groups	232.6	2	116.3	2.7	.07
Residual	5369.4	124	43.3		

Figure 4. These results indicate that most of our subjects were at Piaget's level of concrete operations. Clearly some subjects in this age range are unable to handle questions about experimentation. More concrete questions, concerning results of experiments rather than interpretations may be necessary. Since children participated in the center pretty much as we intended, possibly we could show more progress for our experimental subjects if we were better able to pinpoint their starting point in this area. We are currently taking a deeper look at children's performance in the center to try to answer this question.

Student record keeping

A problem which we find very difficult to resolve is that of student record keeping. Our observation is that students profit from reflecting on what they find out with one set of equipment before going on to another topic. Methods which help students accomplish this are generally perceived negatively by the participants because they involve writing and thinking over what has been done instead of doing something new.

It seems reasonable to request reporting of one sort or another when the student changes activities since this is a natural break in his investigation. In our pilot study we required students to draw or write reports of what they found out using their equipment. Some students complained or did not want to change equipment because they did not want to make reports.

In the present study both interviews and reports were used (Figures 2 and 3). Students were encouraged to fill out the report form before the interview, but these questions were asked during the interview if they had not been answered beforehand. Students enjoyed discussing their experiments with the leader, especially if something unexpected had happened. This system was, therefore, more appealing to the students than the pilot study approach but did not always lead to reflection on what had been done and took a lot of leader time. We asked the classroom teachers what sort of spontaneous reporting was occurring in their classrooms. All had noted isolated instances of reporting. Some students had reported orally to their classes usually describing the steps necessary to solve a challenge in some detail. Some students had displayed evidence of their work in the classroom and discussed it informally with their peers. Teachers had observed small group discussions of what was happening or what had been accomplished at the center. One teacher showed us a bulletin board covered with photographs and descriptions of experiments that had been done at the center. We surmised that this sort of reporting was perceived positively by the students since it was not required. We noted that students spontaneously reported on all types of experiments although the ones which involved a product of some sort (alum crystals, recycled paper) or a surprising result engendered more of this than others. This sort of reporting tended to involve a concrete result or description of a phenomenon rather than a description of a variable. It is clear that the same problems we encounter in asking students to make reports are also important when we use paper and pencil evaluation instruments. In both cases an approach which allowed the student an active role would probably be more effective. Such approaches are very demanding of both staff and student time. We are, however, always trying to find a solution of these problems.

Center leadership

Although the program trials described in this report were carried out with staff members as leaders we were continuously considering the potential role of leaders from regular schools. Both practical and theoretical considerations entered into our deliberations. First of all, we wished to allow the leader to use his or her full potential just as we hoped this was a possibility for the students. Additionally, the monetary situation in the schools today dictated that the leader would be a paraprofessional or parent volunteer.

The goal of making a program 'teacher-free' is sometimes heard from proponents of Computer Assisted Instruction. Piagetian oriented educators often take the other side: asserting that drastic changes in the teacher are needed to create a new programme. Furth and Wachs (1974) spent three weeks in the summer, one week in the fall, and four days a month throughout the year training one teacher to teach children how to think. While this procedure is effective it is both time consuming and expensive.

Our first plan, then, was to devise a rather teacher-free program — one that would work no matter who the leader was. Since we also wanted the full potential of the leader to be realized, however, we had to create a means for this. Thus, we first devised procedures for students to handle the day-to-day problems themselves. Students checked activities in and out, noted when equipment needed to be repaired or replaced, and kept records of what activities they had done. The leader performed only truly essential functions like ordering new supplies and reminding students to return to their classes (a constant and flattering problem). The leader was now free to interview students when they finished their activities. The interview is designed to find out what the child is thinking, not to evaluate. We encouraged the leader to ask any additional questions that would help clarify what the child had done and what it meant. We hope that the leader's experience as an interviewer will prescribe a general role for interaction with the students. The leader will not be providing information but provoking thought.

CONCLUSIONS / The major goal of this study was to explore an approach to instruction in logical thinking and to determine whether children, given a stimulating environment, would independently pursue investigations at their own logical level. We gathered many forms of evidence which all indicate that children can carry out investigations: 1) Children enjoyed the program; 2) children chose projects and pursued them without much leader help; 3) teachers spontaneously incorporated discussions of work in the program into their classes; 4) in at least half of their reports children identified variables by themselves and described the effect of these variables on the experiment they were conducting; 5) pre-tests and post-tests indicated that students in the independent condition were significantly better than controls at interpreting experiments and controlling variables.

We also have evidence that the students in the center were working at their own logical level. Piaget would classify 10- and 11-year-olds as at the level of advanced concrete operations. Our observations indicate that students were performing at this level:

1) Students chose and reported interest in many activities which had concrete objectives such as breaking eggs, making bubbles, making crystals, and building alarms. When students suggested their own challenges, they also listed concrete objectives (e.g., make a rubber cement ball).

2) Students were best able to investigate the effect of variables with which they were familiar such as height, weight, and temperature.

3) Students had difficulty with transitive relationships for unfamiliar variables.

4) Students tended to report on separate events especially results rather than on the role of a particular variable.

5) Students tended to be able to investigate unfamiliar variables in conjunction with familiar variables.

Additionally, our evaluation measures indicate that our subjects were at the level of advanced concrete operations since most subjects could not control variables in experiments, had difficulty recognizing uncontrolled variables but could explain why two identical experiments would not help them find out about a variable.

We have gained a great deal of knowledge about how to design an individualized enrichment program:

1) We have developed a format for an activity based enrichment

center.

2) We have devised a method of presenting activities which encourages independent work.

3) We have profited from many suggestions for revision of activities and apparatus.

4) We have improved methods for student reporting.

5) We have set up procedures for students to handle most of the 'housekeeping' functions in the center such as keeping track of equipment and activities and returning used apparatus.

6) We have developed a possible role for the leader (as an interviewer).

Peer vs. Independent condition

There were no significant differences between the Peer and Independent condition on the evaluation measures. Observations in the center indicated that the Peer condition was slightly less organized probably because the activities were originally designed for one user.

Rather than devising special activities for small groups, at present we feel that having students work on their own project is probably the best approach. To encourage social interaction in a beneficial way we would:

1) encourage informal discussion of activities and results during the operation of the center

2) arrange for students to assist others who need extra hands to carry out a procedure

3) use peer teaching by referring students who have problems with an activity to others who have done it.

Comparison of Pilot Study and Center Trial

There were many differences between the pilot study and the Center Trial. Most importantly, students in the pilot study participated in 36 hours of introduction and experimentation instead of only 10 hours in the Center Trial. Pilot students were from an upper middle class area while Center Trial subjects were from a lower middle class area. Pilot subjects were able to all choose the same activity; experimental subjects could not. Other differences include activity directions, method of reporting, and introduction to science concepts.

The Pilot subjects made much more progress in logical thinking than the Enrichment Center subjects. The most likely reasons for this are (1) that the Pilot subjects were introduced to relevant concepts before doing their experiments, (2) that Pilot subjects spent more time at the center, or (3) that evaluation measures used for pilot subjects were more relevant to their progress than to the progress of the subjects in the Center Trial, since fewer pilot subjects than experimental subjects started at zero on the evaluation measures.

We are currently investigating the effect of our introduction to science concepts on success in the center by comparing students who have studied SCIS to those wo have not studied SCIS. We are lengthening the program slightly for these subjects. We are also currently developing evaluation instruments more relevant to the logical thinking levels of our subjects.

John Dewey, Jean Piaget, and the theoretical foundations of Open Education
R.P. Mai, 1975

The study described a comprehensive theoretical framework for Open Education based upon the epistemological, psychological, and philosophical premises of Dewey and Piaget. The discourse assumed that Open Education requires for itself a more rigorous understanding of the psychological notions and their philosophical implications that currently seem to inform open pedagogy. The author asserts, ' . . . that while an educational reform movement may be carried along initially by the efforts of persuasive critics writing in times of social ferment, and by the examples of a few conspicuously successful experiments in progressive schooling, it must ultimately define itself through its manifest ability to sponsor total development in individual children, and in particular, the development of an active and resourceful intelligence.' Mai sketches a theoretical position from which prescriptions for Open classroom practice may be logically inferred. The evidence is derived largely from the works of Dewey and Piaget and to a lesser extent Kohlberg. 'Strategies for provisioning and organizing Open classrooms are discussed with respect to responsive environmental conditions, and the need for opportunities to act and reflect, and to experience cognitive conflict situations . . . The dynamics of cognitive development suggest that curriculum essentially be thought of as problem-solving activity . . . Curriculum that sponsors problem-solving, inquiry behaviour requires subject matter that is cognitively challenging, and capable of engaging the learner's interests over a substantial period of time . . . the "humanistic" trend in current educational reform, emphasizing the importance of the "helping relationship" for classroom learning and teaching, needs to involve an understanding of developmental psychology and epistemology', p. 6006A.

An application of Piagetian research to the growth of chance and probability concepts with low achievers in secondary school mathematics
M.D. McClenahan, 1975

AIMS / To determine the Piagetian level in the developmental sequence of the acquisition of the concepts of chance and probability among low achievers in secondary school mathematics. Further, the feasibility of inducing such concepts to low achievers in mathematics.

SUBJECTS / N = 23 secondary school pupils.

METHOD / Five tasks on chance and probability as outlined by Piaget and Inhelder in *La Genese de L'Idee de Hasard chez l'Enfant*, were individually administered. Subjects' responses were classified according to the Genevan classification scheme. A training study was then 'designed and implemented based on a task analysis created by ... Shepler. The classroom organization and general teaching approach were derived from implications of Piaget's work as determined by ... Lovell. The ultimate goal of the instruction was that 90 per cent of the Ss score 90 per cent or higher on each of the measured behavioural objectives', p. 686–A.

RESULTS / Twenty-two of the 23 Ss advanced responses indicative of stage II for the majority of the experiments. The remaining subject gave responses indicative of stage III on three of the experiments. '(There) is a strong indication that the low achiever in mathematics may not have attained the formal operational stage, at least as far as the topic of probability is concerned ... Each objective was evaluated in order to determine whether any of the concepts or principles to be learned required formal thought. It was determined that four of the objectives did require formal thought. The Ss had difficulty mastering these objectives and had average percentages below 50 per cent on two of these objectives. For the remaining objectives, there were substantial gains on the post-test, however, the goal that 90 per cent of the Ss should achieve 90 per cent or better on the measured objectives was attained for only three of the fourteen objectives ... some implications for curriculum development. When selecting subject matter for the low achiever, the level of development should be considered. Piaget's developmental psychology appears to give some understanding what can, and what is not likely to, be taught profitably to low achievers in mathematics at the secondary level', McClenahan (1975, p. 686–A).

Piaget, education and teaching
D.W. McNally, 1974

The book is ' . . . designed to present Piaget's theory in terms that can be understood by a student making an initial study of Piaget in Sociology or Education and also with particular reference to the practising teacher'. The book begins with a clear description of how and why Piaget became involved with the development of intelligence and it sets out, in detail, his stages of intellectual development. Piaget's view of knowing, learning, development, language, and memory are closely evaluated followed by the understanding and teaching of number, and the teaching of social studies, science and language. At the end of most chapters there is a useful glossary and the book is illustrated with appropriate diagrams and photographs showing Piaget's ideas in action with children. Implications of Piaget's theory include a consideration whether development can be accelerated. The work of Elkind and Kohlberg with Piaget's theory are considered and McNally sees the difference mainly in the use of the word 'acceleration'. 'When Piaget uses the word it is clear that he means the achievement of optimal rates of natural and spontaneous development'. Tongue (1974) after having reviewed the book states, ' . . . his chapters on Piaget's view of knowing, learning, development, language, memory and their general implications, provide useful ammunition for the supporters of the integrated day', p. 17. In an appendix McNally attempts a defence of Piaget in respect of the outcomes of the Oxford criticism (Bryant, 1972). 'Perhaps the most charitable thing which can be said about this defence is that it alerts the reader to a recent piece of research which takes issue with Piaget on certain aspects of his work', O'Leary (1975, p. 82).

Validity of a reading comprehension test based on the Piagetian model of intelligence *
R.F. Morgan, Jr. and J.P. Esposito, 1976

AIM / To test Piagetian theory and Kretschmer's findings by further investigation of the validity of Kretschmer's experimental test instrument.

SUBJECTS / N = 80, 20 each of seven-, eight-, nine-, and 10-year-olds.

* Gratitude is extended to Dr R.F. Morgan of Old Dominion University and to Dr J.P. Esposito of Virginia University for sending their work to be abstracted.

METHOD / Subjects were administered six Piagetian tasks, Kretschmer's experimental test, and 'commercially prepared reading–thinking exercises in small groups.'

RESULTS / All tests were intercorrelated through Pearson Product-Moment Correlations and as an additional test of construct validity, a factor analysis was computed on the 32 items of the experimental test. Few significant correlations between the experimental test (Kretschmer) and criterion measures, and no clearly interpretable factor pattern of the experimental test were computed. It was concluded that the experimental test lacked both convergent and discriminant validity as well as construct validity. Results substantiated Piagetian theory concerning the cognitive functioning of the concrete operational child. Pedagogical implications from the data were discussed.

Piaget's theory of the development of concrete logical thinking: implications for the elementary curriculum
M.R. Newby, 1973

AIM / The author was intent to discern implications for elementary curriculum vested in Piaget's theory of the development of concrete logical thinking.

SUBJECTS / Children from elementary classes.

METHOD / 'Emergence of the concept of conservation was examined and regarded as a model for developing operations. Logical reasoning is contingent upon the self-structuring of logico-arithmetical operations involving classes, relations, and numbers, and upon the infra-logical operations of space, time, and measurement. The grouping, a logical construct, served as a prototype of operational structures. In the presence of operational structures, a child will unconditionally affirm conservation of the whole of classes, relations, space, and time and can apply operations characteristic of a mathematical group. From this base, he is prepared to pursue deductive reasoning. Five generalizations regarding concrete operational thinking were used as a basis for discussing the implications of Piaget's theory for an elementary school curriculum. Implications focused on operational thinking, learner participation, and social involvement. Further clarification of these implications was attempted through their application to a subject-centered grade school curriculum. Attention was given to alterations in the goal; learning experiences provided in mathematics, science, reading and the language arts, and social studies;

and means of evaluation that would be required to make a conventional school curriculum consonant with Piaget's theory and research', p. 6068A.

RESULTS / The study stresses that schools must recognize each child as the individual constructor of his logical processes. Children should be encouraged to analyze, synthesize, evaluate and coordinate ideas; and the importance of social interaction and question asking for cognitive development, stressed. 'Specific recommendations for implementation included changes in planned learning experiences, teacher preparation courses, administrative practices, and in parent education necessary to promote a more favourable climate in which children can develop . . . logical thinking abilities. It was concluded that Piaget's research has provided a thorough description of the way in which a child structures his intelligence to permit logical reasoning. Piaget's basic theory should guide educators in planning elementary school curricula', p. 6068A.

The effects of selected experiences on the ability of disadvantaged kindergarten and first grade children to use properties of equivalence and order relations
D.T. Owens, 1973

AIM / The author was intent to examine the effects of selected experience on the ability of young children to use properties of equivalence and order relations.

SUBJECTS / N = 47 disadvantaged kindergarten and first grade children.

METHOD / Subjects were administered 16 sessions in which the matching relations, 'as many as', 'more than', 'fewer than', 'as long as', 'longer than' and 'shorter than', were operationally defined through concrete materials. Half the subjects received the pre-tests. 'Then the full treatment group had four lessons on conservation of the matching relations and five lessons on the transitive property of the matching relations. The partial treatment (control group) continued with regular class work. Twelve structured interview post-tests were given to all subjects on Matching (Length) Relations, Conservation of Matching (Length) Relations, Transitivity of Matching (Length), Relations, Symmetric Property of a Matching (Length) Relation, Asymmetric Property of Matching (Length) Relations, and Reversibility . . . of Matching (Length) Relations. An unstructured Transitivity (of a matching relation) Problem was also given', p. 5042A.

RESULTS / Full treatment group performed at the higher levels in contrast to the partial treatment group on the Asymmetric and Transitive Properties of Matching Relations. However, no relationship was observed between being in a treatment group and performance on the Transitivity Problem. Kindergarten subjects performed at the lower levels when compared to the first grade children on Matching Relations, Conservation of Matching Relations, Symmetric Property of a Matching Relation, Asymmetric Property of Matching Relations, Reversibility of Matching Relations and Length Relations. The treatment was not effective in enhancing the ability of the subjects to conserve matching relations. Although the treatment improved the ability of the subjects to perform transitivity tasks very similar to the treatment activities, such an enhancement failed to generalize to the more difficult Transitivity Problem or to the Transitivity of Length Relations. Performance on relations and conservation was slightly higher in the length relational category than in the matching relational category. No relationship was noted between meeting the criterion on conservation and attaining the conservation on transitivity within either relational category.

Curriculum design for junior life sciences based upon the theories of Piaget and Skinner
E.E. Pearce, 1972

AIMS / Two hypotheses were formulated: First, 'to develop experimental curriculum materials utilizing concrete and formal operations levels with secondary reinforcement to facilitate concept attainment in seventh grade level science. Second, to investigate these experimental curriculum materials to determine if they facilitated the learning of more science knowledge than the current classroom learning situation and also facilitated the movement of students into the formal operations level of intellectual performance'.

SUBJECTS / N = 72 seventh grade pupils as at the concrete operations stage by pre-tests.

METHOD / The experimental curriculum materials were drawn from Piaget's cognitive theory and Skinner's theory of secondary reinforcement. 'Four classes ... were selected as the experimental group. These students used the experimental life science curriculum materials. The control group consisted of four classes ... (and) ... did not use the experimental life science curriculum materials.' In order to assess the effects of the experimental curriculum materials on science achievement and intellectual performance — the former was assessed by the administration of the 'Metropolitan Science Test, Advanced Level', while the latter was evaluated by individually administering four Piagetian tasks. The tests were given in a pre-post-test situation.

RESULTS / The data were subjected to Chi-square, t-test, analysis of variance, and Hartley's F — maximum Test. 'The results of . . . study indicate that students learned as much life science content in a curriculum designed for experiences in concrete and formal operations with secondary reinforcement as students in a "traditional" curriculum. The findings support the hypothesis that science experiences in concrete and formal operations facilitate the change of intellectual performance into the formal operations level. The findings give some evidence to support the theory that an active method of instruction which provides experiences for students to operate at their ability levels can be superior to the "traditional" method in providing experiences that facilitate the transition from concrete to formal operations level of intellectual performance', p. 5537A.

The quality of thinking in secondary school subjects
E.A. Peel (Ed.), 1972

Peel (1972) had edited a few researches 'aimed at investigating how the power of thinking, together with the attendant improvement in understanding, develops over the secondary school years. Apart from the last paper, concerned with the promotion of thinking generally, each presents material relating to a specific school subject. These papers include studies of thinking in science, history, geography, mathematics and religion', p. 163.

De Silva (1972) investigated the processes by which adolescents 'ascribe meanings to coded words standing in for historical terms, going on contextual cues alone. A word-context test consisting of ten passages was administered to 160 students taken in equal proportions from those receiving selective and those receiving non-selective education in England', p. 175. Subjects ranged in age from 12 to 16 years. Response categories between grammar school and non-grammar school subjects in respect of all ten passages demonstrated the latter made a high proportion of logically restricted responses while the former showed a high proportion of instances of deductive conceptualization. Significant differences were also computed in the frequency distributions of response categories among the five age groups tested, logically restricted responses decreasing and instances of deductive conceptualization increasing with age. De Silva maintains, 'The evidence from this study may be taken as strongly supporting Peel's (1967, p. 165) assertion: " . . . much of school history is taught through texts and new words are often introduced for fresh ideas and institutions mainly through contextual passages without a precise definition being given. This makes for erroneous concepts",' p.181.

In an attempt to distinguish successive levels of maturity of judgement within the overall framework of development, a set of geographical case-studies were designed for administration to a group of children by Rhys (1972). Subjects ranged in age from nine to 16 years. Five major themes included: Soil erosion in an Andes valley; Masai migration in East Africa; Commercial grain-growing in Manitoba; Intensive rice-cultivation in Japan; and Crofter farming in the Outer Hebrides. Rhys concludes, 'The resolution of geographical problems, through a process of explanation, would seem to require objectivity on two distinct planes. First, in terms of spatial orientation, where some combination of projective and Euclidean concepts has to be employed at an abstract or symbolic level. Secondly, in terms of cultural orientation whereby due attention is paid to local capacities and traditions when appraising the local decision-taking situation. At the most mature level of judgement attained by the children . . . ,whatever constituted the environmental context under review could be organized as a whole from the outset. These older pupils were able to structure and organize the total spatial field, and effectively interweave the component variables, either within a self-contained unit . . . or within the context of a more extensive and elaborate structure . . . At this level human action could be evaluated objectively and critically, where judgements took into account the technical resources and expectations of the local population, and the restraints imposed by their environment as they perceived it. The achievement of equilibrium with respect to symbolic representations of unencountered "worlds" would seem to be critically dependent upon the emergence of a capacity for hypothetico-deductive reasoning', p. 195.

Law (1972) examined the ways in which boys of different ages solved a variety of mathematical problems, some of which were related to school work while others were not. Subjects ranged in age from 11 to 16 years. Results demonstrated 'that ability on problem solving may be related far more closely to intelligence and general academic strength, than to mathematical ability as demonstrated in orthodox school examinations in the subject. It seems likely that the mathematics syllabus has for too long been dominated by the need to learn and reproduce particular techniques. Traditional syllabus work and traditional method of teaching together may over-emphasize such needs, especially in the face of traditional examinations. The newer syllabus . . . Modern Mathematics . . . and the increase in "discovery" methods especially in the primary school, may help to reduce the balance, and may encourage a problem-solving approach. As it is, the ability to solve problems appears to be called upon to a very limited extent in the teaching of mathematics, with the result that very often a pupil's interest in the subject may wane. The high level of interest shown by the subjects . . . may encourage those who are keen to change the emphasis in mathematics teaching from "learning" to "thinking"', p. 210.

Some aspects of adolescents' thinking in science were investigated by Wells (1972). The three experiments were: The rolling of bevelled rolls along a widening and sloping groove; the solubility of ammonia experiments; and the release of open inflated balloons to illustrate space travel. Results demonstrated 'the trend from describer to explainer thinking with increasing age. Mental age was . . . more important than chronological age as an index of quality of thinking. There were comparatively few clear-cut cases of explainers thinking and these were chiefly associated with a mean chronological age of 14 years and above and a mean mental age of 15 years and upwards . . . For each level of thinking there was quite a wide spread about the mean, both for chronological and for mental age. Factors other than age and intelligence were . . . bearing upon the quality of thinking . . . The analysis of responses over the whole range of the investigation suggested the following pattern of developmental changes between describer and explainer levels of thinking . . . Describer Level . . . Extended Describer Level . . . Explainer Thinking Level . . . Use of analogy . . . Inferences . . . and Levels of explanation', p. 222.

Richmond's (1972) study attempted to discover whether the maturity of religious judgement was related to CA. Further, whether there was a relationship between maturity of religious judgement and favourableness of religious attitude. 120 subjects ranged in age from 13 to 16 years of age. The religious judgement passages included: The Bible; Jesus; Love; Religion; Temptations; Adam and Eve; The Beatitudes; and The expression of Jesus' way in man. Attitude to religion was measured by a scale developed by Hyde (1965). Results indicated that the doctrinal statements classified as logically restricted were few. 'A surprising number of answers involved a personal factor relating the hypotheses to a personal experience . . . age differences revealed a significant difference in performance in a progressively rising score from 13 years to 16 years . . . With religious judgements few subjects appeared to achieve the higher levels . . . The coded passages produced a significantly earlier more mature level of judgement than the free passages . . . The results of the attitude test confirmed the findings of other researchers . . . that there is an increasingly unfavourable attitude to religion during adolescence towards the fourth year of secondary school, and then it improves', p. 234.

Individual and group responses of 14- and 15-year-olds to short stories, novels, poems, and thematic apperception tests: case studies based on Piagetian genetic epistemology and Freudian psychoanalytic ego psychology
A.R. Petrosky, 1975

AIMS / The author was intent to investigate two issues: What was the psychological dynamic of response to literature?, and 'By what process does individual, subjective response to literature become shared by a group and in this sense become "objective"?'

SUBJECTS / N = four adolescents.

METHOD / Data were collected from the case studies based on the expressed responses of the four adolescent readers reading the same texts. Responses were recorded verbatim in both individual interview sessions and in group sessions where E was not present. The procedure was followed for 12 works of literature and for the thematic Apperception Tests. 'Using a holistic approach to the case studies, the researcher ties together various aspects of themes in the readers' responses to form a picture of characteristic response styles for each respondent. These patterns of response and the individual's uses of stage-specific operations, as expressed through the responses, are the major foci of the case studies . . . This study identifies and describes five variables that influence response to works of literature: stage-specific operations, identity theme, past experience, expectations, and reading ability', p. 852—A.

RESULTS / The author drew the conclusions as follows: '1) the cognitive and affective parameters of any response in any form are determined by the respondent's stage-specific operations (thought processes) and by the respondent's personality (identity theme); (2) both stage-specific operations and identity theme are intra-individual variables constructed within and with past experiences . . .; (3) response to literature takes a form (or system) that is learned; (4) the learning of a response form . . . , is a direct outcome of the expectations a respondent perceives via the kinds of questions asked of him in order to elicit response; (5) different response forms allow various degrees of freedom (or acceptability); and (6) response to literature evolves into a genuine dialectical experience when the respondents are given the opportunity to articulate and share personal impressions and interpretations in group situations', Petrosky (1975, p. 852–A).

Piaget's logical operations and science content comprehension
H. Polanski, 1975

AIMS / That logical operations, critical thinking, and creative thinking were all components of science content comprehension. Second, that a positive correlation existed between the comprehension model and intelligence of Ss tested; and that the sixth grade Ss would perform at the higher levels of operativity in contrast to the fourth graders.

SUBJECTS / N = 220 fourth and six grade students.

METHOD / The tests administered were: Piaget Comprehension Test constructed by the authors using Piaget's operations of classification, seriation, logical multiplication, and comprehension; Raven Test of Logical Operations; Iowa Comprehension Test, Roberge Critical Thinking Test; and the Torrance Creative Thinking Test.

RESULTS / A correlation coefficient of .62 between the Piaget Comprehension Test and Raven's Test of Logical Operations and a correlation coefficient of .69 between the Piaget Comprehension Test and the Iowa Comprehension Test demonstrated a strong relationship between the types of thinking used. Piaget Comprehension Test and the Roberge Critical Thinking Test computed a correlation coefficient of .46 indicating that comprehension contained a component related to critical thinking. Sixth grade Ss performed at the higher levels than did the fourth grade subjects. 'Examination of a factor score coefficient called a "comprehension factor" gave further support to the basic premises. This factor has significant loadings on two of Raven's subtests, the Piaget Comprehension Test, the Iowa test, and the Roberge test. The presence of this factor suggests that the skills of the Iowa test, the logical operations of the Piaget tests and the critical thinking processes of the Roberge test are all closely related to a factor called "comprehension". The Torrance Creative Thinking Test and the intelligence quotients of the students did not load significantly on this "comprehension factor".

The relationship between children's classification-class inclusion
abilities and geographic knowledge as measured by Piaget's spatial
stages
D.C. Rand, 1974

AIM / To examine children's performance on geographic and spatial
relationships, and to compare that performance with general
classification — class inclusion abilities.

SUBJECTS / N = 120 elementary school stratified by age, sex,
residence and socioeconomic status.

METHOD / Two types of testing measures were used. The first, the
Geographic Stages Test, was a test of children's comprehension of
geographic inclusion concepts and nationality relationships. The second
was administered to evaluate children's understanding in general
classification and class-inclusion concepts (Inhelder and Piaget, 1964).

RESULTS / The data were subjected to three statistical techniques:
chi-square, analysis of variance, and correlational analyses. Results
demonstrated that 'children's observed responses are significantly
different from theoretically expected responses for total sample and for
all subsamples on all subtests and the total test with the exception of
total test score for girls. Further . . . that while children progress
through age-stage relationships similar to those . . . proposed by Piaget,
there is wide variation in children's performance . . . children do differ
significantly according to age, giving support to Piaget's original
contention of age-stage progression . . . while few significant relationships were found between groups of children, evidence clearly suggested
that trends were apparent. Boys outperformed girls, urban children
outperformed rural children, and higher SES children outperformed
lower SES children . . . that the largest single predictor of total
geographic performance was age . . . SES and residence contributed
only negligible amounts . . . significant relationships do exist between
children's performance on general classification-class inclusion measures
and that of geographic concepts of classification and inclusion. Low
correlations ($r = .20 - .36$) exist between single classification abilities
and geographic performance, while moderate correlations
($r = .35 - .54$) exist between multiple classification abilities and
children's performance on geographic concepts. Moderate to high
correlations ($r = .50 - .65$) exist between general class inclusion
abilities and geographic spatial abilities, suggesting that geographic
classification — class inclusion abilities may be a special instance of
those more general abilities . . . Implications for curriculum and

educational practice were discussed . . .', p. 4885—A.

The use of a Piagetian scale of development as a part of growth measure of pre-kindergarten children participating in the Baltimore City public schools*
E. Reid, 1975

The early School Admissions Program has been in operation in the Baltimore City public schools for ten years. It was a Pre-Kindergarten Program for four-year-old and nearly four-year-old children (1260). The goal of the program was to develop skills that would 'open doors' to reading readiness. It was hoped that pupils engaged in the program would demonstrate readiness beyond that of pupils not participating in the Early School Admissions Program (ESAP)[1] upon entering kindergarten.

The ESAP pupils were described as those four-year-olds living within an area defined as inner-city and disadvantaged. Family income, as established by the Office of Economic Opportunity was one determinant for qualifications, other determinants were the limited educational opportunities of adult members of the family, dependency on public assistance and varied problems plaguing the family.

Prior to the school year 1973—4, the program evaluation was based on data gathered through commercially constructed tests. These tests were the intelligence measure, Stanford Binet (Short form), the Verbal Maturity Scale and the Columbia Mental Maturity Scale. These tests proved to be of small value to teachers in their planning for individualization. Teachers needed some form of assessment which would inform them of the child's progress. Somehow this had to be done without 'bogging' teachers down with testing, etc. In cooperation with the Project Manager for ESAP and the Staff Director of the Office of Pupil and Program Monitoring and Appraisal a measure was constructed to assess each program objective and would provide feedback to the teachers by child, class, school and program.

The measure, created as: Pupil Evaluation Measure (PEM), was based on a Piagetian scale of development. Each task, there were nine, was designed to observe pupil growth as he mastered simple tasks and proceeded to the more difficult tasks. In other words he was observed as he began with the concrete and advanced to a more abstract level of cognitive development. The measure was such that a child could be

---

* Published by the kind permission of the author. Gratitude is extended to Dr Ernestine M. Reid of Baltimore City Public Schools, Centre for Planning, Research and Evaluation, Maryland.

1 Early School Admission Program shall be indicated as ESAP, throughout the Paper.

assessed in the latter stages of the sensorimotor period (neonate to two yrs.) to the pre-operational period (two to seven yrs.) and included early stages of the concrete operational period.

The sensorimotor period is the first stage of Piaget's developmental model. It is designated as the time from birth until the beginning of symbolic thought. According to Piaget, the child learns by imitation and repetition and for the most part is in a pre-language period.

The stage with which PEM was most concerned was the pre-operational period. The period, from two to about seven years, is characterized by two things, first, the appearance of the semiotic function which includes language, mental imagery, deferred imitation and drawing. (None of these functions were present previously). The semiotic function, at this point, allows interiorizing of imitation, now the child can now represent to itself an object when it is absent. This in turn permits the development of a new level of intelligence — intelligence in representation and thought. It is no longer restricted to action. At this level the child must reconstruct everything acquired at the level of actions; it has to reconstruct in conceptual terms everything that it has constructed so far in terms of schemes (Evans, 1973).

This entire period is a preparation for the construction of concrete operations. At the sensorimotor level actions take place in space that is immediate and at the present time, while semiotic function actions can and do project into the future. The child, at this level has to not only reconstruct, but he has to deal with the adaptation to a newer and larger field. Everything seen at the sensorimotor plane has to begin anew at this representational plane. This is why operations are not seen immediately. Moreover, it is why conservation is not seen immediately. The child now moves from a presymbol level of conceptualization to a level of actual use of symbols (Evans, 1973).

PEM considered the developmental stages as described and explained by Jean Piaget. If teachers were to understand the developmental stages of children and their effect upon learning, they needed a measure that would help them. They needed to know if the pupils in their classes were growing and the rate of growth. There was an urgent need to know the strengths and weakness of each and every child. In the construction of PEM there was a means to allow observation and an evaluation of each child in the program as well as the overall program itself.

The instrument, based on the nine program objectives, was to provide information that would allow teachers to provide the sorely-needed individualization that everyone talks about, but does little to put it into practice. The information would also make allowances for program change as the program was in operation. Most of all it was hoped this would give some indicators of the growth of children in the pre-school years.

PROCEDURE / A workshop was set up to train teacher assistants[1] in the administering of the measure, PEM (Twenty-five schools were involved (1260) pupils). It was important, as mentioned before, that classroom teachers not be burdened with the added duties of testing and assessment, thus the reason for involving the teacher assistants. The teacher assistants administered the tests monthly on an individual basis. The testing period covered the months of October, 1973 through January, 1974 and again in May, 1974.[2]

When testing was completed, the tests were sent to the Staff Specialist at the Office of Pupil and Program Monitoring and Appraisal (OPPMA). Here they were evaluated and assessed by pupil, by class, by school and by program. Upon completion, each teacher and program official was apprised of the findings and advised accordingly. Extensive record keeping was involved. At the end of the school year 1973–74 an overall report was provided each program participant[3] as well as Baltimore City Public School Officials and the State Department of Education.

FINDINGS / According to PEM data, ESAP pre-kindergarten pupils were growing. The statistics following indicate by objective the number of pupils operating below and / or above the semi-concrete / semi-abstract level of cognitive development in October 1973 and then in May 1974. The scale used to ascertain levels of development follows: 0 to 24 per cent concrete, 25 to 49 per cent semi-concrete, 50 to 74 per cent semi-abstract, 75 to 100 per cent abstract.

The objectives and tasks follow, demonstrating findings according to PEM.

Objective 1: EACH PUPIL WILL DEMONSTRATE THE ABILITY TO IDENTIFY, NAME AND DESCRIBE A VARIETY OF CONCRETE OBJECTS INCLUDING PEOPLE, ANIMALS, TOYS.
Given the concrete objects mentioned the child was first asked to identify, then name and then describe each. As the child progressed from one stage to the next, the stage of performance (i.e. concrete to abstract conceptualizing) was determined.

---

1 Teacher assistants known here as paraprofessionals trained to assist classroom teachers in the reinforcement of skills taught for the purpose of fostering individualization in learning.

2 The teachers' strike interrupted the testing February through April.

3 Program participants include teachers, project manager and others involved in the Early Childhood Education Program.

Time Tested	Below 50%	Above 50%
October	755	262
June	230	845

Objective 2: EACH CHILD WILL DEMONSTRATE INDIVIDUAL DEVELOPMENT OF FURTHERING HIS LANGUAGE ABILITY IN CONVERSATION, SELF-EXPRESSION AND RELATING EXPERIENCES.
The child listens to a story and is asked to relate in a measure of one, two words or sentences, the story back or a related one of his own.

Time Tested	Below 50%	Above 50%
October	632	294
June	185	823

Objective 3: EACH CHILD WILL USE PROBLEM SITUATIONS TO DEVELOP THINKING AND REASONING SKILLS.
He is asked to discuss or perform a means to solve a problem. The degree to which he needs help in solving the problem determines the level of performance.

October	452	664
June	60	1063

Objective 4: EACH PUPIL WILL DEVELOP CLASSIFICATION SKILLS AND WILL BE ABLE TO GROUP CONCRETE OBJECTS BY FORM SIZE COLOUR AND FUNCTION.

The child performs classification skills and will be able to group concrete objects by form, size, color and function.

October	933	357
June	126	655

Objective 5: EACH PUPIL WILL DEVELOP SKILLS IN VISUAL AND AUDITORY PERCEPTION AND WILL BE ABLE TO DISCRIMINATE, MEMORIZE, RECALL AND REPRODUCE.
The child's ability to group according to similarities, discrimination, memorization, recall and reproducing is determined by tasks administered in categories: concrete, semi-concrete, semi-abstract and abstract.

October	927	297
June	141	687

Objective 6: EACH PUPIL WILL DEVELOP MOTOR PERCEPTUAL SKILLS AND WILL BE ABLE TO IDENTIFY, NAME, AND DESCRIBE BODY PARTS AND FUNCTIONS, ORIENT ONE'S BODY TO DIFFERENT KINDS OF SPACES, AND COORDINATE EYE—

HAND AND EYE–FOOT ACTIONS'
The child is asked to perform exercises, identify body parts and to orient his body to certain and varied spaces. In each instance the child begins with concrete aids and as tasks develop in difficulty the use of aids is decreased until he is involved only in abstract reasoning.

Time Tested	Below 50%	Above 50%
October	897	524
June	218	537

Objective 7: EACH PUPIL WILL DEVELOP QUANTITATIVE SKILLS BY BEING ABLE TO IDENTIFY, MATCH, AND COMPARE SETS OF OBJECTS COUNT, AND DEVELOP BASIC UNDERSTANDINGS IN ADDITION AND SUBTRACTION.
The child will develop quantitative skills by being able to identify, match and compare sets of objects, count and develop basic understandings in addition and subtraction. He begins by following demonstrations and then going on to the difficult by performing a task of making sets without a model to follow.

October	798	224
June	301	772

Objective 8: EACH PUPIL WILL DEVELOP WHOLESOME FEELINGS OF SELF.
An assessment of the child's ability to perform tasks as they relate to him as a person and how he feels about himself as he relates to others is determined.

October	934	341
June	174	776

Objective 9: EACH PUPIL WILL HAVE OPPORTUNITIES TO INCREASE THOSE ABILITIES THAT ALLOW HIM TO USE A VARIETY OF ART MEDIA AND MANY ART FORMS.
The pupil shall be able to first (at the concrete stage) name materials needed to perform in the particular art medium, then he is asked to identify and discuss the purpose of (concrete / abstract) materials peculiar to certain art medium. To reach the abstract level the child shall be able to demonstrate and discuss the use of materials.

October	1072	661
June	2	345

The findings were valuable and interesting. In October, 1973, 67 per cent of the pupils were operating at and / or below the level of semi-concrete development, while 33 per cent operated at the semi-abstract level. In May, 1974, 82 per cent of the pupils signified a readiness for reading and kindergarten. (See Appendix for additional reports).

SUMMARY / As a result of the findings demonstrated by the pre-kindergarten pupils, Baltimore City Public School System has found a measure that has the potential to provide a method of following boys and girls throughout their school careers, pre-kindergarten through 12th grade. A measure such as this has provided information concerning children according to socioeconomic conditions, racial backgrounds, and whether or not there is an apparent effect on children, dependent upon one parent, two parents and / or guardian in the home.

Many child psychologists have said much about the racial differences among children effecting achievement. They have said much about the inability of inner-city children to learn and to progress. The children in this study were pre-K, disadvantaged and racially-mixed. Yet, there was growth indicated regardless of backgrounds. (See Appendix). Information was such that kindergarten teachers could receive data that would enable them to plan a program to meet their individual needs.

Children at the pre-school age can be assessed and evaluated to the degree wherein programs for their future educational experiences can be planned and instituted. PEM has proven itself as a measure within the realm of the stages of development among children. If educators could realize the importance of observing and evaluating pupils according to the pupil's own rate of development and growth there is a great possibility of alleviating frustrations that in turn cause failure and drop-outs.

APPENDICES /

Appendix A: Included in the appendices of this paper are the various forms of data collection utilized for distribution by pupils, school, program, sociological background and by ethnic background. Pages 1–25.

Appendix B: Also there is a graph demonstrating data gathered from the Stanford-Binet (Short Form) Intelligence Test and another depicting relationships of the criterion-measure (PEM) and the Binet scoring of the pupils. Pages 1–6.

Appendix C: Procedures for administering and Scoring the PUPIL EVALUATION MEASURE. Pages 1–14.

Piaget in the classroom
M. Schwebel and J. Raph (Eds.), 1973

Piaget has admitted on several occasions that his work has pedagogical implications but that it is up to pedagogues to spell these out, since he considers that his main interest is in the epistemological field. Sinclair, Duckworth, and deMeuron (cited in Schwebel and Raph, 1973) have tried to provide instances of actual classroom practice so that teachers can assimilate a lot of information and gradually draw meaning and inferences. Sinclair cites several learning experiments involving conservation and demonstrates their relationship to teaching number work. Several ways, in which Piagetian insights could be utilized to organize the child's encounters with number in an ordered and accelerated way, have been advanced. Duckworth demonstrates, through examples, as to how the teacher can work with children so as to furnish more material for the learner in order to assemble these together in his head. DeMeuron clarifies, through illustrations, the meaning of such generalities as, 'It is important to ask the right question at the right time', and demonstrates how the classroom world can include Piagetian concepts.

Birns and Golden focus on the importance of the environment for infants in nurseries or day-care centres and state: 'Professionals and non-professionals who plan to work with infants in nurseries . . . should become thoroughly familiar with Piaget's writings on the sensorimotor period . . . not to teach infants such concepts as object permanence, spatial relations, causality etc., but to gain a deeper understanding of how infants, through their own explorations and activities, acquire knowledge about the world. Through such understanding perhaps they can develop a respect for the infant as a scientist-explorer on his voyage of discovery through his new and uncharted world', p. 127. 'Overall, a useful, critical and suggestive book with regard to some of the practical applications . . . closely geared to American educational programmes', Peel (1974, pp. 365–6).

*How to assess science courses**
M. Shayer, 1970

Shayer maintains that, 'When planning new science courses, one must necessarily think of the science first. But in structuring a five-year school course, it must also be kept in mind that the mental capacity of the pupils increases year by year. If taking account of this is not to be

---

* Gratitude is extended to Dr M. Shayer of Chelsea College of the University of London for sending his work to be abstracted.

merely intuitive, a technique to assess the concepts suggested for different stages of the course is needed. Piaget's work might form a basis for such assessment, and examples from the Nuffield O-level chemistry course are used . . . to show how it might be done', p. 182. Shayer continues to maintain that one needs to be aware of the sequence of conceptual development in children, which the work of Piaget can make available. The need is also expressed for the statistics of what proportion of children reach a particular level at varied ages. 'It is . . . possible to see how Piaget's work could be used to assess a projected course. First, the stages of the course ought to follow the same order of increasing logical complexity as are present in the pupils' own development. Secondly, the age range over which the course is taught should match the age range over which these stages develop (even as one recognizes that the course may be a partial means for the pupils' development)', p. 183. The author emphasizes that the technique is 'a negative assessment technique. It will tell you when you cannot teach a certain concept, and it will tell you when you can. But it will not tell you when you should — many other factors govern that. If it was not for the fact that I think many contemporary maths and science courses are full of over-early conceptual material, I would not advocate this technique', p. 184.

Conceptual demands in the Nuffield O-level physics course*
M. Shayer, 1972

Shayer (1970) devised a technique of science courses based on Piaget's conceptual stages. In continuation, Ingle and Shayer (1971) applied the technique to the Nuffield O-level chemistry course. Shayer (1972) employs the findings to the conceptual demands in the Nuffield O-level physics course. Shayer argues that, 'If one teaches science in a highly selective school, and rarely below the third year at that, one will rarely meet any pupils below the 3A stage of formal operations: if one teaches science to average classes in a comprehensive school, and rarely above the fourth year, one is unlikely to have met any pupils whose thinking goes beyond the concrete operations stage. If you try to make someone participate in a process which is taking place at a more complex level than that to which they have access, communication breaks down', p. 29. Shayer continues, ' . . . when Piaget came to study the higher conceptual levels which develop in middle and late adolescence, it seemed that they were either more evident, or at least

*   Gratitude is extended to Dr. M. Shayer of Chelsea College of the University of London for sending his work to be abstracted.

more readily tested, in the context of science experiments than in any other kind of activity. So in *The Growth of Logical Thinking* the tests cover a wide span of representative physics experiments. In each, Inhelder and Piaget list examples of response at each of the four levels (Concrete: 2A and 2B; Formal: 3A and 3B) (used in Figure one). So these were tabulated, and compared with the experiment details and "Teachers Guide" recommendations. Where a section of work had no equivalent in *The Growth of Logical Thinking*, the mathematical operations involved and the style of reasoning were inspected — was it simple classification or seriation? Was a proportionality scheme involved? . . . A rule of thumb used frequently (derived from Piaget's work . . .) was that if a theoretical model was involved — as . . . in the kinetic theory work — this could not be handled as an operative tool at all if the pupil was still at the concrete stage, but could be handled, if given and explained, for making some predictions if the pupil was at stage 3A. And that the active search for, and possible discovery of an explanatory and predictive model was only to be expected at stage 3B', p. 30.

The author concludes that in the Nuffield physics course, especially during the first three years, conceptual development in children was permitted for in a more conscious way than in the planning of the biology or chemistry courses. With respect to the traditional physics teaching, the author maintains that, 'when analyzed in Piaget's terms, some of the traditional routines which may at least have seemed to have the merit of being efficient ways to theoretical competence, can be seen to be regressions — short circuits rather than short cuts', p. 31.

*Conceptual demands in the Nuffield O-level biology course**
M. Shayer, 1974

The author maintains that it is more difficult to assess the thinking involved in a biology course than in one in physics or chemistry. 'Much traditional O-level biology teaching has been of a descriptive kind, and it is possible to achieve a creditable pass without any mathematics or hypothetico-deductive thought at all. This is not to suggest that the activity of organizing information is not a process of thinking: on the contrary, . . . its development is of equal importance, for the intelligent adolescent, to the "possibilistic" thinking described by Piaget as Formal Operational. And it shows up neither in the methods of testing intelligence of the psychometric school nor in the very different

* Gratitude is extended to Dr M. Shayer of Chelsea College of the University of London for sending his work to be abstracted.

methodology of Geneva. But because the presence of so much Formal thought in the Nuffield course makes an analysis possible, I do not want it to be concluded either that I am taking sides in favour of the course for that reason, or because of its apparent difficulty, recommending the traditional approach instead', p. 1. Shayer argues that with the 'Nuffield Physics and Chemistry courses, Formal thinking is used from about half-way through the Third Year, which matches well the age at which the top quarter of the selective school population — those of IQ 125 and over — might be expected to approach this level of thinking. But in the Biology O-level course this level of demand is there from early in the Second Year: indeed, it may even be present in the First year work on classification and keys which involved ways of thought which did not lend themselves to analysis on the basis of Piaget's work', p. 3. Shayer cites examples from the Nuffield O-level biology course, provides graphic presentations, and the conceptual demands in such a course are discussed with respect to the Piagetian conceptual levels.

Relationship between reading achievement and Piaget's conservation tasks for beginning second grade students
J.W. Stanfill, 1975

AIM / The author was intent to determine if there were a relationship between reading achievement and the ability to conserve.

SUBJECTS / N = 160 second grade students.

METHOD / Piagetian conservation tasks of number and continuous quantities were administered. Ss were grouped as achievers or low achievers depending on their scores on the Stanford Reading Test and the Otis-Lennon Mental Ability Test. Data were analyzed and reported for combined sample, achiever group, and low achiever group. Years of formal school, sex, CA, and SES were obtained from school records.

RESULTS / Piagetian conservation proved an appropriate measure to employ in diagnosing a student's readiness to read when used in conjunction with other data. That the formal teaching of reading should not precede the child's ability to conserve. Further, that formal reading instruction in kindergarten was inappropriate for most if not all of the children as the ability to conserve was not attained by children of that age. Students of lower SES who were unable to conserve tended to be unsuccessful with formal reading experiences. Stanfill concluded with the recommendations, 'Replication of this study with a sample which would provide greater variability and thereby increase the number of students in the low achiever group, and . . . replication of this study using measures of conservation which would require additional transformation in the administering of the conservation tasks', p. 122–A.

*A comparative study of selected science teaching materials (ESS) and a textbook approach on classificatory skills, science achievement, and attitudes**
E.P. Vanek and J.J. Montean, 1975

During the past ten years there has been much activity in revising science curricula. Many of the new orientations have come about as a result of a desire to make learning activities be consistent with sound learning theory. According to Piaget, experience with concrete objects facilitates learning (Piaget, 1964). The trend, therefore, has been to change the emphasis from science content to the processes of scientific investigation. The child is no longer seen as a passive learner, receiving information directly from the teacher or from a textbook. Instead, he is actively manipulating materials, developing his own hypotheses, and testing these hypotheses in his own way (Hein, 1968; Zeitler, 1968).

One important scientific process is classification. Classification skills play a major role in the development of reasoning and logic. A child abstracts information from objects or situations, brings together common properties and relations in different objects or events (classifies), abstracts again from classes, and finally creates a logical method of classifying natural phenomena of the world. (Piaget and Inhelder, 1964).

The emphasis on scientific processes not only affects the cognitive domain, but also contributes to the affective domain. One assumes that a child is more likely to have positive feelings about a subject when he is *actively* involved with that subject.

THE PROBLEM / The purpose of this study was to compare the effects of various units of an activity-based curriculum, Elementary Science Study (ESS) (1966, 1969, 1971) and a textbook approach, Laidlaw Science Series (Smith, Blecha and Sternig, 1966), on classification skills, science attitudes, and science achievement.

---

* Written and prepared by the authors for inclusion in this volume. Gratitude is extended to Drs Eugenia P. Vanek and John J. Montean of the University of Rochester.

METHODOLOGY / Fifty-four third graders and 56 fourth graders from a rural school district south of Rochester, New York, were randomly assigned to the two treatment groups at each grade level. Two teachers at each grade level alternated teaching the two curricula.

The study continued for 20 40-minute sessions over a period of six to eight weeks. Units I and II in the third grade were Physical Changes (ESS, Ice Cubes; Laidlaw, pp. 151—167) and Living Things (ESS, Starting With Seeds; Laidlaw, pp. 15—36). Units I and II for fourth grade were Geology (ESS, Rocks and Charts; Laidlaw, pp. 96—129) and Biological Systems (ESS, Mealworms; Laidlaw, pp. 235—58).

TESTING PROCEDURE / Piagetian Tasks as described by Allen (1967) were administered to each child separately in a 20- to 30-minute session before and after instruction. The 11 tasks are:

1. Resemblance sorting (RS)
2. Consistent sorting (CS)
3. Exhaustive sorting (ES)
4. Conservation of classes (CON)
5. Dual class membership (DM)
6. Horizontal reclassification (HS)
7. Hierarchical reclassification (VS)
8. 'Some' and 'All' (SA)
9. Whole is sum of parts $(A + A' = B)$
10. Conservation of hierarchy $(B - A' = A)$
11. Quantitative inclusion $(B{>}A)$

Students were similarly pre- and post-tested on the Science Attitude Scale (SAS) developed by Ralph (1972). The ten subscales of the SAS are:

1. Liking for science class
2. Liking for projects and experiments
3. Liking for scientists
4. Confidence in the ability to do science activities
5. Weighing evidence, suspending judgement, seeking information
6. Critical questioning
7. Interest in diverse information
8. Confidence in methods and procedures of science
9. Open-mindedness, cause-effect
10. Importance of scientific explanations for understanding

After instruction, the Science Test of the Stanford Achievement Primary Battery III (Madden *et al.* 1973) was administered.

Table 1: F-ratio, Piagetian task

Source of Variation	RS	CS	ES	CON	DM	HS	VS	SA	A+A'	B–A'	B>A	TOTAL
Between Grade	0.05	—	0.20	6.62*	0.95	0.49	0.21	0.82	3.16	0.72	3.28	0.01
Between Treatments	0.00	—	1.54	0.81	0.98	0.03	0.00	1.06	0.35	0.12	0.64	0.10
Between Sex	3.32	—	0.02	0.48	0.74	1.11	0.44	0.03	5.32*	0.44	2.17	3.57
Grade X Treatment	2.27	—	0.18	0.05	0.96	0.13	1.08	0.73	0.41	0.04	1.78	0.00
Grade X Sex	0.09	—	0.14	3.05	0.70	1.61	0.07	3.57	1.70	0.12	3.00	0.25
Treatment X Sex	0.09	—	0.43	1.36	0.71	0.34	2.24	0.05	1.05	0.65	3.10	0.70
Grade X Sex X Treatment	0.08	—	0.16	−0.05	0.74	4.47*	0.13	0.30	0.09	0.62	0.55	0.00

* significant at .05 level.

Table II: F-ratios: science attitude scale

Source of Variation					Subscales						TOTAL
	1	2	3	4	5	6	7	8	9	10	
Between Grade	7.06*	15.97*	7.30*	7.51*	10.89*	2.71	8.45*	6.32*	3.30*	5.05*	18.36*
Between Treatments	2.83*	0.30	6.02*	3.61*	2.10	0.24	1.58	0.35	2.03	0.73	7.36*
Between Sex	1.95	1.39	0.13	5.38*	3.32*	3.68*	0.00	0.20	5.03*	0.20	0.69
Grade X Treatment	5.35*	0.53	0.27	0.52	0.74	0.10	0.34	2.71	0.17	1.02	2.13
Grade X Sex	0.10	4.04*	1.67	2.44	1.38	0.94	0.02	1.75	1.32	0.01	1.47
Treatment X Sex	0.06	3.41*	0.54	0.00	0.58	0.01	0.89	0.72	2.85*	0.11	0.22
Grade X Treatment X Sex	2.33	0.23	1.29	1.82	0.03	1.21	1.69	−0.02	0.02	1.86	0.24

* significant at 0.10

Table III: F-ratio, Stanford Achievement Test, Science

Source of Variance	F-ratio
Between Grades	12.95*
Between Treatments	0.05
Between Sex	0.68
Interaction:	
Grade X Treatment	−0.03
Grade X Sex	2.79
Treatment X Sex	0.20
Grade X Treatment X Sex	0.27

*significant at .05 level

ANALYSIS OF THE DATA / A three-way analysis of variance and co-variance, using grade, treatment, and sex, was performed on the data. In the instances where pre-tests were available, these were used as the co-variates. The results of this analysis are summarized in Tables I–III. Statistical significance was determined at a probability of 0.05 for achievement and classification skills and 0.10 for science attitudes.

No significant differences between treatment groups were found in science achievement and on the Piagetian tasks of classification. On the Science Attitude Scale, however, three subscales as well as the total test score reached the level of significance ($p < .10$). In all cases, Elementary Science Study did provide materials and an approach that led to a more positive scientific attitude. ESS students liked science class more, and were more confident in their ability to perform science activities.

Grade effects reached the level of significance ($p < .05$) on the Science Test of the Stanford Achievement Battery. This is to be expected on a norm-referenced test. Grade effects also reached the level of significance ($p < .05$) for the Piagetian task, Conservation of Classes. Since this was the only task that did reach the level of significance, however, one cannot present a strong argument that grade level affects the acquisition of classification skills.

Grade effects were particularly noticeable on science attitudes, where nine out of ten subscales reached the .10 level of significance ($p < .10$). Third grade students possessed more positive attitudes. These results may reflect the differences in previous science instruction, teacher attitudes and practices, and the level of maturity of the students.

The students' difference in sex did not have an effect on science achievement, and was significant on only one task of classification (The Whole is Sum of Its Parts). In this case, girls performed better than boys. Thus, it would appear that sex has little or no effect on development of classification skills or achievement. Differences appeared for four subscales of the Science Attitude Scale. Boys were more confident in their ability to do science activities, but girls were better able to weigh evidence, suspend judgement and seek information. They were also more open-minded and critical in their questioning.

Interaction of grade by treatment by sex proved significant (p<.05) for the Piagetian task of Horizontal Reclassification. Interactions on one subscale of the Science Attitude Scale occurred for grade by treatment and grade by sex, respectively. In the interaction of treatment by sex, ESS proved to be more successful for boys in their liking for science projects and experiments, whereas girls using the textbook said that they liked projects and experiments to a greater extent. Girls, being more passive than boys in school, may feel more comfortable in the textbook approach, which in turn is reflected in their likes and dislikes in performing science experiments. Girls in the ESS group were more open-minded than those in the textbook group. The opposite was true for boys.

DISCUSSION / From the results of this study, it does not appear that the teaching method or materials makes a difference in achievement or classification ability. The proponents of ESS must take a closer look at the evaluation of their program. The effectiveness of a science curriculum cannot be judged on its theoretical framework alone.

This study may have been too short in duration to detect differences in classification ability or science achievement. Similarly, age differences and thus cognitive development may not have been great enough in the study sample. Although field studies are necessary in education, they are subjected to these limitations of age range and duration. More studies with younger subjects may be needed in order to test for changes in classification ability.

An activity-oriented science program, with its emphasis on critical questioning and experimentation, can lead to significant learning, regardless of a child's ability or achievement as measured by standardized tests. It appears that the teaching method makes a difference in scientific attitudes. Children using an activity-based curriculum (ESS) seem to be more willing to explore their world and happier learning about that world. The affective domain has been ignored too long in education at the elementary levels. A more critical look must also be taken at grade and sex differences in scientific attitudes, especially with the trend toward multi-graded classrooms and the abolishment of socialization along sexist lines.

The sequence of development of some early mathematics behaviours
M.C. Wang, L.B. Resnick, and R.F. Boozer, 1971

AIM / To examine the sequence in which children acquire elementary mathematical behaviours of counting, one-to-one correspondence, and numeration.

SUBJECTS / N = 78 with an age range from four years six months to six years.

METHOD / Each child was tested individually on the test prepared for each behaviour specified in the hypothesized hierarchies (Wang, 1968). 'Specific hypotheses concerning the sequence of acquisition of the behaviours under study (counting, one-to-one correspondence, numeration) were derived from a process of behaviour analysis described by Resnick (1967). On the basis of these analyses, the tasks under study were ordered into hierarchies of successively more complex learning tasks, with skill in performing tasks lower in a hierarchical sequence hypothesized to be prerequisite to learning those higher in the same sequence (*cf.* Gagné, 1962). (The predicted hierarchies are shown in figure one on page 1769). In each sequence the task hypothesized to be the most complex appears at the top, with prerequisites shown below, connected by a line. In each box in the figure, the entry above the line describes the stimulus situation and the entry below the line describes the appropriate response,' p. 1768. (Details of the experimental procedure are described elsewhere, Wang, Resnick and Boozer, 1971, pp. 1770–1).

RESULTS / Lingoes' (1963) method of multiple scalogram analysis (MSA) was used to test the scalability of subsets of tests. Results demonstrated a reliable sequence of skills in using numerals; 'the dependence of learning numerals upon prior acquisition of counting skills for sets of the size represented; acquisition of numeral reading for small sets before learning to count larger sets; and the independence of counting and one-to-one correspondence operations in young children', p. 1767. The authors discuss implications of the findings for designing an introductory mathematics curriculum.

The pupil's thinking
F.R. Watson, 1974

The author, after a brief account of the Piagetian stages of intellectual development, draws attention to the importance of action by the pupil. Piaget and his colleagues suggested that much early learning involves the internalization of physical actions performed by the learner, implying that concrete experience is vital at this stage. Watson maintains that much of the current emphasis on 'activity' methods and practical experience in schools stems from this approach. A closer consideration of science teaching in the secondary school is discussed next. That the Geneva school efforts have been largely devoted to examining how the basic concepts of mathematics and science — and of everyday life — such as those of volume, weight, area, density, or velocity develop, for the most part in the stage of concrete operations. Watson maintains that it is only recently that detailed studies of the development of science concepts at the secondary level have been undertaken and cites the work of Inhelder and Piaget (1958), Mealing (1963), Peel (1970), Shayer (1972), and Ingle and Shayer (1971). That the Geneva school have used a variety of examples from physics (e.g., momentum, inverse square law, hydrostatic pressure, a pendulum experiment, etc.). Many of these studies are referred to by Peel (1970) in Part II of *Changes in School Science Teaching*. Peel argues that many of the experimental studies have dealt with concept attainment, in which a S is asked to attain a concept such as 'blue circle' for which he already possesses criteria of classification. This involves processes which are different from those by which secondary school subjects form the more advanced concepts of science, for which they may not have already established intellectual criteria. Ingle and Shayer (1971) and Shayer (1972), have estimated the intellectual demands made on pupils for each topic in the Nuffield O-level Chemistry and Physics courses. From a comparison of each Nuffield experiment with those cited in Inhelder and Piaget (1958), the authors have been able to give each one a rating in terms of the kind of mental operation it involved, if used in the form envisaged in the Teacher's Guides. They have shown that there was a steadier gradation of difficulty in the physics than in the chemistry course — many of the early topics being intelligible for pupils at the concrete operational stage, and most of those dealing in abstractions coming later in the course.

'Detailed information about the proportions of pupils in each age group who are confident (say) in formal operations has not yet been established, but on the best estimates available these two courses appear to be well adapted to the conceptual style of only the top five per cent of the school population if they are used from age 11, and in the manner described. Some topics within them have a much wider intelligibility and no doubt others, by adaptation of teaching method or adjustment of time of teaching, could be made to do so. This type of analysis is leading towards an understanding of why certain topics such as proportion in chemical calculations or surface area to volume relationships, and the use of a key for identifying organisms in biology, are difficult to teach as well as to learn in present day courses', Watson (1974, p. 37).

Reading readiness, a Piagetian enterprise*
L. Weisz, 1975

It is hypothesized that, in a reading readiness program, intervention with specific, hierarchially taught, Piagetian-based Symbol Training (Weisz, 1974, Think * A * Ling Programme) will prepare children better for visual discrimination of word forms than intervention with relevant but random symbol training (e.g. The Croft Program). After eleven weeks, an experimental and a control group of inner-city first grade children (E 18Ss, C 42Ss, and other first grade classes in the same school) were evaluated by three tests:

I   Test of Discrimination of Word Forms (adapted from Croft)
II Test of Discrimination of Piagetian-based Symbols (Weisz)
III Test of Discrimination of Word-Like Forms (from Slingerland)

The percentage of children achieving the criterion score for each test was tabulated and graphed. The means and standard deviations were compared. The results indicate that Piagetian-based Symbol Training can be more effective than eclectic symbol training. Furthermore, it appears probable that there are ten prereading concepts that are necessary before beginning instruction for letter recognition. These Piagetian subconcepts deal with 'directionality', which always evolves from a dot, the simplest mark extant. The perception of directionality seems to occur in a graded progression. It proceeds from a dot to simple symmetrical and then to complex asymmetrical or lateralized changes of the basic dot. All written symbol systems derive from similar variations of marks on a surface. Therefore, training with a Piagetian-based Symbol (Directionality) Series may prepare children to

---

* Written and prepared by the author for inclusion in this volume. Gratitude is extended to Dr Lillian Weisz of Multiple Choice Associates, Inc., Perceptual Discrimination Training, Rhode Island.

differentiate figures in all symbol systems. The instructions for such a program are so elementary that they can be given in 'any language' and to very young children.

The Pennsylvania State University Programme II — Cognitive Developmental*
S.L. Willis, 1975

Willis describes the rationale and activities of the Programme to be based on Piagetian theory and to be categorized into Social—Emotional, Cognitive and Psychomotor developments, with the proviso that Piaget views all phases of learning as a unified process of biological adaptation and that the classroom teacher incorporates all phases of development as a whole in the activities. The Programme is subject to continuous revision and is designed to meet each child at his present developmental level without the assumption that all children should reach the same stage of development within each school session. In elaboration, the emphasis is on giving children opportunities to attain objectives rather than the imposition of fixed requirements.

Within Social—Emotional Development objectives are given as a directive, as goals and reminders for teachers to present opportunities for poor cooperation within the context of many activities also having other objectives. Broad objectives include the increase of skills in interpersonal relationships and the development of intrapersonal skills, incorporating the development of self-management skills and the formation of a favourable self-concept. (Further details are set out in Willis, 1975).

Within the area of Cognitive Development efforts will be made to measure the attainment of objectives for the purposes of the improvement of the Programme. Piaget's delineation of the three areas of knowledge, namely logico-mathematical, social and physical (as interpreted by Kamii, 1970) have been followed. Logico-mathematical knowledge incorporates classification, seriation and number concepts. Recognition of feelings, personal naming-labeling, labeling physical properties of objects and number and letter symbols form the broad areas of objectives within Social knowledge. Physical knowledge refers to the child's receipt of feedback from objects when acted upon by the child and his realization that these objects react in a regular manner. The goal is to let the child discover for himself the consistency of the physical world and his manipulation of it. The verbalization of

* Gratitude is extended to Professor Sherry L. Willis of the Pennsylvania State University for sending her work to be abstracted.

predictions and results enables the teacher to understand his mental actions. Physical knowledge lesson plans include: air, sound, magnification, colour mixing, floating and sinking etc. Representation, actively constructing images, can be encouraged through socio-dramatic play, playdough, painting and blocks. (Detailed content of these objective areas is included in Willis, 1975).

Psychomotor Development includes the increase of control and coordination of the large muscles and gross bodily movements, the strength and agility in use of legs and the control and coordination of small muscles and fine motor skills. The opportunities will again be presented in the context of activities having other goals as well.

*Formative evaluation in a cognitive developmental programme for young children**
S.L. Willis, A.S. Cohen, and J.W. Clement, 1975

The authors describe the attempt to establish an evaluation system for the Cognitive Developmental Early Childhood Programme consistent with the Piagetian assessment approach.

With the understanding that evaluation systems may be categorized into three major types: diagnostic, summative and formative, the compatability between Piagetian methodology and formative evaluation was recognized. (Detailed discussion of these systems is given in Willis *et al.*, 1975).

The development of a formative evaluation system for the Programme is still in an early developmental stage but already has utility. The cognitive domain has been the goal area chosen for initial evaluation. For each curriculum component of Classification, Seriation, Number Concepts, Physical knowledge and Social knowledge a hierarchy of developmental levels has been derived from Piagetian theory and research. These levels are used to guide the teacher in both 'activity presentation and formative data collection'. The teacher asks questions or poses problems 'related to lower levels of the hierarchy and records the child's response before proceeding to higher levels . . . A data card is used to collect data on each activity taught within a given curriculum component' (A sample data card is included in Willis *et al.*, 1975) 'The teacher indicates with checks minuses each level of the hierarchy attempted and/or attained by each child during an activity. Additional comments noted about the child's responses aid in assessing his level of thinking; this information is entered in the column entitled "Comments". The numbers placed by children's names, curriculum components, titles of activities etc. serve as codes for computer storage and retrieval of the data'. (Further details are given in Willis *et al.*, 1975).

---

* Gratitude is extended to Professor Sherry L. Willis of the Pennsylvania State University for sending her work to be abstracted.

The evaluation system generates a series of computer print-outs or reports which provide data on the performance of each child and teacher for each curriculum component being evaluated. The output generated can be classified into three main areas: '1) performance data on each child, 2) performance data on each teacher across all children taught by her and 3) programmatic data concerning differential performance of children as a function of types of materials, instructional formats, etc.' (Elaboration is given in Willis *et al.*, 1975).

'In summary, such an evaluation system is believed to offer a significant contribution to Piagetian methodology and research and application of the theory in a variety of intervention contexts'.

PART TWO

Test Development

a. Introduction

Piaget's definition of intelligence is an *a priori* theoretical one, and it is largely irrelevant to him whether or not it leads to measures of situationally general and longitudinally stable individual differences, as do the traditional psychometric measures. Piaget himself has never been much interested in mental testing or in individual differences. However, his postulation of invariant sequential stages of development has provided a theoretical framework in which researchers have attempted standardization and quantification of Piagetian diagnostic tools and operational scales to assess mental development and predict individual differences in terms of the underlying psychological processes themselves and not merely of their results (Kohlberg, 1968).

Piaget as early as 1947 wrote, 'it is indisputable that these tests of mental age have on the whole lived up to what was expected of them: a rapid and convenient estimation of an individual's general level. But it is no less obvious that they simply measure a "yield" without reaching constructive operations themselves. As Pieron rightly pointed out, intelligence conceived in these terms is essentially a value judgment applied to complex behaviour. Inhelder was able to distinguish moronism from imbecility by the presence of concrete groupings and slight backwardness by an inability to reason formally. This is one of the first applications of a method which could be developed further for determining level of intelligence in general'.

Piaget expects tests based on his theory to theoretically and empirically define basic and general thought processes and assess their level 'better' than do psychometric tests. Psychometric tests assess only the products of thought while Piagetian tests get at the very process of cognition (Kohlberg and DeVries, 1969).

Piaget (1953, 1969) has further elaborated his views that traditional tests are concerned with quantitative measures of behaviour and do not penetrate to the actual qualitative operational mechanisms which govern the behaviour. Piaget therefore indicates that his problem-solving tasks define basic and general thought processes and assess their level more adequately than psychometric tests.

Pinard and Laurendeau (1964) have made one of the strongest contrasts of the Piagetian and traditional psychometric approaches to assessment: 'The usual tests comprise on the one hand problems whose intellectual content is extremely limited (for instance memory span), and on the other hand, problems whose solution requires the intervention of more truly intellectual factors (for example, "absurd" expressions) . . . Even supposing that they all depict the more significant dimensions of the mental function equally well, they are grouped in such a way that they can hardly serve to make known the child's intellectual growth much less intellectual evolution in general. From one age to the other, the problems under consideration are so different that it is impossible to compare validly results obtained by the same child in successive examinations. One is limited, therefore, to a comparison of one child's performance with that of others of the same age in a pattern of intellectual tasks chosen strictly on the basis of their statistical filiation. Thus one ends up with extremely artificial scales!'

Conceptual differences between Piagetian and psychometric conceptions of intelligence have been outlined by Elkind (1969) who maintained that the differences arise from the unique ways that each conception views intelligence and that they are focused on different aspects of intelligent behaviour. He commented on differences with respect to '(a) the type of genetic causality they presuppose; (b) the description of mental growth they provide; and (c) the contributions of nature and nurture which they assess'.

Lester, Muir and Dudek (1970 p. 285) maintained, 'The Piaget Tests seem to measure a range of structures wider than that of the traditional IQ tests. Orientational, spatial and time concepts are involved but also the ability of the child to separate himself from the objective world, to perceive himself from the objective world and to perceive himself as one element in an outside reality'. Stephens, McLaughlin, Miller and Glass (1972) maintained that the Piagetian reasoning tasks involve abilities separate from those measured by standard tests of intelligence and achievement. 'The possibility of unique contributions of Piagetian measurement to psychological assessment and practice is based upon the fact that Piagetian tasks are far richer than traditional forms of assessment in the data they provide about the behaviour of the individual child', Hathaway and Hathaway—Theunissen (1974). The authors continue 'and this greater richness is founded in turn upon the fact that data acquired through Piagetian assessment have meaning in the context of his theory of intelligence. In Piagetian psychometry the tasks are therefore structured and interpreted according to a logic rather than a mere statistical comparison with other children. As such, tasks embedded in the Piagetian developmental theory have the long sought after character of immediately relevant criterion measures of development. This promising criterion-referenced character of Piagetian measures can be made clearer by brief theoretical and empirical comparisons of the traditional psychometric and Piagetian approaches to assessment'.

b. Theoretical and empirical relationship between psychometric and Piagetian conceptions of intelligence

Piagetian tasks and IQ relationships have been reported to be low (Beard, 1960; Dodwell, 1960, 1962). Moderate ones have been demonstrated by Almy *et al.* (1966, 1970); Dudek, Lester, Goldberg and Dyer (1969) and Elkind (1961). Correlations between MA and Piagetian performance at a moderate level have been reported by Freyberg (1966), Kohlberg (1963) and Mannix (1960). Kohlberg and DeVries (1974) in a factor-analytic study demonstrated that Piagetian measures define factors separate from psychometric intelligence factors. In their study involving bright and average six-year-olds, Kohlberg and DeVries found three factors: (a) General psychometric intelligence (11 tests or subjects built from varied psychometric measures); (b) Conservation (liquid, length, ring segment); (c) Classification (sorting and class-inclusion).

Kohlberg and DeVries (*op. cit.*) and Stephens *et al.* (1969) analyses promote the dual suggestion that Piagetian tasks have an element of consistency related to the consistency among traditional tasks through general intelligence, but that the Piagetian tasks likewise, have other elements of consistency only slightly related to the aspects of consistency of traditional measures. Longeot's (1969) investigation involving 17-year-old Ss substantiated the former contention of the inference from Kohlberg's and Stephens' studies. The study by Ross (1971) lent support to the second issue of the earlier suggestion as did the study of Meyers and Orpet (1971).

Five interpretable factors were computed by Stephens, McLaughlin, Miller (1969 *op. cit.*) in the performance of 150 normal and retarded children aged from six to 18 years: (a) Verbal (13 Wechsler and three Wide Range Achievement Test variables); (b) Piagetian reasoning (23 Piagetian measures), CA, MA; (c) Classification (four class-inclusion tasks); (d) Spatial reasoning; (e) Performance (WISC Performance IQ and object assembly). In continuation Stephens McLaughlin, Miller and Glass (1972) noted the following seven factors in the same Ss four years later: (a) Verbal (six WISC verbal subtests and three Wide Range Achievement subscores); (b) Conservation (substance, weight, volume, length, liquid); (c) Performance (five WISC performance subtests); (d) Flexibility of thought processes (MA, CA, four Piagetian spatial reasoning measures); (e) Classification (three class-inclusion tests); (f) Mobility in dealing with concrete and abstract spatial relations (three tasks); (g) Transition from concrete to abstract operational thought (dissolution of sugar, conservation of weight and volume, class-inclusion, transfer from two to three dimensions, and changing mobile perspectives).

The data gathered by Dudek, Lester and Goldberg was analyzed by Hathaway (1973). Ss were 100 children aged from five through eight years of age. Three independent factors were computed: (a) WISC subtests, (b) Seven Piagetian tasks, (c) California Achievement Test subtests, a few WISC subtests, and four Piagetian tasks. Overall, some degree of overlap and some degree of non-overlap of psychometric and Piagetian measures of intelligence is demonstrated by the above studies. However findings remained unclear and Hathaway (1975) examined the question of the unique contributions of Piagetian measurement to diagnosis, prognosis and research of children's mental development in two stages. In the first part the main question considered from the viewpoint of the literature was: 'Is it logically and empirically possible for measurement based on Piagetian theory to add anything unique to what is already measurable by traditional psychometric techniques or does it yield just another, more time consuming and superfluous assessment of psychometric general intelligence?' In the second part four hypotheses dealing with the relationship of traditional psycho-metric and Piagetian assessment were tested. Hathaway maintained that the unique aspects of Piagetian measurement gave promise of unique contributions in three major areas of concern: Education, Clinical practice and Research. In the second part, 104 school children from a homogeneous middle class environment were tested. All Ss yielded data on 21 traditional psychometric and 10 Piagetian variables as well as on 10 scholastic achievement variables. The results indicated that there was a moderate, positive, and statistically significant relationship between the traditional psychometric and the Piagetian measures of mental development. While both types of measures contributed to a first 'general-psychometric and verbally-mediated intelligence' factor, this aspect of mental functioning was largely defined by the psychometric measures. (Fuller details appear later).

Further studies include: Brown (1973); DeVries, (1973); Keating (1973), and Modgil, Dielmann, Cattell and Modgil (1976 described later). However, Webb (1974) contended, 'Perhaps the most comprehensive position is that of Kohlberg and DeVries (1974) who argue that the traditional IQ test has been refined to maximize the contribution of an hereditary component of intelligence roughly equivalent to Spearman's "g", while Piagetian tasks reflect more of the experimental side of an interactive process of intellectual growth and, therefore, might be more relevant to educational assessment. Using a factor-analytic study of six-year-olds, Kohlberg and DeVries (1974) showed that all tests loaded on a first factor which appeared to be "g", but that the Piagetian tests also constituted a second factor which accounted for independent variance. Thus, the Piagetian tasks are related to intelligence in the psychometric sense, but are also independent. Kohlberg and DeVries . . . as well as Brown (1973) interpret the age-related nature of Piagetian tasks as reflecting the time required for experience rather than a maturational factor. With the possible exception of Keating (1973), none of the recent writers have implied that their conclusions might depend on the developmental stage of the child — a surprising omission for people who, for the most part, claim to take Piaget seriously. It is highly probable that the relation of Piagetian measures and IQ tests depends on an interaction of the stage of the child and the tasks selected. If the major Piagetian stages had biological constraints which were essentially maturational in nature, one would not expect a child — no matter how bright in the IQ sense — to develop, say, concrete operations much before the age at which average children do so. However, once the capacity for particular operations were obtained how quickly the new structures were extended to subtle problems might well be a function of IQ (*cf.* Lovell and Shields, 1967). Such an interpretation of the nature of Piagetian stages and the phenomenon of horizontal *décalage* is somewhat unorthodox from a Piagetian point of view where operations are identified with the tasks and implies an underlying competence which is only imperfectly measured by a sample of tasks', p. 294.

The relationship between Piaget's qualitative view and the conventional one is advanced by Tuddenham's (1970) comment 'that conservation tasks correlate more highly when conservation items have more in common with respect to content, a contention that is borne out in the fairly substantial correlations among conservation items that characterize Goldschmid's results. Tuddenham concludes that the notion of conservation, that is, invariance under transformations such as seeing that a change in shape does not alter the amount of plasticine, acts as a sort of general factor, a view that was put forward by Hunt as early as 1961 . . . What Tuddenham is saying is that although tests of conservation would have their principal loading on a general factor, there are significant areas of school performance for which they would have little predictive significance. This seems to be the reasoning behind the construction of the new British Intelligence Scale. The compilers have decided to include items based on the work of Piaget and others so as to obtain scores which also show the qualitative level of thinking attained. In discussing the inclusion of such items in the new test, Warburton (1970) states that while logical operations and sequences can be readily discerned in some areas of ability, it is extremely difficult to extend these concepts to all types of ability and to write appropriate items . . . Tuddenham seems to be moving towards a position where he sees conservation as a manifestation of "g", while those constructing the new British Intelligence Scale seem to see logical operations as a further group factor contributing a qualitative component to a general assessment of intelligence. Both agree, however, that the effect of the progressive development of logical operations or logical structures can be more readily identified as they operate in areas of a logico-mathematical nature and both see the assessment of ability as a multifactor problem . . . "the evidence thus far obtained has about extinguished what hope we might once have held that we could place each child on a single developmental continuum to MA and from this predict his performance on content of whatever kind" ', McNally (1973, pp. 61–2).

The British Intelligence Scale is the first individual test of general intelligence to be developed in Britain. Elliott (1975) * stated, 'It should be said at the outset that there is some force in many of the arguments against intelligence testing. These arguments, however, are based to a large extent on the weaknesses of existing measuring techniques and upon their use (and indeed misuse). In particular, group-administered tests have been heavily criticized, especially for their use in secondary school selection procedures. Perhaps when any such technique becomes an instrument of social policy it is bound to become stigmatized by association if that policy becomes unpopular. The criticism of the use of so-called "IQ" tests in school settings, particularly for the purpose of classifying or categorizing individuals, has led to a more general scepticism regarding the value of intelligence tests. Nevertheless, the British Intelligence Scale is not a group-administered test, and its intended primary function is certainly not to classify or categorize children . . . the scale will not be an "IQ" test as such, as the name of the project might misleadingly imply. The research project is still in the middle of its course, and the various tests which together form the BIS are still in various stages of development and

* Gratitude is extended to Drs Colin Elliott, David Murray and Lea Pearson of the University of Manchester for sending their work to be referenced.

analysis . . . However, if the BIS even partially succeeds in its major aim of being a test of special abilities, it will represent a marked advance on any previously published test and hopefully will enable psychologists to define strengths and weaknesses in the abilities of a child with greater precision and with greater confidence and scientific rigour than is currently possible', p. 460. Murray (1975)* suggested that while 'we cannot hope to construct perfect Rasch subscales for the BIS, in spite of inevitable violations of the model, our hopes for objective scaling by the Rasch model are realistic', p. 25.

In the proposed profile of subscales in the 'BIS' there is a total of 22 subscales and the age range is from two years to 16 years. The 'Formal Operational Thinking' subscale is designed for children from eight to 16 years and is based on Piagetian model, measuring formal logical reasoning. It will be noted that the 'Butch and Slim' items (Ward, 1972; Ward and Pearson, 1973), discussed in Volume Three in the series *Piagetian Research,* have been replaced. The 'Number Concepts' subscale which is Piagetian based includes the concepts of conservation, seriation and reversibility (CA = two to 16 years). The 'Social Reasoning' subscale for children aged five to 16 years involves reasoning about hypothetical social situations. The intent is to produce assessment of development in concrete operational and formal operational thinking, on Piagetian lines. Other subscales are: Block Design; Comprehension; Cubes; Delayed Memory for Objects; Digit Span; Ideational Fluency; Information; Matrices; Number Computation; Picture Vocabulary; Reading; Recall of Designs; Recognition; Similarities; Speed of Problem Solving; Tactile Testing; Visual-Motor; Visual-Spatial; and Vocabulary.

In a paper entitled: 'Developmental Scales in the British Intelligence Scale', Pearson (1975) * concluded, 'No test developer can legislate for the use that will be made of his materials when they are published, and many users may wish to preserve the veil of secrecy; for those who do not, or who would be interested to experiment with a more direct interactive approach to their clients when appropriate, it is hoped that the inclusion of developmental scales will be a helpful, progressive measure, of growing value as validation studies and linked programmes are developed after the publication of the BIS', p. 22.

*   Gratitude is extended to Drs Colin Elliott, David Murray and Lea Pearson of the University of Manchester, for sending their work to be referenced.

c. Piagetian tasks and school achievement

Kaufman (1971) maintains 'Analysis of the tasks used in Piaget's and Gesell's experiments provides one tangible method of learning more about their over-all systems — the interactionist theory of Piaget and the maturationist viewpoint of Gesell. A comparison of the interrelationships among their independently conceived tasks, and an evaluation of the relationships of these tasks to other pertinent variables, might tell much about the psychological meaning of the tasks themselves and, hence, about the theories in which these tasks are rooted'. The data gathered were subjected to a correlation analysis with the following results: the Piaget test and the Gesell school readiness tests correlated fairly well with Lorge-Thorndike mental age and IQ, teething level, chronological age, and Warner's revised scale of father's occupations. (Details of the study appear in Modgil, 1974, pp. 388–9).

In continuation, to compare the effectiveness of tests built from tasks devised by Gesell and Piaget as predictors of first grade achievement, Kaufman and Kaufman (1972) tested 80 children on the Gesell School Readiness Tests, a battery of Piagetian tests, the Lorge-Thorndike Intelligence Tests and the Stanford Achievement Test. The tests were found to be excellent predictors of achievement: the Piaget and Gesell batteries each correlated .64 with Stanford Achievement Test Composite; the Lorge-Thorndike MA correlated .58. A measure of kindergarten teething level proved to be a poor predictor of achievement. (Details follow).

Piaget-based tests likewise, have been shown to be good predictors of arithmetic achievement (Dodwell, 1961; Freyberg, 1966) and of achievement in a variety of school subjects (Almy, Chittenden, and Miller, 1966; Goldschmid and Bentler, 1968; Stephens, Miller and McLaughlin, 1969). 'However, most previous studies either evaluated a Piagetian test of limited coverage or used criteria of achievement that

were not at the same levels of psychometric excellence and broad
curricular coverage as a major achievement battery such as Stanford
Achievement Test', Kaufman and Kaufman (*ibid.,* p. 532). However,
the longitudinal study by Dudek, Lester, Goldberg and Dyer (1969) is
an exception. The authors administered nine of Pinard and
Laurendeau's (1964) tests to 100 kindergarten children to obtain a
broad base of evaluation on Piagetian concepts. Total score on these
tests correlated .63 with composite achievement on the California
Achievement Test in first grade, proving to be best of four predictors
(including two intelligence tests). This strong correlation together with
the virtually identical correlation of the Piagetian battery with the
Stanford Achievement Test in Kaufman and Kaufman's study (*op. cit.*)
lends credence that tests derived from Piaget's tasks are effective
predictors of achievement in school subjects. 'Clearly, tests based on
Piaget's theory would seem to be useful for conventional curriculums
and need not be restricted to those curriculums with a specific Piagetian
orientation,' Kaufman and Kaufman, (*ibid.,* p. 532).

Relationships among Piagetian, IQ, and achievement assessments
were studied by DeVries (1974). The study involved 143 bright and
average children within the age range from five to seven. Factor
analyses of performance on the California Test of Mental Maturity,
Metropolitan Achievement Test, Stanford-Binet, and 15 Guttman-
scaled Piaget-type tasks demonstrated that Piagetian, IQ, and
achievement tests overlapped to some degree, 'but also measure
different aspects of cognitive functioning', p. 746. (Details are given
later).

A developmental index of numerical cognitive performance was
undertaken by Larson (1972) ' . . . objective was to derive several of the
basic characteristics of cognitive – developmental tests from a review
of . . . existing measures and Piaget's theory, and to adapt these basic
constructs to a simplified test form in the area of number concepts
which would be useful in the classroom and still retain a close
correspondence with Piagetian measures themselves'. The operations of
classification, seriation and analogies were cast in the form of subtests
and each of the subtests was divided into a gradient of six levels of
perceptual structure hypothesized to affect the difficulty of numerical
conceptual performance on an array of stimuli. A total of 36 items
were administered to a sample of 46 kindergarten, first and second
grade children. The Wechsler Intelligence Scale for Children (Verbal
Scale) together with a replication of standard Piagetian number
development tasks in conservation and seriation were additionally given
to the Ss. Larson concluded, ' . . . that the cognitive operations and
levels of performance were in general correctly organized . . . the test
was characterized as a homogeneous measure of numerical cognitive

performance highly related to Piagetian number constructs, and correlating significantly with arithmetic ability over and above its relationship to IQ ability'. (Details follow).

Russell (1973) was intent to use a criterion based on Piaget's theory of cognitive development as an alternative criterion to either IQ test scores or achievement test scores for evaluating the effect of pre-school experiences upon the child in the first grade '. . . whether children in the first grade would differ significantly in their scores on the Piaget tests dependent upon whether they had or had not participated in a kindergarten or some other pre-school programme'. Eight Piagetian tasks were administered to first grade Ss. Group one, comprised children who had been in kindergarten; group two, children who had been in Head Start; group three, children with no pre-school experience; and group four children who were repeating first grade. Results demonstrated that children who had pre-school experience tended to perform at higher levels of Piagetian tasks than children who had no such experience. (Details are given later).

d. Standardization of Piagetian tasks

Flavell (1963) has stated, 'Piaget has never bent his talents towards making standardized intelligence tests out of the innumerable cognitive tasks he has created during his professional life time. But such an endeavour would surely be a logical extension of his work and there is some activity in this direction both in Geneva and elsewhere'.

Meyers (1972) has reviewed the major efforts which have attempted to create standardized Piagetian conceptual development tests appropriate to the various Piagetian stages, and Wolff (1974, p. 5) focusing on criticisms of standardized tests hypothesizes the consequences of a possible development of a 'Piaget Developmental Quotient'.

Attempts to 'psychometrize' Piaget include among others Tuddenham (1970), Uzgiris and Hunt (1974) which involve the construction of instruments with traditional psychometric standards of scalability and reliability built from Piagetian tasks. 'While the work with sensorimotor and concrete operations has met with some success, there is clearly no comprehensive Piagetian test of intelligence available at the moment, and relevance of those scales which have been constructed to non-test behaviours or later states has yet to be established', Webb (1974 p. 293). Elkind (1974) contended that ' . . . while there is no question that a scale of Piagetian tasks could be used to differentiate among individuals, it is questionable whether such a scale would be as useful as one which provides a broader profile of individual performance.' 'The skeptic must go further and note that if Piaget were really correct about the universality of his operations, the possibility of such a scale would be by no means obvious', Webb (*op. cit.*, p. 293).

Hathaway and Hathaway-Theunissen (1974) have maintained that 'The ultimate goals of such measurement devices based upon Piaget's developmental theory will be to diagnose not only how rapidly a child acquires particular skills in comparison to other children but also to discover how the child learns, how his intellect develops, where he stands with respect to a scale of development, and, eventually, to make prognosis of how we may best foster his development to advance research supporting both these aims'.

Pinard and Laurendeau's (1964) longitudinal project with a group of 700 French Canadian subjects had two main objectives: to verify the existence of Piaget's stages of mental development, and to construct an ordinal scale of mental development applicable to children aged two to 12 years. A total of 57 subtests together with some 300 behavioural items, designed to elicit mental strategies, are included. The subtests comprise 24 tests of sensorimotor coordination, eight tests of verbal comprehension and 25 Piagetian tasks. Interim results confirm the existence of Piaget's stages. 'However, in certain cases it may well be necessary to eliminate certain levels which the test fails to justify, or perhaps more frequently, to add new ones in order to take into account some totally new answers which apparently cannot be integrated with Piaget's established stages, and which seem authentically to characterize new levels of development'. It is interesting to note that the various developmental stages are generally acquired at slightly later ages by French Canadian children than by the Swiss children. (More recently, Dudek *et al.*, 1969, administered nine tests from the battery devised by Pinard and Laurendeau in their investigation into the relationship of Piaget measures to standard intelligence and motor skills. The tests were found to be equally effective in predicting achievement in young children).

Tuddenham (1968) is engaged in developing a cognitive scale based on Piaget's theoretical formulations. To date, they have made extensive explorations of 15 items on a sample of 350 children of junior school age range with a wide spectrum of socioeconomic levels. Piagetian concepts of quantity, area, number, length, spatial reversals, classification and the transitivity-of-length problem, as studied by Smedslund (1963) are included. Situations in which the child's reasoning may be inferred from what he does rather than from what he says are being established. Some attempt is also being made to develop easier methods of test administration and scoring. Some built-in checks upon the child's understanding of the relational terms 'more', 'less', 'the same', 'longer', 'shorter' are also being examined.

Tuddenham's provisional results indicate that it is possible to categorize children's behaviour patterns into the three Piagetian stages. Their data show some superiority of boys over girls, especially on transitivity, perspectives and most of the conservation items. Race and socioeconomic status were correlated and Negroes did less well than

Whites on every test and on certain tests, the difference is significant at the .01 level. The results also showed intercorrelations between items which, to date, are available only for the sample of 200 children. Although occasional values are as high as .4 and some conservation items intercorrelate .65, the values are generally around .25. 'Data strongly suggest that the attainment of concrete operations on one problem is no guarantee that the child will achieve a comparable level when another problem is posed'.

Tuddenham has partially succeeded in producing a standardized format. However, he states 'I must confess as a differential psychologist, that I am pleased rather than dismayed that the intractable individuality of human beings, which has plagued normative psychologists since Bessel tried to eliminate individual differences in reaction time, continues to assert itself, even in the face of Piaget's elegant normative theory' (Tuddenham, 1969, cited in Cockrell (Ed.), 1970, p.70).

The Nuffield Foundation (1968) have devised 'Check ups' based on Piaget research, the aim of which is stated as ' . . . to try and show that children acquire concepts gradually and to point the difficulties that they are likely to encounter during their progress'. The Foundation maintain that the 'Check Ups' are not tests and that 'there is no question of "right" or "wrong" or marking. They are simply to be given to the children as and when the teacher feels the need to know how far their thinking has progressed'.

The aim of the Social Science Research Council Project (1969—70): 'The Development of Systematic Thinking' under the guidance of Lunzer at Nottingham University is to 'establish a firm body of data on how children progress from intuitive reasoning to systematic thought. One side of the work involves administering a fairly extensive number of individual tests to children at two ages, five and seven to eight. The results of these tests of logical thinking will be compared with various measures of scholastic performance. Particular attention will be paid to the effect of home and school environment, as well as the factor of language development'. A longitudinal follow-up is envisaged to measure the environmental effects on subsequent development. Furthermore, the results, 'should help to clarify the educational significance of laboratory studies on concept development and logical thought'. It is hoped that the data might assist in the construction of a standardized battery of Piagetian tests to assess the development of effective intelligence. (See also Lunzer, 1971—72, 1972, 1973; Lunzer *et al.,* 1973).

The National Children's Bureau (1975) * has devised a develop-

---

*   Gratitude is extended to Margaret Sparrow of the National Children's Bureau, London, for sending the work to be referenced.

mental chart, five to nine years which includes skills and concepts learnt and acquired during the age range. The chart is arranged in six parts, each of which covers a different area of development: motor development, social behaviour, emotional development, development of independence, development of intellectual skills and general information, within the category of intellectual skills, items have been drawn from the work of Piaget.

'The Concept Assessment Kit – Conservation' developed by Goldschmid and Bentler (1968b) was based on Piaget's Systematic developmental theory of cognitive structure depicting a stage-by-stage progress of a child's thinking. 'The Kit measures the concept of conservation which is seen to represent a pivotal construct in the child's cognitive transition from the "pre-operational" stage to "concrete operations". This reflects Piaget's observation that with increasing age the child tends to rely relatively more on such abstract concepts as quantity, volume, and weight and relatively less on such specific attributes of the stimulus object as form and shape. The comprehension of this principle of constancy signals the transition from a prelogical to a logical phase of development. When a child is able to conserve, he realizes that certain properties, such as substance, weight, volume, or number, remain unchanged in the face of certain transformations, such as changing an object's form, shape, colour, or position. Items in the Kit assess such conservation behaviour, i.e., can the child indicate whether a transformation leaves a characteristic of an object the same, as well as assessing his comprehension of the principle involved. While some investigators who have used test materials similar to those of Piaget have successfully validated many of his observations, few attempts have been made to construct standardized procedures to assess these concepts. The Concept Assessment Kit provides such procedures and introduces a psychometrically sound method of measuring conservation . . . The child's level of conservation will serve as an indication of his general development of concept formation, of his readiness to fully comprehend school-related academic subjects, and his verbal ability. Several studies have indicated that conservation is correlated with other cognitive concepts (especially transitivity, probability, and perspective), achievement in school (especially arithmetic and science), mental age, vocabulary, and personality characteristics typically thought of as enhancing cognitive functioning and interpersonal relationships', Goldschmid and Bentler (*op. cit.*).

The Kit consists of three Forms: A, B and C. Forms A and B are parallel forms including tasks measuring conservation of two-dimensional space, number, substance, quantity and weight and discontinuous quantity. Form C measures a slightly different dimension of conservation including conservation of area and length. These assessments could be employed in the classroom situation. The authors describe their scales as 'measures of a general concept of conservation – like a general factor of factor analysis'; and provide strong psychometric evidence to support their interpretation. The Conservation Assessment Kit has been administered in the investigations by Wasik and Wasik (1971) and Harasym, Boersma and Maguire (1971), both described in Modgil, 1974, pp. 75–6 and 55–6 respectively. Figurelli and Keller (1972, p. 296) report: 'It should be noted that all mean scores, with the exception of the post-test scores for the middle class trained group, were somewhat lower than those found in the preliminary norms of the Concept Assessment Kit – Conservation'. However, Fleck (1972) reports encouraging evidence in support of the Kit in an investigation of the relationship of field-independence – dependence and verbal mediation – non-mediation to Piagetian conservation behaviour. Likewise, Goldschmid, Bentler, Kohnstamm, Modgil *et al.* (1973) administered the Conservation Assessment Kit (Scale A) to 25 boys and 25 girls at each age level from four to eight, comprising a total sample of 250 children in each of eight countries. The Concept Assessment Kit appeared to be a reliable indicator of conservation across several cultural groups. (Details of the study appear in Volume Eight in the present series *Piagetian Research*).

A study of the reliability and factor composition of the Concept Assessment Kit – Conservation (Goldschmid and Bentler, 1968b) was undertaken by Galbraith (1975) through the administration of Forms A and B in a counterbalanced manner to 32 girls between the ages of six years four months to seven years four months. The high reliabilities lend weight to the contention that the general format of the Concept Assessment Kit – Conservation is a legitimate method of testing Piaget's theory. 'Objective questioning, standardized patterns of object manipulations and standardized questioning techniques do allow reliable data to be collected. The clustering of variables on the factor analysis indicated that the test has reasonable construct validity. For future research purposes it would be appropriate for the format of the Concept Assessment Kit – Conservation to be adopted. The use of more diverse conservation tasks would be useful in helping to estimate further the degree to which conservation is a generalized or specific ability', Galbraith (*ibid.*, p. 7721–A). (Details follow).

The expediency of such a battery is given further credence by the prolific number of recent researches employing the tests for the Piagetian variable: Boland (1973); Briggs and Elkind (1973); Carlson and Michalson (1973); Clayton (1975); Firlik (1975); Gaudia (1972); Goldschmid and Bentler (1968); Hamel and Riksen (1973); Harris (1974); Holland and Palermo (1975); Hurta (1973); Murray (1972); Pimm (1974); Rardin and Moan (1971); Rosenthal and Zimmerman

(1972); Rubin, Attewell, Tierney and Tumolo (1973); Swize (1972); Than (1974); Thorne (1975); Tumolo (1973); Vicente and Finley (1974); and Zimmerman and Rosenthal (1974, modified version only). However, the Kit has been criticized by DeVries and Kohlberg (1969).

e. Infant sensorimotor scales

Scales of infant psychological development have been constructed within the framework of Piagetian concepts. Such scales have attempted to detect the differentiation of aspects of sensorimotor capabilities, rather than to summarize behavioural competencies of the infant by attaining a single score. In this respect, the efforts have been geared to account for the individual variation among infants in terms of diverse experiences rather than biological factors (Hunt, 1961). Piaget (1967, 1971) however, has pointed out, the differentiation and elaboration of all behaviours, while contingent upon experience, still spring from biological origins.

During the sixties Bell (1968), Casati and Lézine (1968), Escalona and Corman (1967), Gouin-Décarie (1965) and Uzgiris and Hunt (1966) have built infant sensorimotor scales (or series) based on many of Piaget's (1952, 1954) informal experiments with his own children, elaborated in the *Origins of Intelligence in Children* and *The Construction of Reality in the Child*. Corman and Escalona (1969) stated that the rationale for use of the scales is to assess the method and means that infants employ to solve problems.

Bell's (1968) scale of person and object permanence consists of an 11-step scale which is a finely graded series of items that makes it possible to place the S within each of Piaget's stages between stage three, secondary circular reactions, and stage six, the beginning of thought, or in transitional positions between the major stages. Parallel sets of items are used to evaluate the development of person and object permanence. To assess person permanence the adult (mother) or the E hides from the infant behind furniture, doors, or blanket screens. To assess object permanence, small, interesting, unfamiliar toys are hidden under washcloth screens lying on floor during hiding.

Kopp, Sigman, and Parmelee (1974) maintained that all the

sensorimotor scales have limitations. However, Casati and Lézine's (1968) scales meet certain important criteria: it is fairly comprehensive, evaluates sufficient components of sensorimotor stages, is relatively easy to administer and score, and takes a reasonably short time. Further, that the series has been utilized with a large sample of French infants; 'however, the data were obtained cross-sectionally from a heterogeneous sample (Lézine, Stambak, and Casati, 1969)', Kopp, Sigman and Parmelee (*ibid.,* p. 687).

Gouin-Décarie (1965) has developed a standardized version of Piaget's methods and applied it to 90 children, ranging in age from three to 20 months. Her findings concerning object permanence substantiated Piaget's descriptions in all essentials.

Uzgiris and Hunt (1966) stated that their measure 'IPDS' is a provisional instrument and this, in fact, is true of all the sensorimotor scales. 'The scales as well as the theory from which they were derived remain to be validated. Data are insufficient concerning their age, and there are few longitudinal studies. Furthermore, most of the reported research has dealt with only one aspect of sensorimotor behaviour, that relating to object permanence. It is probable that other sensorimotor behaviours may be equally important', Kopp, Sigman, and Parmelee (*ibid.,* p. 687). These latter authors therefore examined a number of aspects of sensorimotor development in a group of normally developing infants from a relatively homogeneous environment. (The study is described more appropriately in Volume One, in the series *Piagetian Research*). In continuation, Uzgiris and Hunt (1974) employed Piaget's schemata as a basis for the construction of the 'Visual Pursuit and Permanence of Objects' series. This 16- task scale is designed to reflect the different, and presumed ordinal, levels of object concept development from 0 to two years of age. The tasks involve showing an infant an object of interest and then placing the object directly under one cover, under super-imposed covers, or under two or three covers consecutively, the child's task being to find the object. The more advanced tasks require placing the object in a small container, moving the container under one or more covers; leaving the object under a cover, then showing the child the empty container, and asking S to find the object. Uzgiris and Hunt computed nearly perfect ordinality scores for the developmental series. Paraskevopoulos and Hunt (1971) have demonstrated that a modified version of the Uzgiris and Hunt scales discriminated between children raised at home and those raised in institutional environments which differed in number of caretakers. However, Miller, Cohen, and Hill (1970) cast doubt on the methodology of the Uzgiris and Hunt study: 'There are several potential problems in the Uzgiris and Hunt methodology . . . which make interpretation of task performance difficult and which rule out

unequivocal support for either Piaget's (1954) theory, or for the
ordinality of the particular 16 tasks studied', p. 61.

In the Kopp, Sigman, and Parmelee (1974) study few significant
intercorrelations were noted between performance level on one subtest
and performance on another subtest. King and Seegmiller (1973,
described later) reported similar findings with the Uzgiris and Hunt
(1966) sensorimotor scales, although they did obtain a higher
percentage of significant intercorrelations. 'Several variables may
explain the low number of intercorrelations found in both studies.
Infants do show more advanced stage-related behaviours sooner on one
subtest than on another. In part this is a function of the structure of
the subtests used in this study. For example, the greatest amount of
task structure occurred in the search for hidden object subtest, and the
infants did reach stage six quite early. In this particular subtest the
infant does not have to be involved with actively manipulating the test
object and is not distracted by any concurrent activities associated with
manipulation and exploration. In some of the other subtests there was
considerably less task structure and more opportunity for the infant to
play. Furthermore, if a task required not only that the infant make the
appropriate response but also inhibit an inappropriate action such as
pulling an incorrect string, then stage progression was also slower . . . In
addition, in the object and support subtest, the infants found the pivot
so fascinating that they ignored their original goal of using the pivot to
obtain a toy and instead played extensively with the pivot. Koslowski
and Bruner (1972) found similar behaviour when testing infants on a
task using a rotating level', Kopp, Sigman, and Parmelee (*ibid.*, p. 694).

In a study entitled, 'Performance of 14- to 22-month-old black,
firstborn male infants on two tests of cognitive development: The
Bayley Scales and the Infant Psychological Development Scale', King
and Seegmiller (*op. cit.*) examined their respective developments. 'The
mean Bayley Mental Score was elevated at 14 months but fell to a level
similar to the standardization sample at 18 months and remained stable
to 22 months. The mean Bayley Psychomotor Score was significantly
greater than that of the standardization sample at all three age levels.
Variability on both the Bayley Mental and Psychomotor Scales was
small at 14 months and increased significantly with age to equal the
standardization sample at 22 months. The Mental Scale showed good
predictive validity, while the Psychomotor Scale showed almost none.
The Uzgiris and Hunt Infant Psychological Developmental Scale appears
to measure specific abilities and to be most applicable below 18 months
of age. Individually, the scales showed almost no predictive validity.
The Bayley Mental Scale showed the greatest number of intercorrelations with all other scales at all age levels. With increasing age,
vocalization and verbal ability became more important determinants of

test performance', (*ibid.*, p. 317). (Details follow).

Performance on the Infant Psychological Development Scales 'IPDS' (Uzgiris and Hunt, *op. cit.*) cannot be measured against a standardization sample, as none exists. 'In future administration of these scales, more discriminatory power would likely be obtained if they were scored not simply pass—fail as Uzgiris and Hunt (1966) indicated and as was done in this study but according to ease of passing as well (Wachs *et al.*, 1971). Furthermore, a better standardization of procedures and materials is needed. However as a first approximation, these data show the subscales to be highly independent as measured by the relatively low degree of intercorrelation among them at all three age levels. Moreover, each subscale seems to be unstable in terms of predictive validity (test-retest) at the ages employed here. As the subscales were reported to have high reliability for scoring and for very brief test-retest reliability (Uzgiris and Hunt, 1966), it is likely that the poor predictive validity results from uneven cognitive growth', King and Seegmiller (*op. cit.*, p. 325).

Lewis (1974) in an article entitled: 'Infant intelligence tests: their use and misuse', argued that, '... If one were affecting object permanence capacity in the young infant by such interventions as peek-a-boo games and showing the children how to find hidden objects, then the type of measurement should not be the Peabody Picture Vocabulary Test or some other verbal task, but rather a specific measure of sensorimotor capacity such as the object permanence scales developed by Hunt and Uzgiris (1966) or Escalona and Corman (1967). Note that King and Seegmiller's (1971) results would argue against using the entire sensorimotor scales since they are not all necessarily related to object permanence', p. 116.

'During infancy ... the few studies providing data concerning the correlations between these scales have not only generated findings at variance with each other, but yielded correlations discrepant from those found during subsequent years (Décarie, 1965; Golden and Birns, 1968; King and Seegmiller, 1973; Lewis and McGurk, 1972). It has been argued that methodological and statistical limitations in these infant studies account for the inconsistent outcomes and such limitations preclude an adequate test of the concurrent relationship between psychometric and Piagetian sensorimotor scales (see Gottfried, 1974; Wilson, 1973). Some of the more critical flaws discussed involve (a) failing to control for age, (b) using psychometric tests which were not standardized on the samples studied, (c) variable rather than constant interperiod time intervals between psychometric and Piagetian testing sessions, and (d) correlation analyses conducted with a lack of variation of test scores', Gottfried and Brody (1975, pp. 379—80). The latter authors therefore in an article entitled, 'Interrelationships between and correlates of psychometric and Piagetian scales of sensorimotor intelligence', were intent to determine the extent to which psychometric and Piagetian scales correlate during infancy and to study the nomological (i.e., correlational) networks of these scales and the degree to which their networks are similar. The sensorimotor scales included the Bayley Scale (Bayley, 1969) and the Escalona—Corman Object Permanence Scale (Corman and Escalona, 1969) and the Uzgiris—Hunt Development of Schemas in Relation to Objects Scale (Uzgiris and Hunt, 1966). Motor development, socio-environmental variables, activity and interaction with objects, and physical development were also evaluated. 'Correlational analyses on 207 infants (mean age 11 months) showed that (a) the correlations between psychometric (i.e. Bayley mental scale) and Piagetian scales were positive, moderate and significant and (b) both types of scales yielded virtually identical correlational networks. Motor and physical development and activity level correlated postively and significantly with sensorimotor development, while socio-environmental variables and measures of interaction with objects accounted for a negligible portion of variance on sensorimotor development. The data indicated that psychometric and Piagetian sensorimotor scales are measures of the same construct. Placing these findings into perspective with the literature on the correlates of intelligence during the later ages provided insight into the failure of infant tests to predict subsequent intellectual functioning', Gottfried and Brody (*ibid.*, p. 379). (Details follow). It is interesting to note that with respect to the Piagetian sensorimotor scales, Gottfried and Brody did not support the findings of Wachs, Uzgiris and Hunt (1971), in which social class was found to be related to operativity on Piagetian scales. However, the resultant patterns supported the results by Golden and Birns (1968) and Lewis and Wilson (1972). These investigators argued that there were no social class differences in sensorimotor development as assessed by either psychometric or Piagetian scales.

In relation to early cognitive development Buss and Royce (1975, p. 98) asserted, 'In considering an individual differences approach to cognitive processes which makes use of a particular methodology, that is, factor analysis . . . it is possible to put the concepts of differentiation and hierarchical integration on a firm empirical foundation'. (The above studies have also been discussed more fully and appear more appropriately within Volume One in the series *Piagetian Research*. See also Modgil, 1974, Chapter Two, pp. 19—30).

f. Psychometric and questionnaire approaches and Piaget's 'clinical' method

Introduction

Many writers have commented upon the common ground between the approaches of developmental psychologists such as Piaget and the work of psychometrists. Elkind (1969) for example, pointed out the strong emphasis that both place upon the process of logical reasoning. Ward (1972) considers that provided a liberal psychometric attitude can be adopted, some of Piaget's experimental situations form a potential source of items which possess the advantage of having a definite rationale. For this reason, the new British Intelligence Scale (Warburton, 1970) provided for the incorporation of materials and procedures from developmental psychology into a multi-factorial framework.

Tuddenham (1970) commented that Piaget's influence upon the mental test movement has been negligible as this *methode clinique*, which enables one to shape the dialogue to the responses of the particular child, is almost antithetical to the traditional mental test emphases upon objectivity, standardization and quantification. However, when one's purpose is not to formulate or substantiate a normative theory, but rather to compare different children under identical conditions, the method of inquiry must not itself risk introducing variability into the results. Moreover, the interrogation required to elucidate the qualitative subtleties of a child's thinking about a single problem, takes too long for the psychologist to sample any variety in a session of reasonable length. When interested in human variability, related to Piaget, it seems appropriate to convert Piagetian experiments into test items meeting strict psychometric criteria, while conserving in so far as possible the essence of the original problems. Tuddenham's method therefore attempted to synthesize Piagetian theory with methods derived from mental tests: for assessing the readiness of particular children for specific educational experience within the context of the Piaget-inspired curricula; for developing appropriate psychometric instruments for making independent evaluations of acceleration attempts; to serve the traditional interest of differential psychologists in the relationships between the variables of age, sex, social class and cognitive level, by providing more extensive data on these problems and with content freer from cultural bias than Stanford-Binet or WISC. A Piagetian psychometric approach might further contribute to a reconstruction of the theory of intelligence, as well as to its measurement. Piaget's demonstration of the logical identity of superficially dissimilar cognitive problems suggested that the logical formulation of items might provide a more definable and systematic basis for item selection than the most haphazard item compilations which comprise the Binet and derivatives. Further, Piaget's contribution might provide a basis for constructing a measure of general ability founded not upon empirical curves of percentages passing, but upon a general theory of cognitive development. Such a measure, if successful, might diagnose a child's cognitive status more precisely than MA or IQ and imply the instructional approach best suited to his needs.

i. Approaches with younger children

Tuddenham's presentation (with children from the kindergarten and first four grades) included multiple-choice items which required the child to select from among several photographs, the one which shows how a small farm would look from various vantage points (spatial). Also presented in multiple-choice format were problems involving the horizontality of water levels, and the identification of the flat patterns which can be folded to produce three-dimensional forms. Tuddenham considers that his items embody the essential idea of the corresponding Piagetian experiments in a much more objective and quantifiable format.

Tanaka, Campbell and Helmick (1970) prepared two forms of experimental materials for 'first graders' which would not require reading ability, could be group administered and which would provide some information tasks which could be related to Piagetian principles. The pictorial material was designed for both instruction and evaluation. Although further validation is needed, for example how the items attempting to translate some of the Piagetian concepts compare with an individualised interview approach, initial studies are 'most encouraging', reliabilities of the 20-item measurements for the different areas being projected from item-test coefficients for unselected items, in the high 80s and low 90s.

Winkelmann (1974) has argued, 'Because Piaget did not carry out correlational analyses, he had little chance to obtain results opposing his postulate. Nevertheless, Braine (1959), who studied the development of the concept of position order and of the transitivity inference, not only found superimposable curves for criterion attainment as a function of age but also found a high correlation between the two tasks. On the other hand, Wohlwill (1963), reviewing the experimental evidence available until 1963, came to the conclusion that "the case for the negative is, however, rather more fully documented". Such negative evidence came. . . . from the investigations of Dodwell (1960, 1962), which showed only a low degree of consistency between various tasks in the area of children's number concept that Piaget had postulated to be closely interrelated. . . Tuddenham (1971) also reports a rather low level of inter-item correlations with items aiming at the transition from the pre-operational stage to the stage of concrete operations and covering a wide range of content. . . . Low correlations between tasks representing one logical concept or several concepts assumed to be related need not be a strong argument against the evidence of a single underlying generalized mental structure because the reliability of the measurement may be low. A more convincing method is factor analysis (e.g., Überla, 1968) which in the case of multi-dimensionability of the underlying cognitive structure, might reveal that several separate and more or less independent cognitive factors, are operative; the degree of reliability would influence only the loadings of the items on the various factors but not the factorial differentiation as such', p. 844. The authors study therefore involved 281 children within the age range from five- to eight-years-old and were adminstered 31 conservation items some using concrete materials and some in paper form. The data, subjected to a factorial analysis, computed four factors: factor one — conservation of substance equality or identity; factor two — conservation of substance inequality; factor three — conservation of number quality, and factor four — conservation of number inequality. These factors were confirmed in separate analyses for the concrete items and for the paper items. The factor structure was cross-validated in a second sample of 280 children aged five to eight to whom the paper items were given with modified instructions. 'These data call the Piagetian concept of *structures d'ensemble* and 'stage' into question', p.843. (Details are given later).

The battery of tests aimed at the age range from five to eight years based on the developmental works of Piaget and his collaborators was constructed by Winkelmann (1975) with the intent to create standardized procedures. for the assessment of different logical operations which play an important part in the transition from intuitive thinking ('pre-operational thinking') to concrete-logical thinking ('concrete operations'). The battery consists of nine individual tests: conservation of substance, conservation of number, class-inclusion, matrices, concepts of verticality — horizontality, asymmetric seriation, ordinal correspondence, transformation, and transitivity of length. Neither a total score for the whole battery nor a global allocation of subjects to certain developmental stages is provided because '. . . . the author, in view of the available empirical evidence, is not convinced of the existence of a generalized congnitive structure (*structure d'ensemble,* overall structure). . . .' for each test, preliminary percentile norms are available for the age groups five, six, seven, and eight. The outstanding characteristic of the test battery is its paper form. Drawings are used instead of real materials. Test and item selection was based on data from a sample of 280 five- to eight-year-old children. Factor analytical methods were applied to the items of each test, to the items of the whole battery, and to the raw scores of all tests. The general result was a relatively high degree of differentiation. In order to verify whether the results of a paper form was comparable to the results of a form using real materials, a corresponding investigation, using a sample of 281 five- to eight-year-old children, was restricted to the two conservation tests. A relatively high correlation between the form using drawings and the forms using concrete materials and a pronounced congruence of the factorial structure of the two modes of presentation were computed. (Details follow).

In continuation, Winkelmann (1975a) in a study entitled, 'Conservation of substance and number in Children's Thinking. I. Reponses of five- to eight-year-old children in tests based on drawings and tests based on concrete materials', tested 281 children. Four tests were administered: conservation of substance (liquids) — Paper Form, CSPF (13 items); conservation of substance — Concrete Form, CSCF (seven items); conservation of number — Paper Form, CNPF (six items); conservation of number — Concrete Form, CNCF (five items). Conservation of number (CN) was easier than conservation of substance (CS) both for the concrete and the paper forms. The forms using concrete materials were less difficult than the forms using drawings for both types of conservation. Correlations between the test forms were rather high, with coefficients amounting to 0.81 for CSPF: CSCF and 0.76 for CNPF: CNCF. 'Test scores were not dependent on sex. The overall distributions of the CS scores were U-shaped; the unimodal overall distribution (with maximum scores being most fequent) found for the CN scores were also interpreted as sections of U-shaped distributions. CSPF tasks with constant visible areas (drawings based on the assumption that glasses have a rectangular base and are constant with regard to the third dimension) were less difficult than tasks with variable areas (drawings based on the assumption that glasses possess a circular base so that the third dimension varies with the breadth of the glasses)', Winkelmann (*op. cit.*). (Details are given later).

Extending his earlier works (1975, 1975a), Winkelmann (1974b) aimed at the classification of two problems: (a) 'Within the domain of the conservation concept, did there exist a generalized cognitive structure (overall "structure, *structure d'ensemble*") as postulated by Piaget's theory?' (b) 'Were conservation tasks using drawings comparable to corresponding tasks using concrete materials within the framework of factor analysis?' The sample comprised 281 five- to eight-year-old children of both sexes. The tasks administered were: Conservation of substance (liquids) — Paper Form, (13 items); Conservation of substance (liquids) — Concrete Form (seven items); Conservation of number — Paper Form (six items); conservation of number — Concrete Form (five items). Each test consisted of conservation of equality (identity or equivalence) items as well as conservation of inequality (difference) items. The paper items demonstrated the same factorial structure as the concrete items. The results contradicted Piaget's notion of a *structure d'ensemble*. The units of cognitive development appeared to be relatively specific. The existence of a cognitive developmental stage (i.e. the stage of 'concrete operations') defined by an integrated system of closely connected cognitive operations was questioned. The sequence of cognitive acquisitions varied from child to child. (Details are given later).

More recently in a paper entitled, 'Modes of information integration and Piagetian measures of concrete operational thought', Carlson and Wiedl (1976) administered Winkelmann's 'Test-batterie zur Erfassung kognitiver Operationen' to a sample of 180, six- to eight-year olds. Factor analysis of the Piaget tests revealed five interpretable factors: conservation of number, conservation of substance-equality, conservation of substance-inequality, class inclusion and matrices. Factor analysis of the marker tests for information integration revealed two factors: simultaneous and successive. All the Piaget measures, with the exception of class inclusion, were related to the simultaneous factor. Class inclusion was weakly related to the successive factor. (Details follow).

To construct a paper-and-pencil test for the evaluation of concrete reasoning ability, Ankney (1975) developed two instruments: the Piagetian Interview Instrument (PII) and The Paper-and-Pencil Test (PPT) — both instruments consisting of conservation of weight, volume, transitivity, class inclusion, and Euclidean space. The written instrument additionally evaluated conservation of length, area, one-to-one correspondence, spatiality, and velocity. One hundred and twenty-nine children within the age range from eight to 14 years were involved. A significant relationship (r = .63), was found between the two instruments. Likewise, a significant relationship was computed between CA of the S and performance on the PII (r = .41), and performance on the PPT (r = .40). (Details are given later).

A group-administered written test of cognitive development was constructed and partially validated (Gray, 1973). Comprising of 36 open-ended items, each logically equivalent to specific Piaget tasks, the test and three Piaget problems were administered in a one-to-one situation. Children were categorized according to Piaget's hierarchy of logical thought development. Convergent and discrimination validation of the scales was mixed, while the item hierarchies for two of the three written scales was 'perfect'. Extending the 1973 work, the development of written items that assessed various aspects of four concrete operational groupings and two variations of two formal operational characteristics was studied by Gray (1975) among 622, nine- to 14-year-old students. Concrete structures assessed were Bi-univocal Multiplication of Classes, Co-univocal Multiplication of Classes, Addition of (increasing) Asymmetrical Relations, Addition of (decreasing) Asymmetrical Relations, and, Bi-univocal Multiplication of Relations. Formal operational structures measured were hypothetical-deductive thinking and combinatorial thinking (combinations and permutations). Eleven factors were extracted. Four factors were exceptionally pure, with each loading only on items assessing a specific concrete or formal logical structure: Hypothetical-deductive reasoning; Combinatorial thinking (permutations); Addition of (increasing) Asymmetrical Relations; and Co-univocal Multiplication of Classes. Gray's contention of the feasibility of a written Piagetian-based test of cognitive development (1973) was given further credibility. (Details are given later).

In *The Development of Adaptive Intelligence*, Feldman et al. (1974) studied logical thought as a product of man's adaptation to his environment. The study focused on the development of thinking in the Eskimo. In particular, the authors used a specially constructed nonverbal test of logical thinking for children aged five years and older, to examine the Piagetian hypothesis that development has the same hierarchical structure in all cultures undergoing successful adaptation. The authors' test consists of a sequence of tasks using coloured blocks — The Coloured Blocks Test. These tasks represent three Piagetian stages and form a series which begins with simple perceptual matching and ends with the abstract operations of symbolic logic. 'The stimulus materials consist of coloured blocks, approximately one-and-a-half inches in diameter. The set of blocks includes four values of each of two characteristics — colour and shape. The four colour values are red, green, yellow and blue; the four shape values are square, circle, diamond, and triangle (16 blocks). There is one complete set of blocks for the subject to use in answering and a set for the tester to use in constructing the problems of the training tasks . . . For the remainder of the test, the problems are drawn on seven-by-twelve-inch cards, and the subject answers from his set of blocks', Feldman *et al.* (*ibid.*, p. 49). In addition to the coloured Blocks Test, there is an analogue task. 'The stimulus and response sets consist of drawings of walruses, seals, bears, and foxes. As in Section I of the Coloured Blocks Test, the subject is presented with a partial matrix with a drawing from the response set', (*ibid.*, p. 62) (Fuller details of the Test are given in Feldman *et al.*, 1974, pp. 48–65). (Details of the Feldman *et al.* study are, more appropriately, given in Volume Eight in the present series, *Piagetian Research.*)

ii. Approaches with adolescents

Tisher (1962, 1971) reports a step in the development, validation and use of a Piagetian questionnaire with secondary school pupils with respect to concrete and formal operational thinking. A group of 232 pupils, 138 males and 94 females formed the experimental sample, ages ranging from 12.0 to 16.9 years and IQs from 71–135, and representatives of Australian grades, seven through nine, being placed in one of three 'cultural enrichment groupings'.

The pencil-and-paper questionnaire contains 24 multiple-choice items based on four scientific phenomena used by Inhelder and Piaget (1958), namely: 'the bouncing ball'; 'equilibrium in a balance'; 'water levels in connected containers' and 'shadows of rings'. Inhelder and Piaget's criteria for concrete and formal stages were used to set the concrete and formal type problems. Before each set of questions was attempted the investigator performed a relevant demonstration. Fifty-seven pupils, 19 in each grade, were randomly selected from the experimental sample and were involved in a 'conversation – interview' situation following Inhelder and Piaget's approaches. The three experiments chosen included 'Invisible Magnetism', 'Combinations of Chemicals' and 'Equilibrium in the Balance'.

Tisher, with respect to the obvious challenge concerning guessing in a multiple-choice situation, elaborates that in the case of a subject presented with 10 formal test items, each containing five choices, the chance of correctly guessing the answer in one item independently of the other items is .2. It was assumed that subjects scoring five or more on the formal items and subjects scoring seven or more on the concrete items were doing better than by guessing and these two scores were taken as criterion levels for classifying subjects as being at the formal stage of mental development. A score of 11+ on the concrete items and eight+ on the formal items was taken to indicate a superior achievement, i.e. 'late formal'. A score of seven+ on the concrete items and four or less on the formal were taken to indicate the subject was in the concrete stage, with a score of below seven and below four being considered as representative of the 'early concrete' stage.

The questionnaire discriminated between concrete and formal levels of thinking in accordance with many other researchers and this was regarded as an indication of the success of the Piagetian questionnaire. Further indication of its success was gained from a comparison of the results with those obtained from the conversation interview. There was a 17 per cent agreement in classification between the two techniques. Tisher concluded that the high percentage of agreement between Questionnaire and Interview classifications indicates that both techniques are measures of the same variable.

Tisher's Piagetian Questionnaire has been examined by the Australian Science Education Project (1972, 1974) and it was concluded that the Questionnaire has validity as a measure of Piagetian developmental level. Field and Cropley (1969) employed Tisher's Questionnaire to yield a measure of stage of mental operations, among 178, 16- to 18-year-old subjects and report that the questionnaire placed 30 of the subjects at the concrete, 104 at the Formal and 44 at 'Late Formal' levels of operational thought. High science achievement appeared to be associated with the ability to apply formal operations. Ross (1974) employing the questionnaire concluded that the general and significant increase in formal thinking from early to middle adolescence gave credibility to the ability of the questionnaire to discriminate between varying levels of logical ability. Further credibility with respect to the discrimination power of the questionnaire is provided by the investigation of Modgil (1975) in which results comparable with other logical operativity studies were obtained among 231 adolescents aged from 14 to 15+ years. (This study has been discussed more fully in the volume concerning Moral Development, under the present *Piagetian Research* series).

Shayer and Wharry (1974) acknowledging the advantages of the Piaget-based task in giving insight into the mental strategies of the individual person, focus on the difficulties of assessing the mental levels of a class of children even though the individual topics of the Nuffield Foundation Courses have been assessed in Piagetian terms. They therefore attempted to develop a method of testing a class which would reveal the level of thinking of the individual pupil in the context of the science teaching that the pupil was receiving. Shayer and Wharry, aware of the difficulties inherent in conventional examination tests: reading ability, visual imagery, recall and thought process and writing ability, therefore endeavoured to develop a testing procedure which minimizes possible effects on the assessment of the child. The criteria therefore included verbal administration with opportunities for supportive reading; visibility of apparatus and its operation; clear demonstration of the problem; the required answer to be short but allowing further elaboration and where appropriate, multiple-choice questions used, to eliminate the need to write at all, together with the liberal use of diagrams. Seven tasks have been given a first trial including Inhelder and Piaget's (1958) 'Shadows' task, 'Balance' task, 'Flexibility of Rods' and 'Floating and Sinking' and the following results were derived. The approach showed differentiation between individual pupils with good levels of consistency between tasks with developmental indications during a 12 months period. Attempts are being made to develop and refine the tasks further. The criteria employed in Shayer and Wharry's approach appear to follow very closely the qualities inherent in the Tisher test, the most noticeable exception being that Shayer and Wharry's assessments follow the opportunities pupils have during various class practical activities in connection with the Nuffield Foundation Combined Science Course to develop concepts and laws. The results however, supported Piaget's contentions that a child's attainment of a concept is dependent upon his stage of readiness. (The study has been discussed more fully in Part I of this Volume).

Dulit (1972) attempted a paper and pencil simulation of the 'Combinations of Coloured and Colourless Chemical Bodies' experiment in view of the time-consuming nature of the actual experiment and concluded from a scrupulous analysis of the reliability that the approach could be identified as a 'different but related' method assessing the same underlying capacities. The impression was gained from a comparison of the orthodox and unconventional approaches that 'it made virtually no difference' for subjects at or near the formal level, who would arrive at the same paper and pencil method on their own, before it was initiated for them. For subjects functioning closer to the concrete level, it may have focused their attention somewhat more on the 'plan' aspect of the problem. However, that would have tended if anything to have improved their performance and since the results appeared in the opposite direction (formal thinking less common than implied by Inhelder–Piaget), Dulit was inclined to conclude little or no difference in the final result due to method.

Burgess (1969) focusing on cognitive investigations being traditionally based on interviews with individual children, considers that any extension in their scope or application depends on the construction of cognitive group tests. This is desirable from the perspectives of statistical interpretation and large scale studies and further, if Piagetian developmental principles are to be of significance in mental testing, it is essential that items based on them can be administered in an equivalent form to present verbal reasoning and similar items thought to indicate certain types of cognitive functioning. Burgess constructed a paper-and-pencil group test in two parts: an abstract concrete combination problem, involving solving a problem and writing another of the same kind and 'three rewrite problems, each representing a different form of irrelevance'. Burgess concluded that the methodology gave a similar type of information on the development of schemata as Piaget's individual studies and in addition the 'make-up' and 're-write' problems appeared to externalise the type of thinking being studied. The greater difficulty of abstract material was in accordance with Piaget's findings together with the general trend in development although the existence of fully formal operational thinking was rare. (Details of the study are given in Modgil, 1974, pp. 387–388).

Bart (1972) describes the construction and validation of paper-and-pencil instruments to test operational thought. Three structurally parallel tests in three content areas and four Piagetian formal thought tasks were administered to 90 scholastically above-average adolescents of 13, 16 and 19 years. Items were six-choice logic items with abstruse and absurd content. The reasoning tests had 'substantial content validity, modest concurrent validity and limited construct validity'. It was recommended that these formal reasoning tests could be employed by educators to select students who are capable of abstract conceptualization and theoretically might profit from a curriculum emphasizing symbolic and verbal instruction and an abstract mode of learning. Bart focuses on the need for validated formal reasoning tests, easy to administer, and postulates that it is quite possible that the evaluation of subject-making achievement and the measurement of the cognitive development will be unified through test construction from a Piagetian framework and could have considerable effect on measurement and evaluation practices in school.

Peel (1971) has constructed verbal situations for assessing the maturity of judgment. The test material designed to assess the developmental changes in adolescent thinking consisted of passages relating to topical, social or intellectual problems followed by a question demanding more for its answer than the information given in the passage. A second question 'Why do you think so?', provided the insight into the maturity of the judgment. The resulting answers were grouped into three main categories: 'Restricted', which were tautological, premise-delaying and irrelevant: 'Circumstantial', which were 'bound solely by the content of the passage, often taking account at first of only one element', and 'Imaginative-Comprehensive' answers which involved the 'invocation and independent ideas and the consideration of the problem in their terms'. This work has been much developed by Peel together with his students in a wide variety of curriculum areas. (The study has been discussed more fully in Part I of this Volume).

Karplus and Peterson (1970) devised a test to determine the level of abstract reasoning children utilize in a ratio and proportion task. Subjects were presented with a drawing of a large stick figure (Mr Tall), the height of which was evaluated with large paper clips ('biggies'). A drawing of a small figure (Mr Short), was then presented and measured with 'biggies'. Subjects were asked to measure Mr Short with small paper clips ('smallies'), to predict the height of Mr Tall in 'smallies', and to advance a written explanation of how they arrived at their prediction. Subsequent modifications made it difficult for S to rely on any perceptual comparisons between the two figures to help them solve the problem because they saw only one figure. Karplus isolated the following response strategies: No explanation; an explanation referring to estimates without reference to the data; an explanation using the data haphazardly; scaling; addition, addition and scaling; incomplete proportion; proportion concrete; addition and proportion; and ratio. The last three response strategies were evidenced as examples of formal operational thought. However, Abramowitz (1975a) has argued, 'The use of a developmental scale to describe the acquisition of proportionality may be questioned. The scale may be relevant only to comparisons involving simple whole numbers. Alternatively, the use of proportions or the idea of comparing numbers by division may not be spontaneous. It may have to be learned. It is possible that students faced with the limitations of their relational reasoning may be more suceptible to learning how to use proportions, as opposed to naturally or innately conceiving of the idea. Lastly, the problem may be one of discrimination. It is possible that children may know how to solve problems which involve proportionality. They may be simply unable to discriminate those situations in which a particular strategy is appropriate. The extent to which the stimulus materials controlled responses in the Karplus work also remains to be determined. The problem used by Karplus, $4/6 = 6/x$, may have biased the children who had an incomplete understanding of proportionality towards the use of an additive mode. The difference between the numerators is two, as is the difference between the numerator and the denominator in the first ratio. The repeated difference of two in this problem may have suggested a strategy that children do not generally employ', p. 5.

More recently, Sills and Herron (1976) attempted to validate an alternative electronic analog task for the Combinations of Chemical Bodies Piagetian problem. 'Both tasks were compared with each other as well as with a Chemistry Placement Exam and an independent Piagetian measure using 29 males and 26 female university first year chemistry students as subjects. The results suggest that the electronic analog task may serve as a simpler test of certain aspects of formal thought. (Details follow).

g. Ordinal scaling of Piagetian tasks

Guttman's scalogram technique to the testing of aspects of Piaget's theory of development in search of an ordinal scale of intellectual assessment has been a popular method, e.g. Peel (1959), Goldman (1965), Kofsky (1966), Siegelman and Black (1969), Schwartz and Scholnick (1970) and Meadows (1975c).

Tests of different types of conservation can be fitted into an ordinal scale by calculating an index or coefficient of homogeneity (Wohlwill, 1960), or by monotonicity analysis (Bentler, 1970). Such scaling procedures have likewise led to the development of a psychometrically acceptable instrument for the evaluation of the general principle of conservation (Goldschmid and Bentler, 1968).

In Hamilton's (1972) study, 'An analysis of present conceptions of conservation capacity suggested that they might be unduly influenced by developmental stage theory, to the extent that continuities and individual differences at one particular stage of development are insufficiently stressed. In order to achieve a finer discrimination between individual differences in conservation of continuous quantity (solid and liquid), a new test instrument was devised. This departs from traditional experimental procedures by being presented largely in pictorial form, and by progressively increasing the number of standards, variables and distributions and redistributions of material. The results indicate that ordinal scaling of conservation at one particular developmental level is possible. It is suggested that the demonstrated individual differences may reflect differences in syllogistic reasoning and information – processing capacity', p. 429. (Details follow). 'Although a highly significant regression of pass rate on assumed order of difficulty was demonstrated, a fully systematic rationale for problem difficulty and between-item intervals was lacking', Hamilton and Moss, (1974, pp. 737–38).

In continuation, method of scaling conservation-of-quantity problems by information content was studied by Hamilton and Moss. 'Conservation of continuous quantity was redefined as a task requiring the sequential processing of equational statements, where each equation represents a step in the analysis and solution of a conservation problem. It was predicted that an increase in the length of a sequence of equations presented by problems will increase the information – processing demands and thus the difficulty level of tasks. The display characteristics of conservation-of-quantity problems which determined their informational content were identified and combined in a formula that reliably quantifies difficulty of individual problems and the between-problem intervals. Applying the formula, a pictorial series of alternate conservation of solid and liquid quantity was constructed and administered to 150 Ss seven- to nine-year-olds. The regression of pass rate on problem difficulty was highly significant. The results are discussed in terms of individual differences in information processing capacity', p. 737. (Details appear later).

Meadows (1975c) used scalogram analysis for data from a longitudinal study of nine Piagetian tasks. The study supported the assumptions that older subjects score higher on the scale than younger and that the scale was valid to the same extent for all ages. Perfect consistency was not however indicated: there was a stable and 'perhaps unidimensional general pattern but much individual variation'. The results were interpreted as indicating less operational generalizability than Piaget has supposed. (Details follow).

h. Clinical practice–mental pathology

Inhelder's (1943) pioneering work ranged from child psychosis, through sensory deficit, to senile dementia. By studying both cognitive and emotional phenomena within the developmental frame of reference she sees promise of improved prognosis and research regarding both normal and abnormal operatory processes. Inhelder suggested that conservation tasks for amount, weight, and volume could differentiate between 'bright' and 'dull' children as defined by their performance on traditional psychometric measures of mental development. Anthony's (1956) work on Piagetian contributions to child psychiatry likewise has indicated the possibility of approaching clinical problems within the developmental framework of Piaget.

Stephens, Miller, and McLaughlin (1969) have employed Piagetian assessment to investigate the moral as well as cognitive development of normals and retardates. Woodward (1959, 1963) has studied the behavioural responses of idiots and of general mental deficiency by Piagetian methods. It has been suggested (Woodward, 1970) that Piaget's approach provides promise for tests for the assessment of the mentally retarded. The application of the Piagetian developmental framework, especially of the sensorimotor stage, to the study of abnormal children have been examined by Tessier (1972), Garfield and Shakespere (1964), and Tabary and Tardieu (1963).

Yates and Richardson (1970) are engaged in an attempt to apply Piaget's theory of cognitive development to the assessment and training of children in a special care unit. The authors have drawn from the work of Woodward (1959, 1961, 1963) towards the construction of simple tests of sensorimotor intelligence 'that would allow a differential profile of cognitive abilities to be projected. The procedures are a mixture of structured tests and observations concerned with the development of operational intelligence, circular reactions, the construction of space and causality'. At present they are mainly concerned with a normal developmental age of about two years. The authors hope eventually to produce a complete developmental scale up to six years of age. However, Elkind (1971) does not agree and concluded that such tests would serve no useful purpose in the classroom because teachers would be unable to interpret them.

However, Hathaway and Hathaway—Theunissen (1974) argued that, 'while the contribution to clinical practice from Piagetian measurement . . . is still problematic and in the very early stages of development, it does offer an alternative to researchers from the usual objective and projective tests. There is reason to hope that development of a widely transferable system of Piagetian measurement might lead to a convergence between those engaged in fundamental research in developmental psychology and those evaluating and treating cognitive deprivation'.

The establishment of a relationship between adverse personality traits suggesting emotional disturbance and Piagetian concept development adds a new dimension to the understanding of the emotionally disturbed child (Modgil, 1974a). The relatively unaffected scholastic performance of these children, together with the fact that IQ was held constant does not reflect their lag in cognitive development as assessed by the Piagetian tasks. It can therefore be suggested that educational psychologists need to broaden their diagnostic measures to include clinical use of Piagetian tasks. A few clinical psychologists have attempted to explore this lag in cognitive development with emotionally disturbed children. The use of Piagetian material to assist in diagnosis has been reported in the literature by at least two authors: Schmid—Kitsikis (1969) and Lefevre (1970). It seems curious that Piaget's theory and method have been so rarely extended to emotionally disturbed children. In part, the reason may reside in the fact that Piaget (1952b, p. 238) himself preferred, ' . . . the study of normalcy and of the workings of the intellect to that of the tricks of the unconscious . . . .' and partly due to its cognitive emphasis. The accumulating evidence, however, presented in Volume Five in the series *Piagetian Research*, especially with reference to Piaget's (1972) reflections, indicates a greater recognition by Piaget of the affective components, within the developing individual. The concept of egocentrism may be utilized by psychologists to explain the finding that emotionally disturbed children of normal intelligence have difficulty with the Piagetian tasks. Pimm (1974a) has hinted that there could be clinical usefulness for Piagetian tasks and has formulated a proposed research study which might investigate: (a) the relationship between a variety of Piagetian tasks and the diagnostic category 'emotional disturbance'; (b) the argument that an emotionally disturbed child does poorly on Piagetian operativity and has social problems because he is egocentric, is still not very useful. We need to develop research which will probe the antecedents conditions which assist us in knowing the processes by which a child becomes less egocentric. We also need to understand more clearly in exactly which dimensions of cognitive development the emotionally disturbed child is deficient.

Nolen (1974) in a discussion paper entitled, 'Piaget and the school psychologist', opens with a quotation from Dodgson (1963) and maintains, 'Asking what Piaget has to say to the school psychologist is like asking a ten-year-old what time the clock says. Those who have been around children of this age know that the child's reply is predictable: "The clock doesn't say anything. You have to read it". Piaget does not volunteer anything directly to the school psychologist, either. Like the clock, he must be read. Unlike the clock, Piaget must be thought about as well for his answers to questions that may concern school psychologists are likely to be given as parables'. The paper is a discussion of an application of Piagetian understandings to the interpretive diagnosis of a learning disabled child's, Wechsler Intelligence Scale for Children protocol. Nolen focused her analyses on the identification of correspondences among: (i) characteristic thought patterns of children in the concrete — operational stage, (ii) demonstrated thought strategies as sampled by the WISC and (iii) cognitive information processing demands from reading, spelling and arithmetic in the primary school age range. Behavioural and cognitive test interpretations were contrasted with the conclusion that intelligence and academic test interpretations were often fragmentary and incomplete without Piagetian theory to integrate and supplement the findings. (Details are given later).

Abstracts

The development of a Piagetian paper-and-pencil test for assessing concrete operational reasoning
P.M. Ankney, 1975

AIM / To construct a paper-and-pencil test for the evaluation of concrete reasoning ability.

SUBJECTS / N = 129 aged eight to 14 years.

METHOD / The two instruments developed were the Piagetian

Interview Instrument (PII) and the Paper-and-Pencil Test (PPT). The former consisted of five concrete reasoning tasks while the latter in addition to the identical five concrete reasoning tasks included another five. The Piagetian tasks on both instruments were: conservation of weight, volume, transitivity, class inclusion, and Euclidean space. The written instrument additionally evaluated conservation of length, area, one-to-one correspondence, spatiality, and velocity.

RESULTS / A significant relationship ($r = .63$) was computed between performance on the PII and PPT. A significant relationship was observed between CA and performance on the PII ($r = .41$), and performance on the PPT ($r = .40$). Children aged eight years and five months to 10 years five months did less well on the PPT than hypothesized. No significant relationship was found between performance on either instrument and sex, type of community, or cultural background. Ankney, when discussing the implications concluded, 'Assessment of concrete stage development does appear amenable to objectification, subject to the limitations imposed by reading levels. The flexibility of the clinical interview cannot easily be built into an objective test. Nevertheless, the reproducibility of a test holds promise for periodic measurement of increments in cognitive ability. Experiences in clinical interviewing should be included in preservice teacher training to offer insights into how children think. In-service teachers, however, will probably have more interest in an efficient method of appraising the cognitive skills of an entire class. In this connection the facility of a paper-and-pencil measure is evident'.

*Modes of information integration and Piagetian measures of concrete operational thought * ***
J.S. Carlson and K.H. Wiedl, 1976

The relationship between stage and structure from a Piagetian

* Published with the kind permission of the authors. Gratitude is extended to Professor Jerry S. Carlson of University of California, Riverside, and Dr Karl Heinz Wiedl of University of Trier, Federal Republic of Germany.

** This study was supported partially from a research grant from the University of California, Riverside and a research award from the Alexander von Humboldt-Stiftung granted to the first author. The authors are grateful to Annely Ennen and Wolfgang Loth for their aid in data collection. We also wish to express our gratitude to Professor Dr Leo Montada, Fachbereich I, Psychologie der Universität Trier for his aid and support as well as to the Kultusministerium des Landes Rheinland-Pfalz and the Schulbehorde der Stadt Trier for their cooperation. Reprint requests should be sent to Jerry S. Carlson, Department of Education, University of California, Riverside, California 92502 or Karl Heinz Wiedl, Fachbereich I, Psychologie, der Universität Trier, D—5500 Trier, Federal Republic of Germany.

standpoint has been dealt with by several authors (Flavell, 1971; Flavell and Wohlwill, 1969; Pinard and Laurendeau, 1969; Brainerd, 1972; Wohlwill, 1963; Bart and Smith, 1974; Overton, in press). A central issue is the degree of concurrent development of same-stage Piagetian concepts. Some authors (e.g., Flavell, 1971) argue that relatively little within-stage synchrony is called for by Piagetian theory. Others (e.g., Brainerd, 1972; Pinard and Laurendeau, 1969; Seiler, 1973; Weinreb and Brainerd, 1975), suggest that the theory requires high levels of synchrony.

Empirically, most investigations of concrete operational thought have shown that asynchrony is the rule rather than the exception (Dodwell, 1962; Lunzer, 1960; Smedslund, 1964; Brainerd, 1972; Weinreb and Brainerd, 1975). In a recent study by Winkelman (1974), tests of conservation of substance and number were administered to 280 children. Factor analysis revealed four orthogonal factors: conservation of substance (equality), conservation of substance (inequality), conservation of number (equality), and conservation of number (inequality). He concluded that Piaget's notions of *structures d'ensemble* and stage are of questionable validity.

The study of information integration is a possible method of effecting a compromise between the synchrony and asynchrony viewpoints. It might be, as Oerter (1971) has suggested, that even if Piaget measures do test different aspects of thought, they might nonetheless require similar modes of dealing with the information. On this point, the work of Das (1972, 1973a, 1973b) is helpful. He has isolated two basic modes of information integration: simultaneous and successive. The distinction derives from the work of Luria and reflects both task demands and incipient problem solving strategies. According to Das, these modes of information integration are parallel and reflect different cognitive strategies. Das defines them as follows: 'In simultaneous synthesis, one is required to arrange stimuli in a simultaneous manner in order to arrive at a judgment. In successive synthesis, stimuli must be arranged in a sequence to make a decision' (1972, p. 10). Description of the marker tests which define these dimensions may help to clarify the distinction.

The simultaneous dimension is best defined by the Raven Progressive Matrices, Cross-modal Coding, Graham-Kendall's Memory-for-Designs and Figure Copying. The successive dimension is defined by tests of Short-term Visual Memory, Serial Recall and Free Recall (Das, 1973a). These tests are stable marker tests for the dimensions involved.

The purpose of this investigation was to examine Das' distinction between simultaneous and successive processing and relate the distinction to performance on a variety of tests of concrete operational thought. We wished to examine the possibility that although the Piaget tests may be multifactorial, they might require a similar mode of information integration for solution, one which we could define as simultaneous.

SUBJECTS / One hundred and eighty children ages 6 to 8 were tested. The mean age was 7 years, 5 months. All children attended regular public schools in the city of Trier, West Germany.

VARIABLES / Five marker tests for simultaneous and successive information integration were administered. The simultaneous tests were: Raven Coloured Progressive Matrices Test (Raven, 1965) and the Memory-for-Designs Test (Graham and Kendall, 1960). The former test is well known and need not be described here. The Memory-for-Design Test requires the subject to draw from memory straight-line geometric forms or designs. There is a total of 15 such designs. Each design is shown to the subject for 5 seconds, after which he draws the design from memory. There is no restriction on drawing time. Each drawing is scored on a four-point scale: a score of 0 is given if the design is accurately reproduced: 1, if two or more easily identifiable errors are made; 2, if orientation is correct but errors of closure and spacing are detected; and 3, if the figure is reversed or rotated. Objective scoring is facilitated by a test manual (Graham and Kendall, 1960).

The marker tests for successive information integration were a visual short-term memory test, a serial recall test, and a free recall test. The visual short-term memory test was adapted from Das (1972, 1973b). A total of 22 cards was presented. Each card had five numbers ranging from 1 to 9. The numbers were randomly selected and placed on the card. Three of the numbers were arranged horizontally; 2 vertically, intersecting the middle horizontal number. The first two cards served as practice items. The subject was shown each card for five seconds. This was followed by a colour-naming task used to prevent rehearsal. The subject was then asked to write the numbers on a blank stimulus grid in exactly the same position as he saw them. The total number of digits placed in correct position was the score obtained for each item. The serial and free recall tasks consisted of twenty-four sets of items of five words each. In half of the cases (12) the words were closely related (example: mother, father, brother, sister, aunt); in half they were not (example: house, ocean, tiger, broom, forest). The related and unrelated items were intermixed. Each set of words representing an item was presented orally to the subject, immediately after which he was asked to repeat the list in the order given. Serial recall scoring was based on the number of words which the subject recalled in the correct order. Free recall was scored by the number of words correctly repeated, regardless of order.

The Piaget tests were all taken from Winkelmann's *Test-batterie zur Erfassung kognitiver Operationen* (Winkelmann, 1975). The tests were conservation of substance, identity (4 items) and equivalence (5 items) equal, (4 items unequal); conservation of number, equality (4 items), inequality (2 items); matrices (8 items); and class inclusion (6 items). Each item was presented in the standard format of the test and scored 0 for an incorrect answer, 1 for a correct answer. The subject was not asked to give a verbal explanation of his answer.

PROCEDURE / All Ss were tested individually in two sessions, each lasting approximately 45 minutes. The individual tests were presented in random order. The Raven Coloured Progressive Matrices score was divided into subparts: a score for those items which are perceptual in nature and a score for conceptual items. The reason for this division is that the test is not homogeneous (see Müller, 1970; Carlson, *et al.*, 1974). The Memory-for-Designs Test was scored by two independent judges. The interrater agreement was very high (r = .98). Where disagreement did occur, an average of the two scores was used. Scoring for all the other tests was straightforward and total scores for tests and subtests were calculated.

RESULTS / The Piaget items were factor analyzed using Bentler's (1971) monotonicity coefficients to control for item difficulty. In this and the subsequent factor analysis, the number of factors was determined by applying the Scree test (Cattell, 1966). Commonalities were estimated by R^2 and rotation was done according to the Varimax criterion. Five orthogonal factors were extracted which accounted for 69 per cent of the total variance. As can be seen in Table 1, the loadings of the various tests are high and consistent on the factor which they define. The factors can be identified as follows: Factor I, Conservation of Number — equality and inequality; Factor II, Class Inclusion; Factor III, Conservation of Substance, equivalence-equality and identity; Factor IV; Conservation of Substance, inequality; and Factor V, Matrices. It can be seen that conservation of substance separated on the dimension of equality-inequality, not on the identity-equivalence dimension. The proportion of common variance contributed by each factor is 20, 18, 34, 13, and 15 per cent, respectively.

These results replicate those of Winkelmann (1974, 1975). The only difference is that conservation of number, equality and inequality, loaded on a single factor in the present study. Winkelmann's results showed separate factors for each. The small number of items could account for this, however.

To define successive and simultaneous modes of information integration, the tests assumed to define these dimensions were factor

Table 1: Factor patterns for Piagetian test items*

Variables	I	II	III	IV	V
Conservation of Substance					
1. − identity	.19	.06	.65	.12	.18
2. − identity	.09	.16	.71	−.01	.16
3. − equivalence, equality	.16	.05	.64	.05	.27
4. − equivalence, inequality	.15	.12	.12	.86	.10
5. − equivalence, inequality	.23	.07	.08	.76	.20
6. − equivalence, inequality	.05	.09	.60	.51	.06
7. − equivalence, inequality	.18	−.07	.29	.66	.11
8. − identity	.30	.06	.85	.06	.14
9. − identity	.12	.11	.81	.13	.11
10. − equivalence, equality	.16	.11	.90	.19	.07
11. − equivalence, equality	.20	.08	.87	.10	.13
12. − equivalence, equality	.22	.08	.87	.10	.13
13. − equivalence, equality	.20	.14	.82.	.14	.06
Conservation of Number					
14. − equality	.69	−.02	.19	.24	.16
15. − equality	.66	.05	.31	.28	.18
16. − inequality	.42	.12	.14	.34	.38
17. − equality	.70	−.09	.25	.30	.29
18. − inequality	.57	.00	.25	.35	.41
19. − equality	.81	.04	.38	−.07	.07
20. Class Inclusion	.04	.85	.06	−.02	.13
21. Class Inclusion	−.02	.79	−.03	.13	.06
22. Class Inclusion	.14	.89	.17	.07	−.00
23. Class Inclusion	.08	.73	.11	.00	.01
24. Class Inclusion	.05	.58	.29	.09	−.04
25. Class Inclusion	−.05	.69	.06	−.05	.05
26. Matrices	.27	−.00	.15	.09	.56
27. Matrices	.63	.17	.18	.19	.14
28. Matrices	.22	.08	.08	.03	.33
29. Matrices	.33	.07	.19	−.00	.44
30. Matrices	.58	.05	.07	−.12	.43
31. Matrices	−.05	.12	.12	.19	.76
32. Matrices	.16	−.11	.15	.09	.78
33. Matrices	.17	.05	.14	.11	.64
Proportion of Common Variance	19.7	18.0	33.6	13.3	15.4

* Factor loadings rounded to two places in this and all other tables.

Table 2: Factor patterns for marker tests

	Variables	I	II
1.	Raven-perceptual	.35	.77
2.	Raven-conceptual	.15	.59
3.	Memory-for-Designs	−.15	−.31
4.	Serial Recall	.87	.28
5.	Free Recall	.86	.29
6.	Visual Short-term Memory	.63	.45
	Proportion of Common Varience	59.7	40.3

Abstracts   237

analyzed. The results are reported in Table 2. The two factors extracted
account for 94 per cent of the total variance. ·

The serial recall, free recall and visual short-term memory tests load
highly and consistently on Factor I, successive information integration.
The Raven Matrices, perceptual and conceptual, and Memory-for-
Designs tests mark Factor II, simultaneous information integration. The
proportion of the common variance accounted for by Factors I and II is
59.7 and 40.3 per cent, respectively.

The relationship of the two defined dimensions, simultaneous and
successive information integration, and the various Piaget tests were
derived from factor analysis (see Table 3) and correlations of the Piaget
measures with the most salient of the marker tests (see Table 4).

Table 3: Factor analysis of marker and Piaget tests

	Variables	I	II
1.	Conservation of Substance-equality	.54	.38
2.	Conservation of Substance-inequality	.64	.13
3.	Conservation of Number-equality	.67	.18
4.	Conservation of Number-inequality	.74	.18
5.	Class Inclusion	.07	.38
6.	Matrices	.62	.29
7.	Raven Perceptual	.70	.38
8.	Raven Conceptual	.45	.22
9.	Memory-for-Designs	−.34	−.13
10.	Serial Recall	.26	.91
11.	Free Recall	.38	.80
12.	Visual Short-term Memory	.49	.62
	Proportion of Common Variance	57.1	42.9

Two orthogonal factors were isolated which account for 94 per cent
of the total variance. All of the Piaget tests, except for class inclusion,
and the marker tests which define simultaneous processing, load on
Factor I. This factor accounts for 57.1 per cent of the common
variance. The tests which load on Factor II, which accounts for the
other 42.9 per cent of the variance, are those defined as marker tests
for successive information integration. Class inclusion also loads
moderately (.38) on this factor.

Table 4 reports the correlations between the various Piaget tests with
the marker tests which have the highest loadings on the factors which
they define (see Tables 2 and 3). These are the Raven Progressive
Matrices — perceptual for simultaneous information integration (factor
loadings of .77 and .70), and Free Recall for successive (factor loadings
.87 and .91). All the correlations, with the exception of class inclusion

and Raven-perceptual, are significantly different from zero. But this is of less significance than the fact that the correlations of the Piaget tests, except class inclusion, with the two marker tests differ consistently and significantly in the expected direction (thus one-tail z-tests were used) and show higher correlations between the Piaget measures and Raven-perceptual than between the Piaget tests and free recall. The corresponding z values are as follows: conservation of substance-equality, $z = 2.59$, $p < .05$; conservation of substance-inequality, $z = 2.38$, $p < .05$; conservation of number-equality, $z = 2.62$, $p < .05$; conservation of number-inequality, $z = 1.75$, $p < .05$, class inclusion, $z = 0.85$, ns; matrices, $z = 3.93$, $p < .05$.

Table 4: Correlations of Piaget tests with most salient marker tests[1]

	Marker Tests	
Piaget Tests	*Raven-perceptual*	*Free Recall*
Conservation of Substance	.51*	.28*
Conservation of Substance	.46*	.24*
Conservation of Number	.43*	.18*
Conservation of Number	.45*	.29*
Class Inclusion	.08	.17*
Matrices	.58*	.24*

1 Correlation between Raven-perceptual and Free Recall .18*
* sig., p.< .05

These results show that although the Piaget tests are multifactorial, they require a similar mode of information integration (simultaneous). The exception is class inclusion which seems to be related more, although rather weakly, to successive than to simultaneous processes.

DISCUSSION / Many of the investigations which have dealt with the issue of the relationship of various tasks of concrete operational thought have shown that tight, easily definable synchronies probably do not exist. The main purpose of the present investigation was to approach the problem of within-stage correspondence from the perspective of modes of information integration that may 'tie together' what appear to be different capabilities. That is, we do not doubt the validity of the several correlational and factor analytic studies which show within-stage correspondence to be minimal at best. (In fact one of our intents was to replicate and extend Winkelmann's work which gave clear, unambiguous results showing the multifactorial natures of the tests used.) What we do doubt, however, is that the capabilities assessed by the several measures are really as independent and separate as these studies might lead one to believe.

The result of the replication and extension of Winkelmann's work showed unambiguously the same factor patterns as he found. In addition, the factor patterns show that class inclusion and matrices are dimensions separate from each other and from the conservation tests employed. In passing, it should be noted that the conservation of substance equality and inequality items loaded on separate factors, whereas no separation was detected for identity-equivalence items. This result, although the same as Winkelmann's, is nevertheless surprising inasmuch as the evidence that identity conservation is different from and precedes equivalence conservation seemed unequivocal (Elkind, 1967; Hooper, 1969).

The statistical verification of the two modes of information integration, simultaneous and successive, showed that the serial and free recall tests were the best marker tests for successive information integration, the Raven Coloured Progressive Matrices, both perceptual and conceptual subtests, for simultaneous processing (see Table 2).

The results of the factor analysis reported in Table 3 showed that the conservation of substance, number, and matrices tests load consistently and highly on the same factor as those tests identified as marker tests for simultaneous information integration. The class inclusion test, on the other hand, does not appear on this factor. It loads, though only moderately, on the same factor as the successive information marker tests. The weak relationships between class inclusion and the two most salient of the marker tests, Raven-perceptual for simultaneous, free recall for successive, indicates that not only is class inclusion separate from the other Piagetian tests in terms of the mode of information integration demanded, but also that it is not highly related to successive processing either. A similar lack of relationship of class inclusion to other Piaget measures of concrete operational thought has been reported by Stephens *et al.* (1972).

What the above results indicate can be relatively simply stated. Various Piaget tests of concrete operational thought such as conservation of number, conservation of substance, matrices and class inclusion do show different factor patterns. These are consistent and easily interpretable. This does not necessarily mean, however, that these measures are entirely unrelated as conservation of number, conservation of substance, and matrices all require a common mode of information integration which can be defined as simultaneous. Class inclusion, on the other hand, apparently does not require this form of information integration.

Relationships among Piagetian, IQ, and achievement assessments
R. DeVries, 1974

AIMS / Two hypotheses were advanced: the degree to which IQ tests and Piaget-type tasks measure the same intelligences and to what extent tests of achievement and Piaget-type tasks measure the same knowledge.

SUBJECTS / N = 143. High-IQ and average-IQ subjects were chronologically aged between five to seven years and the low-IQ children were chronologically aged between six to 12 years and mentally aged five to seven years.

METHOD / Fifteen Piaget-type tests were administered as follows in three sessions:

Session one included: Guessing game (DeVries, 1970), mass conservation, sibling egocentrism, left-right perspective, constancy of generic identity (De Vries, 1969), and class-inclusion.

Session two included: Number conservation, constancy of sex, identity (DeVries, 1969; Kohlberg, 1963), conservation of mass in the context of the ring-segment illusion (Jastrow effect), dream interview, and length conservation.

Session three included: length transitivity, liquid conservation, magic interview (Kohlberg, 1963), object sorting (Kohlberg, 1963).

'Piaget never studied (Guessing Games, Constancy of Generic and Sex Identity, Ring Segment Conservation and Magic). Nevertheless, these were inspired by Piaget's work and are similar in focus and method to Genevan tasks. tasks and scoring are described in detail elsewhere (DeVries, 1971)', DeVries, 1974, P.749.

Scores on the California Test of Mental Maturity and the Metropolitan Achievement Test were obtained from the school records.

RESULTS / Factor analyses of performance on the Californian Test of Mental Maturity, Metropolitan Achievement Test, Stanford-Binet and 15 Guttman-scaled Piaget-type tests demonstrated that 'Piagetian tasks do appear to measure a different intelligence and a different achievement than do psychometric tests. This finding suggests examination of the nature of this difference and the implications for assessment of intelligence, for education, and for research on children. Two primary differences can be noted between Piagetian and psychometric measures. First, they differ in their general perspective; and second, they differ specifically in how they assess intelligence', pp.

751–753. However, Piagetian, IQ, and achievement tests overlap to some degree. Finally the results are discussed with other related studies (McClelland, 1973; Inhelder, 1943 (1968); Stephens, 1972; Kamii and DeVries, 1975 and Kohlberg and Mayer, 1973).

A study of the reliability and factor composition of the Concept Assessment Kit — Conservation
K.W. Galbraith, 1975

AIM / To assess the psychometric properties of the Concept Assessment Kit — Conservation (CAK–C).

SUBJECTS / N = 32 girls between the ages of six years four months to seven years four months.

METHOD / Forms A and B of the CAK–C (Goldschmid and Bentler, 1968b) were administered in a counterbalanced manner to the Ss. Analysis of two subsamples was made, the first dealing with Ss aged six years four months to six years eight months and the second composed of Ss six years eight months to seven years four months. The Metropolitan Readiness Test scores, within one standard deviation of the mean, were available for the Ss. The reliability of the instrument was examined by generating reliability coefficients for the subjects' true score, interjudge agreement and parallel forms.

RESULTS / The reliability coefficients based upon variance estimates computed from an analysis of variance all exceeded the .90 level. 'This indicated that the reliability of the CAK–C is within levels expected for an individually administered instrument. The true score, parallel form and interjudge reliability coefficients were all acceptable. The factor analysis of the items revealed that a single factor did account for at least 50 per cent of the variance. This indicated that the ability to conserve is a generalized function. However, other factors identified indicated that the specific item's content was important. Depending upon the content of the item and form of the questioning, somewhat different abilities are measured', Galbraith (*ibid.*, p. 7721–A).

Interrelationships between the correlates of psychometric and Piagetian scales of sensorimotor intelligence
A.W. Gottfried and N. Brody, 1975

AIMS / To determine the extent to which psychometric and

Piagetian scales correlate during infancy; and to study the nomological (i.e. correlational) networks of these scales and the degree to which their networks were similar.

METHOD / The sensorimotor scales administered included the Bayley Scales of Infant Development (Bayley, 1969); the Escaloma-Corman Object Performance Scale (Corman and Escalona, 1969); and the Uzgiris-Hunt Development of Schemes in relation to Objects Scale (Uzgiris and Hunt, 1966). Motor developments, socio-environmental variables, activity and interaction with objects, and physical development were also evaluated. (Fuller details of the experimental procedures are given in Gottfried and Brody, 1975, pp 380–381).

RESULTS / The correlations between psychometric (i.e. Bayley mental scale) and Piagetian scales were positive, moderate, and significant. Both types of scales yielded virtually identical 'correlational networks'. 'Motor and physical development and activity level correlated positively and significantly with sensorimotor development, while socio-environmental variables and measures of interaction with objects accounted for a negligible portion of variance on sensorimotor development. The data indicated that psychometric and Piagetian sensorimotor scales are measures of the same construct. Placing these findings into perspective with the literature on the correlates of intelligence during the later ages provided insight into the failure of infant tests to predict subsequent intellectual functioning', Gottfried and Brody (*ibid.*, p. 379).

The factor structure of concrete and formal operations: a confirmation of Piaget *
W.M. Gray, 1975

AIM / Piaget has hypothesized that concrete and formal operations can be described by specific logical models and assessed via a variety of physical problems (Inhelder and Piaget, 1955 / 1958, 1959 / 1969; Piaget, 1953 / 1957). Unfortunately, most of the research that has focused on concrete and formal operations has been concerned with the content of the problems rather than logical models they represent. Because of the content orientation, there has been little work on devising different means (e.g., written items) of assessing the various logical models, irrespective of content, with the exception of that done

---

* Written and prepared by the author for inclusion in this volume. Gratitude is extended to Professor William M. Gray of the University of Dayton, Ohio.

by Bart (1971) and Gray (1973, 1974). The present research is part of a continuing program directed toward evaluating the various concrete and formal logical models via the traditional Piagetian tasks and written items. Its specific focus was on the development of written items that assess various aspects of four concrete operational groupings and two variations of two formal operational characteristics.

SUBJECTS / N = 622, nine- to 14-year-old students participating in the Human Sciences Program curriculum designed by Biological Sciences Curriculum Study (BSCS) were the subjects. Average age was 12.09 years, with a standard deviation of .537.

INSTRUMENT / Two 15-item written tests consisting of items assessing various concrete and formal operational structures were used. Concrete structures assessed were Bi-univocal Multiplication of Classes, Co-univocal Multiplication of Classes, Addition of (increasing) Asymmetrical Relations, Addition of (decreasing) Asymmetrical Relations, and Bi-univocal Multiplication of Relations (including direct and inverse correspondence); formal operational structures measured were hypothetical-deductive thinking (making correct implications and denying incorrect implications) and combinatorial thinking (combinations and permutations). Approximately one-half of the items included drawings; and approximately one half were open ended, with the other half being multiple choice.

METHOD / During May 1974, subjects were given Form A of the test on one day and Form B on the next. Because each form was given on a different day, only 578 of the original 622 subjects took both forms; and the analysis was performed on the 578.

For analysis, the combined results of both forms were considered as one test. An order analysis (Bart and Krus, 1973) of the thirty items eliminated seven items (four from Form A and three from Form B). The remaining twenty-three items were factor analyzed via incomplete image analysis (Harris, 1962) and the initial factor matrix was obliquely transformed using Hofmann's Orthotran (Hofmann and Pruzek, 1974).

RESULTS / Eleven factors were extracted, of which four were considered trivial. Four factors were *exceptionally* pure, with each loading *only* on items assessing a specific concrete or formal logical structure: Hypothetical-deductive reasoning (including both making correct and denying incorrect implications); Combinatorial thinking (permutations); Addition of (increasing) Asymmetrical Relations; and Co-univocal Multiplication of Classes. Two factors were described in terms of specific logical structures [addition of (increasing) Asymmetrical Relations and Combinatorial thinking (combinations)]. The remaining factor tended to load on items assessing correspondence.

DISCUSSION / Several implications were derived from the results. First, there is a confirmation of Piaget's conceptions on the existence of various cognitive structures and their logical foundations. Second, because the confirmation was obtained on written non-Piagetian type tasks, powerful support is provided for the generalizability of the Piagetian system. Finally, Gray's contention of the feasibility of a written Piagetian-based test of cognitive development (1973) is given greater support.

Currently the items are undergoing revision with the ultimate aim of developing ones which will assess specific characteristics of each concrete operational grouping (e.g., associativity, reversibility, etc.) or the four-group of formal operational transformations. Target date for next testing is Spring 1976. Also, available data is being reanalysed using Multiple Hierarchical Analysis, a synthesis of Guttman scalogram analysis and ordering theory (Bart and Krus, 1973).

Continuities and individual differences in conservation
V. Hamilton, 1972

AIMS / Hamilton tested two predictions: (1) 'that conservations of solid and liquid quantity are best described as continuous dimensions of cognitive ability which depend on the individual's capacity to handle progressively more complex information in displays of increasing complexity; (2) that there is a significant positive relationship between age and solving conservation problems of increasing order of difficulty, as defined', p. 435.

SUBJECTS / N = 85 selected from kindergarten, first, second and third grades with mean age five years 11 months, six years eight months, seven years nine months, and nine years respectively. Full scale Wechsler IQs ranged from 111.2 to 113.6.

METHOD / Hamilton maintains, 'An analysis of present conceptions of conservation capacity suggested that they might be unduly influenced by developmental stage theory, to the extent that continuities and individual differences at one particular stage of development are insufficiently stressed. In order to achieve a finer discrimination between individual differences in conservation of continuous quantity (solid and liquid), a new test instrument was devised. This departs from traditional experimental procedures by being presented largely in pictorial form, and by progressively increasing the number of standards, variables and distributions and redistributions of material', p. 429. (Fuller details of the tests, experimental procedures and diagrammatical examples are described in Hamilton, 1972, pp. 430–34).

RESULTS / The two hypotheses stated above were fully substantiated — that ordinal scaling of conservation at one particular developmental level is possible. The study suggests that the demonstrated individual differences may reflect differences in syllogistic reasoning and information-processing capacity '. . . that individual differences in conservation of continuous quantity are not fully described by the limited standard procedures. Problems aimed at one specific level of cognitive capacity may contain so many variations on the basic theme of dimensional change that neither multiplication of relations nor reversibility operations may be adequate for the task. We seem to be dealing with a scalable skill dependent on the progressive development of the capacity for handling and processing amounts of information which is required for a "necessary" deduction of invariance', p. 439.

A method of scaling conservation — of — quantity by information content
V. Hamilton and M. Moss, 1974

AIMS / The authors advanced two hypotheses: (a) 'that there is a highly significant negative correlation between the information content of a conservation-test series (the n [steps] index and subjects percentage pass rate; (b) that older compared with younger children achieve higher pass rates on problems with systematically increasing information — processing demands', p.742.

SUBJECTS / N = 150 children, 50 subjects in each age group seven, eight and nine of average ability.

METHOD / 'Conservation of continuous quantity was redefined as a task requiring the sequential processing of equational statements, where each equation represents a step in the analysis and solution of a conservation problem. It was predicted that an increase in the length of a sequence of equations presented by problems will increase the information — processing demands and thus the difficulty level of tasks. The display characteristics of conservation-of-quantity problems which determined their informational content were identified and combined in a formula that reliably quantifies the difficulty of individual problems and the between-problem intervals. Applying the formula a pictorial series of alternate conservation of solid and liquid quantity was constructed and administered . . . ', p. 737. (Fuller details of the tests, procedures and diagrammatical examples are described in Hamilton and Moss, 1974, pp. 738–42).

RESULTS / Hypothesis (a) stated above was fully substantiated. The regression of pass rate on problem difficulty was highly significant. Hypothesis (b) above was rejected. 'It is our opinion that we have been directing attention to a processing variable which is related not only to the acquisition or maturation of knowledge or skills but perhaps more to the general efficiency of the conceptual-processing apparatus in dealing with increasing amounts of intellectual work. Differences in sorting playing cards and in coding operations by subjects respectively scoring high or low on conservation as measured by the problem series described here . . . provide the basis for this tentative conclusion. Our findings appear to be complementary to those of Osler and Kofsky (1965), who demonstrated that the capacity to process bits of information is a function of age and conceptual development, and to those of Pascual-Leone (1970)', p. 744.

*The unique contributions of Piagetian measurement to diagnosis, prognosis, and research of children's mental development**
W.E. Hathaway and A. Hathaway-Theunissen, 1975

This paper examines the question of the unique contributions of Piagetian measurement to diagnosis, prognosis and research of children's mental development in two stages. In the first part of the paper three relevant questions are considered from the viewpoint of the literature:

1. Is it logically and empirically possible for measurement based on Piagetian Theory to add anything unique to what is already measurable by traditional psychometric techniques or does it yield just another, more time consuming and superfluous assessment of psychometric general intelligence?
2. What progress has been made in the construction of systems of

* Written and prepared by the authors for inclusion in this volume. Gratitude is extended to Drs Walter E. Hathaway and Anneke Hathaway-Theunissen of Portland Public Schools, Oregon.

Piagetian measurement?

3. What are the unique uses in prognosis, diagnosis, and research to which systems of Piagetian measurement may be put?

In the second part of the paper an original empirical study is reviewed. In this study four hypotheses dealing with the relationship of traditional psychometric and Piagetian assessment were tested. The results of that study add weight to the evidence supporting a positive response to the first question above and thus give further encouragement to efforts similar to those described in the response to the second and third questions.

Part One
Possibility of unique contributions of Piagetian measurement

The theoretical and empirical evidence reviewed strongly suggests that Piagetian assessment tasks reach into areas of mental functioning of importance to educators and clinicians (and the children they serve) but which are not not adequately assessed by existing psychometric techniques.

Systems of Piagetian measurement

Major efforts to create standardized Piagetian conceptual development tests appropriate to the various Piagetian stages have been carried forward extensively since 1959, notably by Inhelder, Vinh-Bang, and their colleagues at Geneva; by Pinard and Laurendeau *et al.* at Montreal; by Tuddenham; and by Goldschmid and Bentler. There has been no major change in these four serious efforts to develop Piagetian scales since they were excellently described by Meyers at the Second Annual Conference on Piagetian Theory and the Helping Professions (1972). Less formal or less comprehensive systems have also been developed by numerous others.

Uses of Piagetian systems of measurement

The unique aspects of Piagetian measurement give promise of unique contributions in three major areas of concern to the helping professions and especially some of their subareas outlined below:

1. Education
   a. Assessment of readiness
   b. Acceleration of cognitive development and fostering of conceptual growth
2. Clinical practice
   a. Diagnosis and alleviation of mental pathology
3. Research

a. Relationship of variables such as chronological age, sex, race, and social-cultural environment to cognitive level

b. Extension of the theory of intelligence and of measurement

Part Two

As the discussion of questions 2 and 3 reveals, Piaget inspired tests are increasingly being constructed and used along with or in place of traditional psychometric measures of mental development for theoretical and practical reasons. This is occurring in spite of the fact that Piaget has been centrally concerned with establishing the regularities of cognitive development among children rather than with the extent and range of the differences among them. And in the discussion of question 1 theoretical evidence was reviewed which suggests a relationship between traditional psychometric and Piagetian measures in which each type of measure assesses both common and unique parts of a child's total mental maturity. In this study was investigated the degree of that relationship and its nature. And the question of which aspects of general mental development each type of test uniquely assesses were explored. In this way it was hoped to provide information to encourage and facilitate the continued development of Piagetian measures and the appropriate selection and use of each type of measure and combinations of them for diagnosis (understanding children's present behaviours), prognosis (planning for children's general and specific mental development), and for research leading to the constructing and maintaining of optimal developmental environments.

PROCEDURES AND METHODS / The total sample consisted of 104 school children from a homogeneous middle class environment. All subjects yielded data on three occasions (K, I, II) on 21 traditional psychometric and 10 Piagetian variables, as well as on 10 scholastic achievement variables on two occasions (I, II). Descriptive statistics, correlations, factor analysis, canonical correlations, and stepwise multiple regression were employed to analyze the degree and nature of the relationship between the traditional psychometric and the Piagetian measures.

SUMMARY / The results of this study indicate that there is a moderate, positive, and statistically significant relationship between the traditional psychometric and the Piagetian measures of mental development (Hypothesis I). While both types of measures contribute to a first 'general-psychometric and verbally-mediated intelligence' factor, this aspect of mental functioning is largely defined by the psychometric measures (Hypothesis II).

The existence of the second (Piagetian) factor of operational thought suggests, however, the uniqueness of the Piagetian tasks and the aspects of mental development they reflect. The existence of the third (Piagetian) experimental, logical-classification, seriation, and education factor suggests the richness as well as the uniqueness of the aspects of a child's thought processes that we may approach by Piagetian means (Hypotheses III and IV).

The Piagetian measures responsible for the consistent superiority of the Piaget total in predicting achievement in the regression (which articulates the overwhelming and dominant concurrent association of the third factor with measures of school achievement) possibly point a way to new and possibly more valid and reliable predictors and developmental aids to children's achievement.

Tests built from Piaget's and Gesell's tasks as predictors of first grade achievement
A.S. Kaufman and N.L. Kaufman, 1972

AIMS / The authors were intent to compare the effectiveness of tests built from Gesell and Piagetian tasks as predictors of first grade achievement.

SUBJECTS / N = 80, mean age 66.8 months and mean Lorge-Thorndike IQ = 108.

METHOD / Children were adminstered the following tests:
(a) Gesell School Readiness Tests (predictor 1) (Ilg and Ames, 1965).
(b) Piaget battery (predictor 2) included number conservation (Piaget, 1952b); logic (Inhelder and Piaget,1964); space (Piaget and Inhelder, 1956); and geometry (Piaget, Inhelder and Szeminska, 1960).
(c) Lorge-Thorndike Intelligence Tests, Level 1, Form A (predictor 3).
(d) Teething level (predictor 4).
  (Fuller details are described in Kaufman and Kaufman, 1972, pp. 524–526; and Kaufman, 1971. The details of the 1971 study are also given in Modgil, 1974, pp. 388–389).

RESULTS / The results demonstrated that the tests were excellent predictors of achievement. The Piaget and Gesell batteries each correlated .64 with the Stanford Achievement Test Composite. The Lorge-Thorndike MA correlated .58. The measure of teething level tended to be a poor predictor of achievement. The authors compare their results with other relevant studies and draw practical and theoretical implications of their results.

Performance of 14- to 22-month-old black, first born male infants on two tests of cognitive development: the Bayley Scales and the Infant Psychological Development Scale
W.L. King and B. Seegmiller, 1973

AIM / To present data obtained from black male infants on the Bayley Mental and Psychomotor Scales and on the Uzgiris and Hunt Infant Psychological Development Scale.

SUBJECTS / N = 51, aged between 14- and 22-months. Ss were chosen from the black population American mothers residing in the Harlem area. Further subject requirements were: a five-minute Apgar of eight or better (Apgar and James, 1962), birth weight of five pounds or more, absence of maternal disease or drug addiction during pregnancy, and lack of congenital disorder in the infant.

METHOD / The batteries administered were: the Bayley Scale of Infant Development (Bayley, 1969), and the Infant Psychological Development Scale (Uzgiris and Hunt, 1966). The former comprises two scores, providing a measure of general mental and general psychomotor ability. The latter was constructed to reflect a variety of specific abilities, consisting of seven scales: Schemata, Means, Causality, Object, Space, Gestural and Vocal Imitation.

RESULTS / 'The mean Bayley Mental Score was elevated at 14 months but fell to a level similar to the standardization sample at 18 months and remained stable to 22 months. The mean Bayley Psychomotor Score was significantly greater than that of the standardization sample at all three age levels. Variability on both the Bayley Mental and Psychomotor Scales was small at 14 months and increased significantly with age to equal the standardization sample at 22 months. The Mental Scale showed good predictive validity, while the Psychomotor Scale showed almost none. The Uzgiris and Hunt Infant Psychological Developmental Scale appears to measure specific abilities and to be most applicable below 18 months of age. Individually, the scales showed almost no predictive validity. The Bayley Mental Scale showed the greatest number of intercorrelations with all other scales at all age levels. With increasing age, vocalization and verbal ability became more important determinants of test performance', p. 317.

A developmental index of numerical cognitive performance
J.C. Larson, 1972

AIM / The author was intent 'to derive several of the basic characteristics of cognitive-developmental tests from a review of . . . existing measures and Piaget's theory, and to adapt these basic constructs to a simplified test form in the area of number concepts which would be useful in the classroom and still retain a close correspondence with Piagetian measures themselves'.

SUBJECTS / N = 46 from kindergarten, first, and second grades.

METHOD / The tasks involved classification, seriation and analogies. Each of these tasks was divided into 'a gradient of six levels of perceptual structure hypothesized to affect the difficulty of numerical conceptual performance on an array of stimuli. These six levels of performance included, from easiest to hardest; global dimensions; low number / high structure; low structure; and relational dimensions. Two items were developed for each level within the three subtests . . . the total test contained 36 items'. The WISC (verbal scale) and a replication of standard Piagetian number development tasks in conservation and seriation were used for the validity of the test.

RESULTS / Larson concludes, ' . . . the cognitive operations and levels of performance were in general correctly organized, however, some excessive error variance was detected in several items which detracted slightly from the strength of the test constructs. From the pattern of correlations with concurrent measures, the test was characterized as a homogeneous measure of numerical cognitive performance highly related to Piagetian number constructs, and correlating significantly with arithmetic ability over and above its relationship to IQ ability. The primary correlations were as follows: total test score with Piagetian tasks, $r = .70$; total score with age, $r = .69$; total score with IQ, $r = .41$; total score with WISC Arithmetic subtest, $r = .58$ . . . IQ with Piagetian tasks, $r = .25$ . . . ' Larson asserts that the developmental index of numerical cognitive performance would be a useful instrument in broad-scale curriculum evaluation.

Scalogram analysis of nine concrete operations tests *
S. Meadows, 1975c

AIM / Scalogram analysis has been much used in the field of cognitive development. The basic premise of such use is that scalability of responses to a set of problems indicates a single developmental continuum. Clearly there must be an independent validation of the psychological dimension defined by the items, and the ranking of subjects on this dimension should correspond with psychological development. Thus there should be a significant association between rank order position and age; Wallace (1965) suggests that with increasing age there should be a change in the direction of a higher scale type, and any given subject should respond in accordance with the scale whenever he is tested. A longitudinal study of nine Piagetian tasks provides data on which to test these predictions.

METHOD / N = 120 children aged between five years one month and 10.10 at first testing were given tests of conservation of amount, weight and volume (Elkind, 1961), multiplicative and additive classification (respectively Lovell, Mitchell and Everett, 1962; Calvert, 1972) left-right discrimination and coordination of perspectives (Laurendeau and Pinard, 1970), reciprocal relationships and role inclusion (Piaget, 1926). Testing was repeated after six months and after a year. The data from each testing were analysed using the computer program BMD 05S. In each analysis the number of items was 9, the number of levels on each item 4, the number of subjects 120. The results of the analyses are shown in Tables 1 and 2.

RESULTS / The scale resulting from the analysis of the first testing has nineteen levels, a coefficient of reproducibility of .892, a minimum marginal reproducibility of .426 and a coefficient of scalability of .811. Looking at the matrix of ranked responses (Table 2), it is found that 17 per cent of cases fall into the bottom three categories, failing all the tests; a further 14 per cent pass only the easiest test, Re, 10 per cent two tests Re and A. The next easiest tests are R.M and W; a further 31 per cent pass some or all of these tests in addition to Re and A. Nineteen per cent also pass C, forming scale-level 4; the top three categories take up 9 per cent of cases.
Analysis of the results of the second testing gave rise to a scale with seventeen levels, with a coefficient of reproducibility of .890, a

* Written and prepared by the author for inclusion in this volume. Gratitude is extended to Dr Sara Meadows of Bedford College of the University of London.

Table One: Scalogram Analysis: Task order

First, second and third testings: 9 items

Task	1	2	3		Task
Conservation of volume	V			V	Conservation of volume
Co-ordination of perspectives	Pe			Pe	Co-ordination of perspectives
Left-right position	Po			Po	Left-right position
Class inclusion	C			C	Class inclusion
Conservation of weight	W			W	Conservation of weight
Multiplication of relations (matrix)	M			R	Role Inclusion
Role Inclusion	R			A	Conservation of amount
Conservation of amount	A			M	Multiplication of relations (matrix)
Reciprocal relationships	RE			RE	Reciprocal relationships

$$1_2 = .98 \qquad 2_3 = .98 \qquad 1_3 = .95$$

Table Two: Scalogram Analysis: Summary of Levels

First testing

Level	Freq.	Fraction	Tasks achieved (cumulative)
19	10	.0833	None or almost none
18	7	.0583	
17	3	.0250	
16	12	.1000	Re
15	5	.0417	
14	2	.0167	
13	2	.0167	A
12	8	.0667	
11	8	.0667	R
10	1	.0083	
9	8	.0667	M
8	4	.0333	
7	5	.0417	W
6	6	.0500	
5	5	.0417	
4	23	.1917	C
3	1	.0083	Po
2	6	.0500	Pe
1	4	.0333	V

Rep. = .892
Coefficient of scalability = .81

Second Testing

Level	Freq.	Fraction	Tasks achieved (cumulative)
17	5	.0417	None or almost none
16	6	.0500	
15	1	.0083	
14	5	.0417	Re
13	5	.0417	
12	1	.0083	A or M
11	1	.0083	
10	9	.0750	
9	9	.0750	A & M
8	16	.1333	
7	2	.0167	R
6	17	.1417	W
5	6	.0500	C
4	14	.1167	Po
3	9	.0750	Pe
2	5	.0417	
1	9	.0750	V

Rep. = .890
Coefficient of scalability = .79

Third Testing

Level	Freq.	Fraction	Tasks achieved (cumulative)
16	2	.0167	None
15	2	.0167	
14	2	.0167	Re
13	4	.0333	M
12	4	.0333	
11	4	.0333	A
10	3	.0250	
9	8	.0667	R
8	3	.0250	
7	1	.0083	W
6	18	.1500	
5	8	.0667	C
4	10	.0833	
3	30	.2500	Pe, Po
2	6	.0500	
1	15	.1250	V

Rep. = .918
Coefficient of scalability = .66

minimum marginal reproducibility of .482 and a coefficient of scalability of .787. There is little change in the order of the tests, which is the same as in the first testing except that M and R have changed places and M is now the easier. On this testing only 10 per cent of cases fell into the bottom three categories, failing all tests; a further 25 per cent passed Re and either A or M or both. The next easiest test was R; 13 per cent passed A, M, Re and R, 15 per cent also passed W, 5 per cent added C, 12 per cent Po. A further 8 per cent passed Pe, forming the fourth level; the top three levels, 12 per cent, were differentiated by their responses to V, ranging from total failure to success.

The third testing produced still fewer levels, sixteen only; the coefficient of reproducibility was .918, the minimum marginal reproducibility .582 and the coefficient of scalability .66. This time only two children failed all the tests, only four passed only the easiest, Re a total of 5 per cent. Six per cent passed Re and M, 6 per cent A, M and Re, 9 per cent A, M, R and Re. Sixteen per cent passed five tests, most commonly A, M, R, Re and W; 15 per cent passed six tests, usually failing V, Pe and Po. The remaining 43 per cent were differentiated in level mainly by their response to V; 25 per cent failed the test completely, 5 per cent partially, and 13 per cent passed it.

DISCUSSION / It may be seen from these results that there was a general improvement in performance between testing sessions. The rank order of items was very stable ($\uparrow_{12}$ = .98, $\uparrow_{23}$ = .98, $\uparrow_{13}$ = .95), the rank order of subjects slightly less so (r_{12} = .65, r_{23} = .72, r_{13} = .62). The results of this study, like those of Versey (1974), support the assumptions that older subjects score higher on the scale than younger and that the scale is valid to the same extent for all ages. Although the coefficients of reproducibility are in the cases of the first two testings just under the .9 recommended by Guttman as a minimum level, the coefficients of scalability are for each scale well over Green's suggestion of .6. They are far short however of the value of 1.00 which indicates perfect consistency. There is a stable and perhaps unidimensional general pattern but much individual variation. This variation may have been due in part to a lack of reliability of some or all of the tests. Low Reps. are often taken as indicating that several subscales are present rather than one homogeneous scale; in this case they may be indicative of less operational generalizability than Piaget has supposed.

A factor analytic investigation of personality, attitudinal, and cognitive variables in 7- and 8-year-old children [1]
S.L. Modgil, T.E. Dielman, R.B. Cattell and C. Modgil, 1975

In an earlier investigation (Modgil, 1969), children classified as emotionally unstable on the basis of their Bristol Social Adjustment scores (Stott, 1958) were inferior in their performance on tests of conservation to children classified as emotionally stable, even when the two groups were matched for CA and IQ. In addition, both low conservation and maladjustment were positively associated with ignoring, high dominance, and possessiveness scores on a parental attitude scale (Shoben, 1949) by the children's mothers.

The current investigation is in part an extension of Modgil's (1969) study and has the further exploratory purpose of the inclusion of several measures of 'emotional stability' and 'conservation' in order to examine the amount of common variance obtaining among the different measures. In the hypothesis testing sense, all measures of 'emotional stability' should load one factor and all measures of conservation another. Further, if children who receive higher scores on emotional stability also receive higher scores on the conservation measures, then a positive loading on the 'conservation factor' should obtain for each measure of emotional stability. The mother's high dominance, ignoring, and possessiveness variables would be expected to exhibit negative loadings on both the emotional stability and conservation factors.

In addition to measures of emotional stability, conservation, and parental attitudes, other variables included were age, sex, tests of academic achievement, IQ, peer preference, attitudes towards school subjects and teachers, and a number of additional child personality scales.

METHOD / The sample included 258 children ranging in age from 7-0 to 8-4 and their parents and teachers. The 44 variables employed in the study and a brief description of their nature, when not self explanatory, are listed in Table 1. The children were group tested on the Early School Personality Questionnaire (ESPQ; Coan and Cattell, 1966), the battery of Schonell group tests of five areas of academic achievement (Schonell, 1960), the ten individual tests of reasoning derived from the work of Piaget and administered in a standardized form based on a pilot study by Lunzer (1970), the Sleight Non-Verbal Intelligence Test (Sleight, 1949), the four attitudes towards teachers and school (Modgil, 1969), the three measures of anxiety (Biggs, 1962),

1 This research was supported in part by Public Health Service Research Grant MH1733 from the National Institute of Mental Health.

and the peer preference variable. The latter consisted of assigning each child a score based on the number of times he was chosen as 'liked' or 'disliked' during individual testing of members of his peer group. In addition, the Bristol Social Adjustment Guide (Stott, 1958) was completed for each child by his teacher, and both parents of each child independently completed the parental attitude scales (Shoben, 1949) to yield the measures of dominance, possessiveness, and ignoring. Complete data were available for all children.

Table 1: List of variables employed

---

1. Age in Months
2. Sex (1 = male, 0 = female)
3. Sleight Non-Verbal IQ Score
4. Schonell Mechanical Arithmetic Score
5. Schonell Problem Arithmetic Score
6. Schonell Silent Reading Score
7. Schonell Spelling Score
8. Schonell Composition Score
9. Lunzer Number Conservation Score
10. Lunzer Substance Conservation Score
11. Lunzer Area Conservation Score
12. Lunzer Length Conservation Score
13. Lunzer Class Inclusion Classificatory Reasoning Score
14. Lunzer Classificatory Anticipation Classificatory Reasoning Score
15. Lunzer Cross-Classification Classificatory Reasoning Score
16. Lunzer Haptic Recognition Spatial Operativity Score
17. Lunzer Linear and Circular Order Spatial Operativity Score
18. Lunzer Horizontal and Vertical Co-Ordinates Spatial Operativity Score
19. Total Piaget Score
20. Shoben Dominance Score
21. Shoben Possessiveness Score
22. Shoben Ignoring Score
23. Stott Social Adjustment Score
24. Biggs General Anxiety Score
25. Biggs Number Anxiety Score
26. Biggs Test Anxiety Score
27. ESPQ Factor A (Reserved vs. Outgoing)
28. ESPQ Factor B (Low Intelligence vs. High Intelligence)
29. ESPQ Factor C (Affected by Feelings vs. Emotionally Stable)
30. ESPQ Factor D (Phlegmatic vs. Excitable)
31. ESPQ Factor E (Obedient vs. Assertive)
32. ESPQ Factor F (Sober vs. Happy-Go-Lucky)
33. ESPQ Factor G (Expedient vs. Conscientious)
34. ESPQ Factor H (Shy vs. Venturesome)
35. ESPQ Factor I (Tough-Minded vs. Tender-Minded)
36. ESPQ Factor J (Vigorous vs. Doubting)
37. ESPQ Factor N (Forthright vs. Shrewd)
38. ESPQ Factor O (Placid vs. Apprehensive)
39. ESPQ Factor Q4 (Relaxed vs. Tense)
40. Peer Preference Score
41. Modgil Attitude towards Reading
42. Modgil Attitude towards Arithmetic
43. Modgil Attitude towards School
44. Modgil Attitude towards Teacher

Product moment correlations were computed among the 44 variables. Seventeen factors were indicated by application of the scree test (Cattell, 1966) to the plot of the eigenvalues, which accounted for 73 per cent of the accountable variance. The highest correlation in each column was taken as the estimate of communality and inserted in the diagonal element. Seventeen principal axes factors were extracted and initially rotated to the Oblimax criterion (Saunders, 1961), followed by Rotoplot — assisted visual rotation (Cattell and Foster, 1963) until an unimprovable ±.10 hyperplane count of 83 per cent was reached.

RESULTS AND DISCUSSION / The seventeen primary factors along with the salient variable (V_{FP} values $\geqslant$ .20) and their associated loadings are presented as Table 2.

Factor I in Table 2 is clearly a 'Conservation' factor, with the high loadings from the Lunzer Number and Substance Conservation variables. The only other variables approaching ±.20 loadings on this factor were the Lunzer Horizontal and Vertical Coordinates Spatial Operativity Score (.19), ESPQ Factor E−, or 'Obedience' (−.19), and ESPQ Factor O+, or 'Apprehensive' (.18).

Factor II again receives its highest loadings from three of the Lunzer variables, although it should be noted that the two measures of 'Spatial Operativity' load in opposite directions, with one 'Classificatory Reasoning' variable loading in a positive direction. Another anomaly here is that the Modgil 'Attitude towards Teacher' shows a positive loading while the 'Attitude towards School' is in a negative direction. In addition, the ESPQ Factors A+ ('Outgoing'), D− ('Phlegmatic'), and H+ ('Venturesome') made sizable contributions to this factor.

Factor III is also in a sense anomalous, with the Sleight Non-Verbal IQ and the ESPQ Intelligence scores making contributions in opposite directions. The other salient variables appearing on this factor, however, are in partial confirmation of the hypothesis concerning the relationship between emotional stability and parental practices, with positive loadings appearing in the case of the parental possessiveness score and the Biggs general and number anxiety scores.

The fourth factor listed in Table 2 received high loadings from the ESPQ factors H+ (venturesome) and O+ (apprehensive) and a moderate loading from ESPQ factor Q_4+ (tense), but negative loadings from the Shoben dominance and the Biggs test anxiety variables. This would indicate that the Biggs score and the ESPQ factors which enter the second-order anxiety factor are not measuring the same sort of 'adjustment' and that while the Shoben dominance score is positively related to one of the Biggs anxiety scores, as hypothesized, it is negatively related to some of the ESPQ factors which enter the second

Table 2: Rotated primary factor pattern values ⩾.20

Variable No.	Variable Identification	Vf Value
	Factor I	
9	Lunzer Number Conservation Score	0.62
10	Lunzer − Substance Conservation Score	0.80
	Factor II	
13	Lunzer Class Inclusion Classificatory Reasoning Score	0.46
17	Lunzer Linear and Circular Order Spatial Operativity Score	0.41
18	Lunzer Horizontal and Vertical Co-Ordinates Spatial Operativity Score	−0.53
27	ESPQ Factor A (Reserved vs. Outgoing)	0.28
30	ESPQ Factor D (Phlegmatic vs. Excitable)	−0.24
34	ESPQ Factor H (Shy vs. Venturesome)	0.34
43	Modgil Attitude towards School	−0.36
44	Modgil Attitude towards Teacher	0.27
	Factor III	
3	Sleight Non-Verbal IQ Score	−0.28
21	Shoben Possessiveness Score	0.52
24	Biggs General Anxiety Score	0.22
25	Biggs Number Anxiety Score	0.34
27	ESPQ Factor A (Reserved vs. Outgoing)	0.28
28	ESPQ Factor B (Low Intelligence vs. High Intelligence)	0.30
33	ESPQ Factor G (Expedient vs. Conscientious)	−0.23
	Factor IV	
3	Sleight Non-Verbal IQ Score	−0.43
5	Schonell Problem Arithmetic Score	−0.41
13	Lunzer Class Inclusion Classificatory Reasoning Score	−0.21
18	Lunzer Horizontal and Vertical Co-Ordinated Spatial Operativity Score	−0.23
20	Shoben Dominance Score	−0.23
26	Biggs Test Anxiety Score	−0.25
28	ESPQ Factor B (Low Intelligence vs. High Intelligence)	0.23
34	ESPQ Factor H (Shy vs. Venturesome)	0.51
37	ESPQ Factor N (Forthright vs. Shrewd)	0.28
38	ESPQ Factor O (Placid vs. Apprehensive)	0.53
39	ESPQ Factor Q^4 (Relaxed vs. Tense)	0.20
43	Modgil Attitudes towards School	−0.33

Table 2 Cont'd

Factor V

3	Sleight Non-Verbal IQ Score	0.41
4	Schonell Mechanical Arithmetic Score	0.66
5	Schonell Problem Arithmetic Score	0.77
6	Schonell Silent Reading Score	0.86
7	Schonell Spelling Score	0.68
8	Schonell Composition Score	0.73

Factor VI

3	Sleight Non-Verbal IQ Score	−0.39
15	Lunzer Cross-Classification Classificatory Reasoning Score	−0.21
16	Lunzer Haptic Recognition Spatial Operativity Score	0.38
18	Lunzer Horizontal and Vertical Co-Ordinates Spatial Operativity Score	0.69
19	Total Piaget Score	0.23
23	Stott Social Adjustment Score	−0.43
24	Biggs General Anxiety Score	−0.33
40	Peer Preference Score	0.34

Factor VII

1	Age in Months	0.28
14	Lunzer Classificatory Anticipation Classificatory Reasoning Score	−0.69
17	Lunzer Linear and Circular Order Spatial Operativity Score	0.31

Factor VIII

1	Age in Months	−0.23
10	Lunzer Substance Conservation Score	0.20
27	ESPQ Factor A (Reserved vs. Outgoing)	−0.22
29	ESPQ Factor C (Affected by Feelings vs. Emotionally Stable)	−0.54
30	ESPQ Factor D (Phlegmatic vs. Excitable)	−0.60
31	ESPQ Factor E (Obedient vs. Assertive)	−0.61

Factor IX

19	Total Piaget Score	−0.21
20	Shoben Dominance Score	−0.55
22	Shoben Ignoring Score	0.93
23	Stott Social Adjustment Score	0.39
25	Biggs Number Anxiety Score	0.90
26	Biggs Test Anxiety Score	0.73

Factor X

1	Age in Months	−0.39
3	Schonell Composition Score	−0.39
13	Lunzer Class Inclusion Classificatory Reasoning Score	−0.31
33	ESPQ Factor G (Expedient vs. Conscientious)	0.22

Table 2 Cont'd

	Factor XI	
11	Lunzer Area Conservation Score	−0.76
12	Lunzer Length Conservation Score	−0.65

	Factor XII	
15	Lunzer Cross-Classification Classificatory Reasoning Score	−0.57
16	Lunzer Haptic Recognition Spatial Operativity Score	−0.52
17	Lunzer Linear and Circular Order Spatial Operativity Score	0.28
19	Total Piaget Score	−0.21
41	Modgil Attitude towards Reading	−0.29

	Factor XIII	
2	Sex (1 = Male 0 = Female)	0.76
23	Stott Social Adjustment Score	0.20
26	Biggs Test Anxiety Score	−0.23
27	ESPQ Factor A (Reserved vs. Outgoing)	0.21
28	ESPQ Factor B (Low Intelligence vs. High Intelligence)	−0.22
32	ESPQ Factor F (Sober vs. Happy-Go-Lucky)	−0.85
36	ESPQ Factor J (Vigorous vs. Doubting)	0.99
37	ESPQ Factor N (Forthright vs. Shrewd)	0.46
40	Peer Preference Score	−0.77
41	Modgil Attitude towards Reading	−0.40
42	Modgil Attitude towards Arithmetic	0.72
43	Modgil Attitude towards School	−0.29
44	Modgil Attitude towards Teacher	0.30

	Factor XIV	
7	Schonell Spelling Score	0.23
15	Lunzer Cross Classification Classificatory Reasoning Score	0.31
17	Lunzer Linear and Circular Order Spatial Operativity Score	0.36
18	Lunzer Horizontal and Vertical Co-Ordinates Spatial Operativity Score	0.38
19	Total Piaget Score	0.44
28	ESPQ Factor B (Low Intelligence vs. High Intelligence)	0.37
33	ESPQ Factor G (Expedient vs. Conscientious	0.37

	Factor XV	
2	Sex (1 = Male 0 = Female)	−0.28
10	Lunzer Substance Conservation Score	−0.20
24	Biggs General Anxiety Score	0.24
32	ESPQ Factor F (Sober vs. Happy-Go-Lucky)	0.34
34	ESPQ Factor H (Shy vs. Venturesome)	0.28
37	ESPQ Factor N (Forthright vs. Shrewd)	0.32
41	Modgil Attitude towards Reading	0.36
44	Modgil Attitude towards Teacher	0.43

Table 2 Cont'd

	Factor XVI	
34	ESPQ Factor H (Shy vs. Venturesome)	−0.22
35	ESPQ Factor I (Tough-Minded vs. Tender-Minded)	0.77
37	ESPQ Factor N (Forthright vs. Shrewd)	−0.26
39	ESPQ Factor Q4 (Relaxed vs. Tense)	−0.60
43	Modgil Attitude towards School	0.39
44	Modgil Attitude towards Teacher	0.22
	Factor XVII	
2	Sex (1 = Male 0 = Female)	−0.24
23	Stott Social Adjustment Score	−0.29
28	ESPQ Factor B (Low Intelligence vs. High Intelligence)	0.26
29	ESPQ Factor C (Affected by Feelings vs. Emotionally Stable)	−0.26
38	ESPQ Factor O (Placid vs. Apprehensive)	−0.44

order anxiety factor. Again, the ESPQ B factor (intelligence) and the Sleight Non-Verbal IQ variable exhibited loadings which were opposite in sign. The Schonell problem Arithmetic variable and the Lunzer Class inclusion and spatial coordinates variables entered this factor with loadings in the same direction as the Sleight Non-Verbal variable and the Biggs test anxiety and Shoben dominance variables, but opposite in sign to the ESPQ 0 and Q4 factors, thus supporting the hypothesis of a negative relationship between the Piagetian measures and 'emotional stability' if one accepts the ESPQ 0+ and Q4+ dimensions as definitions of such a concept, but not if one prefers to define the concept by the Biggs test anxiety score.

Factor V includes all of the achievement scores as well as the Sleight Non-Verbal IQ score which we shall take as a general intelligence factor. The sixth factor exhibits negative loadings from both the Stott Social adjustment scale and the Biggs general anxiety score, as well as the Sleight IQ score and one classificatory reasoning score, and positive loadings from peer preference, total Piaget score, and two spatial operativity scores. This pattern calls into question the efficacy of the Sleight IQ score inasmuch as past evidence indicates that less intelligent children are less socially adjusted and less accepted by their peers rather than more so. Factor VII is a small triplet including positive loadings from age in months and a spatial operativity score but a large negative loading from the classificatory anticipation score, which calls the validity of the latter into question.

The eighth factor in Table 2 is primarily the ESPQ second order 'introversion' factor, with small loadings from age in months (negatively) and the substance conservation score (positively). Factor IX is primarily a social adjustment — anxiety score, except that high anxiety would appear to go with high adjustment, which again causes one to question the validity of the measures. In terms of our hypotheses, we have here a negative loading from the Shoben 'dominance' scale and a positive one from the 'ignoring' score, indicating that, if these scales are valid measures of the constructs, the two certainly do not go together and while the ignoring parent tends to have a more anxious (but more socially adjusted?) child, the dominant parent tends to have a less anxious (but less socially adjusted?) child. The total Piaget score exhibited a small negative loading here, lending some evidence to the hypothesized relationship of the Biggs scores and the Shoben 'ignoring' score and the Piagetian concepts, but not the Stott scale or the Shoben 'dominance' scale.

Factors X through XII are small and self explanatory and the reader can easily grasp their meaning through inspection of Table 2.

Factor XIII is composed primarily of ESPQ scales and the Modgil attitude scales, with additional loadings from peer preference (low), test anxiety (low), Stott social adjustment (high), and male sex. The pattern of the ESPQ loadings are in the direction of 'reserved', 'low intelligence', 'sober', 'doubting', and 'shrewd'. The reading and school attitudes exhibit negative loadings, while the arithmetic and teacher attitudes rendered positive contributions. Factor XIV is primarily a 'Lunzer' factor, with positive loadings from three of the Lunzer variables and the total Piaget score. Also contributing, in a positive direction, were the Schonell spelling score, ESPQ B+ ('high intelligence'), and ESPQ G+ ('Conscientious').

Factor XV is composed of female sex,' positive loadings from the Modgil attitudes towards reading and teacher, ESPQ N+ ('shrewd'), H+ ('Venturesome'), and F+ ('happy-go-lucky'), and the Biggs general anxiety score and a negative loading by the Lunzer Substance Conservation score. Factor XVI is again primarily ESPQ and Modgil attitudes, with positive attitudes towards school and teacher, ESPQ H− ('shy') I+ ('tender-minded'), N− ('forthright') and Q_4− ('relaxed'). The last factor in Table 2 seems to be a 'lack of social adjustment' factor, with a negative loading from the Stott social adjustment scale and ESPQ factor C ('affected by feelings'). However, the results here are clouded by the negative loading from ESPQ factor C ('placid'), and a positive loading from ESPQ factor B ('more intelligent').

To summarize, the analysis indicated a lack of convergence of the measures of 'social adjustment' which were employed. They were, in fact negatively related. Further, the measures of conservation did not exhibit a satisfactory degree of convergence. As a consequence, the relationship among the measures of parental behaviour, emotional stability and conservation depends upon the particular measure one chooses to use.

Piaget and the school psychologist *
P. Nolen, 1974

> *'The question is,' said Alice, 'whether you can make words mean*
> *so many different things.'*
> *'The question is,' said Humpty Dumpty, 'which is to be master —*
> *that's all.' (Dodgson, 1963)*

Asking what Piaget has to say to the school psychologist is like
asking a ten-year-old what time the clock says. Those who have been
around children of this age know that the child's reply is predictable:
'The clock doesn't say anything. You have to read it.' Piaget does not
volunteer anything directly to the school psychologist, either. Like the
clock, he must be read. Unlike the clock, Piaget must be thought about
as well, for his answers to questions that may concern school
psychologists are likely to be given as parables.

Parables are greatly honoured in certain philosophic traditions, and
as a method of teaching, they are not without precedent. Yet they are
hardly accustomed nourishment for those who cut their teeth on the
hard data of tests and measurements. It is not that they are difficult to
understand. On the contrary, Piaget's parables invite the reader to think
within narrative examples that lead to understanding. They deliberately
involve the reader in a discovery process that the author believes is
characteristic of how people learn best. Yet the reader can be so caught
up in the scope and originality of Piaget's views, that it may be difficult
to divorce a Piagetian principle from the parable context in which it is
embedded. For example, unless readers make a conscious effort,
subsequent references to conservation after reading Piaget's first
discussions are likely to conjure up images of clay and flasks of liquids.
The abstract understanding that certain aspects of an object or event
remain unchanged despite variations in shape or position is all but lost
in the vividness of the original situational context. Nor is a reader's
thinking pointed in a more general direction by the many duplications
of Piaget's studies which dot professional journals. In replications
exploring the parameters of Piagetian theory, extensions to problem
classes broader than the originals are still the exception, rather than the
rule.

Translating parables is difficult. But still more difficult may be
Piaget's choice of a language of mathematics and logic to make his
views precise. It is a language into which few have been initiated, so
that many members of the helping professions must approach Piaget

---

* Published by the kind permission of the author. Gratitude is extended to
Professor Patricia Nolen of the University of Washington.

only through someone else's exegesis of his text. Most of the writing about Piaget stays close to the spirit and illustrative examples of the original. As practice is not the primary purpose in explication of theory, 'Applications in Education' are usually left to blush unseen in chapters toward the back. Thus readers with a bent toward application can find themselves overwhelmed by contextual detail or language differences if they follow a normal reading progression, or they may be disappointed in the scantiness of conclusions if they reverse their usual reading order.

There is of course, no more justification in criticizing Piaget or his translators for failure to consider a school psychologist's preferences in reading than there is in criticizing a clock for being late in the day. The burden of responsibility lies with the reader, and the fact that the helping professions may sometimes evaluate Piagetian understandings as interesting, but of limited relevance, reflects not at all on the theory. The helping professions must acknowledge that they are judging within their own frames of immediate reference, a kind of professional egocentrism. They must make an effort to find those parts of the theory that relate to their concerns, asking only if more can be understood with the help of Piaget than without.

Much of Piaget's writing has concerned the course of children's thinking in the elementary school years, an age group of special interest to school psychologists as well. While Piaget seeks evidence of *similarities* in the way children of this age handle experiences, they come to a school psychologist's attention because of their *individual differences* in thinking and performance. Piaget's purpose in interviewing children is to establish the *universal course* of the development of thought. But a school psychologist's interview is to establish a *particular course* of thought for an individual child. Yet despite their differences, the work of Piaget and the school psychologist is in fundamental correspondence. *Both look at a child from the standpoint of the kinds of learning possible at any one point in a child's development.*

Questions about a child's basic ability to learn after his failure in the classroom is a common reason for referring a child to a school psychologist. Expectations about children's learning capacities within broad age groups are among Piaget's contributions. Bringing together a school psychologist's school-oriented hindsight questions with anticipatory theoretical answers is a difficult venture at best. There is always the possibility that answers may be supplied for questions that were not asked, or that questions that are asked can be answered best by traditional means. For the helping professions, judgments of theoretical relevance will depend on the extent to which expectations about children's thinking can be given practical consequence.

When a school psychologist is asked to assess the learning problems of an elementary school child, it is with the tacit understanding that he will produce prescriptions for change. Profound shifts have taken place of late in beliefs that change is possible. Evidence for the modifiability of intelligence and demonstrated success in matching school tasks to learners rather than the other way around are examples. School psychologists must know not only aspects of how a child thinks and learns, but also what kinds of thinking and learning are demanded in various school activities. From this knowledge base they can prescribe courses of action which are likely to produce change.

The exact procedures in an evaluation of an elementary school child's learning problem will vary according to school districts and a psychologist's professional training. Customarily measures are taken of a child's intelligence, his school performance and of factors contributing to how he feels about himself as a learner. Results from intellectual, social and school achievement measures are analyzed and placed in a diagnostic framework with possible causes and promising remedies for the learning difficulty identified. The preliminary work of a school psychologist in report form may look something like this:

NAME: John   AGE: 7

SCHOOL: Briarcrest Elementary   GRADE: 2

TESTS ADMINISTERED /   *Bender Test of Visual Motor Gestalt;*
                             Diagnostic Reading Tests;
                             Educational Achievement Battery;
                             Wechsler Intelligence Scale for Children

REASON FOR REFERRAL: John has not acquired reading and number skills commensurate with those his age. His teacher reports that he has had special help in reading, but that he does not retain letter sounds and their corresponding symbols from one day to the next. His arithmetic papers show much reworking with little understanding of basic addition and subtraction processes. His spelling often seems to be a random assortment of letters. In the light of repeated failure John is said to have lost confidence in himself and no longer uses his time to his own advantage.

RESULTS /
1. WISC

Verbal Subtests	Scaled Scores	Performance Subtests	Scaled Scores
Information	9	Picture Completion	10
Comprehension	11	Picture Arrangement	11
Arithmetic	9	Block Design	13
Similarities	10	Object Assembly	10
Digit Span	8	Digit Symbol	10
Vocabulary	10	Mazes (not given)	
Total	57	Total	54
Prorated	48		
Verbal IQ	97	Performance IQ	106
	Full Scale IQ 101		

2. BENDER

John understood test directions readily. He seemed to perceive the figures accurately, but have some difficulty in reproducing them as shown by his running commentary and erasures so that his drawings would 'look just like yours'. While the quality of his figures did not always meet standards for a child of 7, there were no gross distortions or alterations to suggest perceptual motor dysfunctions.

3. READING

John's instructional reading level is at middle first grade. He attempts to sound out the majority of words he reads in lists or connected text. Most of the words he is able to sound out, he is unable to blend into a meaningful whole. Those words he attempts by sight appear to be recalled on the basis of distinctive letter configurations (basket / breakfast; red / ride; the / there) and initial letter cues. Comprehension questions asked John following material he has read were likely answered on the basis of information he has had prior to reading.

4. SPELLING

John's spelling achievement was recorded at first grade level. Beyond those few words he spelled correctly (cat, man, go) his attempts showed either incorrect associations between speech sounds and letter symbols or were a random assortment of correct letters in incorrect sequence. John showed little carry over of letter correspondences he identified correctly in his phonic word attacks in reading. Examples of John's spelling were hcicn / chicken, care / carry, grl / girl and wih / which.

5. ARITHMETIC

John has beginning second grade arithmetic skills with his written work showing more understanding of addition and subtraction processes than his replies to oral arithmetic questions on the WISC. However, John makes many mistakes in recalling number combinations and does not seem to have established a firm understanding of place value in either addition or subtraction. The following are samples of John's work:

Addition:

4	16	26	32	8	34
+3	+2	+13	+54	+23	+6
7	9	39	86	13	13

Subtraction:

42	64	17	34	39	43
−25	−29	−9	−21	−16	−19
23	45	8	13	23	36

Since Piaget has had little to say directly about motivation or social adjustment, just those measures that deal with the quality of a child's thinking within an academic setting have been included in the preliminary report. From an academic standpoint interpretation of the report is likely to proceed as an exercise in elimination of hypotheses. For example, adjustment of academic expectancies for John on the grounds of less than average intelligence is not necessitated, given his full scale IQ index. A hypothesis of perceptual dysfunction based on John's idiosyncratic spellings or failure to make progress in reading is not fully supported by John's Bender performance of his relatively high scores in the visual analysis section of the WISC. Few school psychologists today will cling to a perceptual or symbolic deficit explanation (dyslexia) where there are either reasonable alternatives or discrepancies among perceptual measures. This leaves John's immediate problems in reading, spelling and arithmetic to be related to his relatively low scores in auditory memory. The reasoning is that whatever was behind a child's difficulties in reciting digits heard must also be behind his failure to remember sequences of sounds in reading or rules of operation' in arithmetic. And whatever was behind John's ease of handling visual problems in the formal tests will also be available to John in acquiring those academic skills he has missed. Recommendations likely will include an emphasis on visual perception in all areas needing remedial instruction.

The school psychologist may suggest changing from a sound-symbol reading approach relying on auditory memory to a word family method where there is a redundancy among visual patterns. Probably in arithmetic there will be suggestions taking into account both problems in conceptual understanding and John's feelings toward his repeated failures. Reteaching with the use of concrete examples and devices for manipulation will make use of John's preferred modality for learning and supply the real world of objects representative of place value understandings and number combinations. John's spelling may be puzzling at first. How is it that a child with adequate visual memory skills according to the performance section of the WISC, did so poorly on a task which is basically visual memory? One way to reconcile these data within accepted frameworks for educational interpretation is to see John's lack of success in phonic analysis in reading carried over to his spelling. Recommendations for his spelling program undoubtedly will be based on the axiom that no child needs to learn to spell words that he does not yet read. A sight approach to spelling probably will be reinstituted although with a different selection of words to correspond with those in John's reading tasks.

Reports embodying interrelations among possible causes and remedial suggestions like those above have demonstrated usefulness. Though the patterns among scaled scores vary and different arrangements of academic strengths and weaknesses emerge for different children, the diagnostic process usually begins with looking to one set of performances for an explanation of the other. Resulting prescriptions commonly specify increased attention to the learner, direct teaching to his strongest avenue for reception, adjustment of pace with many experiences of success, and ample time for the remedies to be practiced so that the reinforcing aspects of success may take effect. Time is on the side of the school psychologist writing the remedial prescriptions. Most children profit soon after suggested changes are made and where program changes are not effective at once, a policy of wait and see often produces the desired result. Why some children must endure a time lag before benefits accrue has not been a major concern of school psychologists. Crowded calendars, repeated demonstrations of success in continued practice and desired changes for the majority of children all suggest strength in waiting rather than any weakness in the diagnosis. In accounting for a time lapse between prescription and practice, patience has been a useful hypothesis for the school psychologist.

Piaget's expectancies for children's ways of handling information at various times in their development however, might suggest that patience as an explanatory construct was of limited usefulness. Piaget would be interested in what it was children were doing during the time lag, what mental operations were available to them and what cognitive structures and strategies they had between the time the remedial plan was instituted and the time it took effect. These are questions that are not often asked by school psychologists, but they are the answers to be found in reading Piaget. Perhaps what Piaget has to say to the school psychologist can only be found if questions of this kind are asked.

Asking questions about children's cognitive strategies is not the same as asking whether children are to be classified as visile or audile learners. Questions about the former refer to broad characteristics of children's thinking that may transcend any one sense modality. In considering Piaget's answers a school psychologist might do well to review how Piaget has characterized the thinking of the approximate age group represented by the child who has been referred to him. According to Piaget, John is either in or approaching the stage of concrete operational thought. Once a child has mastered this stage he can:

consider two separate aspects of objects or events simultaneously (decentration)

group objects different on one dimension into classes on the basis of a second, shared dimension (classification)

understand the logical relationship between parts and whole (class inclusion)

represent internally sequences of events through time (mental representation)

distinguish between elements and relate them in a series (ordering)

retain the identity of an object or situation on one aspect although another aspect is transformed (conservation)

grasp the idea that operations on objects or situations in the environment or in thought can be nullified by an inverse operation (reversibility) or by a compensating action (reciprocity)

form generalizations from particular instances he has experienced (inductive reasoning) (Gorman, 1972)

The concrete operational child cannot:

perform the above operations on a purely verbal or abstract level

deduce exemplary instances from learned generalizations (deductive reasoning)

always differentiate his own hypotheses or assumptions from fact (egocentrism) (Elkind, 1973)

Before seeking to reconcile test data and theory it should be recalled that the systematization of thought that occurs in the early elementary school years appears within a broad age range that can span the years from five to eight. Also characteristic of the cognitive skills detailed above is a sequence to their appearance and organization with capabilities acquired earlier, that is individual for the individual child. While some ordered succession is necessitated as in perceiving multiple dimensions prior to making alternative classification, the same thinking skills are not always available to a child over several classes or problems.

At times an elementary child's thinking attainments seem to be quite task specific (Lovell, 1968). He may be able to 'conserve' quantity, but not weight, or to integrate parts and wholes in space, but not time. Further, any limitations on a child's perceptual or memory capacities may produce still other differences in the organization of his thought. For example, if a child's visual memory is limited, his ability to retain and classify on visual dimensions will also be limited. Thus children seem to be in the concrete operational stage by reason of age and normal intelligence in one area. Their classifications may be dominated by immediate experience or their learning patterns based on rote memory in one set of tasks despite their use of logical organization in solving problems of a different kind. Overall, Piaget's outline of children's thinking emphasizes its rule governed nature whatever stage it is found. Children's actions and attitudes are seldom random. They only seem so to an adult whose thinking follows a different set of rules.

Bringing cognitive theory to bear on John's performance samples supports certain of the diagnostic interpretations and clarifies others. First, it is apparent that despite John's 'advanced' age of seven years, he has not achieved synchronous development of all the thinking skills of the concrete operational stage. Specifically, in reading, John does not:

consider two separate aspects of events simultaneously: Words are analyzed by letter—sound associations *or* by configuration. John does not integrate the two methods of word recognition.

group situations different on one dimension into classes on the basis of a second, shared dimension: John does not seem to recognize that his superordinate language meaning classes can take two different subordinate forms: words in speech and words in print.

represent internally sequences of events in time: Blending does not produce a meaningful word even when attempts are overt. John cannot yet internalize into a mental operation what he cannot do in reality.

distinguish between elements and relate them in a series: John has discriminated word elements but has not yet brought them together in a serial relationship.

retain the identity of a situation on one aspect although another aspect is transformed: John does not retain the language understanding associated with words when they are transformed from sound to a set of visual symbols.

grasp the idea of reversibility in reading: On a general level, John does not seem to recognize that thought can be represented in writing and that writing represents thought. On a particular plane, phonic analysis is also a kind of reversible thinking. It depends upon the ability to

understand the logical relationship between parts and wholes: John has learned to speak in 'wholes'. He does not seem to have acquired the understanding that speech words are sound groups that can be further analyzed into their component phonemes. Put another way, John probably would not recognize that the word *eel* is the same as the word *heel* without its first sound or the word *he* without its sound ending.

reason inductively: John has tried to derive phonic generalizations from concrete instances in reading, but he has been more successful in applying his 'organizational' rules to spelling.

In sum, reading as it has been taught to John at his particular stage of cognitive development does not seem to have been a meaningful process for him, bearing little relationship to either his own concerns or to his abilities in thinking. The phonics method has asked John to analyze and synthesize while his cognitive strategies were based on a non-analytical syncretistic way of dealing with information. John has tried to learn phonic rules as schemes for action with no corresponding mental structures to give them stability. He has not yet acquired the ability to trade off space for a time. Add to this some deficit or developmental lag in John's auditory abilities and his reading difficulties are predictable. With some supplementary recommendations involving John in the active construction of sentences for reading and experiences to guide his discovery of the nature and relationship of speech sounds to written symbols, the school psychologist's remedial program shows promise.

Viewed from a traditional interpretative framework, John's spelling patterns may mask the kind of thought processes he is using. Yet he is more successful in analyzing his own speech sounds in spelling than he is in reading. His 'rules' appear to be a fusion of remembered letter sequences and sound-symbol correspondences derived inductively from his speech. For John, some letter names represent their corresponding sounds. Other sound associates have been acquired by his careful attention to his teacher. The letter *h*, for example, contains in its name the sound spelled *ch*, and the letter *n* when pronounced by his teacher in isolation contains a vowel. Together with the recalled visual sequence of *ck* for the *k* sound, John spells chicken as *HCKN,* or *which* as *WIH.*

Spelling is a meaningful process to John, but given the interference of competing phonic correspondences he has generalized on his own and those he has tried to acquire in his reading, it is little wonder that John has become discouraged. The school psychologist's recommendation for spelling instruction matched to reading requirements is commendable. From a Piagetian point of view understanding the 'rules' John is following adds only the necessity to take into account in John's program the considerable unlearning required before progress is possible.

In a similar light, John's arithmetic solutions are no more random than his spelling. He also appears to be further along in the concrete operational stage of thought with regards to mathematics symbols than he is with verbal symbols. Number has been abstracted as a specific aspect of objects or events separate from their size or arrangement in space. Addition and subtraction 'combinations' are known, probably first by the process of counting and secondly, by rote. In order to understand the concept of number John has attained skills in decentering, classifying, ordering and conserving. His grasp of reversibility, however, has been sidetracked, again by rules that John appears to have reasoned out on his own to fit a special set of number circumstances. As in spelling, John's idiosyncratic 'rules' work some of the time, and thus are tenacious in their hold by reason of intermittent reinforcement. That rules of this kind can interfere with a child's progress toward mature forms of concrete operational thought is apparent. For John, the rules of addition take the form 'Add digits in column sequences. Where columns are incomplete, construct one.' Thus John added $32 + 54$ correctly for a sum of 86, but attempted $34 \div 6$ as $4 \div 6 \div 3$ for 13. John's rule for subtraction may be a repetition of something he has heard: 'Take the smaller number from the larger.' And like Epaminodas, John literally does just that: $43 - 19$ or $9 - 3$ and $4 - 1$ for a difference of 36. Add to the fact that the rules often produce correct answers, a second fact that rules can also be forgotten in the haste or anxiety of tests, John's work papers in arithmetic are understandable if not commendable; even by his rules, John has done the best he can. And, like many children, once John has worked out a hypothesis or predictive rule on his own, he tends to hold onto it even in the face of conflicting evidence, a kind of 'cognitive conceit.' (Elkind, 1973). It makes a good case for the school psychologist's recommendations emphasizing a return to concrete devices for demonstrating the properties of place value. Once again, the original recommendations are supplemented, rather than replaced.

Intelligence tests have been constructed to measure a child's ability to profit from experience. They emphasize more what a child has taken from his environment, and to a lesser degree how it is he has acquired it. Without academic records, John's WISC scores suggest some problem in memory or attention. With academic records, the classroom effects of attentional or memory deficits are demonstrated. Once insight into how thinking develops is included in the school psychologist's interpretation, the diagnostic picture of what and with what effect is rounded out to include the how and why. Remedial planning can then take into account any necessity for unlearning and any sources of interference from earlier learning along with matching a child's current learning requirements to his needs and abilities. Nothing is supplanted, there is only a broadening of focus.

What Piaget says to the school psychologist then are reminders of some things he has always known: First, children's behaviour always means, even their errors have intent. What children's behaviour means at any one time may vary. Behavioural understandings are probably among the most useful a school psychologist has at his command. Yet the power of reinforcement and the web of contingency relationships operating in the school do not fully take into account the strategic necessities by which children act and organize their learning. For this, Piaget is heeded in the cognitive domain, just as still other theories may be required to interpret a child's social behaviour. Only when the behavioural explanations are made relative to the developmental course of children's thought or social interactions is anything like a complete understanding provided.

Second, Piaget newly reminds the school psychologist of the distinction between children's learning for themselves and learning for another. It is a distinction that is nowhere more apparent than it is with children in academic difficulty. In learning for themselves, children do not go blindly astray, as John's work in spelling and arithmetic has shown. A peculiar combination of lag in hearing memory, incomplete cognitive structure allowing analysis and dual classifications, skills in inductive reasoning and a certain egocentrism in the face of contrary evidence were all at work. Had John's errors been only those of failure to memorize what he had been taught, their configuration would not have been the same. There would have been no constructive aspect to John's performances, no pattern exhibited, no suggestion of the 'rules' he seemed to be using. Admittedly on somewhat limited evidence there is yet reason to believe that John's attempts in reading were not learning for himself but learning to please another. Cognitive strategies and structures of which he was in part capable had not yet been brought to bear on verbal symbols, and the majority of his resources reflected characteristics of an earlier stage of thinking. Perceptual memory factors may have been influencing John's first year in school as well, but many of these perceptual 'problems' are also becoming newly understood with reference to children's developmental rules of handling information, (Goodnow, 1972).

The third thing Piaget reminds the school psychologist is that there are no equations for diagnosis of learning problems, no recipes for remedial programs, and no interpretive umbrellas that will shield him from the responsibility of ferreting out the patterns that are maintaining or may modify a disability in learning. For these reasons, Piaget's parables are well designed. They are less answers to questions a school psychologist presently may put and more a guide to additional questions he yet may need to ask. The nature of a parable is to suggest, and suggestions rather than proclamations are what Piaget has provided. Those who write interpretive diagnoses and prescriptions for children have always known that they give a picture of a child several steps removed from reality. Regardless of current enthusiasms or professional preferences, the dynamic, behavioural or cognitive 'laws' used to describe the learning without only hint of the learning within. Piaget has provided one more set of laws whose implications must be taken into account, relative to all else that is known of children's learning and development.

In reply to Alice, a school psychologist *must* be able to read many different things into children's behaviour and records. The more he brings to his understandings of children the more checks there are upon a human predisposition to oversimplify. Without Piaget a school psychologist is likely to be at the mercy of words and test scores. Humpty Dumpty is right. The question is which is to be master — that's all.

Effect of preschool experience on performance of Piaget tasks in first grade
W.L. Russell, 1973

AIM / The author was intent 'to use a criteria based on Piaget's theory of cognitive development as an alternate criteria to either IQ test scores or Achievement test scores for evaluating the effect of pre-school experiences upon the child . . . interested in determining whether the children in the first grade would differ significantly in their scores on the Piaget tests dependent upon whether they had or had not participated in a kindergarten or some other pre-school programme'.

SUBJECTS / Four groups of children participated in the study: Group I were first grade children who had attended the kindergarten; Group II first grade children attended the Head Start programme; Group III first grade children with no pre-school experience; and Group IV first grade children who were repeating first grade.

METHOD / Piagetian tasks were administerered. Each child was seen individually and all responses were recorded verbatim.

RESULTS / 'An analysis of covariance was made using the scores from the Piaget test as the dependent variable (Y) and the Kuhlmann — Finch IQ score as the covariate (X). Three main factors were considered: (1) Group (G) with the four levels mentioned above; (2) Sex (s); and (3) Socioeconomic (E) with two levels. First order (two-way) interactions and second order (three-way) interactions were investigated. One significant difference was found in the main effects. The Newman-Keuls Table of Ordered Means was constructed to investigate where that difference occurred. The significant difference was found to be between first grade children who had been in kindergarten and first grade children with no pre-school experience. It was found that first grade children who had had kindergarten scored significantly higher on performance of the Piaget tasks than did first grade children who had had no pre-school experience', p. 3157A.

Piaget in the classroom: Part I: Testing a whole class at the same time *
M. Shayer and D. Wharry, 1974a

AIM / The authors assert, 'Although the individual topics of the Nuffield Foundation courses in the sciences have been assessed in Piagetian terms (Shayer, 1970; Ingle and Shayer, 1971; Shayer, 1972), it is at present not possible to assess the mental level of a particular class with much precision . . . we attempted to develop a method of testing a class which would reveal the level of thinking of the individual pupil in the context of the science teaching that the pupil was receiving', p. 447.

SUBJECTS / N = 35, with an age range from 12 to 13 years and 'with a class of very low ability in a comprehensive school in a semi-rural area'.

METHOD / The tasks administered were as follows and 'are in the context of a course based on the Nuffield Foundation Combined Science Course'. (a) Drawing task; (b) Shadows task — both patterned after Piaget and Inhelder (1956); (c) Balance task; (d) Support on land test; (e) Floating and sinking; (f) Dissolving task — these modelled after Inhelder and Piaget (1958); and (g) Volume and its measurement (Piaget, Inhelder and Szeminska, 1960).

---

* Gratitude is extended to Drs M. Shayer and D. Wharry of Chelsea College, of the University of London for sending their work to be abstracted.

RESULTS / Initial results of this first phase that some pupils (CA 12 to 13) showed 'some signs of beginning the transition from concrete to formal operations, . . . Several pupils who showed stage one in the first one or two tasks . . . appear to have developed as one might hope they should — their varying results, going as high as 2B / 3A . . . , might be taken to indicate what Piaget has termed a *décalage*, i.e., a variation of stage with the topic concerned. This . . . might also be related to their attendances at school and to their inconsistent behaviour patterns while in class . . . that these tasks will . . . allow the teacher to be his own psychologist in that the results themselves and psychological information and need no further translation. They should therefore help the teacher by giving instant feedback on the probable success of a course he is using or may have designed himself, and this should help to make his teaching self-correcting', pp. 455—457.

Study of an electronic analog to the combinations of chemical bodies Piagetian task*
T.W. Sills and J.D. Herron, 1976

INTRODUCTION / Recent educational research (Athey, 1970; Field and Cropley, 1969; Goodnow and Bethon, 1966; Mermelstein and Schulman, 1967; McDaniel et al., 1973; Nelson, 1969; and Sigel and Hooper, 1968) has shown that the tasks originally formulated by Piaget (Inhelder and Piaget, 1958) and his colleagues are very useful measures of learning ability and predictors of student performance. The Piaget task that this study is concerned with is the Combinations of Colored and Colorless Chemical Bodies task (Inhelder and Piaget, 1958, p. 107) hereafter referred to as the chemical task.

In this task four bottles containing colorless liquids labeled 1, 2, 3, and 4, respectively, along with a fifth bottle labeled g are presented to the subject. It is then demonstrated that addition of g to samples from the four bottles may or may not produce a yellow coloration. The subject is then asked to take the solution and duplicate the yellow coloration. The complete solution to this task consists of the determination that solutions 1 and 3 combined with g produce the yellow coloration, solution 2 has no effect on the yellow coloration, and solution 4 has the effect of removing the yellow coloration.

AIM / The purpose of this study was to determine the validity of an electronic analog to the chemical task. This electronic analog consists of

* Published by the kind permission of the authors. Gratitude is extended to Drs Thomas Sills and J. Dudley Herron of Purdue University.

a small plain box which has a series of four momentary push buttons and an indicator light bulb (Figure 1). It is demonstrated to the subject that the light will go on when the buttons are properly pressed (Figure 2). The subject is then presented with the task of taking the box and making the light bulb go on. The solution to this task consists of the determination that buttons 1 and 3 must be pushed simultaneously and held down to make the light bulb go on and stay on, button 2 has no effect on the light, and button 4 has the effect of extinguishing the light when pushed. It is hereby proposed that addition of solution g to a solution or combination of solutions in the chemical task is equivalent to the subject pressing a button or combination of buttons in the electronic analog task.

Figure 1: A view of the Sills Electronic Analog as the subject is presented with the task.

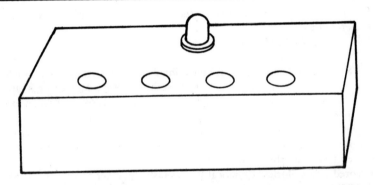

Figure 2: Before the subject is given the task it is demonstrated that the light will go on without revealing how.

The electronic analog has several more desirable features than the chemical task. The time of administration of the electronic analog task is less than half that of the chemical task. Where the electronic analog requires only inexpensive, expendable batteries, the chemical task requires more expensive, expendable chemicals. Another advantage of the electronic analog is the ease of administration in comparison with the potentially awkward and messy chemical task.

METHOD / In this study the two tasks described above were compared. Scores on these two tasks were compared with scores on a Chemistry Placement Exam and an independent Piagetian measure. The subjects in this study were university first year chemistry students from five different courses. Twenty-nine of the 55 subjects were male and 26 were female. Thirty-three subjects were selected randomly from a cross-section of abilities established from a score on the Chemistry Placement Exam. This 40 item exam of 12 mathematics, 6 physics, and 22 chemistry questions has a KR−20 reliability coefficient of .72 based on a sample of a few thousand students. To sample a variety of courses, 22 additional subjects were randomly selected from courses that had not given the Chemistry Placement Exam. All subjects were presented both the chemical and electronic analog tasks. One half of the subjects were presented the chemical task first, and one half of the subjects were presented the electronic analog task first. Two different task administrators administered the two different tasks to each subject. These two administrators randomly alternated between the chemical and electronic analog tasks for each of the two subgroups. These two tasks were scored identically on a 10 point scale as follows: Concrete IIA (1−2 points), Concrete IIB (3−5 points), Formal IIIA (6−8 points), and Formal IIIB (9−10 points).

Piagetian levels were determined independently for all subjects using a combination of other tasks. The independent measure was scored on a 13-point scale using the ratings used by Piaget and others. Four tasks were used: The Conservation of Weight Using Clay, (Piaget and Inhelder, 1962,−2 points; the Conservation of Volume Using Metal Cylinders, (Karplus and Lavatelli 1969),−3 points; Separation of Variables, (Inhelder and Piaget, 1958), p.46)−4points; and Equilibrium in the Balance (Inhelder and Piaget, 1958, p. 164)−4 points. To eliminate examiner bias, subject performance on both the Chemistry Placement Exam and independent Piagetian measures were unknown to the task administrator.

RESULTS / Table 1 shows various task correlations with the Chemistry Placement Exam. Equivalence of task administrators was estimated by computing the correlation between the subject's task score by each administrator and the subject's Chemistry Placement Exam score. These correlations were $r = .37$ and $r = .41$ for administrator A and administrator B, respectively. Correlations between the Chemistry Placement Exam and the chemical task and between the Chemistry Placement Exam and the electronic analog task were found to be similar and significant with respective values of $r = .36$ and $r = .42$. Because of the similarity between the chemical task and the electronic analog task, an attempt to minimize a carry over effect between the first and second task administered was made by the use of two different task administrators as well as a numerical reordering of the chemical task bottles. However, the correlation between the subject's first task and the Chemistry Placement Exam was found to be $r = .50$ and significant at $p = .01$. The correlation between the subject's second task and the Chemistry Placement Exam was found to be $r = .27$ which is not significant. The independent Piagetian score which is a composite of four tasks showed a higher correlation with the Chemistry Placement Exam score of $r = .61$ and was significant at $p = .01$.

Various task correlations with the independent Piagetian score were computed. Equivalence of task administrators was again demonstrated with observed significant correlations of $r = .53$ and $r = .49$ for administrators A and B, respectively. Correlations between the independent Piagetian measure and both the chemical task and the electronic analog task were again found to be similar and significant with respective values of $r = .54$ and $r = .48$. The correlation between the subject's first task and the independent Piagetian measure was $r = .62$ where the correlation between the subject's second task and the independent Piagetian measure was $r = .41$. The correlation between first task scores which are chemical tasks and the independent Piagetian measure shows an increased value of $r = .66$. Similarly the correlation between the first task scores which are electronic analog tasks and the independent Piagetian measure shows an increased value of $r = .58$. A direct correlation between the chemical task score and the electronic analog task score was found to be $r = .39$ significant at the $p = .01$ level. The electronic analog and the chemical tasks' respective average times of administration were 3.1 minutes and 7.4 minutes significant at $p = .01$.

The classification into Piagetian levels by the electronic analog task and the chemical task is presented in Table 2. In this table the Piagetian level established by the first task administered to each subject is tabulated. Twenty-seven subjects took the electronic analog task first, and 28 subjects took the chemical task first. This comparison of electronic analog task and the chemical task in Table 2 yields $X^2 = .38$. Thus, one is not able to reject the hypothesis that each task results in classification of students at the same Piagetian level and lends support to our contention that the electronic analog may be substituted for the chemical task.

Table 1: Correlations between task scores and other measures

Correlates	r	n	Confidence limits
Chemistry Placement Exam Score *vs.*			
Subject Task Score by Task Administrator A	.37*	30	.07 < p < .61
Subject Task Score by Task Administrator B	.41*	36	.15 < p < .62
Chemical Task Score	.36*	33	.09 < p < .59
Electronic Analog Task Score	.42*	33	.16 < p < .64
Subject's First Task Score	.50**	33	.24 < p < .69
Subject's Second Task Score	.27	33	−.02 < p < .52
Independent Piagetian Score	.61**	33	.39 < p < .77
Independent Piagetian Score *vs.*			
Subject Task Score by Task Administrator A	.53**	52	.34 < p < .68
Subject Task Score by Task Administrator B	.49**	58	.31 < p < .64
Chemical Task Score	.54**	55	.36 < p < .68
Electronic Analog Task Score	.48**	55	.29 < p < .64
Subject's First Task Score	.62**	55	.46 < p < .95
Subject's Second Task Score	.41**	55	.21 < p < .58
First Task Scores Which Are Chemical Tasks	.66**	28	.44 < p < .81
First Task Scores Which Are Electronic Analog Tasks	.58**	27	.31 < p < .77
Chemical Task Score *vs.*			
Electronic Analog Task Score	.39**	55	.18 < p < .56

Note: Task Administrator B administered both chemical and electronic tasks to three subjects.

* p = .05
** p = .01

Table 2: Number of subjects at each Piagetian Level as determined by the first task administered

	Electronic Analog Task	Chemical Task	Total Sample
Concrete IIA (1−2 points)	0	0	0
Concrete IIB (3−5 points)	6	5	11
Formal IIIA (6−8 points)	9	10	19
Formal IIIB (9−10 points)	12	13	25
Total	27	28	55

DISCUSSION / In Table 1 it is interesting to note that the correlation between the Chemistry Placement Exam and the chemical task was not greater than the correlation between the Chemistry Placement Exam and the electronic analog task. Also, it is thought that the magnitude of both of these correlations were lowered by an observed carry-over effect between the first and second task administered. All correlations between the subject's first task score and other variables in Table 1 show a larger value than correlations between the subjects' second task score and these same variables. Thus, the direct correlation between the chemical task score and the electronic analog task score ($r = .39$) can be expected to be lowered by this observed carry over effect. It is also worth noting that the first seven correlations in Table 1 are affected by the KR-20 reliability of .72 of the Chemistry Placement Exam.

The study was done with a relatively small sample. As a consequence, the stability of the correlations which are reported is in some doubt. However, the similarity between the correlations obtained between the chemical task and other variables and the correlations between the electronic analog and these same variables suggest that the electronic analog may serve as a simpler test of certain aspects of formal thought. Those who wish to use the electronic analog task may obtain further descriptive information by addressing the authors at the Department of Physics, Purdue University, West Lafayette, Indiana, 47907, or Stoelting Company, 1350 South Kostner Avenue, Chicago, Illinois, 60623.

Stoelting's

CAT. NO. 31260

SILLS ELECTRONIC ANALOG

By THOMAS W. SILLS

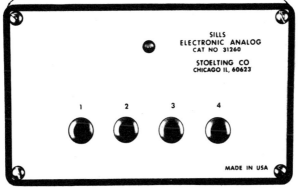

The Sills Electronic Analog is a more easily administered highly valid alternate task for the Combinations of Colored and Colorless Chemical Bodies Piagetian task (Inhelder and Piaget, 1958).

The Sills Electronic Analog has several features which make it superior to the chemical task administration-wise.

1. The time of administration of the Sills Electronic Analog is less than half that of the chemical task.
2. The Sills Electronic Analog requires only an inexpensive, expendable battery; the chemical task requires more expensive, expendable chemicals.
3. The task is more easily administered.
4. The chemical task is awkward and messy.
5. All of the above combine to make it by far the more practical instrument to use when a large number of subjects are to be tested.

THIS ANALOG REPLACES THE CHEMICAL BODIES PIAGETIAN TASK.

STOELTING COMPANY - 1350 S. KOSTNER AVE - CHICAGO, ILLINOIS 60623

(Area Code 312) 522–4500   CHS-487-1   Printed in U.S.A.

Testbatterie zur Erfassung kognitiver Operationen (TEKO). Piaget-orientierte tests für Kinder im Alter von etwa 5—8 Jahren. (Developmental Test Battery of Cognitive Operations. Piaget-oriented tests for children aged about 5 to 8.)* Braunschweig: Georg Westermann Verlag, 1975. (Available from: Testzentrale, Wildbader Str. 4, 7 Stuttgart-Bad Cannstatt, Federal Republic of Germany.)
W. Winkelmann, 1974

AIM / This battery of tests is based on the developmental works of Piaget and his collaborators. It was constructed with the intent to create standardized procedures for the assessment of different logical operations which play an important part in the transition from intuitive thinking ('pre-operational thinking') to concrete-logical thinking ('concrete operations').

AGE RANGE; USES / Initially, the construction of the test battery was aimed at the age range from 5 to 8 years. From the data gained during test and item analysis, it seems reasonable to extend the age range of some of the tests to four-year-old or nine-to-ten-year-old children; this will have to be considered in the collection of further normative data planned for the future.

The following fields of application of the TEKO may be pointed out:

— assessment of cognitive development,
— contributions to the diagnosis of intelligence,
— planning of individualized cognitive training procedures,
— efficiency control of Piaget-oriented cognitive training procedures or cognitive curricula,
— inclusion into psychological and educational research projects.

STRUCTURE / The battery consists of nine individual tests which can be applied and scored independently of each other. Since the author, in view of the available empirical evidence, is not convinced of the existence of a generalized cognitive structure (*structure d'ensemble*, overall structure), neither a total score for the whole battery nor a global allocation of subjects to certain developmental stages is provided. The outstanding characteristic of the test battery is its paper form. Drawings are used instead of real materials. The nine tests refer to the following operations:

---

*   Written and prepared by the author for inclusion in this volume. Gratitude is extended to Dr Wolfgang Winkelmann of Projektgruppe Kleinkindforschung an der Pädagogischen Hochschule Rhineland, Abteiling Köln, Germany.

1. Conservation of Substance (Liquids) (13 items)
2. Conservation of Number (6 items)
3. Class Inclusion (6 items)
4. Matrices (Multiplication of Classes) (8 items)
5. Concepts of Verticality-Horizontality (6 items)
6. Asymmetric Seriation (12 items)
7. Ordinal Correspondence (10 items)
8. Transformation (e.g. Inversion) or Positional Order (16 items)
9. Transitivity of Length (7 items)

SCORING / For each test, preliminary percentile norms are available for the age groups 5, 6, 7, and 8. For each of the two conservation tests, a differential scoring for (a) conservation of equality or identity and (b) conservation of inequality or of a difference is suggested. For some of the tests a criterion-referenced classification is recommended. The collection of further normative data in future investigations is planned.

In most of the tests, scoring is based on the child's choice from a number of verbal or graphic alternatives. In the test which examines the concept of verticality-horizontality, a drawing response is requested. In the transitivity of length test, in case of a correct choice response, the child is also asked for án explanation of his choice.

TEST CONSTRUCTION AND ANALYSIS / Test and item selection was based on data from a sample of 280 five- to eight-year-old children. Three of the initial twelve tests were eliminated. One of these tests, the Perspectives Test, turned out to be too difficult, so that a fundamental revision and additional research will be necessary with regard to this test. For the final version of the test battery, indices of reliability (split-half and internal-consistency coefficients) were determined. The reliability estimations and the preliminary norms reported both originate from the sample which also served for items analysis and for item selection.

Factor analytical methods were applied to the items of each test, to the items of the whole battery, and to the raw scores of all tests. The general result was a relatively high degree of differentiation. Therefore it appeared reasonable to confine the scoring procedure to the determination of test-specific scores (in some cases even the determination of scores for parts of a test is recommended). The feasibility of a generalized score for the whole battery was discarded.

SUPPLEMENTARY INVESTIGATIONS / Several investigations were carried out in immediate connection with the construction of the test battery. Three investigations referred to the transitivity test. One of their aims was the analysis and control of certain artifact eventualities. Since the initial version of the transitivity test had to be modified, also the norm informations for the modified version were drawn from the data of one of these investigations (sample size: 308).

Prior to the construction of the TEKO, a question of fundamental importance had to be clarified: Are the results of a paper form comparable to the results of a form using real materials? Since this problem was particularly salient with regard to the two conservation tests, a corresponding investigation, using a sample of 281 5- to 8-year-old children, was restricted to the conservation items. The general results of this study were (a) a relatively high correlation between the form using drawings and the forms using concrete materials and (b) a pronounced congruence of the factorial structure of the two modes of presentation. This investigation, comprising also other aspects of the development of conservation, is reported in detail in Appendices I and II of the manual (see special abstracts). In English, a brief report on the factor analytical aspect of this research is available (Winkelmann, 1974).

From two educational-evaluative investigations, in which, besides other tests, also the TEKO was applied, as a by-product, a fair amount of information could be gathered concerning the relationship between the TEKO-tests and a considerable number of different cognitive tests. Samples of more than 500 children each were tested. In one study, the majority was five-years-old, in the other, the majority was six-years-old. As a general conclusion, it can be said that the TEKO-tests, above all, are tests of logical (or logico-mathematical) thinking and that factors of verbal and perceptual intelligence are only of minor importance in these tests. The results of the two investigations are reported in Appendices III and IV of the TEKO-manual.

Die Invarianz der Substanz und der Zahl im kindlichen Denken. I. Das Verhalten 5—8 jähriger Kinder bei Tests in Papierform und bei Tests mit konkretem Material. * *(Conservation of substance and number in children's thinking. I. Responses of five- to eight-year-old children in tests based on drawings and tests based on concrete materials.) In: Manual — 'Testbatterie zur Erfassung kognitiver Operationen (TEKO)', Appendix I, 67—81. Braunschweig: Georg Westermann Verlag, 1975a. (Available from: Testzentrale, Wildbader Str. 4, 7 Stuttgart-Bad Cannstatt, Federal Republic of Germany.)*
W. Winkelmann, 1975a

* Written and prepared by the author for inclusion in this volume. Gratitude is extended to Dr Wolfgang Winkelmann of Projektgruppe Kleinkindforschung an der Pädagogischen Hochschule Rhineland, Abteilung Köln, Germany.

AIMS / The author investigated various aspects of the development of conservation of substance and number. Part I of the corresponding research report pertains to the following aspects: (a) comparison of conservation of substance and conservation of number concerning their average probabilities of a correct response, (b) dependence of the conservation response on age and sex, (c) form of distributions of conservation test scores, (d) effects of certain item characteristics, (e) response tendencies, (f) comparison of two modes of presentation of conservation tasks, one using drawings and the other using real materials. The main practical starting point and motive of the investigation was the last aspect (f). The concern was to obtain basic informations serving the purpose of the construction of a developmental test battery of concrete operations (TEKO) in paper form. The factor analytical aspects of the study are treated in part II of the research report (see special abstract).

SUBJECTS / N=281 children aged five to eight. The sample was about equally divided between the four age groups (5–6–7–8) and between the two sexes.

METHOD / Four tests were administered: Conservation of Substance (liquids) − Paper Form, CSPF (13 items); Conservation of Substance − Concrete Form, CSCF (7 items); Conservation of Number − Paper Form, CNPF (6 items); Conservation of Number − Concrete Form, CNCF (5 items).

RESULTS / Age curves based on the average probabilities of a correct response were determined. There was a continuous and generally marked increase from five to eight years. Conservation of number (CN) was easier than conservation of substance (CS) both for the concrete and the paper forms. The forms using concrete materials were less difficult than the forms using drawings for both types of conservation. Correlations between the test forms were rather high, with coefficients amounting to 0.81 for CSPF:CSCF and 0.76 for CNPF:CNCF. Test scores were not dependent on sex. The overall distributions of the CS scores were U-shaped; the unimodal overall distributions (with maximum scores being most frequent) found for the CN scores were also interpreted as sections of U-shaped distributions. CSPF tasks with constant visible areas (drawings based on the assumption that glasses have a rectangular base and are constant with regard to the third dimension) were less difficult than tasks with variable areas (drawings based on the assumption that glasses possess a circular base so that the third dimension varies with the breadth of the glasses). It was shown that there is a certain tendency in children to choose the last-named alternative of the experimenter's question; this means that either correct or incorrect responses can be favored depending on the respective instructions. An analysis of incorrect responses revealed that they are more often centred on height than on width in the CS tests and more often on length than on density in the CN tests. No clear evidence was gained concerning the difficulty relation between identity conservation and equivalence conservation, but the data suggested that the difference, if there is any, is probably not very great.

DISCUSSION / The main point of discussion was the bearing of the results on the construction of standardized tests of conservation of substance and conservation of number in paper form.

Die Invarianz der Substanz und der Zahl im kindlichen Denken. II. Faktorenanalyse der Reaktionen auf verschiedene Invarianzaufgaben. * *(Conservation of substance and number in children's thinking. II. Factor analysis of responses in different conservation situations.)* ** *In: Manual — 'Testbatterie zur Erfassung kognitiver Operationen (TEKO)', Appendix II, 82—95. Braunschweig: Georg Westermann Verlag, 1975b. (Available from: Testzentrale, Wildbader Str. 4, 7 Stuttgart-Bad Cannstatt, Federal Republic of Germany.)* W. Winkelmann, 1975b

AIMS / With this study, the author aimed at the clarification of two problems, one more theoretical in nature and the other more of practical importance. (a) Within the domain of the conservation concept, does there exist a generalized cognitive structure (overall structure, *structure d'ensemble*) as postulated by Piaget's theory? (b) Are conservation tasks using drawings comparable to corresponding tasks using concrete materials within the framework of factor analysis? Problem (b) was regarded to be particularly relevant to the construction of a developmental test battery of concrete operations in paper form (TEKO). Other aspects of this investigation are treated in part I of the research report (see special abstract).

* Written and prepared by the author for inclusion in this volume. Gratitude is extended to Dr Wolfgang Winkelmann of Projektgruppe Kleinkindforschung an der Pädagogischen Hochschule Rhineland, Abteilung Köln, Germany.
** Brief report in English: Winkelmann, W. (1974)'Factorial analysis of children's conservation task performance,' *Child Developm.*, 45, 843—48.

SUBJECTS / N = 281 five- to eight-year-old children of both sexes, about equally divided between the four age groups (5, 6, 7, and 8 years old).

METHOD / Four tests were administered: Conservation of Substance (liquids) — Paper form, CSPF (13 items); Conservation of Substance (liquids) — Concrete Form, CSCF (7 items); Conservation of Number — Paper Form, CNPF (6 items); Conservation of Number — Concrete Form, CNCF (5 items). Each test consisted of conservation of equality (identity or equivalence) items as well as conservation of inequality (difference) items.

RESULTS / When all 31 items were factor-analysed on the basis of phi-coefficients, there emerged four factors. The factorial structure was extraordinarily distinct and could be unequivocally interpreted. The factors were defined in the following way: Factor I: CSE — Conservation of Substance Equality (Identity or Equivalence); Factor II: CSI — Conservation of Substance Inequality (Difference); Factor III: CNE — Conservation of Number Equality (Equivalence); Factor IV: CNI — Conservation of Number Inequality (Difference). There was no factorial separation of the items using drawings and the items using concrete materials. Additional factor analyses were applied to different sets of items resulting from each possible combination of only two of the four tests. The factors determined in these analyses (two or four factors, depending on the respective combination) were always consistent with the outcome of the overall factor analysis. The 19 paper items were also administered with modified instructions to a second sample of 280 five- to eight-year-old children (sample used for the standardization of the TEKO). The same four factors as before were replicated. To take also sequential regularities into account, several analyses were carried out again on the basis of the monotonicity coefficient recommended by Bentler (1971) and on the basis of Loevinger's homogeneity coefficient for two items instead of phi-coefficients. Again, the same four factors were identified. However, the angular separation of the item clusters defining the factors I (CSE) and III (CNE) was smaller in this case; this was explained by the fact that the difference in average item difficulty between the two clusters was prevented from manifesting itself in form of a diminished correlation.

DISCUSSION / From the results, the following conclusions were drawn: (a) The paper items have the same factorial structure as the concrete items; this outcome is of importance for the construction of conservation tests in paper form. (b) The results contradict Piaget's notion of a *structure d'ensemble,* i.e., his assumption that the 'concrete operations' develop in unison. In contrast, the units of cognitive development appear to be relatively specific. Consequently, the existence of a cognitive developmental stage (i.e. the stage of 'concrete operations') defined by an integrated system of closely connected cognitive operations is also called into question. (c) The sequence of cognitive acquisitions may vary from child to child. (d) Educational objectives within the domain of cognitive operations should be defined with a high degree of specification.

Factorial analysis of children's conservation task performance
W. Winkelmann, 1974

AIM / To investigate whether the 'paper form' yielded results comparable to those based on concrete materials, using the data of another study collected in the preparation of a standardized battery of Piagetian operations (Winkelmann, 1975a).

SUBJECTS / N = 281 with an age-range from five to eight years inclusive.

METHOD / The tests administered were as follows:
(a) *Conservation of substance — paper form.* The test comprised 13 items purporting to measure liquid conservation. Nine items tested the conservation of an equality relation or of identity; four items measured the operativity of an inequality relation.
(b) *Conservation of substance — concrete form.* 'The seven items with variable areas of visible liquid (round glasses) of the paper form were also administered using real glasses and lemonade. Two of the items involved conservation of an inequality relation', p. 844.
(c) *Conservation of number — paper form.* The test comprised six items — four items tested the conservation of the correspondence by pairs between two sets of objects and the remaining two items tested the conservation of a numerical difference relation.
(d) *Conservation of number — concrete form.* The five items were similar to the first five items of the paper form. Three of these were equality and two inequality items.

(Fuller details of the experimental procedure including diagrammatical sequences of the above tests are described elsewhere, Winkleman, 1974, pp. 844–845).

RESULTS / All 31 items were subjected to factor analysis. Cattell's

(1966a, 1966b) 'Scree test' for the number of factors demonstrated four factors: factor I — conservation of substance equality or identity, factor II — conservation of substance inequality, factor III — conservation of number equality, and factor IV — conservation of number inequality. 'These factors were confirmed in separate analyses for the concrete items and for the paper items. The factor structure was cross-validated in a second sample of 280 children aged five to eight to whom the paper items were given with modified instructions. These data call the Piagetian concept of *structures d'ensemble* and "stage" into question', p. 843.

ABBREVIATIONS USED IN THE BIBLIOGRAPHY
(under the series *Piagetian Research*, Vols. 1—8)

Acta Psychol.	Acta Psychologica (Holland)
Adol.	Adolescence
Aging and Hum. Develop.	Aging and Human Development
Alberta J. Ed. Res.	Alberta Journal of Educational Research
Am. Ed. Res. Assoc.	American Educational Research Association
Am. Ed. Res. J.	American Educational Research Journal
Am. J. Ment. Def.	American Journal of Mental Deficiency
Am. J. Orthopsych.	American Journal of Orthopsychiatry
Am. J. Psych.	American Journal of Psychology
Am. J. Soc.	American Journal of Sociology
Am. Psych.	American Psychologist
Am. Psych. Assoc.	American Psychological Association
Am. Soc. Rev.	American Sociological Review
Ann. Rev. Psych.	Annual Review of Psychology
Arch. Dis. Child.	Archives of the Diseases of Childhood (UK)
Archiv. Gen. Psychiat.	Archives of General Psychiatry
Arch. de Psychol.	Archives de Psychologie
Aust. J. Psych.	Australian Journal of Psychology
Aust. J. Soc. Issues	Australian Journal of Social Issues
Brit. J. Clin. & Soc. Psych.	British Journal of Clinical and Social Psychology
Brit. J. Ed. Psych.	British Journal of Educational Psychology
Brit. J. Psych.	British Journal of Psychology
Brit. J. Stat. Psych.	British Journal of Statistical Psychology
Brit. J. Psych. Stat.	British Journal of Psychology — Statistical Section
Brit. J. Soc.	British Journal of Sociology
Brit. Med. Bull.	British Medical Bulletin
Brit. J. Med. Psych.	British Journal of Medical Psychology
Bull. Danish Inst. for Ed. Res.	Bulletin of the Danish Institute for Educational Research
Calif. J. Ed. Res.	Californian Journal of Educational Research
Can. Educ. Res. Dig.	Canadian Educational and Research Digest
Can. J. Behav. Sci.	Canadian Journal of Behavioural Science
Can. J. Psych.	Canadian Journal of Psychology
Can. Psychol.	Canadian Psychology
Child. Developm.	Child Development (USA)
Child Study Journ.	Child Study Journal
Childhood Psych.	Childhood Psychology (UK)
Cogn.	Cognition
Cogn. Psych.	Cognitive Psychology
Contemp. Psych.	Contemporary Psychology (USA)
Dev. Psych.	Developmental Psychology (USA)

Diss. Abstr.	Dissertation Abstracts (USA)
Educ. of Vis. Handicap.	Education of the Visually Handicapped
Educ. & Psych. Measmt.	Educational and Psychological Measurement (USA)
Ed. Res.	Educational Research (UK)
Ed. Rev.	Educational Review (UK)
Educ. Stud. Maths.	Educational Studies in Mathematics
El. Sch. J.	Elementary School Journal (USA)
Eug. Rev.	Eugenics Review (UK)
Excep. Child.	Exceptional Children
Forum Educ.	Forum Education
Gen. Psych. Mon.	Genetic Psychological Monographs (USA)
Harv. Ed. Rev.	Harvard Educational Review
Human Developm.	Human Development (Switzerland)
Hum. Hered.	Human Heredity
Inst. Child Welf. Monogr.	Institute of Child Welfare Monographs
Int. J. Psych.	International Journal of Psychology (France)
Int. Rev. Educ.	International Review of Education (Germany)
Int. Soc. Sci. Bull.	International Social Science Bulletin (France)
Jap. J. Ed. Psych.	Japanese Journal of Educational Psychology
Jap. Psych. Res.	Japanese Psychological Research
J. Abnorm. Soc. Psych.	Journal of Abnormal and Social Psychology (USA)
Journ. Amer. Acad. Child Psychiat.	Journal of American Academy of Child Psychiatry
J. Am. Stat. Assoc.	Journal of American Statistical Association
J. App. Psych.	Journal of Applied Psychology (USA)
J. Compar. Psychol.	Journal of Comparative Psychology
J. Comp. and Physiolog. Psych.	Journal of Comparative and Physiological Psychology
J. Child Psych. Psychiatr.	Journal of Child Psychology and Psychiatry
J. Clin. Psych.	Journal of Clinical Psychology (USA)
J. Consult. Psych.	Journal of Consultant Psychology (USA)
J. Cross. Cult. Psych.	Journal of Cross-Cultural Psychology (USA)
J. Ed. Psych.	Journal of Educational Psychology (USA)
J. Ed. Res.	Journal of Educational Research (USA)
J. Ed. Stud.	Journal of Educational Studies (USA)
J. Exp. Child Psych.	Journal of Experimental Child Psychology (USA)
J. Exp. Educ.	Journal of Experimental Education
J. Exp. Psych.	Journal of Experimental Psychology

J. Gen. Psych.	Journal of Genetic Psychology (USA)
J. Gerontol	Journal of Gerontology
J. Home Econ.	Journal of Home Economics
Journ. Learn. Disabil.	Journal of Learning Disabilities
J. Math. Psych.	Journal of Mathematical Psychology
J. Ment. Sub.	Journal of Mental Subnormality
J. Negro Ed.	Journal of Negro Education (USA)
J. Pers.	Journal of Personality (USA)
J. Pers. Soc. Psych.	Journal of Personality and Social Psychology (USA)
J. Pers. Assessm.	Journal of Personality Assessment (USA)
J. Psych.	Journal of Psychology (USA)
J. Res. Maths. Educ.	Journal of Research in Mathematics Education
J. Res. Sci. Teach.	Journal of Research in Science Teaching (USA)
J. Soc. Iss.	Journal of Social Issues (USA)
J. Soc. Psych.	Journal of Social Psychology (USA)
J. Soc. Res.	Journal of Social Research
J. Spec. Ed.	Journal of Special Education (USA)
Journ. Struct. Learn.	Journal of Structural Learning
J. Teach. Ed.	Journal of Teacher Education (USA)
J. Verb. Learn. Verb. Behv.	Journal of Verbal Learning and Verbal Behaviour (UK/USA)
J. Youth Adolesc.	Journal of Youth and Adolescence
Math. Teach.	Mathematics Teacher (USA)
Maths. Teach.	Mathematics Teaching
Merr.-Palm. Quart.	Merrill-Palmer Quarterly (USA)
Mon. Soc. Res. Child Dev.	Monographs of the Society for Research in Child Development (USA)
Mult. Beh. Res.	Multivariate Behavioural Research
New Zealand Journ. Educ. Stud.	New Zealand Journal of Educational Studies
Ped. Sem.	Pedagogical Seminary
Pedag. Europ.	Pedogogica Europaea
Percep. Mot. Skills	Perceptual and Motor Skills
Psych. Absts.	Psychological Abstracts
Psych. Afric.	Psychologica Africana
Psych. Bull.	Psychological Bulletin (USA)
Psych. Iss.	Psychological Issues
Psych. Mon.	Psychological Monographs (USA)
Psych. Mon. Gen. and Appl.	Psychological Monographs: General and Applied (USA)
Psychol. Rec.	Psychological Record
Psych. Rep.	Psychological Reports (USA)
Psych. Rev.	Psychological Review (USA)
Psychol. Sch.	Psychology in Schools
Psych. Sci.	Psychological Science (USA)
Psychomet.	Psychometrika
Psy.-nom. Sc.	Psychonomic Science
Psy. Today	Psychology Today
Publ. Opin. Quart.	Public Opinion Quarterly (USA)

Quart. J. Exp. Psych.	Quarterly Journal of Experimental Psychology (UK/USA)
Rev. Educ. Res.	Review of Educational Research
R. Belge de Ps. Ped.	Review Belge de Psychologie et de Pédagogie (Belgium)
Rev. Suisse Psych.	Revue Suisse de Pschologie (Switzerland)
Scan. J. Psych.	Scandinavian Journal of Psychology
Sch. Coun. Curr. Bull.	Schools Council Curriculum Bulletin
Sch. Sci. Maths.	School Science and Mathematics
Sci.	Science
Sci. Americ.	Scientific American
Sci. Ed.	Science Education (USA)
Scot. Ed. Stud.	Scottish Educational Studies
Sem. Psychiat.	Seminars in Psychiatry
Soc. Psychi.	Social Psychiatry
Soviet Psych.	Soviet Psychology
Teach. Coll. Contr. Ed.	Teachers' College Contributions to Education (USA)
Theo. into Pract.	Theory into Practice
Times Ed. Supp.	Times Educational Supplement
Train. Sch. Bull.	Training School Bulletin
Vita. Hum.	Vita Humana
WHO Mon.	World Health Organization Monographs
Wiener Arb. z. pad. Psychol.	Wiener Arbeiten zur pädagogischen Psychologie (Austria)
Yearbook Journ. Negro Educ.	Yearbook of the Journal of Negro Education
Zeitschr. f. ang. Psychol.	Zeitschrift für angewandte Psychologie und Charakterkunde (Germany)
Zeitschr. f. pad. Psychol.	Zeitschrift für pädagogische Psychologie und Fugendkunde (Germany)

BIBLIOGRAPHY

ABRAMOWITZ, S. (1975a) Adolescent understanding of proportionality. PhD thesis, Stanford University. Also personal communication.

ALLEN, L.R. (1967) An examination of the classificatory ability of children who have been exposed to one of the New Elementary Science Programmes. PhD thesis, the University of California, Berkeley.

ALLMAN, P.D. (1973) 'A validation study of a Piagetian type diagnosis of community college students' cognitive functioning abilities', *Diss. Abstr.* 33, 10, 5343A–5882A (5463A), Xerox University Microfilms.

ALMY, M. (1964) 'Young children's thinking and the teaching of reading'. In: CUTTS, W. (Eds.) *Teaching young children to Read: Proceedings of a Conference, Nov. 14–16.* Bulletin No. 19, US Dept. of Health, Education and Welfare, Office of Education, Washington, D.C., pp. 97–102.

ALMY, M., CHITTENDEN, E., and MILLER, P. (1966) *Young Children's Thinking.* New York: Teachers College Press.

ALMY, M. *et al.* (1971) *Logical Thinking in Second Grade.* New York: Teacher's College Press, Columbia University.

ANDERSON, D.R. (1967) 'An investigation into the effects of instruction on the development of propositional thinking in children', *Dip. Child. Psych.*, research, Birmingham University.

ANKNEY, P.H. (1975) 'The development of a Piagetian paper-and-pencil test for assessing concrete-operational reasoning', *Diss. Abstr.* 35, 9, 5581A–6281A (5947–A).

ANTHONY, E.J. (1956) 'The significance of Jean Piaget for child psychiatry', *Brit. J. Child Psych.*, 50, 255–69.

ATHEY, I.J. (1970) *Educational Implications of Piaget's Theory.* Waltham, Mass: Ginn-Blaisdell.

ATKINSON, R.C. (1969) *The Computer is a Tutor: Readings in Psychology.* CRM del Mar, California.

AUSTRALIAN SCIENCE EDUCATION PROJECT (1974) 'Report on the trial of two Piagetian Tests'. Unpublished report, in private communication with L. Dale, Australian Science Education Project, Director, Melbourne, Australia.

AYERS, J.B., ROHR, M.E., and AYERS, M.N. (1974) 'Perceptual-motor skills, ability to conserve, and school readiness' *Percept. Mot. Skills*, 38, 491–4.

BANKS, S.H. (1958) How students in a secondary modern school induce scientific principles from scientific experiments. Unpublished PhD thesis, Birmingham University.

BARROS, N.R. (1972) 'Applications of Piaget's theory to education: a critical study', *Diss. Abstr*, Order No. 72–11823 (5664A), Xerox University Microfilms.

BART, W.M. (1971) 'The factor structure of formal operations', *Brit. J. Ed. Psych.*, 41, 70–7.

BART, W.M. (1972) 'Construction and validation of formal reasoning instruments', *Psych. Rep.*, 30, 663–70.

BART, W.M., and KRUS, D.J. (1973) 'An ordering-theoretic method to determine hierarchies among items', *Educ. and Psych. Measmt.*, 33, 291–300.

BART, W.M. and SMITH, M.B. (1974) 'An interpretive framework of cognitive structures' *Human Development*. 17, 161–75.

BARTON, P.C. (1975) 'The effects of a Piagetian geometry model on beginning school children', *Diss. Abstr.*, 35, 8, pp. 4757A to 5579A, (p. 4972A).

BASS, H. (1975) 'Topological understandings of young children'. In: ROSSKOPF, M.F. (Ed.) *Children's Mathematical Concepts: Six Piagetian Studies in Mathematics Education.* New York: Teachers College Press, Columbia University.

BAUTISTA, L.B. (1975) 'The relationship between intellectual levels and achievement in the comprehension of concepts classified according to a scheme derived from the Piagetian model', *Diss. Abstr.*, 35, 9, 5581A–6281A (5948–A).

BAYLEY, N. (1969) *Bayley Scales of Infant Development: Birth to two years.* New York: Psychological Corporation.

BEARD, R.M. (1960) 'The nature and development of concepts', *Ed. Rev. (Birmingham)*, 13, 12–26.

BELL, S.M. (1968) The relationship of infant-mother attachment to the development of the concept of object-permanence. Unpublished PhD thesis, Johns Hopkins University.

BENTLER, P.M. (1970) 'Evidence regarding stages in the development of conservation', *Percep. Mot. Skills*, 31, 855–859.

BENTLER, P.M. (1971) 'Monotonicity analysis: an alternative to linear factor and test analysis'. In: GREEN, D.R., FORD, M.P. and FLAMER, G.B. (Eds.), *Measurement and Piaget.* New York: McGraw Hill, pp. 220–44.

BEREITER, C. (1970) 'Educational implications of Kohlberg's cognitive developmental view', *Interchange*, 1, 1, 25–33.

BERZONSKY, M.D. (1971) 'The role of familiarity in children's explanations of physical causality', *Child Developm.*, 42, 705–15.

BETH, E.W., and PIAGET, J. (1966) *Mathematical Epistemology and Psychology.* Dordrecht, Holland: D. Reidel Publishing Company.

BIGGS, E.E. and MACLEAN, J.R. (1969) *Freedom to Learn.* Addison–Wesley.

BIGGS, J.B. (1962) *Anxiety, Motivation and Primary School Mathematics*. Slough: NFER.

BINGHAM-NEWMAN, A.M. (1975) 'Development of logical operations abilities in early childhood: a longitudinal comparison of the effects of two preschool settings', *Diss. Abstr.* 35, 9, 5581A–6281a (5916–A).

BOLAND, S.K. (1973) 'Conservation tasks with retarded and non-retarded children', *Exceptional Children*, 40, 209–11.

BOYER, C.B. (1939) *The Concepts of the Calculus*. New York: Columbia University Press.

BOYLE, D.G. (1975) 'Has psychology anything to offer the teacher?', personal communication.

BRAINERD, C.J. (1972) 'Structures of thought in middle childhood: recent research on Piaget's concrete-operational groupements'. Paper presented at the Third Annual Meeting on Structural Learning, Philadelphia, March.

BRAUCHLER, C.E. (1975) 'An investigation of the feasibility of using a measure of conservation as a predictor of reading comprehension', *Diss. Abstr.*, 35, 9, 5581A–6281A (5917–A).

BREKKE, B.W., (1972) 'An investigation of what relationships exist between a child's performance of selected tasks of conservation and selected factors in reading readiness', *Diss. Abstr..*, order No. 72–1815A, Xerox University Microfilms.

BREKKE, B.W., and WILLIAMS, J.D. (1974) 'Conservation and reading achievement of second grade bilingual American Indian children', *J. Psych.*, 86, 65–9.

BREKKE, B.W., and WILLIAMS, J.D. (1975) 'Conservation as a predictor of reading achievement', *Percep. Mot. Skills*, 40, 95–8.

BREKKE, B.W., WILLIAMS, J., and HARLOW, S. (1973) 'Conservation and reading readiness', *J. Gen. Psych.*, 123, 133–8.

BRIGGS, A., and ELKIND, D. (1973) 'Cognitive development in early readers', *Dev. Psych.*, 9, 279–280.

BROCK, S.A. (1975) 'Facilitating psychological growth in post-adolescents: a cognitive-developmental curriculum intervention and analysis', *Diss. Abstr.*, 35, 8, pp. 3677B–4295B, (p. 4140–B).

BROWN, A.L. (1973) 'Conservation of number and continuous quantity in normal, bright, and retarded children', *Child Developm.*, 44, 376–9.

BRUNER, J.S. (1966) *Toward a Theory of Instruction*. Cambridge, Mass: Harvard Univ. Press.

BRUNER, J.S., OLVER, R.R., and GREENFIELD, P.M. (1966) *Studies in Cognitive Development*. New York: Wiley.

BRYANT, P.E. (1972) 'The understanding of invariance by very young children', *Can. J. Psych.*, 26 (1), 78–95.

BURGESS, J.W. (1969) Alternate paths: An inquiry into the development of adult reasoning. MEd thesis, Edinburgh University.

BUSS, A.R., and ROYCE, J.R. (1975) 'Ontogenetic changes in cognitive structure from a multivariate perspective', *Dev. Psych.*, 11, 1, 87–101.

BUSSIS, A. *et al.* (1969) 'Teaching classification concepts to disadvantaged preschool children'. Paper presented at the annual meeting of AERA, February.

BYBEE, R. and McCORMACK, A. (1970) 'Applying Piaget's Theory', *Sci. and Children*, Dec., 14–7.

CAMBRIDGE CONFERENCE ON SCHOOL MATHEMATICS (1963) *Goals for School Mathematics.* Boston: Houghton Mifflin.

CARLSON, J. *et al.* (1974) 'Der Effekt von Problemverbalisation bei verschiedenen Aufgabengruppen und Darbietungsformen des "Raven Progressive Matrices Test" ', *Diagnostica,* 20, 133–41.

CARLSON, J.S., and MICHALSON, L.H. (1973) 'Methodological study of conservation in retarded adolescents', *Am. J. Ment. Def.*, 78, 3, 348–53.

CARLSON, J.S. and WIEDL, K.H. (1976) 'Modes of information integration and Piagetian measures of concrete operational thought'. Paper presented at the Sixth International Interdisciplinary Seminar, Piagetian Theory and its Implications for the Helping Professions, 30th January. Also personal communication.

CARPENTER, T.P. (1975) 'Measurement concepts of first- and second-grade students', *J. Res. Maths. Educ.*, 6, 3–13.

CARROLL, C.A. (1975) 'Low achievers' understanding of logical inference forms'. In: ROSSKOPF, M.F. (Ed.) *Children's Mathematical Concepts: Six Piagetian Studies in Mathematics Education.* New York: Teachers College Press, Columbia University.

CASATI, I., and LEZINE, I. (1968) Les étapes de l'intelligence sensorimotrice', Paris: Editions du centre de psychologie appliquée. (English translation, E. Ristow, unpublished manuscript).

CASE, D., and COLLINSON, J.M. (1962) 'The development of formal thinking in verbal comprehension', *Brit. J. Ed. Psych.*, 32, 103–11.

CASE, R. (1972) 'Learning and development: a neo-Piagetian interpretation', *Human Developm.*, 15, 339–58.

CATHCART, W.G. (1971) 'The relationship between primary students' rationalization of conservation and their mathematical achievement', *Child Developm.*, 42, 755–65.

CATTELL, R.B. (1966a) 'The meaning and strategic use of factor analysis'. In: CATTELL, R.B. (Eds.) *Handbook of Multivariate Experimental Psychology.* Chicago, Rand-McNally.

CATTELL, R.B. (1966b) 'The scree test for the number of factors', *Mult. Beh. Res.*, 1, 245–76.

CATTELL, R.B., and COAN, R.W. (1966) *Guidebook for the Early School Personality Questionnaire — ESPQ*. Champaign, Illinois: Inst. for Personality and Ability Testing.

CATTELL, R.B., and FOSTER, M.J. (1963) 'The rotoplot programme for multiple singleplane, visually-guided rotation', *Behav. Sc.*, 8, 156—65.

CHARLESWORTH, R.N. (1975) 'Cognitive development: guiding principles for early childhood programmes', *Diss. Abstr.*, 35, 7, 3941A—4780—A (4311—A).

CLAYTON, D.M. (1975) 'An investigation into the relationship of non-intellective factors to cognitive functioning and development', *Diss. Abstr.*, 35, 8, pp. 3677B to 4295B, (pp. 4163—4164—B).

COLLIS, K.F. (1971) 'A study of concrete and formal reasoning in school mathematics', *Aust. J. Psych.*, 23, 289—296.

COLLIS, K.F. (1972) A study of concrete and formal operations in school mathematics. Unpublished PhD thesis, University of Newcastle (New South Wales).

COLLIS, K.F. (1973) 'A study of children's ability to work with elementary mathematical systems', *Aust. J. Psych.*, 25, 2, 121—30.

COLLIS, K.F. (1974) 'The development of a preference for logical consistency in school mathematics', *Child Developm.*, 45, 978—83.

COLTON, T. (1972) 'The role of classification skills in children's acquisition of concrete operational thought', *Diss. Abstr.*, order No. 72—11331, Xerox University Microfilms.

CORMAN, H.H., and ESCALONA, S.K. (1969) 'Stages of sensorimotor development: a replication study', *Merr.-Palm. Quart.*, 15, 351—61.

CRONBACH, L.J., and SNOW, R.E. (in press) *Aptitudes and Instructional Methods*. New York: Irvington.

DALE, L.G. (1975) 'Some implications from the work of Jean Piaget'. In: GARDNER, P.L. (Ed.) *The Structure of Science Education*. Australia: Longman Australia Pty Limited, pp. 115—40.

DAS, J.P. (1972) 'Patterns of cognitive ability in nonretarded and retarded children', *Am. J. Ment. Def.*, 77, 6—12.

DAS, J.P. (1973a) 'Patterns of cognitive abilities: simultaneous and successive information integration'. Paper presented at the Western Psychological Association Meeting, Anaheim, California.

DAS, J.P. (1973b) 'Structure of cognitive abilities: evidence for simultaneous and successive processing', *J. Ed. Psych.*, 65, 103—8.

DAVIES, G.B. (1964) Concrete and formal thinking among adolescent children of average ability. Unpublished MEd thesis, Birmingham University.

DAVIS, R.B. (1964) 'Films on the Madison Project: "Infinite sequences" "Bounded sequences"; and "What is convergence?" ' Madison Project.'

DE MEURON, M. (1974) 'The use of clinical and cognitive information in the classroom'. In: SCHWEBEL, M. and RAPH, J. (Eds.), *Piaget in the Classroom*. London: Routledge and Kegan Paul.

DE SILVA, W.A. (1972) 'The formation of historical concepts through contextual cues', *Educ. Rev.*, 24, 3, 174—83.

DeVRIES, R. (1969) 'Constancy of generic identity in the years three to six', *Mon. Soc. Res. Child Dev.*, 34, 3, (Serial No. 127).

DeVRIES, R. (1970) 'The development of role-taking as reflected by behaviour of bright, average, and retarded children in a social guessing game', *Child Developm.*, 41, 751—70.

DeVRIES, R. (1973) 'The two intelligences of bright, average, and retarded children'. Meeting of the Society for Research in Child Development, Philadelphia.

DeVRIES, R. (1974) 'Relationships among Piagetian, IQ, and Achievement assessments', *Child Developm.*, 45, 746—56.

DeVRIES, R., and KOHLBERG, L. (1969) 'The Concept Assessment Kit Conservation', *J. Ed. Measur.*, 6, 4, 263—9.

DEWEY, J. (1963) *Experience and Education.* New York: Collier.

DIAMOND, H. (1973) 'An investigation of the efficacy of Piaget curriculum elements integrated into a traditional Head Start programme', *Diss. Abstr.*, 34, 1, 1A—451 (167A), Xerox University Microfilms.

DIENES, Z.P. (1959) 'The growth of mathematical concepts in children through experience', *Ed. Res.*, 2, 9—28.

DOCHERTY, E.M. (1974a) 'Identifying concrete and formal operational children'. Paper presented at the Fourth Special Invitational Interdisciplinary Seminar on Piagetian Theory and Its Implications for the Helping Professions, University of Southern California, February 15th.

DODGSON, C. (1963) 'Through the Looking Glass', in *The Annotated Alice*. Cleveland: World Publishing Company.

DODWELL, P.C. (1960) 'Children's understanding of number and related concepts', *Can. J. Psych.*, 14, 191—205.

DODWELL, P.C. (1961) 'Children's understanding of number concepts: characteristics of an individual and of a group test', *Can. J. Psych.*, 15, 29—36.

DODWELL, P.C. (1962) 'Relations between the understanding of the logic of classes and of cardinal number in children', *Can. J. Psych.*, 16, 152—60.

DOLAN, T. (1975) Review of 'Thinking goes to school', *Brit. J. Ed. Psych.*, 45, 1, 97, (Review).

DUCKWORTH, E. (1964) 'Piaget rediscovered', *J. Res. Sci. Teach.*, 2, 172—5.

DUCKWORTH, E. (1974) 'The having of wonderful ideas', In:

SCHWEBEL, M. and RAPH, J. (Ed.) *Piaget in the Classroom.*
London: Routledge and Kegan Paul.
DUDEK, S.Z., LESTER, E.P., GOLDBERG, J.S., and DYER, G.B.
(1969) 'Relationship of Piaget measures to standard intelligence and
motor scales', *Percep. Mot. Skills*, 28, 351–62.
DULIT, E. (1972) 'Adolescent thinking à la Piaget: the formal stage', *J.
Youth and Adoles.*, 1, 4, 281–301.
DUNN, L.M. (1965) *The Peabody Picture Vocabulary Test.* Circle
Pines, Minnesota: American Guidance Service.
DYER, G.B. (1968) A longitudinal study with five Piaget tests among
children in kindergarten, grade one and grade two. Unpublished
masters thesis, University of Montreal.
ELEMENTARY, SCIENCE STUDY (1966) *Teacher's Guide for
Behaviour of Mealworms.* New York: McGraw-Hill Books Company.
ELEMENTARY SCIENCE STUDY (1969) *Teacher's Guide for Ice
Cubes.* New York: McGraw-Hill Books Company.
ELEMENTARY SCIENCE STUDY (1969) *Teacher's Guide for Rocks
and Charts.* New York: McGraw-Hill Books Company.
ELEMENTARY SCIENCE STUDY (1971) *Teacher's Guide for Starting
from Seeds.* New York: McGraw-Hill Books Company.
ELKIND, D. (1961) 'Quantity conceptions in junior and senior high
school students', *Child Developm.*, 32, 551–60.
ELKIND, D. (1967) 'Piaget's conservation problems: a logical analysis',
Child Developm., 38, 15–27.
ELKIND, D. (1969) 'Piagetian and psychometric conceptions of
intelligence', *Harv. Ed. Rev.*, 2, 319–37.
ELKIND, D. (1969a) *Studies in Cognitive Development.* Oxford:
Oxford University Press.
ELKIND, D. (1971) 'Two approaches to intelligence: Piagetian and
psychometric'. In: GREEN, D.R., FORD, M.P. and FLAMER, G.B.
(Eds.) *Measurement and Piaget.* New York: McGraw-Hill, pp.
12–33.
ELKIND, D. (1973) 'Cognitive structure in latency behaviour'. In:
WESTMAN, J.C. (Ed.) *Individual Differences in Children.* New
York: John Wiley and Sons.
ELKIND, D. (1974) 'Two approaches to intelligence'. In: ELKIND, D.
Children and Adolescents: Interpretive Essays on Jean Piaget. 2nd
Edition, London: Oxford University Press.
ELKIND, D., LARSON, M.E., and DOORNINCK, W.N. (1965) 'Per-
ceptual learning and performance in slow and average readers', *J. Ed.
Psych.*, 56, 1, 50–6.
ELLIOTT, C. (1975) 'The British Intelligence Scale: Final report before
standardisation, 1975–1976', personal communication. Also Paper
presented at the Annual Conference of the British Psychological

Society, 4th April.

ELLIOTT, C. (1975a) 'Innovation and decision-making in psychological assessment: a further reply to Gillham', personal communication. Also Paper presented to the Annual Conference of the British Psychological Society, 4th April.

ERIKSON, E.H. (1972) *Young Man Luther.* New York: Basic Books Inc.

ESCALONA, S., and CORMAN, H. (1967) 'The validation of Piaget's hypothesis concerning the development of sensorimotor intelligence: methodological issues'. Paper presented at the biennial meeting of the Society for Research in Child Development, New York, March.

EVANS, R.I. (1973) *Jean Piaget, the Man and his Ideas.* New York: E.P. Dutton.

FELDMAN, C.F., *et al.* (1974) *The Development of Adaptive Intelligence.* Jossey-Bass, Inc.

FESTINGER, L. (1957) *A Theory of Cognitive Dissonance.* Evanston, Ill.: Row, Peterson.

FIELD, T.W., and CROPLEY, A.J. (1969) 'Cognitive style and science achievement', *J. Res. Sci. Teach.,* 6, 2–10.

FIGURELLI, J.C., and KELLER, H.R. (1972) 'The effects of training and socioeconomic class upon the acquisition of conservation concepts', *Child Developm.,* 43, 293–8.

FIRLIK, R.J. (1975) 'Mixed-age grouping and performance on standard conservation tasks', *Diss. Abstr.* 35, 8., 4751a–5579A (4858A).

FISCHBEIN, E. (1973) 'Intuition, structure and heuristic methods'. In: HOWSON, A.G. (Ed.) *Developments in Mathematical Education.* Cambridge University Press.

FISCHER, H. (1964) 'The psychology of Piaget and its educational applications', *Int. Rev. Ed.,* 10, 431–9.

FLAVELL, J.H. (1963) *The Developmental Psychology of Jean Piaget.* New York: Van Nostrand Reinhold.

FLAVELL, J.H. (1971) 'Stage-related properties of cognitive development', *Cogn. Psych.,* 2, 421–53.

FLAVELL, J.H. (1973) 'The development of inferences about others'. In: MISCHEL, T. (Ed.) *Understanding Other Persons.* Oxford: Blackwell, Basil and Mott.

FLAVELL, J.H. and WOHLWILL, J.F. (1969) 'Formal and functional aspects of cognitive development'. In: ELKIND, D. and FLAVELL, J.H (Eds.) *Studies in Cognitive Development; Essays in Honour of Jean Piaget.* New York: Oxford University Press.

FLECK, J.R. (1972) 'Cognitive styles in children and performance on Piagetian conservation tasks', *Percep. Mot. Skills,* 35, 747–756.

FLECKMAN, B. (1975) 'Spontaneous vs. scientific concepts', personal communication. Also Paper presented at the fourth annual international interdisciplinary conference on Piagetian theory and the Helping Professions, Children's Hospital, Los Angeles, California, 24th January.

FREYBERG, P.S. (1966) 'Concept development in Piagetian terms in relation to school attainment', *J. Ed. Psych.*, 57, 3, 164—8.

FROST, J.L. (1973) *Revisiting Early Childhood Education: Reading.* New York: Holt, Rinehart and Winston.

FULLER, F.F., and MANNING, B.A. (1973) 'Self-confrontation reviewed: a conceptualization for video playback in teacher education', *Rev. Ed. Res.*, 43, 4, 469—528.

FURTH, H.G. (1970) *Piaget for Teachers.* New York: Prentice Hall.

FURTH, H.G. and WACHS, H. (1974) *Thinking goes to School: Piaget's Theory in Practice.* London: Oxford University Press.

GAGNE, R.M. (1962) 'The acquisition of knowledge', *Psych. Rev.*, 69, 355—65.

GALBRAITH, K.W. (1975) 'A study of the reliability and factor composition of the Concept Assessment Kit-Conservation', *Diss. Abstr.* 35, 12, pt I, 7447A—8068A (p. 7721—A).

GARFIELD, A., and SHAKESPERE, R. (1964) 'A psychological and developmental study of mentally retarded children with cerebral palsy', *Developm. Med. and Child Neurol.*, 6, 485—94.

GAUDIA, G. (1972) 'Race, social class, and age of achievement of conservation on Piaget's tasks', *Dev. Psych.*, 6, 1, 158—65.

GAUDIA, G. (1974) 'The Piagetian dilemma: what does Piaget really have to say to teachers?', *El. Sch. J.*, 74, 8, 481—92.

GENKINS, E.F. (1975) 'The concept of bilateral symmetry in young children'. In: ROSSKOPF, M.F. (Ed.) *Children's Mathematical Concepts: Six Piagetian Studies in Mathematics Education.* New York: Teachers College Press, Columbia University.

GINSBURG, H. and OPPER, S. (1969) *Piaget's Theory of Intellectual Development: An Introduction.* Prentice-Hall.

GOLDEN, M., and BIRNS, B. (1968) 'Social class and cognitive development in infancy', *Merr.-Palm. Quart.*, 14, 139—49.

GOLDMAN, R. (1964) *Religious Thinking from Childhood to Adolescence.* London: Routledge and Kegan Paul.

GOLDMAN, R.J. (1965) 'The application of Piaget's schema of operational thinking to religious story data by means of a Guttman scalogram', *Brit. J. Ed. Psych.*, 35, 158—71.

GOLDSCHMID, M.L., and BENTLER, P.M. (1968) 'The dimensions and measurement of conservation', *Child Developm.* 29, 3, 579—89.

GOLDSCHMID, M.L., and BENTLER, P.M. (1968b) *Manual: Concept Assessment Kit-conservation.* San Diego, California: Educational and Industrial Testing Service.

GOLDSCHMID, M.L., BENTLER, P., DEBUS, R., RAWLINSON, R.,

KOHNSTAMM, G., MODGIL, S., *et al.* (1973) 'A cross-cultural investigation of conservation', *J. Cross-Cult. Psych.*, 4, 1, 75–88.

GOODACRE, E.J. (1971) *Children and Learning to Read.* London: Routledge and Kegan Paul.

GOODNOW, J. (1972) 'Rules and repertories, rituals and tricks of the trade: social and informational aspects to cognitive and representational development'. In: FARNHAM-DIGGORY, S. (Ed). *Information Processing in Children.* New York: Academic Press.

GOODNOW, J., and BETHON, G. (1966) 'Piaget's tasks: the effects of schooling and intelligence', *Child Developm.*, 37, 573–582.

GORDON, W.J.J. (1971) *The Metaphorical Way of Learning and Knowing.* Cambridge: Porpoise Books.

GORMAN, R.M. (1972) *Discovering Piaget.* Columbus: Charles E. Merrill.

GOTTFRIED, A.W. (1974) Interrelationships between and nomological networks of psychometric and Piagetian measures of sensorimotor intelligence. PhD thesis, New School for Social Research. Also *Diss. Abstr.*, 35, 2989–B.

GOTTFRIED, A.W., and BRODY, N. (1975) 'Interrelationships between and correlates of psychometric and Piagetian scales of sensorimotor intelligence', *Dev. Psych.*, 11, 3, 379–87.

GOUIN-DECARIE, T. (1965) *Intelligence and Affectivity in Early Childhood.* New York: International University Press.

GRAHAM, F. and KENDALL, B. (1960) 'Memory-for-Designs Test: revised general manual', *Percep. Mot. Skills*, Monog. Suppl. 2–7, 11, 147–88.

GRAY, K. (1972) 'Thinking abilities as objectives in curriculum development', *Educ. Rev.*, 24, 3, 237–50.

GRAY, W.M. (1973) 'Development of a Piagetian-based written test: a criterion-referenced approach'. Paper presented at the annual meeting of the American Educational Research Association, New Orleans, February.

GRAY, W.M. (1974) 'The integrated cognitive structures of EMH (Educationally Mentally Handicapped) children'. Paper presented at the fourth special invitational interdisciplinary seminar on Piagetian theory and its implications for the Helping Professions, Los Angeles.

GREEN, B.F. (1956) 'A method of scalogram analysis using summary statistics', *Psychometrika*, 21, 79–88.

GRIFFITHS, D.H. (1974) 'The study of the cognitive development of science students in introductory level courses', *Diss. Abstr.*, 34, 7, 3613A–4477A (3989A), Xerox University Microfilms.

GYR, J.W. *et al.* (1973) 'Children's attention to mathematically ordered transforming stimuli', *Percep. Mot. Skills*, 36, 463–75.

GYR, J.W., WILLEY, R., GORDON, D., and KUBO, R.H. (1974) 'Do mathematical group invariants characterize the perceptual schema of younger and older children?', *Human Developm.*, 17, 176–86.

HADAMARK, J. (1949) *The Psychology of Invention in the Mathematical Field.* New York: Dover Pub. Inc.

HALL, E.A. (1970) 'A conversation with Jean Piaget and Barbel Inhelder', *Psych. Today*, 3, 25–31, 54–6.

HALL, J.R. (1973) 'Conservation concepts in elementary chemistry', *J. Res. Sc. Teach.*, 10, 2, 143–6.

HALLAM, R.N. (1967) 'Logical thinking in history', *Ed. Rev.*, 19, 183–202.

HALLAM, R.N. (1969) 'Piaget and moral judgements in history', *Ed. Res.*, 11, 200–6.

HALLAM, R.N. (1969a) 'Piaget and the teaching of history', *Ed. Res.*, 12, 1,

HAMEL, B.R., and RIKSEN, B.O.M. (1973) 'Identity, reversibility, verbal rule instruction, and conservation', *Dev. Psych.*, 9, 66–72.

HAMEL, R., and van der VEER, M.A.A. (1972). 'Structures d'ensembles, multiple classification, multiple seriation and amount of irrelevant information', *Brit. J. Ed. Psych.*, 42, 319–25.

HAMILTON, V. (1972) 'Continuities and individual differences in conservation', *Brit. J. Psych.*, 63, 3, 429–40.

HAMILTON, V., and MOSS, M. (1974) 'A method of scaling conservation-of-quantity problems by information content', *Child Developm.*, 45, 737–45.

HARASYM, C.R., BOERSMA, F.J., and MAGUIRE, T.U. (1971) 'Semantic differential analysis of relational terms used in conservation', *Child Developm.*, 42, 767–79.

HARRIS, C.M. (1962) 'Some Rao-Guttman relationships', *Psychometrika*, 27, 247–63.

HARRIS, D.B. (1963) *Children's Drawings as Measure of Intellectual Maturity.* New York: Harcourt, Brace and World.

HARRIS, H.L. (1974) 'Piagetian task performance as a function of training', *Diss. Abstr.*, 4479A–5379A, (4869A), Xerox University Microfilms.

HATHAWAY, W.E. (1973) 'The degree and nature of the relations between traditional psychometric and Piagetian developmental measures of mental development'. Paper presented at the annual meeting of the American Educational Research Association, March.

HATHAWAY, W.E. (1975) 'The unique contributions of Piagetian measurement to diagnosis, prognosis, and research of children's mental development', personal communication. Also an invited Paper read at the fourth annual conference on Piaget and the Helping Professions, Los Angeles, California, Feb. 15, 1974.

HATHAWAY, W.E., and HATHAWAY-THEUNISSEN, A. (1974) 'The

unique contributions of Piagetian measurement to diagnosis, prognosis, and research of children's mental development'. Paper presented at the fourth annual conference on Piaget and the Helping Professions, Los Angeles, California, February 15th.

HAWKINS, D. (1973) 'Nature, man and mathematics'. In: HOWSON, A.G. (Ed.) *Developments in Mathematical Education.* Cambridge University Press.

HAYSOM, J., and SUTTON, C. (Ed.), (1974) *Theory into Practice: Activities in School for Student Teachers.* Maidenhead: McGraw-Hill.

HEIN, G. (1968) 'Children's Science in another culture', reprinted from *Tech. Rev.*, 71, 2, December.

HILDRETH, G.H., GRIFFITHS, N.L., and McGAUVRAN, M.E. (1969) *Manual of Directions Metropolitan Readiness Tests.* New York: Harcourt, Brace and World.

HOFMANN, R.J., and PRUZEK, R.M. (1974) 'Factor analysis: stretching our roots and twisting our vectors'. Paper presented at the annual meeting of the American Educational Research Association, Chicago, April.

HOMME, L.E., and KLAUS, D.J. (1962) 'Laboratory studies in the analysis of behaviour', *Albuquerque*, TM 1.

HOMME, L.E., deBACA, P., DEVINE, J.V., STEINHORST, R., and RICKERT, E.J. (1963) 'Use of the Premack Principle in controlling the behaviour of nursery school children', *J. Exp. Anal. Behav.*, 6, 544.

HOOPER, F.H. (1969) 'Piaget's conservation tasks: the logical and developmental priority of identity conservation', *J. Exp. Child Psych.*, 8, 234–49.

HUGHES, M.M. (1965) A four-year longitudinal study of the growth of logical thinking in a group of secondary modern schoolboys. MEd thesis, University of Leeds.

HUNT, J. McV. (1961) *Intelligence and Experience.* New York: Ronald Press.

HUNT, J. McV. (1969) 'The impact and limitations of the giant of developmental psychology', In: ELKIND, D. and FLAVELL, J.H. (Eds.), *Studies in Cognitive Development.* New York: Oxford University Press. pp. 3–66.

HURTA, M.J. (1973) 'The relationship between conservation abilities on selected Piagetian tasks and reading ability', *Diss. Abstr.*, 33, 9, 4587A–5342A (4941A), Xerox University Microfilms.

HYDE, K.E. (1965) 'Religious learning in adolescence', *Educ. Monogs. VII*, London: Oliver and Boyd.

ILG, F.L., and AMES, L.B. (1965) *School Readiness.* New York: Harper and Row.

INGLE, R.B., and SHAYER, M. (1971) 'Conceptual demands in

Nuffield O-level chemistry', *Educ. in Chemist.*, 8, 5, 182–3.

INHELDER, B. (1943) *Le Diagnostic du Raisonnement chez les Debiles Mentraux.* Neuchatel: Delachaux et Niestlé.

INHELDER, B. (1968) *The Diagnosis of Reasoning Processes in the Retarded.* New York: John Day Company.

INHELDER, B., and PIAGET, J. (1955) *De la Logique de l'Enfant à la Logique de l'Adolescent.* Paris: Presses Universitaires de France.

INHELDER, B., and PIAGET, J. (1958) *The Growth of Logical Thinking from Childhood to Adolescence.* London: Routledge and Kegan Paul.

INHELDER, B., and PIAGET, J. (1959) *La Genèse des Structures Logiques Elémentaires.* Neuchatel: Delachaux et Niestlé.

INHELDER, B., and PIAGET, J. (1964) *The Early Growth of Logic in the Child.* London: Routledge and Kegan Paul.

JAGODA, E., and ROBISON, H. (1975) 'The relationship of teaching competence to teacher performance and children's learning of classification skills', personal communication.

JENKINS, E. and WHITFIELD, R. (Ed.), (1974) *Readings in Science Education.* London: McGraw-Hill, pp. 42–50.

JIMENEZ, J. (1976) 'Piaget and synectics'. Paper presented at the Sixth International Interdisciplinary Seminar Piagetian theory and its implications for the helping professions, January 30th. Personal communication.

JUSTIZ, T.B. (1969) 'A reliable measure of teacher effectiveness', *Educ. Leader.*, 3, 1, 49–55.

KAGAN, J. (1971) *Understanding Children: Behaviour, Motives and Thought.* New York: Harcourt, Brace, Javanovich.

KAMII, C. (1970) 'Piaget's theory and specific instruction: A response to Bereiter and Kohlberg', Interchange: *J. Ed. Stud.*, Pub. by the Ontario Institute for Studies in Education, 1, 1, 33–9.

KAMII, C. (1971) 'Evaluation of learning in preschool education'. In: BLOOM, B. *et al.*, (Eds.) *Formative and Summative Evaluation in Student Learning.* New York: McGraw Hill.

KAMII, C. (1974) 'Pedagogical principles derived from Piaget's theory: relevance for educational practice'. In: SCHWEBEL, M. and RAPH, J. (Eds.) *Piaget in the Classroom.* London: Routledge and Kegan Paul.

KAMII, C. (1974a) 'Piaget's interaction and the process of teaching young children'. In: SCHWEBEL, M. and RAPH, J. (Eds.) *Piaget in the Classroom.* London: Routledge and Kegan Paul.

KAMII, C., and DeVRIES, R. (1975) 'Piaget for early education'. In: PARKER, R. and DAY, M. (Eds.) *Preschool in action.* Boston: Allyn and Bacon.

KARPLUS, R. (1964) Relativity and Motion. Science Curriculum improvement Study, California University (mimeographed).

KARPLUS, R. (1964) 'The science curriculum improvement study – Report to the Piaget Conference', *J. Res. Sci. Teach.*, 2, 236–40.

KARPLUS, R., and LAVATELLI, C. (1969) *The Developmental Theory of Piaget: Conservation.* San Francisco: John Davidson Film Producers.

KARPLUS, R., and PETERSON, R.W. (1970) 'Intellectual development beyond elementary school II: Ratio, a survey', *Sch. Sc. and Mathm.*, 70, 9, 813–20.

KAUFMAN, A.S. (1971) Comparison of tests built from Piaget's and Gesell's tasks: an analysis of their psychometric properties and psychological meaning. Unpublished doctoral dissertation, Teachers College, Columbia University.

KAUFMAN, A.S., and KAUFMAN, N.L. (1972) 'Tests built from Piaget's and Gesell's tasks as predictors of first-grade achievement', *Child Developm.*, 43, 521–35.

KEATING, D. (1973) Precocious development at the level of formal operations. PhD thesis, Johns Hopkins University.

KENT, A.H. (1973) 'The relationships of reading comprehension, conservation ability, auditory discrimination, and visual-motor development of third-grade pupils', *Diss. Abstr.* 34, 6, 2809A–3611A (2924A), Xerox University Microfilms.

KEPHART, N.C. (1964) 'Perceptual-motor aspects of learning disabilities', *Except. Child.*, 31, 201–6.

KESSEN, W., and KUHLMAN, C. (Eds.), (1962) 'Thought in the young child', *Mon. Soc. Res. Child. Dev.*, 27, 2, (whole No. 83).

KILPATRICK, J. (1964) 'Cognitive theory and the SMSC programme'. In: RIPPLE, R.E. and ROCKCASTLE, V.N. (Eds.) *Piaget Rediscovered: A report of the conference on Cognitive Development, 1964* Ithaca, NY: School of Education, Cornell University, 128–33.

KILPATRICK, J. (1975) 'Commentary'. In: ROSSKOPF, M.F. (Ed.) *Children's Mathematical Concepts: Six Piagetian Studies in Mathematics Education.* New York: Teachers College Press, Columbia University.

KIMBALL, R. (1968) *A Science Concept Study in Malawi.* Domasi, Malawi: The Science Centre.

KIMBALL, R. (1970) *San Luis, Teoloxolco: Aborita.* San Leandro: Educational Science Consultants.

KIMBALL, R. (1971) *Substances and Mixtures and Liquids and Powders.* San Leandro: Educational Science Consultants.

KIMBALL, R. (1972) 'A test of a theory of development in Uganda: implications for intellectual growth of school children in less technologically developed nations'. Paper presented at the 15th

Annual meeting of the African Studies Association, Philadelphia, Nov. 8—11.

KIMBALL, R. (1972a) *You and Me*. San Leandro, California, Educational Science Consultants.

KIMBALL, R.L. (1973) 'The teaching and understanding of formal operations'. Paper delivered to the Third Annual Conference on Piaget and the Helping Professions, Children's Hospital, Los Angeles.

KIMBALL, R.L. (1974) 'Some aspects of the role of affective development in cognitive development: relating formal operations learning to emotional maturity'. Paper delivered to the Fourth Annual Conference on Piaget and the Helping Professions: Children's Hospital, Los Angeles, California, February.

KIMBALL, R. (1975a) *NEW: Hope, Love, Life: Understanding, Trust, Responsibility*. San Leandro: Educational Science Consultants.

KING, W.L., and SEEGMILLER, B. (1971) 'Cognitive development from 14 to 22 months of age in black, male, first-born infants assessed by the Bayley and Hunt-Uzgiris scales', *Proc. Soc. Res. Child Develop. Meet.*, Minneapolis.

KING, W.L., and SEEGMILLER, B. (1973) 'Performance of 14- to 22-month-old Black firstborn male infants on two tests of cognitive development: The Bayley Scales and the Infant Psychological Development Scale', *Dev. Psych.*, 8, 317—26.

KNOTT, D. (1974) 'The development of scientific concepts in pupils of the first two years of a secondary school', personal communication.

KOFSKY, E. (1966) 'A scalogram study of classificatory development', *Child Developm.*, 37, 191—204.

KOHLBERG, L. (1963) 'The development of children's orientations toward a moral order: I, Sequence in the development of moral thought', *Vita Humana*, 6, 11—33.

KOHLBERG, L. (1968) 'The child as a moral philosopher', *Psych. Today*, 2, 4, 24—31.

KOHLBERG, L. (1968a) 'Early education: a cognitive-development view', *Child Developm.*, 39, 1013—63.

KOHLBERG, L. (1970) 'Stages of moral development as a basis for moral education'. In: BECK, C. and SULLIVAN, E. (Eds.) *Moral Education*. Toronto: University of Toronto Press.

KOHLBERG, L. and DeVRIES, R. (1969) 'Relations between Piaget and psychometric assessments of intelligence'. Paper presented at the conference on the Natural Curriculum of the Child, Urbana, Illinois.

KOHLBERG, L., and DeVRIES, R. (1974) 'Relations between Piaget and psychometric assessments of intelligence'. In: LAVATELLI, C. *The Natural Curriculum of the Child*. Urbana: University of Illinois Press.

KOHLBERG, L., and MAYER, R. (1972–1973) 'Development as the aim of education', *Harv. Ed. Rev.*, 42, 4, November.

KOPP, C.B., SIGMAN, M., and PARMELEE, A.H. (1974) 'Longitudinal study of sensorimotor development', *Dev. Psych.*, 10, 5, 687–95.

KOSLOWSKI, B., and BRUNER, J. (1972) 'Learning to use a lever', *Child Developm.*, 43, 790–9.

KOWITZ, G.T. (1975) 'Review of: J. Rest (1974) "Developmental Psychology as a Guide to value education: a review of "Kohlbergian" programmes",' *Child Developm. Abstrs. and Bibliog.*, Summer Issue, p. 196.

LANGFORD, P.E. (1974) 'Development of concepts of infinity and limit in mathematics' *Arch. de Psycholog.*, 42, 311–22.

LARSON, J.C. (1972) 'A developmental index of numerical cognitive performance', *Diss. Abstr.*, (order no. 72–14913), Xerox University Microfilms.

LAVATELLI, C.S. (1970) Cited in review of, 'Piaget in the classroom: or is he?', by C.S. Lavatelli, 1974, *Contemp. Psych.*, 19, 5, pp. 365–366.

LAW, E.G. (1972) 'The growth of mathematical thinking during the secondary school years', *Ed. Rev.*, 24, 3, 197–211.

LEE, L.C. (1971) 'The concomitant development of cognitive and moral modes of thought: a test of selected deductions from Piaget's theory', *Gen. Psych. Mon.*, 83, 93–146.

LEFEVRE, A. (1970) 'A propos d'un cas de "dyscalculie" de la rééducation à la psychothérapie', *Perspectives Psychiatriques*, 4, 30, 39–56.

LEWIS, D.G. (1967) *Statistical Methods in Education.* University of London Press.

LEWIS, D.G. (1968) *Experimental Design in Education.* University of London Press.

LEWIS, M. (1974) 'Infant intelligence tests: their use and misuse', *Hum. Developm.*, 108–18.

LEWIS, M. and McGURK, H. (1972) 'Evaluation of infant intelligence scores – true or false?', *Science*, 178, 1174–7.

LEWIS, M. and WILSON, C.D. (1972) 'Infant development in lower-class American families', *Human Developm.*, 15, 112–27.

LEZINE, I., STAMBAK, M., and CASATI, I. (1969) *Les Etapes de l'Intelligence Sensorimotrice* (Monographie No. I). Paris: Les Editions du Centre de Psychologie Appliquée.

LINDVALL, C.M. and LIGHT, J.A. (1974) 'The use of manipulative lessons in primary grade Arithmetic in a programme for individualized instruction'. Paper presented at the meeting of the American Education Association, Chicago.

LINGOES, J.C. (1963) 'Multiple scalogram analysis: a set theoretic model for analyzing dichotomous items', *Educ. and Psych. Meast.*, 23, 501—24.

LINN, M.C. and THIER, H.D. (1975) 'The effect of experiential science on development of logical thinking in children', *J. Res. Sci. Teach.*, 12, 1, 49—62.

LINN, M.C., CHEN, B., and THIER, H.D. (1975) 'Personalization in science: Can we teach children to interpret experiments'. Advancing Education through Science-Oriented Programmes, Report PSc—4. Also personal communication.

LINN, M.C., CHEN, B., and THIER, H.D. (in press) *Personalization in Science*. Instructional Science.

LOUGHRAN, R. (1975) Review of 'Thinking goes to school: Piaget's theory in practice', *Educ. Stud.*, 1, 1, 81, (Review).

LOVELL, K. (1968) 'Piaget in perspective: The experimental foundations'. Paper read at the Conference 'Piaget in Perspective' at University of Sussex, 5th and 6th April.

LOVELL, K. (1971) *Intellectual Growth and Understanding Mathematics*. Columbus, Ohio: ERIC Information Analyses Center for Science and Mathematics Education, February.

LOVELL, K. and SHIELDS, J.B. (1967) 'Some aspects of the study of the gifted child', *Brit. J. Ed. Psych.*, 37, 201—8.

LUNZER, E.A. (1960) *Recent Studies in Britain Based on the Work of Jean Piaget*. Slough: NFER, (New Edit. 1973).

LUNZER, E.A. (1960a) 'Some points of Piagetian theory in the light of experimental criticism', *J. Child Psych. and Psychiat.*, 1, 191—202.

LUNZER, E.A. (1969—70) 'The Development of Systematic Thinking' 'Annual Report', Social Science Research Council. pp. 173—74.

LUNZER, E.A. (1970) 'Construction of a standardized battery of Piagetian tests to assess the development of effective intelligence', *Research in Educ.*, 3, 53—72, Manchester University Press.

LUNZER, E.A. (1971—1972; 1973) 'The Development of Systematic Thinking', 'Research Supported', Social Science Research Council. p. 158 and pp. 234—35, respectively.

LUNZER, E.A. (1972) 'An enquiry into the development of systematic thinking. In: MONKS, F.J., HARTUP, W.W., and deWIT, J. (Eds.) *Determinants of Behavioural Development*. Academic Press

LUNZER, E.A. *et al.* (1973) 'Factors affecting cognitive behaviour of children in their first year of schooling'. Paper presented at Biennial Conference of Society for the Study of Behavioural Development, Ann Arbor, Michigan, USA.

MADDEN, E. *et al.* (1973) *Stanford Achievement Test, Primary Level III, Form A*. New York: Harcourt, Brace, Jovanovich, Inc.

MAEHR, M.L. (1968) 'Learning theory, some limitations of the application of reinforcement theory to education', *Sch. and Soc.*,

Feb., 108—10.

MAI, R.P. (1975) 'John Dewey, Jean Piaget, and the theoretical foundations of open education', *Diss. Abstr.* 35, 9, 5581A—6281A, (6006—A).

MALPAS, A.J. and BROWN, M. (1974) 'Cognitive demand and difficulty of GCE O-level mathematics pretest items', *Brit. J. Educ. Psych.*, 44, 155—62.

MANNIX, J.B. (1960) 'The number concepts of a group of ESN children', *Brit. J. Ed. Psych.*, 30, 80—1, also MEd thesis of same title, Manchester University.

MARTIN, J.L. (1975) 'A test with selected topological properties of Piaget's hypothesis concerning the spatial representation of the young child', *Diss. Abstr.*, April, 35, 10, pp. 6283A—6852A (6368—A).

McCLELLAND, D.C. (1973) 'Testing for competence rather than for "intelligence" ', *Amer. Psych.*, 28, 1, 1—14.

McCLENAHAN, M.D. (1975) 'An application of Piagetian research to the growth of chance and probability concepts with low achievers in secondary school mathematics', *Diss. Abstr.*, 686A.

McCURDY, E. (Ed.) (1923) *Leonardo da Vinci's Note Books*. NY: Empire State Book Co.

McDANIEL, E., FELDHUSEN, J., WHEATLEY, G., and HOUTZ, J. (1973) *Measurement of Concept Formation and Problem-Solving in Disadvantaged Elementary School Children*. West Lafayette, Indiana: Purdue Educational Research Center.

McNALLY, D.W. (1974) *Piaget, Education and Teaching*. Sussex: New Education Press.

MEADOWS, S. (1975c) Scalogram analysis of nine concrete operations test. Personal communication and PhD thesis, Bedford College London University.

MEALINGS, R.J. (1963) 'Problem solving and science teaching', *Ed. Rev.*, 15, 194—207, (1961, Unpublished MA thesis, Birmingham University).

MERMELSTEIN, E., and SCHULMAN, L. (1967) 'Lack of formal schooling and the acquisition of conservation', *Child Developm.*, 38, 39—52.

MEYERS, C.E. (1972) 'Can Piaget's theory provide a better psychometry? Proceedings of the second annual UAP Conference on Piagetian theory and the Helping Professions, Los Angeles, January, pp. 5—10.

MEYERS, C.E., and ORPET, R.E. (1971) 'Ability factor location of some Piagetian tasks at 5½ years'. Proceedings of the 79th Annual Convention of the American Psychological Association.

MILLER, D., COHEN, L., and HILL, K. (1970) 'A methodological investigation of Piaget's theory of object concept development in the sensorimotor period', *J. Exp. Child Psych.*, 9, 59—85.

MODGIL, C. (1975) Piagetian operations in relation to moral development. MPhil thesis, University of Surrey.

MODGIL, S. (1969) The relation of emotional adjustment to the conservation of number. Unpublished Masters thesis, University of Manchester.

MODGIL, S. (1974) *Piagetian Research: A Handbook of Recent Studies*. Windsor: NFER.

MODGIL, S. (1974a) The patterning of cognitive development in relation to parental attitude. PhD thesis, King's College, London University.

MODGIL, S., DIELMAN, T., CATTELL, R.B., and MODGIL, C. (1975) 'A factor analytic investigation of personality, attitudinal and cognitive variables in 7 and 8 year old children'. In press.

MORGAN, R.F. (Jr.). (1975) 'Validity of a reading comprehension test based on the Piagetian model of intelligence', *Diss. Abst.*, 35, 8, pp. 4757A to 5579A, (p. 4989—A)

MORGAN, R.F. and ESPOSITO, J.P. (1976) 'Validity of a Reading Comprehension Test based on the Piagetian model of Intelligence' Personal communication.

MÜLLER, R. (1970) 'Eine kritische empirische Untersuchung des "Draw-a-Man Test" und der "Coloured Progressive Matrices" ', *Diagnostica*, 16, 138—47.

MURRAY, D. (1975) 'Rasch item analysis and scaling', personal communication. Also Paper presented to the Annual Conference of the British Psychological Society at Nottingham, 4th April.

MURRAY, F.B. (1972) 'Acquisition of conservation through social interaction', *Dev. Psych.*, 6, 1—6.

NATIONAL CHILDREN'S BUREAU (1975) 'Developmental Chart 5—9 years'. Personal communication.

NELSON, R.J. (1969) 'An investigation of a group test based on Piaget's concepts of number and length conservation and its ability to predict first-grade arithmetic-achievement'. Unpub. PhD thesis, Purdue University.

NEWBY, M.R. (1973) 'Piaget's theory of the development of concrete logical thinking: implications for the elementary curriculum', *Diss. Abstr.*, 33, 11, 5883A—6507A (6068A), Xerox University Micro-films.

NOLEN, P. (1974) 'Piaget and the school psychologist'. Personal communication. Also Paper presented at the Fourth Annual UAP Conference on Piagetian Theory and the Helping Professions, University of Southern California, February.

NUFFIELD JUNIOR SCIENCE (1967) *Teachers Guide 1 & 2*. William

Collins
NUFFIELD MATHEMATICS PROJECT (1967) *I Do and I Understand*. London: Chambers and Murray.
NUFFIELD MATHEMATICS PROJECT (1968) *Check Ups*. London: Chambers and Murray.
OERTER, R. (1971) *Psychologie des Denkens*. Donauwörth: Auer.
O'LEARY, M.P. (1975) Review of 'Piaget, education and teaching', *Educ. Stud.*, 1, 1, 82, (Review).
ORTON, A. (1970) A cross sectional study of the development of the mathematical concept of a function in secondary school children of average and above average ability. MEd thesis, Leeds University.
OSLER, S.F., and KOFSKY, E. (1965) 'Stimulus uncertainty as a variable in the development of conceptual ability', *J. Exp. Child Psych.*, 2, 264–79.
OVERTON, W. (in press) 'General systems, structure and development'. In: RIEGEL, K. (Ed.) *Issues in Developmental and Historical Structuralism*. New York: Wiley.
OWENS, D.T. (1973) 'The effects of selected experiences on the ability of disadvantaged kindergarten and first grade children to use properties of equivalence and order relations', *Diss. Abstr.*, 33, 9, 4587A–5342A, (5042A), Xerox University Microfilms.
PARASKEVOPOULOS, J. and HUNT, J. McV. (1971) 'Object construction and imitation under differing conditions of rearing', *J. Gen. Psych.*, 119, 301–21.
PARKER, R.K. (1972) *The Preschool in Action*. Boston: Allyn and Bacon.
PASCUAL-LEONE, J. (1970) 'A mathematical model for the transition rule in Piaget's developmental stages', *Acta Psychol.*, 32, 301–45.
PASCUAL-LEONE, J. and SMITH, J. (1969) 'The encoding and decoding of symbols by children: a new experimental paradigm and a neo-Piagetian model', *J. Exp. Child Psych.*, 8, 328–55.
PEARCE, E.E. (1972) 'Curriculum design for junior life sciences based upon the theories of Piaget and Skinner', *Diss. Abstr.*, 5537A, order No. 72–12911, Xerox University Microfilms.
PEARSON, L. (1975) 'Developmental scales in the British Intelligence Scale', personal communication. Also Paper presented to the Annual Conference of the British Psychological Society, 4th April.
PEEL, E.A. (1959) 'Experimental examination of some of Piaget's schemata concerning children's perception and thinking, and a discussion of their educational significance', *Brit. J. Ed. Psych.*, 29, 89–103.
PEEL, E.A. (1960) *The Pupil's Thinking*. London: Oldbourne Book Company Limited.
PEEL, E.A. (1966) 'A study of differences in the judgments of

adolescent pupils', *Brit. J. Ed. Psych.*, 36, 77—86.

PEEL, E.A. (1967) 'Method for investigating children's understanding of certain logical connectives used in binary propositional thinking', *Brit. J. Math. Statis. Psych.*, 20, 81—92.

PEEL, E.A. (1971) *The Nature of Adolescent Judgment.* New York: Wiley-Interscience.

PEEL, E.A. (1971a) 'Generalising and abstracting', *Nature*, 230, 296—300.

PEEL, E.A. (1971b) 'Adolescent concept formation'. In: *Interdisciplinary Approaches to Language.* Centre for Information in Language Teaching Reports and Papers No. 6, Paper 2, 21—29.

PEEL, E.A. (Ed.) (1972) 'The quality of understanding in secondary school subjects', *Educ. Rev.,* 24, 3, 163—251, School of Education University of Birmingham.

PEEL, E.A. (1974) Review of 'Piaget in the classroom', *Brit. J. Ed. Stud.*, 22, 3, 365—6. (Review).

PEEL, E.A. (1975) 'Predilection for generalising and abstracting', *Brit. J. Ed. Psych.*, 45, 177—88.

PEEL, E.A. (1975a) 'The analysis of comprehension and judgment from textual material', *Ed. Rev.*, 27, 100—113.

PETROSKY, A.R. (1975) 'Individual and group responses of fourteen and fifteen year olds to short stories, novels, poems and thematic apperception tests: case studies based on Piagetian genetic epistemology and Freudian psycho-analytic ego psychology'. *Diss. Abstr.*, 36, 2, 579A—1131A (p. 852—A).

PIAGET, J. (1950) *Psychology of Intelligence.* London: Routledge and Kegan Paul.

PIAGET, J. (1952b) *The Child's Conception of Number.* London: Routledge and Kegan Paul.

PIAGET, J. (1954) *The Construction of Reality in the Child.* New York: Basic Books.

PIAGET, J. (1957) *Logic and Psychology.* New York: Basic Books, Inc.

PIAGET, J. (1962) *The Origins of Intelligence in Children.* New York: Norton.

PIAGET, J. (1964) 'Development and learning', *J. Res. Sc. Teach.*, 2, 176—186.

PIAGET, J. (1967) *Six Psychological Studies.* New York: Random House.

PIAGET, J. (1969) *The Mechanisms of Perception.* New York: Basic Books.

PIAGET, J. (1970) *Science of Education and the Psychology of the Child.* New York: Viking Press.

PIAGET, J. (1971) *Biology and Knowledge.* Edinburgh: Edinburgh University Press.

PIAGET, J. (1971a) 'The theory of stages in cognitive development'. In: GREEN, D.R., FORD, M.P. and FLAMER, G.B. (Eds.) *Measurement and Piaget*. New York: McGraw-Hill.

PIAGET, J. (1972) *The Principles of Genetic Epistemology*. New York: Basic Books.

PIAGET, J. (1973) 'Comments on mathematical education'. In: HOWSON, A.G. (Ed.) *Developments in Mathematical Education*. Cambridge University Press.

PIAGET, J., and INHELDER, B. (1956) *The Child's Conception of Space*. London: Routledge and Kegan Paul.

PIAGET, J., and INHELDER, B. (1962) *Le Developpment des Quantities Physiques chez l'Enfant*. Neuchatel, Switzerland, Delachaux and Niestle.

PIMM, J.B. (1974) 'The performance of the emotionally disturbed child on Piaget's conservation tasks', personal communication.

PIMM, J.B. (1974a) 'The clinical use of Piagetian tasks with emotionally disturbed children. Paper presented to Fourth Annual UAP Conference on Piagetian Theory and the Helping Professions Children's Hospital of Los Angeles, Feb. 15.

PINARD, A., and LAURENDEAU, M. (1964) 'A scale of mental development based on the theory of Piaget', *J. Res. Sc. Teach.*, 2, 253–60.

PINARD, A. and LAURENDEAU, M. (1969) '"Stage" in Piaget's cognitive-developmental theory: exegis of a concept', In: ELKIND, D. and FLAVELL, J.H. (Eds.) *Studies in Cognitive Development: Essays in Honour of Jean Piaget*. New York: Oxford Univ Press.

POLANSKI, H. (1975) 'Piaget's logical operations and science content comprehension', *Diss. Abstr.*, 35, 9, 5581A–6281A.

PRIOR, F.M. (1959) The place of maps in the junior school. Unpublished PhD thesis, Birmingham University.

RALPH, R.O. (1972) The development and analysis of an instrument to measure attitudes about science of upper elementary pupils. Phd thesis, Kent State University.

RAMSEY, G.A. and DALE, L.G. (1971) 'The Australian Science Education Project: Its rationale', *J. Aust. Sci. Teach.*, 17, 3, 51–57.

RAND, D.C. (1974) 'The relationship between children's classification class inclusion abilities and geographic knowledge as measured by Piaget's spatial spaces', *Diss. Abstr.*, 34, 8, 4479A–5379A, (4885A), Xerox University Microfilms.

RARDIN, D.R. and MOAN, C.E. (1971) 'Peer interaction and cognitive development', *Child Developm.*, 42, 1685–99.

RAVEN, J. (1965) *Guide to Using the Coloured Progressive Matrices, Sets A, Ab, B*. Dumfries: Grieve & Sons.

RAVEN, R., and SALZER, R. (1971) 'Piaget and reading instruction', *Reading Teach*, 24, 630—639.

REID, E.M. (1975) 'The use of a Piagetian scale of development as a part of growth measure of pre-kindergarten chidren participating in the Baltimore City Public Schools', personal communication. Also Paper prepared for the Piagetian Society Conference held at the Children's Hospital, Los Angeles.

RESNICK, L.B. (1967) 'Design of an early learning curriculum'. Working Paper 16, Pittsburgh: Learning Research and Development Center: University of Pittsburgh.

REST, J. (1974) 'Developmental psychology as a guide to value education: a review of "Kohlbergian" programmes', *Rev. Educ. Res.*, 44, 241—59.

RHYS, W.T. (1972) 'Geography and the adolescent', *Ed. Rev.*, 24, 3, 183—96.

RICHMOND, R.C. (1972) 'Religious judgment between the ages of 13 and 16', *Ed. Rev.*, 24, 3, 225—36.

RIPPLE, R.E., and ROCKCASTLE, V.N. (Eds.) (1964) 'Piaget Rediscovered: A Report of the Conference on Cognitive Studies and Curriculum Development'. U.S. Office of Education.

ROBISON, H., JAGODA, E., and BLOTNER, R. (1974) 'Competency-based teacher training: Skinner vs. Piaget in classification'. Paper read at the Fourth Annual Piaget Conference on Feb. 15, at the University of Southern California, jointly sponsored by the Children's Hospital of Los Angeles and the University of Southern California.

ROSENTHAL, T. and ZIMMERMAN, B. (1972) 'Modelling by exemplification and instruction in training conservation', *Dev. Psych.*, 6, 3, 392—401.

ROSS, E. (1971) An investigation of verbal and nonverbal expression of reading comprehension skills and classification abilities at the concrete operations stage. Unpublished dissertation, Philadelphia, Pennsylvania: Temple University.

ROSS, J.E. (1959) An inquiry into the ability of junior and first-year secondary modern children to reason about sound. Unpublished PhD thesis, Birmingham University.

ROSS, R.J. (1974) 'The development of formal thinking for high and average achieving adolescents'. Paper presented at the 4th Annual Conference, at University Southern California and Los Angeles Children's Hosp., 15th Feb. Also personal communication.

ROSSKOPF, M.F. (Ed.) (1975) *Children's Mathematical Concepts: Six Piagetian Studies in Mathematics Education*. New York: Teachers College Press, Columbia University.

ROSSKOPF, M.F., STEFFE, L.P. and TABACK, S. (Eds.) (1971)

Piagetian Cognitive-Development Research and Mathematical Education. Washington, D.C.: National Council of Teachers of Mathematics.

RUBIN, K.H., ATTEWELL, P.W., TIERNEY, M.C., and TUMULO, P. (1973) 'Development of spatial egocentrism and conservation across the life span', *Dev. Psych.*, 9, 3, 432.

RUSSELL, W.L. (Jr.) (1973) 'Effect of preschool experience on performance of Piaget tasks in first grade', *Diss. Abstr.*, 34, 6, 2809A–3611A, (3157A), Xerox University Microfilms.

SAUNDERS, D.R. (1961) 'The rationale for an "oblimax" method of transformation in factor analysis', *Psychometr.*, 26, 317–24.

SCANDURA, J.M. (1968) 'Research in psycho-mathematics', *The Maths. Teach.*, 61, 581–91.

SCANDURA, J.M. (1970) 'Role of rules in behaviour: toward an operational definition of what (rule) is learned', *Psych. Rev.*, 77, 516–33.

SCHMID-KITSIKIS, E. (1969) *L'Examen des Opérations de l'Intelligence.* Delachaux et Niestlé, Neuchatel/Swisse.

SCHONELL, F.J., and SCHONELL, E.G. (1960) *Diagnostic and Attainment Testing.* 4th Edition. London: Oliver and Boyd.

SCHWARTZ, M.M., and SCHOLNICK, E. (1970) 'Scalogram analysis of logical and perceptual components of conservation of discontinuous quantity', *Child Developm.*, 41, 695–705.

SCHWEBEL, M., and RAPH, J. (Eds.) (1973) *Piaget in the Classroom.* New York: Basic Books, p. 310.

SCIENCE CURRICULUM IMPROVEMENT STUDY (1970) *Material Objects.* Chicago: Rand McNally.

SECONDARY SCHOOL MATHEMATICS CURRICULUM IMPROVEMENT STUDY (1968) *Unified Modern Mathematics: Course II, Part I.* New York: Teachers College Press.

SEILER, Th. B. (1973) 'Die Bereichsspezifität formaler Denkstrukfurenkonsequenzen für den pädagogischen Prozess. In: FREY and LANGE (Eds.) *Kognitionspsychologie und Unterricht.* Bern: Huber.

SELMAN R.L. (1975) Book review of 'Thinking goes to school: Piaget's Theory in Practice', *Harv. Ed. Rev.*, 45, 1, 127–34.

SHAYER, M. (1970) 'How to assess science courses', *Educ. in Chemist.*, 7, 5, 182–6.

SHAYER, M. (1972) 'Conceptual demands in the Nuffield O-level physics course', *Sch. Sc. Rev.*, 186, 54, 26–34.

SHAYER, M. (1972) Piaget's work and science teaching. Masters thesis, Leicester University.

SHAYER, M. (1974) 'Conceptual demands in the Nuffield O-level biology course', *Sch. Sc. Rev.*, 195, 1–11.

SHAYER, M., and WHARRY, D. (1974a) 'Piaget in the classroom: Part

I: Testing a whole class at the same time', *Sch. Sc. Rev.*, 194, 447—57.

SHEPPARD, J.L. (1974) 'Concrete operational thought and developmental aspects of solutions to a task based on a mathematical three-group', *Dev. Psych.*, 10, 116—23.

SHOBEN, E.J. (Jr.) (1949) 'The assessment of parental attitudes in relation to child adjustment', *Gen. Psych. Mon.*, 39, 102—48.

SIEGELMAN, E., and BLOCK, J. (1969) 'Two parallel sets of Piagetian tasks', *Child Developm.*, 40, 3, 951—6.

SIGEL LE., and HOOPER, F.H. (1968) *Logical Thinking in Children: Research Based on Piaget's Theory.* New York: Holt, Rinehart and Winston.

SILLS, T.W., and HERRON, J.D. (1976) 'Study of an electronic analog to the combinations of chemical bodies Piagetian task', Paper presented at the 6th Annual Interdisciplinary International Conference on Piagetian Theory and the Helping Professions, Los Angeles, California, January 30th. Also personal communication.

SILVAROLI, N.J. (1972) *Classroom Reading Inventory.* Dubuque, Iowa: Brown.

SIME, M. (1973) 'Implications of the work of Piaget in the training of students to teach primary mathematics'. In: HOWSON A.G. (Ed.), *Developments in Mathematical Education.* Cambridge University Press.

SINCLAIR, H. (1971) 'Piaget's theory of development: the main stages'. In: ROSSKOPF, M.F., STEFFE, L.P. and TABACK, S. (Eds.) *Piagetian Cognitive-Development Research and Mathematical Education.* Washington, DC: National Council of Teachers of Mathematics.

SMEDSLUND, J. (1963) 'The concept of correlation in adults', *Scan. J. Psych.*, 4, 165—73.

SMEDSLUND, J. (1964) 'Concrete reasoning: a study of intellectual development'. Monographs of the Society for Research in Child Development, 29, (2, Whole No. 43).

SMITH, H., BLECHA, M., and STERNIG, J. (1966) *Science Four: Laidlaw Science Series.* River Forest: Illinois.

SMITH, L.T. (1959) The role of maturity in acquiring a concept of limit in mathematics. PhD Thesis, Stanford University. Ann Arbor, Mich: University Microfilms, 1967, No. 59—3671.

SMITH, L.T. (1959a) 'The role of maturity in acquiring a concept of limit in mathematics', *Diss. Abstr.*, 20, 1288—89, 4.

STAFFORD, D.G. and RENNER, J.W. (1971) 'SCIS helps the first grade to use simple logic in problem solving', *Sch. Sc. and Maths.*, 71, 159—64.

STANFILL, J.W. (1975) 'Relationship between reading achievement and Piaget's conservation tasks for beginning second grade students', *Diss. Abstr.* 36, 1, 1A–577A (p. 122A).

STEPHENS, W.B., MILLER, C.K., and McLAUGHLIN, J.A. (1969) 'The development of reasoning, moral judgment and moral conduct in retardates and normals'. Report on Project No. RD–2382–P, Philadelphia, Pennsylvania: Temple University, May.

STEPHENS, W.B., McLAUGHLIN, J.A., MILLER, C.K. and GLASS, G.V. (1972) 'Factorial structure of selected psycho-educational measures and Piagetian reasoning assessments', *Dev. Psych.*, 6, 343–8.

STONES, S.K. (1965) 'An analysis of the growth of adolescent thinking in relation to their comprehension of school history material', *Dip. Child Psych.*, dissertation, Birmingham University.

STOTT, D.H. (1958) (3rd Ed. 1966) *Social Adjustment of Children Bristol Social Guides.* University of London Press.

SUCHMAN, J.R. (1961) 'Inquiry training: Building skills for autonomous discovery', *Merr.-Palm. Quart.*, 7, 3, 147–69.

SUCHMAN, J.R. (1964) 'The Illinois studies in inquiry training', *J. Res. Sci. Teach.*, 2, 230–2.

SULLIVAN E.V. (1967) *Piaget and the School Curriculum.* Toronto: OISE.

SWIZE, M.T. (1972) 'Prediction of Piagetian conservation for second grade Mexican-American and Anglo-American children', *Diss. Abstr.*, order No. 72–13331, (5624A), Xerox University Microfilms.

TABA, H., DURKIN, M.C., FRAENKEL, J.R., and McNAUGHTON, A.H. (1971) *A Teacher's Handbook to Elementary Social Studies.* 2nd Edition, California: Addison-Wesley, Menlo Park.

TABACK, S.F. (1969) The child's concept of limit. PhD thesis, Teachers College, Columbia University. Also in ROSSKOPF, M.F. (Ed.) *Children's Mathematical Concepts: Six Piagetian Studies in Mathematics Education.* New York: Teachers College Press, Columbia University.

TABARY, J.C., and TARDIEU, G. (1963) 'Application of Piaget's genetic psychology to the education of children suffering cerebral palsy'. Paper presented at the 9th World Congress on Rehabilitation, Copenhagen.

TAMBURRINI, J. (1975) 'Implications of Piaget's theory for in-service education', *Maths. Teach.*, 72, 4–10. (Based on the lecture first delivered at the First American Conference on Teachers' Centres in Mathematics Education in St. Louis in April 1974.).

TANAKA, M., CAMPBELL, J.T., and HELMICK, J.S. (1970) 'Piaget for first-grade teachers: written exercises for assessing intellectual development', *Educ. Testing Service Res. Memorandum*, July.

TESSIER, F.A. (1972) 'The development of young cerebral palsied children according to Piaget's sensorimotor theory'. Proceedings of the Second Annual UAP Conference on Piagetian Theory and the Helping Profession, Los Angeles, January.

THAN, A.A. (1974) Cognitive development in a sample of Burmese Primary School children assessed by the concept of assessment kit, (Goldschmid and Bentler). MA dissertation, London University.

THOMAS, D.I. (1967) 'Children's understanding of archaeological material'. Unpublished research, Birmingham University reported by Peel in BURSTON, W.H. and THOMSON, D. (Eds.) *Studies in the Nature and Teaching of History*. Routledge and Kegan Paul.

THOMAS, H.L. (1975) 'The concept of function'. In: ROSS-KOPF, M.F. (Ed.) *Children's Mathematical Concepts: Six Piagetian Studies in Mathematics Education*. New York: Teachers College Press, Columbia University.

TISHER, R. (1971) 'A Piagetian questionnaire applied to pupils in a secondary school', *Child Developm.*, 42, 1633—6. Unpublished BA thesis, 1962.

TOMLINSON-KEASY, C. (1972) 'Formal operations in females from 11 to 54 years of age', *Dev. Psych.*, 6, 2, 364.

TONGUE A. (1974) Review of 'Piaget, Education and Teaching', *The Teacher*, 25, 19, November 8th, p. 17, (Review).

TUDDENHAM, R.D. (1968) *New Ways of Measuring Intelligence*. Chicago: American Educ. Res. Assoc. Conven.

TUDDENHAM, R.D. (1968a) 'Psychometricizing Piaget's Méthode Clinique'. Revised paper and cited in ATHEY, I.J. and RUBADEAU, D.O. (Eds.) *Educational Implications of Piaget's Theory*. Ginn-Blaisdell Company, 317—24.

TUDDENHAM, R.D. (1969) 'A Piagetian test of cognitive development', Paper presented at the Symposium on Intelligence, Ontario, Toronto, May. In: DOCKRELL, W.B. (ed) (1970) The Toronto Symposium on Intelligence. London: Methuen.

TUDDENHAM, R.D. (1970) 'A "Piagetian" test of cognitive development'. In: DOCKRELL, B. (Ed) *On Intelligence*. Toronto: Ontario Institute for Studies in Education, pp. 49—70, London: Methuen.

TUDDENHAM, R.D. (1971) 'Theoretical regularities and individual idiosyncrasies'. In: GREEN, D.R., FORD, M.P. and FLAMER, G.B. (Eds.) *Measurement and Piaget*. New York: McGraw-Hill.

TURSI, P.A. (1973) 'Exposition, analysis and implication of selected presuppositions inherent in Piaget's theory', *Diss. Abstr.*, 34, 2, 453A—927A, (673A), Xerox University Microfilms.

ÜBERLA, K. (1968) *Faktorenanalyse*. Berlin: Springer.

UZGIRIS, I.C. and HUNT, J.M. (1966) 'An instrument for assessing infant psychological development'. Unpublished manuscript, University of Illinois, Champaign, Illinois.

UZGIRIS, I.C. and HUNT, J. McV. (1972) 'Towards Ordinal Scales of Psychological Development in Infancy. Unpublished manuscript.

UZGIRIS, I.C. and HUNT, J. McV. (1974) *Towards Ordinal Scales of Psychological Development in Infancy.* Urbana: University of Illinois Press.

VALERY, P. (1971) *The Collected Works of Paul Valéry.* Volume 3. Princeton: Princeton University Press.

VANEK, E.P. and MONTEAN, J.J. (1975) 'The effect of two science programmes (ESS–Laidlow) on student classification skills, science achievement and attitudes', personal communication.

VICENTE, J.M. and FINLEG, G.E. (1974) Cited in *Crosscultural Inventory of Piagetian Studies,* compiled by DASEN, P and SEAGRIM, G.N.

VICTORIAN EDUCATION DEPARTMENT (1969) 'Primary School Science: Course of Study; Beginning Science; Following on; Branching Out'.

VICTORIAN EDUCATION DEPARTMENT and ACER (1966) *Backgrounds in Mathematics.*

VYGOTSKY, L.S. (1962) *Thought and Language.* Mass: MIT Press.

WACHS, T., UZGIRIS, I., and HUNT, J. McV. (1971) 'Cognitive development in infants of different age levels and from different environmental background: an explanatory investigation', *Merr.-Palm. Quart.,* 17, 283–319.

WAGMAN, H.G. (1975) 'The child's conception of area measure'. In: ROSSKOPF, M.F. (Ed.) *Children's Mathematical Concepts: Six Piagetian Studies in Mathematics Education.* New York: Teachers College Press, Columbia University.

WANG M.C. (Ed.) (1973) Criterion-Referenced Achievement Tests for the Early Learning Curriculum of the Primary Education Project. Pittsburgh: Learning Research and Development Center, University of Pittsburgh.

WANG, M.C., RESNICK, L.B., and BOOZER, R.F. (1971) 'The sequence of development of some early mathematics behaviours', *Child Developm.,* 42, 1767–8.

WARBURTON, F.W. (1970) 'The British Intelligence Scale', In: DOCKRELL, W.B. (Ed.) *On Intelligence.* London: Methuen.

WARD J. (1972) 'The saga of Butch and Slim', *Brit. J. Ed. Psych.,* 42, 267–89.

WARD, J. and PEARSON, L. (1973) 'A comparison of two methods of testing logical thinking', *Can. J. Beh. Sci/Rev. Can. Sci. Comp.,* 5, 4, 385–98.

WASIK, B.H. and WASIK, J.L. (1971) 'Performance of culturally deprived children on the concept assessment kit-conservation', *Child Developm.,* 42, 1586–90.

WATSON, F.R. (1974) 'The pupil's thinking'. In: SUTTON, C.R. and HAYSOM, J.T. (Eds.) *The Art of the Science Teacher*. London: McGraw-Hill, pp. 31–40.

WEBB, R.A. (1974) 'Concrete and formal operations in very bright 6- to 11-year-olds', *Human Developm.*, 17, 292–300;

WEIKART,   (1967) Cited in review of 'Piaget in the classroom: or is he?' by C.S. Lavatelli (1974), *Contemp. Psych.*, 19, 5, pp. 365–6.

WEINREB, M. and BRAINERD, C.J. (1975) 'A developmental study of Piaget's groupement model of the emergence of speed and time concepts', *Child Developm.*, 46, 176–85.

WEISZ, L. (1974) 'Test of discrimination of Piagetian-based symbols (Weisz "VT") — Weisz THINK*A* LING worksheets and manual' Multiple Choice Associates, Inc.

WEISZ, L. (1975) 'Reading readiness, a Piagetian enterprise', personal communication.

WELLS, J. (1972) 'Some aspects of adolescent thinking in science', *Ed. Rev.*, 24, 3, 212–224.

WICKENS,   (1971) Cited in review of, 'Piaget in the classroom: or is he?', by C.S. Lavatelli, 1974, *Contemp. Psych.*, 19, 5, pp. 365–366.

WILLIS, S. (1973) 'A framework for the development of goals and curriculum for a Piagetian-based early childhood education programme'. Mimeo.

WILLIS, S. (1975) 'The Pennsylvania State University Programme II — Cognitive developmental'. Personal communication.

WILLIS, S. and CLEMENT, J. (1973) 'Goals and objectives for a Piagetian-based early childhood education programme'. Mimeo.

WILLIS, S., COHEN, A., and CLEMENT, J. (1975) 'Formative evaluation in a cognitive developmental programme for young children'. Personal communication. Also Paper presented at the 4th Annual USC Piagetian Conference, 1974.

WILSON, R.S. (1973) 'Testing infant intelligence', *Science*, 18, 734–6.

WINKELMANN, W. (1974) 'Factorial analysis of children's conservation task performance', *Child Developm.*, 45, 843–8;

WINKELMANN, W. (1975) 'Testbatterie zur Erfassung kognitive operationen (TEKO). Piaget-orientierte Tests für im Alter von etwa 5–8 Jahren. (Developmental Test Battery of Cognitive operations. Piaget-oriented tests for children aged about five to eight). Braunschweig: Georg Westermann Verlag. (Available from: Testzentrale Wildbader Str. 4, 7 Stuttgart-Bad Cannstatt, Federal Republic of Germany).

WINKELMANN, W. (1975a) 'Die Invarianz der Substanz und der Zahl im kindlichen Denken. I, Das Verhalten 5–8 jähriger kinder bei Tests in Papierform und bei Tests mit Konkretem Material.

(Conservation of substance and number in children's thinking I. Responses of five- to eight-year-old children in tests based on drawings and tests based on concrete materials). In: Manual — *Testbatterie zur Erfassung kognitiver Operationen (TEKO)*, Appendix I, 67—81. Braunschweig: Georg Westermann Verlag. (Available from: Testzentrale, Wildbader Str. 4, 7 Stuttgart-Bad Cannstatt, Federal Republic of Germany.)

WINKELMANN, W. (1975b) 'Die Invarianz der Substanz und der Zahl im kindlichen Denken II. Faktorenanalyse der Reaktionen auf verschiedence Invarianzanfgaben. (Conservation of substance and number in children's thinking II. Factor analysis of responses in different conservation situations.) In: Manual — *Testbatterie zur Erfassung kognitiver operationen (TEKO)*. Appendix II, 82—95. Braunschweig: Georg Westermann Verlag. (Available from: Testzentrale, Wildbader Str. 4, 7 Stuttgart-Bad Cannstatt, Federal Republic of Germany).

WINKELMANN, W. (1975c) *Testbatterie zur Erfassung Kognitiver Operationen (TEKO)*. Piaget-orientierte Tests für kinder im Alter von etwa 5—8 Jahren. (Developmental Test Battery of Cognitive Operations. Piaget-oriented tests for children aged about 5 to 8). Braunschweig: Georg Westermann Verlag. (Available from: Testzentrale, Wildbader Str. · 4, 7 Stuttgart-Bad Cannstatt, Federal Republic of Germany. To be published April 1975.

WOHLWILL, J.F. (1960) 'A study of the development of ·the number concept by scalogram analysis', *J. Gen. Psych.*, 97, 345—77.

WOHLWILL, J.F. (1963) 'Piaget's system as a source of empirical research', *Merr.-Palm. Quart.*, 9, 253—62.

WOLFF, P.H. (1974) 'What Piaget did not intend'. Paper presented at the fourth annual conference at the University of Southern California and Los Angeles Children's Hospital, 15th Feb.

WOODWARD, M. (1959) 'The behaviour of idiots interpreted by Piaget's theory of sensori-motor development', *Brit. J. Ed. Psych.*, 29, 60—71.

WOODWARD, M. (1961) 'Concepts of number of the mentally subnormal studied by Piaget's methods', *J. Child Psych. Psychiat.*, 2, 249—59.

WOODWARD, M. (1963) 'The application of Piagetian theory to research in mental deficiency'. In: ELLIS, N.R. (Ed.) *Handbook of Mental Deficiency*. New York: McGraw-Hill.

WOODWARD, M. (1970) 'The assessment of cognitive processes: Piaget's approach'. In: MITTLER, P. (Ed.) *The Psychological Assessment of Mental and Physical Handicap*. London: Methuen.

YATES, J., and RICHARDSON, J. (1970) 'An attempt to apply Piaget's theory of intelligence to the assessment and training of children in a special care unit'. Invited paper, BPS Conference at Nottingham University.

ZEITLER, W.R. (1968) 'The changing role of the elementary school teacher'. Address presented at NSTA meeting, Washington, DC.

ZIMMERMAN, B.J., and ROSENTHAL, T.L. (1974a) 'Observational learning of rule-governed behaviour by children', *Psych. Bull.*, 81, 29–42.

INDEX